Communications
in Computer and Information Science 276

Editorial Board

Anupam Agrawal   R.C. Tripathi
Ellen Yi-Luen Do   M.D. Tiwari (Eds.)

Intelligent Interactive Technologies and Multimedia

Second International Conference, IITM 2013
Allahabad, India, March 9-11, 2013
Proceedings

 Springer

Volume Editors

Anupam Agrawal
Indian Institute of Information Technology
Allahabad 211 012, India
E-mail: anupam@iiita.ac.in

R.C. Tripathi
Indian Institute of Information Technology
Allahabad 211 012, India
E-mail: rctripathi@iiita.ac.in

Ellen Yi-Luen Do
Georgia Institute of Technology
School of Interactive Computing
Atlanta, GA 30332-0477, USA
E-mail: ellendo@gatech.edu

M.D. Tiwari
Indian Institute of Information Technology
Allahabad 211 012, India
E-mail: mdt@iiita.ac.in

ISSN 1865-0929   e-ISSN 1865-0937
ISBN 978-3-642-37462-3   e-ISBN 978-3-642-37463-0
DOI 10.1007/978-3-642-37463-0
Springer Heidelberg Dordrecht London New York

Library of Congress Control Number: 2013934294

CR Subject Classification (1998): I.4, H.5, H.3, I.2.6-7, I.2.10, H.2.8

Typesetting: Camera-ready by author, data conversion by Scientific Publishing Services, Chennai, India

Printed on acid-free paper

Springer is part of Springer Science+Business Media (www.springer.com)

Preface

The Indian Institute of Information Technology Allahabad (IIIT-A) was privileged to organize the Second International Conference on Intelligent Interactive Technologies and Multimedia (IITM 2013) on its campus during March 9–11, 2013. This conference is a forum for presenting and discussing the latest research and development in the areas of intelligent interactive technologies, human–computer interaction, and multimedia. The objective is to explore possibilities and future directions in the field. Equally encouraging is the fact that the conference received the full support of Springer, Germany, with the proceedings of the conference being made available in Springer's CCIS digital library at www.springerlink.com.

With the increase in global awareness of the importance of interactive technologies, there has been a corresponding rise in the contributions made by techniques providing innovative solutions for various complex problems. It is expected that the next generation of interactive technologies will empower people who are physically challenged or economically and educationally disadvantaged. There should also be a driving force to "bridge the rural and urban divide," which is more prominent in developing countries. This conference aims to provide a major point of confluence of researchers, engineers, and practitioners working in its various conference tracks, coming from national and international academic institutes, government research and development laboratories, and the respective industries.

This conference had great support from the research community and received more than 90 papers. The Program Committee had a very challenging task of selecting high-quality submissions. The technical committee initially screened each paper to find its suitability to the conference themes and topics. In addition, an internal plagiarism check was carried out using the IIITA-developed plagiarism detection tool to select papers suitable for the review process. To evaluate each submission, a double-blind evaluation method was followed using the EasyChair Conference Management system. To this end, each paper was reviewed by two or more experts from the Program Committee as well as by some members of Technical Advisory Committee. Only high-quality submissions were accepted and the overall acceptance rate was about 30%. Finally, a total of 27 contributory papers were selected for presentation and publication, out of which 15 are full papers and 12 are short papers based on the reviewers' grading. There were also four keynote papers from world-renowned experts in the field.

We would like to express our thanks, first of all, to the authors of the technical papers, whose work and dedication made it possible to put together a program that we believe is a landmark of high scientific quality contributions. Next, we would like to thank all the members of the Technical Advisory Committee and the Program Committee, who helped us with their expertise and time.

We would also like to thank the invited speakers for their invaluable contribution and for sharing their visions of the field. We extend our sincere thanks to Honorable Chancellor Professor Goverdhan Mehta for his wholehearted support of this conference. We are grateful to our faculty and staff members as well as our students for their invaluable contribution in organizing this conference. Finally, we are also thankful to the ACM IIIT Allahabad Professional Chapter, the CSI Allahabad Chapter, and the North India ACM SIGCHI Chapter. Our special thanks are due to the Department of Electronics and IT (DEITY), Ministry of Communication and Information Technology, Government of India, New Delhi, for their timely financial and technical support of this conference.

We hope that you enjoy these proceedings of IITM 2013.

March 2013   M.D. Tiwari

IITM 2013 Committees

Chief Patron

M. D. Tiwari   Director, IIIT-A, India

General Chair

Ellen Yi-Luen Do   Director ACME, Georgia Tech, USA

General Co-chair

R. C. Tripathi   Divisional Head-HCI, IIIT-A, India

Program Chair

Anupam Agrawal   Chairman ACM Chapter, IIIT-A, India

Track Co-chairs

Track 1: Interaction Design, Innovative Methods and Devices of IITM
Gerrit Meixner   DFKI, IFS, Kaiserslautern, Germany
Sitaram Ramachandrula   Hewlett-Packard Labs, Bangalore, India

Track 2: Graphics, Animation, Image and Multimedia Technologies
Santanu Chaudhury   IIT, Delhi, India
Nadia Magnenat-Thalmann   Nanyang Technological University, Singapore

Track 3: Cognitive Models, Softcomputing, AI and Machine Learning
G.C. Nandi   IIIT, Allahabad, India
Qiang Shen   Aberystwyth University, Wales, UK

Track 4: Speech and Language Processing Technologies
Rajesh M Hegde   IIT, Kanpur, India
Veton Këpuska   Florida Institute of Technology, Melbourne, USA

Technical Advisory Committee

Rama Chellappa	University of Maryland, USA
Nadia Magnenat-Thalmann	Nanyang Technological University, Singapore
Anirudha N. Joshi	IDC, IIT Bombay, Mumbai, India
Narayanan Srinivasan	CBCS, University of Allahabad, Allahabad, India
Santanu Chaudhury	IIT, Delhi, India
M. Radhakrishna	IIIT, Allahabad, India
Andrew M. Dearden	Sheffield Hallam University, UK
R.K. Shyamasundar	TIFR, Mumbai, India
Valentina Emilia Balas	AurelVlaicu University of Arad, Romania
U.B. Desai	IIT, Hyderabad, India
Chang Wen Chen	University at Buffalo, SUNY, USA
Sivaji Bandyopadhyay	Jadavpur University, Kolkata, India
Takashi Omori	Tamagawa University, Japan
Pushpak Bhattacharyya	IIT, Mumbai, India
Sankar K. Pal	ISI, Kolkata, India
Aparajita Ojha	IIITDM, Jabalpur, India
Anupam Basu	IIT, Kharagpur, India
David Benyon	Napier University, Edinburgh, UK
C. Chandra Shekar	IIT Madras, Chennai, India
Satish Babu	ICFOSS, CSI National President, Trivandrum, India

Program Committee

Josef Kohout	University of West Bohemia, Czech Republic
Preeti Rao	IIT Bombay, Mumbai, India
Fuli Wu	Zhejiang University of Technology, P.R. China
Nishchal K. Verma	IIT, Kanpur, India
Gerrit Meixner	DFKI, IFS, Kaiserslautern, Germany
Rajesh M. Hegde	IIT, Kanpur, India
A.V. Subramanyam	IIIT, Delhi, India
Pabitra Mitra	IIT, Kharagpur, India
S. Sanyal	IIIT, Allahabad, India
Shirshu Verma	IIIT, Allahabad, India
B.S. Sanjeev	IIIT, Allahabad, India
Pinaki Roy Chowdhury	DTRL, DRDO, Delhi, India
O.P. Vyas	IIIT, Allahabad, India
David Raneburger	Vienna University of Technology, Austria
Mahua Bhattacharya	ABV-IIITM, Gwalior, India
Samit Bhattacharya	IIT, Guwahati, India
C. Saravanan	NIT, Durgapur, India
Kaladhar Bapu	UXINDIA & UMO, USA
Dharmendra Singh	IIT, Roorkee, India

Rajesh K. Pandey	IIITD&M, Jabalpur, India
Krishna Prasad	IIT, Gandhinagar, India
Amit A. Nanavati	IBM Research Lab, New Delhi, India
Rakesh C. Balabantaray	IIIT, Bhubaneswar, India
Anupam Agrawal	IIIT, Allahabad, India
M. Radhakrishna	IIIT, Allahabad, India
Suman Mitra	DAI-ICT, Gandhinagar, India
Pritee Khanna	IIITD&M, Jabalpur, India
Amitava Das	University of North Texas (UNT), Texas, USA
Narendra Chaudhari	IIT, Indore, India
Shekhar Verma	IIIT, Allahabad, India
Rama Vennelakanti	HP Labs India, Bangalore, India
Sonali Agrawal	IIIT, Allahabad, India
Triloki Pant	IIIT, Allahabad, India
K.P. Singh	IIIT, Allahabad, India
Sheetal K. Agarwal	IBM Research, Bangalore, India
Aruna Tiwari	IIT, Indore, India
Ankur Sardana	Samsung Design, Delhi, India
Neeta Nain	MNIT, Jaipur, India
Anne Boyer	LORIA – University of Nancy, France
Anupam Shukla	ABV-IIITM, Gwalior
M. Hima Bindu	JIIT, Noida, India
J. Kreutel	Beuth University of Applied Sciences Berlin, Germany
Lajish V.L.	University of Calicut, Kerala, India
Rahul Banerjee	BITS, Pilani, India
Ravibabu Mulaveesala	IIT, Ropar, India
B. Sivaselvan	IIITD&M, Kancheepuram, India
Archana M. Rajurkar	M.G.M. College of Engineering, Nanded, India
A. Vadivel	National Institute of Technology, Tiruchirappalli, India
Srini Ramaswamy	University of Arkansas at Little Rock, Arkansas, USA
R.C. Tripathi	IIIT, Allahabad, India
G.C. Nandi	IIIT, Allahabad, India
V.B. Singh	University of Delhi, New Delhi, , India
Peeyush Tewari	Birla Institute of Technology, Noida, India
Paolo Bottoni	"La Sapieza" University of Rome, Italy
Sanjay Kumar Dwivedi	Baba Saheb Bhimrao Ambedkar University, Lucknow, India
Suneeta Agarwal	MNNIT, Allahabad, India
Vrijendra Singh	IIIT, Allahabad, India
Neetesh Purohit	IIIT, Allahabad, India

Special Thanks

Organizing Institute:

 Indian Institute of Information Technology, Allahabad (IIIT-A), India

Gold Sponsors:

 Department of Electronics and Information Technology (Deity), Ministry of Communication & Information Technology, Government of India, New Delhi

Technical Sponsors:

 Springer CCIS, Heidelberg, Germany

 ACM IIIT Allahabad Professional Chapter

 North India ACM SIGCHI Chapter, Allahabad

Knowledge Partners:

School of Interactive Computing, Georgia Institute of Technology, Atlanta, Georgia, USA

Dept. Design, Manufacture and Engg. Management, University of Strathclyde, Glasgow, Scotland

Table of Contents

Keynote Papers

Full Papers

Short Papers

Designing Interactive Computing for Happy Healthy Life

Ellen Yi-Luen Do

School of Industrial Design & School of Interactive Computing
Georgia Institute of Technology, Atlanta, Georgia 30332, USA
ellendo@gatech.edu

Abstract. The future of design computing is in the making of intelligent and interactive technologies for a smart living environment. This chapter explores the concepts of technology as magic and provides examples of creative design computing projects to illustrate the opportunities and challenges for making smart objects, interactive furniture and responsive environments.

Keywords: design, interactive computing, human-computer interaction.

1 Introduction

The age of ubiquitous/pervasive/ambient computing is upon us. What does this mean when we have computing without computers, where information processing has diffused into everyday life, and become invisible? This chapter describes the vision and efforts toward a smart living environment, in which the built environment is responsive and interactive, with ubiquitous sensors and actuators as part of the building material, to support everyday happy, healthy living in the forms of things that think, spaces that sense, and places that play.

In this paper we will first briefly review the concepts of wellness and human centered computing before discussing the integration of design and computing for a physically and computationally enhanced environment. We then describe the 3 B's – the Brick, Bench, and Bionic Building paradigms with example projects ranging from intelligent objects, interactive furniture to responsive walls. Design implementation, methodologies and principles would be discussed for the framework of the built environment as an interface for information, communication and wellbeing, designing a smart living of tomorrow.

1.1 Smart Living of Tomorrow

Your dream comes to a sweet ending. It's six o'clock in the morning. Your eyes open to the sunshine that was carefully let in by the window blinds. You feel rested and happy to jump out of the bed. Your pillow notices that you have gotten up and talks to the coffee maker to make a fresh brew. You gesture to the wall and your favorite song starts to play and follows you. The bathroom mirror gives you the traffic report and the meeting schedule of the day while you brush your teeth. Then your slippers blink

A. Agrawal et al. (Eds.): IITM 2013, CCIS 276, pp. 1–13, 2013.

lights to indicate that you have just received a love note in your email inbox. How nice! You tell your house to remember to make a romantic dinner reservation. You open the refrigerator and happily discover that your refrigerator has already ordered fresh milk and orange juice for you. Before you sit down, the breakfast table had prepared a plate of two eggs, sunny side up, just the way you like them. While you are reading the dynamically displayed local news on the kitchen wall, the house slowly turns off all the climate control in all other rooms knowing that you will soon leave the house and go to work. The story goes on...

Is this too good to be true? Is this a lullaby? We all have heard it many times in the popular media or product commercials. There are plenty of imaginary worlds depicted in science fiction with the theme of how computer technology is going to help us save time, and to be more efficient. At the same time, we are also concerned that using intelligent information appliances and smart houses might make us less intelligent, or become more isolated from the society. We all want a good life. The idea of a futuristic smart living space is therefore enticing. It will probably involve all sorts of engineering innovations. We can definitely solve the technical problems. However, the real question is not what we can do with technology, but what kind of life do we want to live?

Not surprisingly, I have a vested interest in the future of smart living spaces, because I plan on living there. We have a once in a lifetime opportunity to truly integrate intelligent computing and architecture to create wonderful environments for future generations to enjoy. The remarkable opportunities are here now. The 21st century would be the era for the designers, the architects, and the engineers who have vision to make beautiful imagination a reality for the world.

Let me try to sketch that imaginary picture for you. Let's think about a compelling vision of what the world will be like tomorrow. Alan Kay is quoted as saying that "the best way to predict the future is to invent it [1]." I believe the process of inventing the future is also a process of observing the present, and seeing the challenges and opportunities to innovate. What we are seeing today is that information is moving out of traditional computer setups and into the world around us. This world had evolved from the industrial society into the information society. Then the information society we are now in is rapidly transforming into the communication society, and heading toward the creative society.

1.2   Technology as Magic

It was magic when Watson first heard Bell's calling through the electric instrument. To see for the first time a horseless carriage with an internal combustion engine moving on the road is magic. To hear musical melodies coming out from a black box or watch tiny persons talking and dancing behind a glass plane is certainly magic. We can look to the history of technology to see how innovation such as books and recorded music, central heat, electric light and the telephone were designed, redesigned, and gradually assimilated. All this magic has faded into the fabric of life we now take for granted.

Technology is like magic. An advanced technology often appears to be indistinguishable from magic. When technology is smart and close enough to people it then disappears. The mechanism and user interface in a good mechanically designed bicycle or piano are so closely integrated that we cannot distinguish the form and function. We can use them easily without thinking about them as technology or even thinking about them at all. A technology becomes invisible when we stop noticing it. Invisibility should be the goal for technology. What if the computers disappear and our built environment and our world become our interface? This chapter paints a picture of embedding intelligent computing in the built environment as creating magic.

1.3 Unveiling Magic

As a researcher and educator, I have been working with people to do magic through the field that is known as Design Computing. I have engaged people in topics on human-computer interaction, tangible interface, physical computing, smart toys, and home of the future. We worked on creating "not-in-your-face" ubiquitous and pervasive computing. We worked on subtle information visualization that is known as ambient intelligence. It's not just about having computing anywhere and everywhere, but to make it intuitive, invisible, and unobtrusive. We have attempted to create magical moments for smart living space by using sensing-based technology to support human-centered creative work.

Let me first tell you the spirit of our work before showing you a collection of projects. I should like to call the type of Design Computing we are doing as "fun computing" in that we create "playful inventions" for people. The "play" component as an essential facility for design is pretty much described in Paul Rand's article "Design and the Play Instinct" [2]. We explore bridging the digital and physical worlds. We combine personal passion and intellectual pursuits. We encourage people to use their senses to make sense of the world around us.

2   Intelligent Computing for Wellness

What's the first sentence you would say when you greet a friend (besides Hi, Hello or Howdy)? A couple examples come to mind: How are you? How have you been? Good Morning! Nice to see you! No doubt you can come up with a couple more that are similar in the spirit. There are of course cultural and situational differences and people may express their greetings both audibly and physically, such as handshaking, hugging, cheek kissing, or gesturing a wave or giving a high-five. How about the parting words? Good-bye! See you later! Have a nice day! Good luck! Take care!

As evidenced in the social greeting and parting rituals, we human beings intentionally communicate our awareness of each other's presence and show interest in other people's welfare or happiness. The idea of wellness is related to human condition and potential. What is wellness? Wellness is the presence of wellbeing. Wellness is about being active, alive and vital. It concerns individuals, communities as well as the surrounding environments.

Wellness is multi-dimensional. The popular notion considers wellness as consisted of six inter-related dimensions: physical, emotional, occupational, social, intellectual and spiritual [3]. The physical dimension refers to dietary and physical activities. The emotional dimension recognizes awareness and acceptance of feelings and behaviors. The occupational dimension considers achievement and enrichment through work. The social dimension encourages contribution to the environment, community and the world. The intellectual dimension seeks creative and stimulating activities. The spiritual dimension recognizes the search for values, meaning and purpose in life.

The Grand Challenge of achieving wellness is upon us. As human beings we aim to develop and cultivate our untapped potential for a happy, healthy, creative and fulfilling life. We are concerned about the quality of life issues for ourselves and for our society. Technological innovation may be just the key to unlock human potential for the Holy Grail of wellness.

The human centric view for smart living environments is the commitment to improving the human condition through advanced science and technology. With Design Computing, we are in a culture of possibilities. To briefly demonstrate the spirit and the scope of the types of the research efforts, the rest of this chapter will focus on three paradigms of interest – the Brick, Bench, and Bionic Building, each illustrated by a couple projects, to form part of the picture of "unlocking human potential through technological innovation" to create "Things that Think, Spaces that Sense, and Places that Play."

3   Brick, Bench, and Bionic Building Paradigm

Before we talk about the various projects, let me use a framework to put them in context. I am calling this the Brick, Bench, and Bionic Building paradigm. The classification is based on the relative scale of the artifacts - objects, furniture and environments can be symbolized and represented as the Brick, Bench, and Bionic Building Paradigm.

3.1   The Brick Paradigm - Intelligent Objects

The Brick paradigm covers a range of different design computing building blocks. For example, a computationally enhanced block could serve as an interface for people to navigate and explore the digital and imaginary worlds, a tangible construction kit could enable people to "think with their hands" by providing feedback or simulations in different domains.

3.1.1 Navigational Blocks and Storytelling Cubes

Navigational Blocks [4] is a tangible user interface that facilitates retrieval of historical stories from a multi-media database. Each face of each block represents a subcategory. For example, the Who block has a face representing the "founding fathers," and another face "the merchants." The When block has a face for 1850's and another one for 1920's. A face of the What block represents an historical event and a face of the Where block represents a location. Orientation, movement, and relative positions of wooden blocks provide a physical embodiment of digital information through tactile manipulation and haptic feedback.

Electromagnets embedded in the Blocks and wireless communication encourages rapid rearrangement to form different queries into the database. With similar forms and functions of the Navigational Blocks, Storytelling Cubes [5] enable young children to create animated cartoon stories displayed by a computer. Each face of the cubes depicts a different character (e.g., cat, pig), a different scene (e.g., tree house, igloo) or an action (e.g., eating, hiking). The orientation sensor and wireless transmitter inside each cube tell the host computer which side of each cube is facing up. Children can create their own stories by picking up and playing with the cubes and narrate for their cartoon characters. Figure 1 left shows that a visitor can rotate Who, What, When, Where Navigational Blocks to retrieve historical data in a tourist kiosk. Similarly, the Story Telling Cubes as shown in Figure 1 right, could be a block with each side representing a different activity for a character, the Monkey, or a combination of a Character block and an Environment block to trigger different animations on the computer.

Fig. 1. Navigational Blocks and Storytelling Cubes

3.1.2 FlexM and Posey

FlexM is a hub-and-strut toy for making and manipulating geometric models with computer models and simulations [6]. Sensors and microprocessors embedded in the hubs determine the topology and geometry of the model the user assembles. With flexible joints on the hubs, the designer can make models that transform dynamically. The hubs transmit parametric information to the computer, which renders the model on the screen in real time. This enables the designer to create complex forms with the fun and directness of playing with a toy. Posey [7] enhanced the hub-and-strut topology with optocouples ball and socket joints that determine the poses (roll, pitch and yaw of connections) of the struts and use Zigbee to transmit data wirelessly to activate different applications running on a host computer. The host computer displays a representation and configuration of the physical model in real time as the user plays with the Posey interface. The representation can trigger different applications in different domains. For example, posing Posey as a skeleton of a puppet, one can control the movement of a virtual dinosaur for an online puppet show. Or using Posey's hub and strut to represent the atoms and bonds for molecule, a molecule modeling application can retrieve information of molecules of similar configurations. Figure 2 shows the hub-and-strut construction toy FlexM (left) and the real time update of the onscreen geometry, the components (struts, ball and socket joints) of Posey (center), and an online puppet show of a dinosaur created with Posey (right).

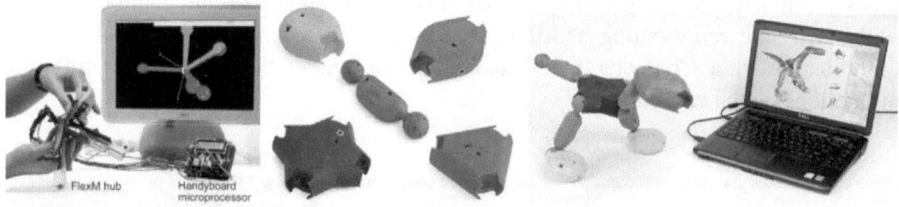

Fig. 2. FlexM is a computationally enhanced hub-and-strut construction toy. Posey is an interface of optocouples ball and socket joints and struts that can transmit wirelessly to different domain applications such as an online puppet show.

3.1.3 Mobile Music Touch

Mobile Music Touch [8, 9] is a light-weight glove that facilitate passive haptic learning of piano playing. When the music is playing, the glove taps corresponding finger for each key so one can learn to play music while doing household chores or on the move. The Mobile Music Touch is outfitted with vibration motors to cue users which finger to use to play the next note. Figure 3 shows a user's hand with the music glove playing on a lighted keyboard, a version in a converted golf glove, and a fingerless version with strap-on hardware box. A pilot study with students with no musical backgrounds shows that the songs that were cued with the glove have lesser

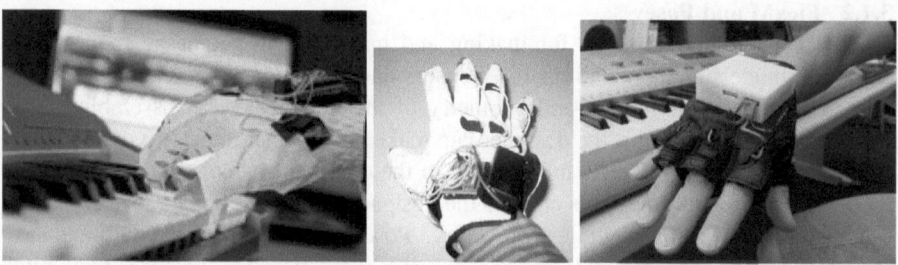

Fig. 3. Vibrating motors of Mobile Music Touch cue which fingers to play

finger key mistakes than the ones without. A study with quadriplegic patients shows that a short-term use of the glove improved sensation and mobility for people with spinal cord injury [10]. It's encouraging that a wearable device like this could be an engaging and pervasive hand rehabilitation as well as music learning.

3.2   The Bench Paradigm - Responsive Furniture

In the scale of the human body what types of forms and functions conform to our movements and activities? Can we imagine having chairware, tableware, and everyware [11]?

3.2.1 MouseHaus Table and TeleTables

MouseHaus Table [12] is an interface to pedestrian movement simulation. It uses a video camera to capture images of paper cutouts representing urban elements on a table, as collaborating designers add, remove, and rearrange them to propose configurations of buildings, streets, and parks. A visual simulation of pedestrian behavior is projected on top of these arrangements, allowing the designers to understand the effects of their proposed arrangements. Instead of using a structured editor to input urban elements, users of MouseHaus Table cut out colored papers with scissors and arrange them on the table to see real-time simulation feedback. TeleTables [13] are a pair of networked table that capture shadows cast and respond in blinking lights, it's a telepresence project that connects people of remote places by using wireless communication between the tables to sense shadows that are cast on one table to be mirrored and represented with light on the other table. A person sitting down on an interactive table to eat a meal would activate yellow light on that table to reflect the shadow and movement of the activity and transmit that to the remote table while the other table user's motions would in turn displayed in another table. By having traces of lights on both tables, the presence of both parties were subtly conveyed and created a bi-locative interface.

3.2.2 Window Seat and Music Under Pressure

Window Seat is a chairware interface to control remote camera motion [13]. This project uses the rock and swivel of a chair as an interface for a pan and tilt camera. A rocking chair controls the up/down tilt and a set of pressure sensors to control the left/right pan. A tiny camera is placed inside an architectural model, and a projector mounted inside the chair and a mirror displays the camera's current viewpoint on the wall in front of the chair. The chair's occupant can visually occupy a scale model or remote space (Figure 4 left). The Music Under Pressure project [15] used conductive foam and washers to act as pressure sensors embedded under the cushions of the couch and each sensor is mapped to a specific MIDI sound in a part of a musical ensemble (Figure 4 right). Infrared rangefinders and tap sensors are embedded in the arms and seat backs of the couch as part of this playful environment that could in turn motivate embodied interaction for the seated.

Fig. 4. Window Seat rocking chair's up/down and left/right motion controls a remote camera. A girl plays cartwheel on a musical couch embedded with pressure sensors triggers specific sound in Music Under Pressure.

3.2.3 Patient Interactive Communication and Learning System

The Patient Interactive Communication and Learning System (PILS) combines communication tools in a hospital into a bedside foldable railing tablet [14]. This easy-to-use system, as shown in Figure 5, has a one-touch call button that connects to videophones for nurses, and family teleconferencing. Vital signs, entertainment and educational video as well as medical and clinician visitation record can all be activated in this "command post" for easy access and communication to alleviate the stress of the patients, family and care givers.

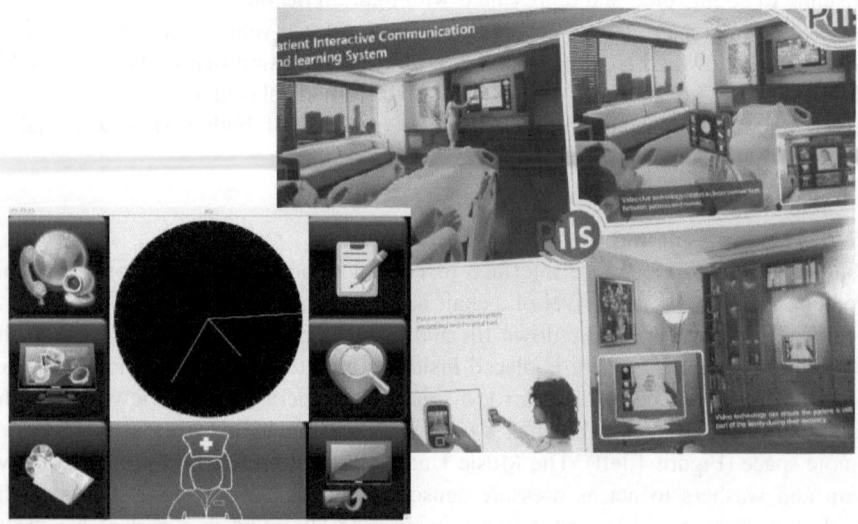

Fig. 5. Patient Interactive Communication & Learning System mounted on the bedside connects patients, care givers & family members at home, monitors vital signs and provides learning opportunities

3.3   The Bionic Building Paradigm - Interactive Environments

Beyond the brick and bench paradigms, the next level of interaction happens in the scale of life like building scale. The bionic building paradigm houses interesting, interactive and transformative environments in building components.

3.3.1 Plant Tiles and Alphabet Space

Plant Tiles [15] translate people's movement on the floor into control of video playing (Figure 6 left). A six by ten foot platform sits in front of a rear-projected screen showing time-lapse video of plant growth. When you step onto the platform, a projected video sequence plays to a key frame. Walking toward the screen plays the sequence forward; walking backward reverses it. Side to side movement triggers different video segments. The Alphabet Paint Space [15] is an interactive mural in public space painted by the movements of passers by. The software captures the colors of people's clothing and renders fading traces or watercolor effects in the large projected canvas wall. The result is a spontaneous play in which the audience are at the same time the authors of the interactive art.

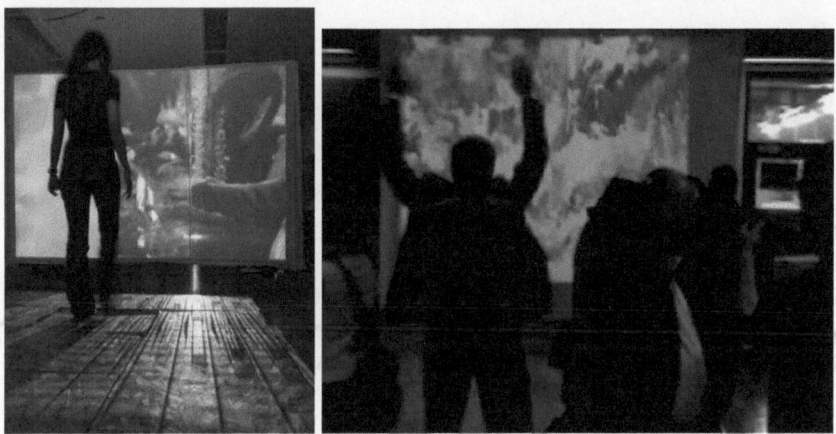

Fig. 6. Left: Floor tile sensors create an interactive platform space in PlantTiles. Right: Interactive mural created with people's movement in the Alphabet Paint Space.

3.3.2 Espresso Blocks and Digital Animation Museum

The goal of Architectural Robotics is to meet human needs and comfort. Espresso Blocks [16] are self-assembling building blocks that build dynamic structures (Figure 7 left) such as a live/work espresso stand that can respond to the occupants' desires and needs and transforms itself throughout the day.

The Digital Animation Museum [17] project explores the notion that architectural spaces and forms can be influenced by ubiquitous and wireless information technology to provide flexibility in spatial programming. The building experience can be manipulated in a variety of ways to interact with and respond to visitor interests and preferences. Each unit space in the museum can automatically reconfigure itself to form space and change the exhibit display by identifying the preference and behavior of the viewers. In this way, buildings and visitors can collaborate to produce a unique and individualized experience of the visit and the space.

Figure 7 (right) shows a 3D view of a reconfigurable unit space in which partition and display walls are changeable to enclose a room with variable numbers of units. The floor plan (top right) shows a grid system in which different size rooms can be formed between the structure columns. The diagram illustrates variation of paths through the museum taken by different visitors.

If for example, an urban plaza has a similar grid plan layout so that each of the unit square is the size of a floor tile and each tile block is instrumented with a spring-tilt mechanism [18] so it could go up and down, and lock at different height positions, we can then push up and down different unit tile blocks to reconfigure the plaza to accommodate different occasions such as seating for intimate conversations, family picnic gathering, or a tiered stadium concert seating. With Architectural Robotics, the plaza could be self-configuring based on the context by sensing behavior patterns or direct instructions from the people.

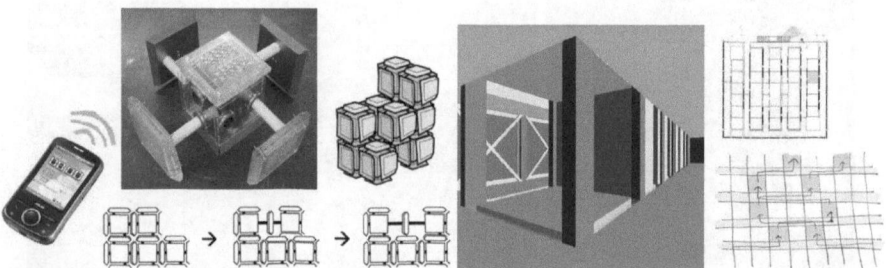

Fig 7 Left: Self assembling Espresso Blocks. Right. A unit space, the floor plan grid, and different paths through the building in Digital Animation Museum.

3.3.3 Transformer Architecture

Employing modular robotics techniques, an architectural space, or an architectural robotic structure, can cycle through different structures to accommodate different activities such as an espresso stand during the day and an entertainment room in the evening. The occupant can rearrange the blocks with their remote control to create new configurations, save them, and even trade designs with others.

TransDorm [19] is a convertible multi-purpose two-person dormitory unit that supports transformation of sleeping quarter into living, study, or a place to play and entertain. Figure 8 shows that elevated beds, desks, cabinets, sofa and media wall, etc. can be arranged to accommodate different activities. Care On Rail [20] extends the functionality of a hospital ER or OR into an acuity-adaptable room by providing mobile, sharable medical resources mounted on the ceiling sliders (Figure 8 right) to eliminate equipment clutter that hinder care and operations. Caregivers can choose sliders from different equipment zones, adjust the slider height and location, detach or connect different instruments (e.g., masks, hooks, operating lamp, monitor, defibrillator or ultrasound machine) as needed for different setup, operation and maintenance.

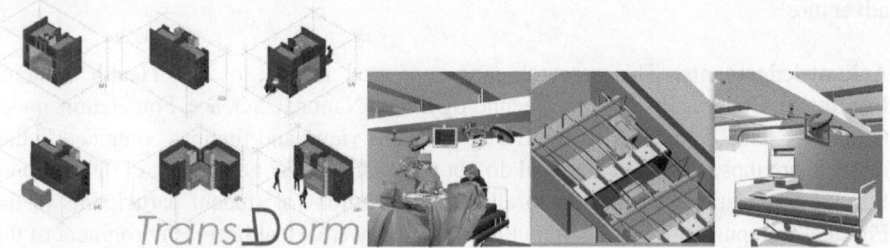

Fig. 8. Left: Different spatial arrangements in TransDorm. Right: Care On Rail, adaptable equipment sliders.

4   Toward a Smart Living Environment

4.1   Living Machines

The notion of an architecture machine for living is not new. "A house," stated Le Corbusier, "is "a machine for living in" [21]. Eastman's Adaptive-Conditional Architecture includes "a sensing device, a control algorithm, a change mechanism, and a control setting" [22]. Negroponte [23] described in his Soft Architecture Machines that a "responsive architecture" is an environment that takes an "active role," initiates changes "as a result and function of complex or simple computations" but also "knows me" and the context it is in. Archigram proposed an entire neighborhood could relocate and move with the economical fluctuations and lifestyle changes in the form of a Walking City [24].

4.2   Towards Happy Healthy Living

To create structures composed of dynamic materials like Espresso Blocks, or to operate transformer architecture like TransDorm or Care on Rail, we need interfaces that are easy and intuitive. To specify a desired design form, perhaps one can demonstrate by stacking up the blocks, and a planning algorithm can automatically generate a rule set to produce that form. To transform a living space or a patient room, perhaps multi-modal inputs such as voice commands and gestures, combined with the identification of the context and the past experience sensed by the environment, different rule sets could be selected and run on the physical and robotic architecture.

4.3   Discussion and Future Work

We hope a vision of a future living space can emerge from this effort to become much more responsive, accessible, and expressive, and delightful. We want our living space smart, but also wise.

Reading about magic is like reading about food. There is no substitute for the real thing and real experience. We hope many of you would join us in this magic making adventure!

Acknowledgements. This research was supported in part by the Health Systems Institute at Georgia Institute of Technology, and National Science Foundation under Grant ITR-0326054 and CCLI DUE-0127579. The views and findings contained in this material are those of the authors and do not necessarily reflect the views of the National Science Foundation. Thank you to all the contributions of student participants in the Physical Computing, Design Computing and Everyware, Healthcare Environment of the Future, and Happy Healthy Home courses over the years.

References

1. Kay, A.: The best way to predict the future is to invent it. Mathematical Social Sciences 30(3), 326 (1995)
2. Rand, P.: Design and the Play Instinct. In: Kepes, G. (ed.) Education of Vision, Studio Vista, London, pp. 156–174 (1965)
3. Hettler, B.: Six Dimensions of Wellness, National Wellness Institute (1976), http://www.nwi.org, http://www.hettler.com/sixdimen.htm
4. Camarata, K., Do, E., Gross, M., Johnson, B.: Navigational Blocks: Tangible Navigation of Digital Information. In: ACM Conference on Human Factors (SIGCHI), pp. 751–752. ACM Press (2003)
5. Camarata, K., Gross, M., Do, E.Y.-L.: A Physical Computing Studio: Exploring Computational Artifacts and Environments. International Journal Architectural Computing 1(2), 169–190 (2003)
6. Eng, M., Camarata, K., Do, E.Y.-L., Gross, M.D.: FlexM: Designing a Physical Construction Kit for 3D Modeling. In: Cheng, N., Pinet, C. (eds.) IJAC – International Journal of Architectural Computing, June 1, vol. 4(2), pp. 27–47. Multi-Science Publishing Co. Ltd. (2006); (Eng: M Arch student, Camarata: former MS student, Gross: faculty colleague), doi:10.1260/1478-0771.4.2.27
7. Weller, M.P., Do, E.Y.-L., Gross, M.D.: Tangible Sketching in 3D with Posey. In: Ext Abstracts of 27th International Conference on Human Factors in Computing (CHI 2009) Session: Interactivity: Touch & Feel, Boston, MA, USA, April 5-9, pp. 3193–3198 (2009)
8. Huang, K., Do, E.Y.-L., Starner, T.: PianoTouch: A Wearable Haptic Piano Instruction System For Passive Learning of Piano Skills. In: ISWC 2008, 12th IEEE International Symposium on Wearable Computers, Pittsburgh, Pennsylavania, September 28-October 1, pp. 41–44 (2008), http://www.iswc.net/
9. Huang, K., Starner, T., Do, E., Weiberg, G., Kohlsdorf, D., Ahlrichs, C., Leibrandt, R.: Mobile music touch: mobile tactile stimulation for passive learning. In: Proceedings of the 28th International Conference on Human Factors in Computing Systems (CHI 2010), pp. 791–800. ACM, New York (2010), http://doi.acm.org/10.1145/1753326.1753443, doi:10.1145/1753326.1753443

10. Markow, T., Ramakrishnan, N., Huang, K., Starner, T., Eicholtz, M., Garrett, S., Profita, H., Scarlata, A., Schooler, C., Tarun, A., Backus, D.: Mobile Music Touch: Vibration Stimulus as a Possible Hand Rehabilitation Method. In: Proceedings of the 4th International Pervasive Health Conference, Munich, Germany (March 2010)
11. Greenfield, A.: Everyware: The Dawning Age of Ubiquitous Computing. New Riders Publishing
12. Huang, C.-J., Do, E.Y.-L., Gross, M.D.: MouseHaus Table: A Physical Interface for Urban Design. In: UIST, User Interface Software and Technology, Conference Supplement, November 2-5, pp. 41–42. UIST, Vancouver
13. Oh, Y., Camarata, K., Weller, M.P., Gross, M.D., Do, E.Y.-L.: TeleTables and Window Seat: Bilocative Furniture Interfaces. In: Theng, Y.-L., Duh, H.B.L. (eds.) Ubiquitous Computing: Design, Implementation, and Usability. Information Science Reference, ch. 11, pp. 160–171. IGI Global, Hershey (2008) ISBN-13: 978-1-59904-693-8 (hardcover) ISBN-13: 978-1-59904-695-2 (e-book) reference
14. Do, E.Y.-L., Jones, B.D.: Happy Healthy Home. In: Maitland, J. (ed.) The Handbook of Ambient Assistive Technologies for Healthcare, Rehabilitation and Well-being, vol. 11, pp. 195–210. IOS Press, Amsterdam (2012), doi:10.3233/978-1-60750-837-3-195
15. Camarata, K., Gross, M.D., Do, E.Y.-L.: Physical Computing, a design studio that bridges art, science, and engineering. In: ICLS 2002, The Fifth International Conference of the Learning Sciences, Seattle, October 23-26, pp. 520–521 (2002)
16. Weller, M.P., Do, E.Y.-L.: Architectural Robotics: A New Paradigm for the Built Environment. In: De Paoli, G., Zreik, K., Beheshti, R. (eds.) EuropIA.11, 11th International Conference on Design Sciences & Technology, Digital Thinking in Architecture, Civil Engineering, Archaeology, Urban Planning and Design: Finding the Ways, Montreal, Quebec, Canada, Europia, September 19-21 (2007)
17. Chen, J.: DAM: Digital Animation Museum. M. Arch thesis, University of Washington, Seattle (2002)
18. Shelton, E.: Adaptable Urban Plaza Seating, Digital Design Studio, University of Washington (Spring 2000)
19. Sivcevic, E.: Trans-Dorm: transformable space. In: Happy Healthy Home Class 2009. Georgia Tech. (2009), http://wiki.cc.gatech.edu/designcomp/index.php/Happy_Healthy_Home
20. Al-Emam, F., Kuo, C.-L., Masse, D.: Care On Rail: Extendable Adaptable Sliders, Emergency Room of the Future 2008 (2008), http://www.hsi.gatech.edu/erfuture/
21. Corbusier, L.: Towards a New Architecture (original title: Vers une architecture). Eng. Trans. (1923)
22. Eastman, C.: Adaptive-Conditional Architecture. In: Design Participation, Proc. Design Research Society's Conference, pp. 51–57. Academy Editions (1971, 1972)
23. Negroponte, N.: Soft Architecture Machines. MIT Press (1976)
24. Herron, R., Harvey, B.: A Walking City. Archigram 5 (1964)

Computing the Incomputable with Human Processing Units

Jonathan Corney[1,*], Gokula Annamalai Vasantha[1], Andrew Lynn[1],
Ananda Jagadeesan[1], Nuran Acur[1], Marisa Smith[1], and Anupam Agarwal[2]

[1] Design Manufacture and Engineering Management, University of Strathclyde, Glasgow, UK
{Jonathan.corney,Gokula.annamalai-vasantha,
Andrew.lynn,Ananda.jagadeesan,Nuran.acur,M.k.smith}@strath.ac.uk
[2] Information Technology Division, Indian Institute of Information Technology Allahabad,
India
anupam@iiita.ac.in

Abstract. Initially commercial crowdsourcing services (such as Amazon's Mechanical Turk) were focused largely on providing micro-labor services for tasks such as image labeling and text processing. However it is becoming increasingly apparent that these services can also be regarded as providing parallel, on-demand, networks of (so-called) 'Human Processing Units' (HPUs). Such services are able to provide specialist computational facilities in a manner analogous to the way Graphics Processing Units (GPUs) support the specialist process of high speed rendering. This paper describes how this new technology could extend the functionality of mechanical CAD/CAM or PLM systems. Crucial to the commercial feasibility of such systems is the ability to access networks of HPUs where engineering data can be processed securely (unlike open crowdsourcing sites such as mTurk). The paper reports the initial results of work done to establish the feasibility of a proposed architecture for integrating HPUs into desktop CAD that uses established BPO centers in rural India to provide a secure source of geometric intelligence.

Keywords: Crowdsourcing, Human Processing Units, CAD/CAM, BPO.

1 Introduction

In many jobs machine intelligence is already emerging as a pivotal technology. But while AI systems are well established in are as such as translation, navigation and speech recognition, manufacturing has yet to find cost effective method of automating many common reasoning tasks. Next-generation cost effective manufacturing systems aim to increase efficiency and effectiveness of overall production processes. Rigidity of the production system and limitations of artificial intelligence (AI) technologies are some of the important hindrances to achieve this aim. Shea [1] argues that a key to creating a highly adaptable and flexible manufacturing system is embedding on-line,

---

* Corresponding author.

A. Agrawal et al. (Eds.): IITM 2013, CCIS 276, pp. 14–24, 2013.

cognitive capabilities in the machines and the production control. This argument stresses requirement for support mechanisms to facilitate the unique interaction between human cognition and programmed machine controls. So such systems should aim to provide intelligent support rather than total automation. However this paper makes the case that industrial system should also provide an integrated environment for distributed, online problem solving. Such, so called, Crowdsourcing is an emerging concept which aims to use the power of people to solve problems that range from micro-tasks (e.g. image labeling and text processing) to making creative decisions (e.g. design generation). In other words Crowdsourcing is an online, distributed problem-solving and production model that has emerged in recent years [2].

In commerce the term crowdsourcing is commonly used to describe "a new web-based business model that harnesses the creative solutions of a distributed network of individuals through what amounts to an open call for proposals" [3]. The Crowdsourcing approach is exemplified by Amazon's "Mechanical Turk" (mturk.com) site that provides an online, automated, marketplace that co-ordinates the use of human intelligence to perform tasks which computers are unable to do. While computing technology continues to improve, there are still many things that human beings can do much more effectively than computers. Crowdsourcing has the potential to revolutionize the way jobs requiring human judgments are performed by offering a 'virtual automation' of tasks. Core advantages of this crowdsourcing approach are 24/7 labor market open, with a diverse workforce available to perform tasks quickly and cheaply. The crowdsourcing market is growing at an accelerated rate (~75% in 2011) and the number of crowdsourcing workers is growing in excess of 100% per annum [4]. Contrary to a commonly held view crowdsourcing as a transfer of low-skill work to low cost locations, the analysis carried out by Crowdsourcing.org shows that the majority of crowdsourcing workers are 18-40 years old, well-educated, with almost 60% living in developed countries [4]. It has been pointed that almost two thirds of Crowdsourcing market revenues are coming from three industry sectors: Internet Services, Media and Entertainment, and Technology. Stalwarts of traditional outsourcing, like Financial Services, Manufacturing and Government are significantly behind in terms of adoption, presenting significant potential for crowdsourcing providers [4]. It has been reported that only few industrial applications of Crowdsourcing have been reported in literature [5]. This is surprising because many of the reasoning and planning tasks inherent in CAD/CAM involve 2 or 3D problems that are difficult to automate computationally.

To demonstrate Crowdsourcing as a tool to facilitate machine intelligence in a knowledge-based factory, we have chosen the geometric reasoning tasks (2D part nesting) associated with many industrial processes and engineering computations. The belief is based on the observation that humans, regardless of their educational or social background, are adept at manipulating and reasoning about shapes, a task that computers find extraordinarily difficult to do. The authors have previously reported how workers on an open, public crowdsourcing service (i.e, mTurk) can produce more effective packing layouts than the best algorithms, but practical implementation requires that such work is done in a secure environment. Consequently this paper reports the results of an initial investigation to establish if similar performance could be obtained from BPO centers in rural India.

Business process outsourcing emerged over thirty years ago as a subset of outsourcing that involves the contracting of the operations and responsibilities of specific business functions (or processes) to a third-party service provider. The BPO industry is well established and according to McKinsey [6], the global "addressable" BPO market is worth $122 – $154 billion across of which around 70% is associated with retail banking and insurance businesses. India has revenues of $10.9 billion from offshore BPO and $30 billion from IT. Although about a million workers are employed in the Indian BPO industry almost all of those jobs are in cities (70% of Indian's 1 Billion citizens live in rural areas that are largely remote from BPO operations). Rural BPOs are emerging in the developing countries where outsourcing to rural workers could provide a sustainable source of skilled employment that gives opportunity to the majority of the population regardless of their educational background.

This work is motivated by the vision of exploiting an innate human ability (found in both rural and urban workforces) to reason about shape being employed remotely to improve the efficiency of manufacturing industry. The hypothesis is that such a scheme could make a significant economic contribution to rural populations through a long term source of high value, "distributable" work that does not demand professional levels of numerical or linguistic skills. The remaining sections of this paper present a high level schematic overview of interaction between, CAD/CAM systems whose intelligence is boosted by HPUs organized to provide a secure (i.e. private) Crowdsourcing facility. Subsequent sections describe the research focus and methodology used to produce a systematic comparison of the results obtained from open (mTurk) and closed (BPO) Crowdsourcing platforms and algorithms. The paper closes with a discussion of the work and draws some conclusions.

2   Schematic View to Aid Interaction between AI and HPUs

Many of the combinatorial problems found in functions such as Operations Management (e.g. job-shop scheduling, route planning and container packing) software can only produce "good" rather than optimum solutions [7]. Because of this it is

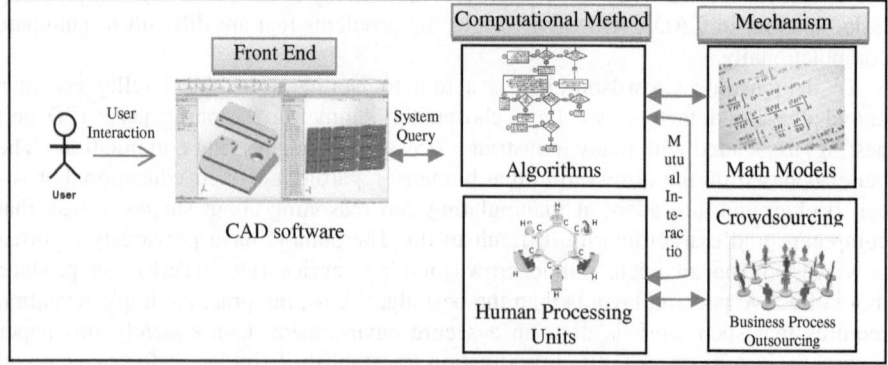

Fig. 1. Schematic view to aid Interaction between AI and HPUs

frequently possible for humans to improve on the algorithmically generated solutions computed by CAD/CAM software [8]. Figure 1 illustrates the interaction required between human cognition and AI technologies to improve on the algorithmically generated solutions.

Although researchers have developed numerous computational approaches to reasoning and knowledge representation, their implementations are always limited to specific applications (e.g. assembly planning, fault diagnosis or production scheduling) for which bespoke knowledge bases or algorithms have been created. However, "cloud computing" has made irrelevant both the physical location and internal processes used by machine intelligence. In other words, the Internet encourages functional processes to be treated as 'black boxes' with which users need only be concerned with posing the right question and interpreting the response. The system asking the questions does not need to know how answers are generated, only that they are available in an appropriate time frame. A direct consequence of this methodology is that rather than systems requiring, say, rule-bases, inference-engines, fitness functions or databases of "case" examples, the focus becomes the construction of queries for the crowd and the development of statistical methods for the aggregation of their responses. Thus parallel, on-demand, networks of (so-called) 'Human Processing Units' (HPUs) act as an aid to enhance the algorithmically generated solutions. The recent work at MIT [9] that has shown when the crowd are allowed to incrementally review and refine solutions to difficult optimization or recognition problems, the overall effect is much more than simply the sum of individual efforts. If the proposed approach could be established that enabled Crowdsourcing infrastructures to be used to enhance the algorithmically generated solutions, the scope of potential establishment is huge with the global market for CAD/CAM systems is estimated to be around \$26.3 billion in 2010 [10].

3   Research Focus and Methodology

To investigate the feasibility of implementing Crowdsourcing methods in a Rural BPO outsourcing, in this paper we used 'Expert' tasks. In general, these are difficult problems where some individuals exhibit an exceptional ability and computational approaches are NP-complete (i.e. have infinite search space that cannot be fully explored by even the most powerful computers). We used 2D packing (i.e. nesting) problems to illustrate possible enhancement of the algorithmically generated solutions through Open Crowdsourcing and BPO infrastructures.

The 2D packing (i.e. nesting) problems have been extensively studied for several decades because of the numerous industrial applications where there is a need to place a variable number of arbitrary shapes into the smallest space to minimize wasted material or maximize bin capacity. For example, in the manufacture of sheet metal stampings, material can represent 75%, or more, of the total cost consequently even small changes in material usage can directly impact on the profit of an enterprise [11]. Similar economic considerations exist in the wood, clothing, glass and paper industries, where 2D shapes have to be cut from large sheets of raw material. In all cases, the aim is to reduce the cost by minimizing the amount of waste left after the desired shapes have been removed from the raw material. Computation of a theoretically optimum solution for 2D part nesting is known to be NP-complete and consequently numerous "good" and "near optimum" solution are used in practice. However the ability to improve on even a good solution can often have significant economic benefits (e.g. less waste, higher productivity).

The aim is to investigate (costs, performance, speed) of Industrial 2D nesting problem using real data. The use of engineering data will allow the value of the Crowdsourcing and BPO work to be quantified for different levels of performance and provide vital input to the business study. To investigate this possibility, we created an experiment that asked mTurk workers and rural BPO workers to pack 2D shape into the smallest possible area. This experiment intends to establish the capabilities of crowd workers and rural BPO workers to do a 2D geometric reasoning task. The results obtained from the Crowdsourcing infrastructures are compared with the results of the best current computational approaches found in commercial CAD/CAM software.

Corney et al. [12] suggest three possible categorizations for the classification of Crowdsourcing tasks based upon: nature of the task (creation, evaluation and organization tasks), nature of the crowd ('expert', 'most people' and 'vast majority') and nature of the payment (voluntary contribution, rewarded at a flat rate and rewarded with a prize). The sample problem undertaken in this work lies in the creation task. 'Most people' and 'Vast majority' crowd sets have been used to illustrate the benefits of the Crowdsourcing approach. The packing problem occurs in many different applications from container transportation to the 2D stamping of complex profiles on CNC machines [13]. The task tests the crowd's ability to interactively optimize a problem with many complex interactions (and provides a numerical measure of success) by asking workers to create the most compact layout of a set of profiles. The packing task is seeking the best amongst many attempts. Like many design tasks, results cannot be averaged or aggregated in the packing task.

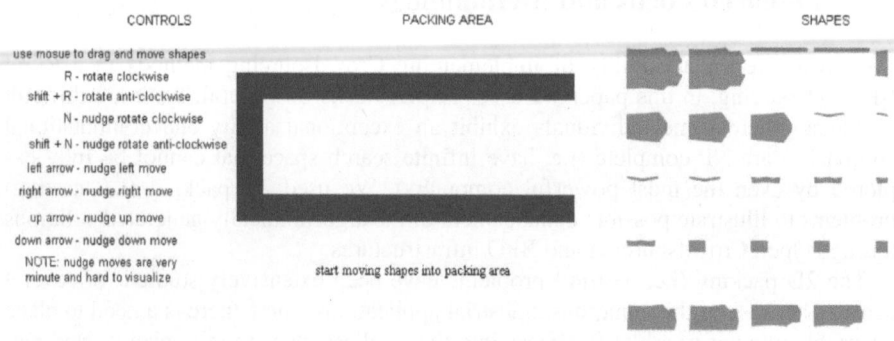

Fig. 2. The 2D-packing task

Table 1. Albano problem definition

Number of different pieces	Total number of pieces	Vertices by piece (by average)	Plate width
8	24	7.25	4900

Figure 2 illustrates the design of the 2D-packing task used in this study. In order to quantify the effectiveness and performance of the Crowdsourcing approach for two-dimensional strip packing, several experiments were conducted using the Albano data sets [14] from the textile industry and comprises a total of 24 items (Table 1). This design of this task was developed using "Flash" software. The workers were provided with the task of packing objects of different shapes into a rectangular space on the webpage, while ensuring that the overall length of the space used was as small as possible. The shapes of the objects used in the packing task shown belong to the Mumford-Valenzuela benchmark data set [15].

The green shapes could be dragged into the space provided within the red boundaries. The workers were able to rotate and nudge the objects to allow denser packing. The length of the space used was displayed dynamically while the objects were packed, so the worker could manipulate their positions and orientations in order to get an efficient packing. Once they were satisfied with the packing they could upload the results using the "Submit" button in the designed Flash page. The work submitted was scored and classified depending on the density of their packing, in %, and the time employed to return the task. Table 2 describes the experiment parameters used in the Open Crowdsourcing platform and rural BPO. The results obtained from the Open Crowdsourcing and Rural BPO approaches are compared with the best results available from the literature, which corresponds to the simulated annealing hybrid algorithm (SAHA) [16] and an extended local search algorithm (ELS) [17]. The next section discusses the results obtained from these three different approaches.

Table 2. Parameters distinguish between Crowdsourcing and Rural BPO

Parameters	mTurk Crowdsourcing platform	Rural BPO
Number of workers	10	40
Payment	$3 per worker	Paid $1-3 per worker to the BPO organization, not to the workers directly
Time allotted	Not restricted to time limits	Time limited to one hour due to organization constraints
Bonus	A bonus of $0.5 per 0.5% of improvement on the 'best result'	No bonus provided

4   Results

The results generated from the three different approaches namely: Computer Algorithms, Open Crowdsourcing and Rural BPO are discussed in this section. Firstly a hybrid algorithm (SAHA) and an extended local search algorithm (ELS) proposed in the literature to solve Irregular Strip Packing problems are presented. Gomes and Oliveira [16] proposed the metaheuristic simulated annealing to guide the search over the solution space while linear programming models are solved to generate neighbor-hoods during the search process. The linear programming models are used to locally optimize the layouts, derive from the application of compaction and separation algo-rithms. The proposed simulated annealing hybrid algorithm produced 87.43% efficiency in the average time of 2257 seconds for the Albano 2D-packing task in the computational tests consisted on 20 runs for each instance. The computational tests were performed on a personal computer with a Pentium IV processor running at 2.4GHz and with 512Mb of RAM. In 2012, Leung et al. [17] present an extended local search algorithm (ELS) for the irregular strip packing problem. It adopts two neighborhoods, swapping two given polygons in a placement and placing one poly-gon into a new position. The tabu search algorithm is used to avoid local minima, and a compact algorithm is presented to improve the result. The proposed ELS algorithm produced 88.48% efficiency in the average time of 1203 seconds for the Albano 2D-packing task in the computational tests consisted on 10 runs for each in-stance with same computational power used by Gomes and Oliveira [16]. Figure 3 illustrates the efficient packing layout generated by the SAHA and ELS algorithms. These best layouts are compared later with the solutions generated by the Crowdsourcing and Rural BPO workers.

Table 3. Best layout generated by the SAHA and ELS algorithms

SAHA Algorithm [16]	ELS Algorithm [17]

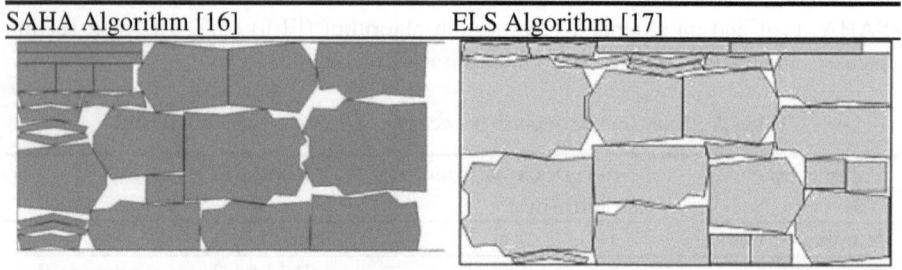

Best efficiency - 87.43% (2257 seconds)	Best efficiency - 88.48% (1203 seconds)

For the Open crowdsourcing approach through mTurk.com, two sets of experi-ments were conducted. In the first set, the crowd workers were given the Albano 2D-packing task without showing the best solution. In the second set, the workers were presented with the best solution generated before and asked them to improve the solution. In both the sets of experiments, 10 mTurk workers were involved. Figure 3 illustrates the efficiency of 2D-packing task by the mTurk crowdsourcing workers before and after the best solution was shown to them.

Performance of Crowdsourcing against the Albano benchmark produced the best efficiency of 89.41% in the time of 4018 seconds. Figure 3 illustrates that this highest efficiency was reached after the best solution generated from the first set was shown to the mTurk workers. The average in the second set (84.8%) is considerably in-creased compared to the first set (80.15%) where the best solution was not shown.

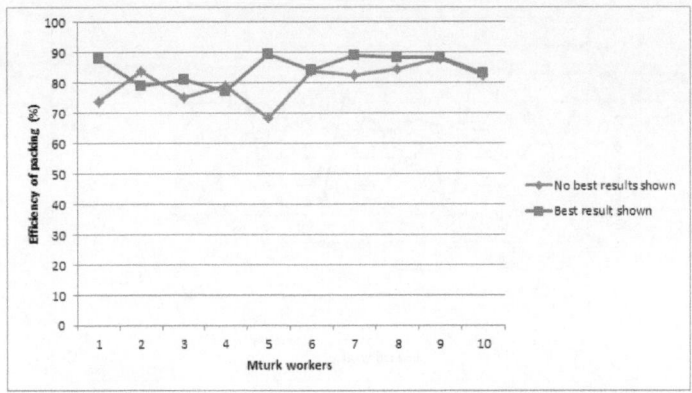

Fig. 3. Efficiency of packing by the mTurk crowdsourcing workers

The correlation between the efficiency of packing and the time taken by the crowd workers in first and second sets are 0.65 and 0.53 respectively. Table 4 represents the best layout generated by a mTurk worker.

Table 4. Best layout generated by the mturk crowdsourcing and Rural BPO worker

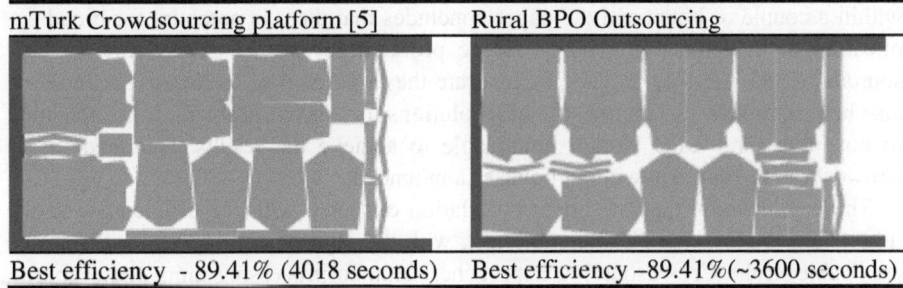

mTurk Crowdsourcing platform [5]	Rural BPO Outsourcing
Best efficiency - 89.41% (4018 seconds)	Best efficiency –89.41%(~3600 seconds)

For the rural BPO outsourcing, we have chosen two rural BPO organizations located in two different states of India. The 2D-packing task was assigned for twenty rural BPO workers in each centre through the internet. The percentage of efficiency received from these two rural BPO centres are plotted in Figure 4. The Rural BPO – 2 workers (average: 84.1, Min: 78, Max: 89.41) performed better compared to the Rural BPO – 1 centre (average: 81.9, Min: 76.82, Max: 85.54). But variation in the results is much wider in the Rural BPO – 2 centre. The best 2D-packing layout produced for the Albano problem is tabulated and compared with Crowdsourcing mTurk worker's best solution in Table 4. These results from the Crowdsoucing platform and Rural BPO centres demonstrate that their performance is found to be superior to reported computational algorithms in both cases.

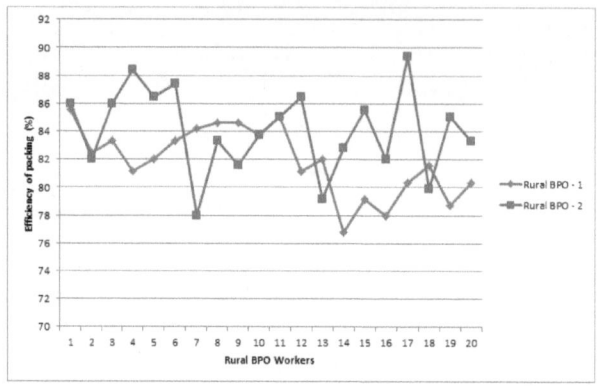

Fig. 4. Efficiency of packing by the Rural BPO workers

5　Discussion and Future Work

From these results it can be observed that the Open CrowdSourcing and Rural BPO approaches, although considerably slower, improved on the best algorithmic result published in the literature for this data set. In all these cases results were returned within a couple of hours and the paper concludes that there is potential for broad application of Crowdsourcing to geometric problem solving in CAD/CAM. Crowdsourcing could not only be used to generate the large pool of 'solutions' needed but also help retrieve (e.g. identify) the best solutions for a given problem. It is interesting to note that rural BPO worker could able to achieve the results generated in the Crowdsorucing platform without bonuses announced.

The results show that the linear correlation expected with the efficiency and the time taken to solve the NP-complete task with the algorithmic approach will not be applicable in the Crowdsourcing approaches. Human processing units could able to find better solutions much quicker if provided with the best possible solution to improve upon [19]. There was not a strong correlation between the outcome of this experiment and the educational background of the 'workers', their age, time spent at mTurk, or even the country where they lived [5].

Demonstration of availability of intelligence in the Open Crowdsourcing and rural BPO approaches could act as a unique selling point other than low wages to enable the spread of knowledge economy to rural areas. Also the results demonstrate the constant availability of sufficient quantity, and quality, of on-line workers crucial to any industrial use of Crowdsourced "human intelligence". Our results suggest that the Internet is now sufficiently large and globally distributed well that commercial Crowdsourcing sites and rural BPO centres can easily provide results in only a few hours on a 24/7 basis. However, finding the "right" crowd, especially if the task to solve requires a 'special talent' could be a challenge. The quantification of the Crowd's performance will help give confidence that the "right" workers are being employed.

The paper presents the early results of Crowdsourced part nesting where not only do the results improve upon those generated by commercial CAM systems but could, potentially, also provide insights into how automate system could be improved. Through continuous learning loop from human cognition to machine algorithms helps to update algorithms with new knowledge models. In addition to recognizing the value of having "human's in the loop", enterprises wishing to exploit Crowdsourcing will also have to tackle the issues of confidentiality. Rural BPO approach provides substantial platform to handle the issues of confidentiality. It has been observed that the crucial aspect was to formulate the right question and carefully consider the instructions provided to the mTurk and BPO workers. The formulation of appropriate questions could be channeled towards the harness of the crowd's judgment and knowledge, so the system can react at any given scenario when a problem arises, with the most appropriate solution in each case provided by the crowd.

Further work in this area includes the exploitation of Crowdsourcing in the gathering of solution strategies and examples rather than just recording the end result. Indeed understanding the problem solving process used by humans is often a first step towards teaching machines how to learn and acquire the knowledge to support the process [18]. Currently we are working to quantify potential economic benefits for both manufacturing industry and crowdsourcing workforce to solve various industrial optimization tasks. The extension of this work as the potential to impact on several established areas of academic research into process optimisations (ie. CNC machining, stamping, FEA analysis, process planning, process costing, etc). A research question "how to embed knowledge-based resources in a company's systems (e.g. work flow)" is yet to be answered. There is also considerable scope for further academic investigation of the reward schemes used to motivate the Crowd. The relationship between payment levels, speed of response and quality of results will require large scale, sustained trials.

Acknowledgement. This research was collaboratively funded by EPSRC, UK (Grant EP/J000728/1) and DST, India (Grant DST/SEED/INDO – UK/005/2011/C) as part of the research project "Distributing Industrial Optimization Tasks To Rural Workers".

References

1. Shea, K.: Editorial of the cognitive factory. Advanced Engineering Informatics 24, 241–242 (2010)
2. Brabham, D.C.: Crowdsourcing as a Model for Problem Solving: An Introduction and Cases. Convergence: The International Journal of Research into New Media Technologies 14(1), 75–90 (2008)
3. Howe, J.: The Rise of Crowdsourcing. Wired 14(6), (2006), http://www.wired.com/wired/archive/14.06/crowds.html (accessed February 10, 2012)
4. Crowdsourcing Industry report, Enterprise Crowdsourcing: Market, Provider and Worker Trends. Research report, Crowdsourcing.org (February 2012)

5. Corney, J.R., Torres-Sánchez, C., Jagadeesan, A.P., Yan, X.T., Regli, W.C., Medellin, H.: Putting the crowd to work in a knowledge-based factory. Advanced Engineering Informatics 24, 243–250 (2010)
6. Richardson, R., Belt, V.: Saved by the Bell? Call Centres and Economic Development in Less Favoured Regions Economic and Industrial Democracy, vol. 22, pp. 67–98. SAGE, London (2001)
7. Heady, R.B., Toma, A.G., Ristroph, J.H.: Evaluation of carton packing rules for high volume operation. Journal of Operations Management 13(1), 59–66 (1995)
8. Hill, V.: An experimental comparison of human schedulers and heuristic algorithms for the travelling salesman problem. Journal of Operations Management 2(4), 215–223 (1982)
9. Iterative Tasks on Mechanical Turk,TurKit, http://groups.csail.mit.edu/uid/turkit/ (accessed January 11, 2011)
10. Global leaders in PLM Consulting, CIMdata, http://www.cimdata.com/ (accessed January 11, 2011)
11. Venkata, R.R.: Evaluation of Metal Stamping Layouts Decision Making (2007) ISBN 978-1-84628-818-0
12. Corney, J.R., Torres-Sánchez, C., Jagadeesan, P., Lynn, A., Regli, W.: Outsourcing labour to the cloud. International Journal of Innovation and Sustainable Development 4(4), 294–313 (2009)
13. Puchinger, J., Raidl, G.R.: Models and algorithms for three-stage twodimensional bin packing. European Journal of Operational Research 183(3), 1304–1327 (2007)
14. Albano, A., Sapuppo, G.: Optimal allocation of two-dimensional irregular shapes using heuristic search methods. IEEE Transactions on Systems, Man and Cybernetics 10, 242–248 (1980)
15. Mumford-Valenzuela benchmark data (2001), http://dip.sun.ac.za/~vuuren/repositories/levelpaper/WebpageData/nice1.25.xls
16. Miguel, G.A., Oliveira José, F.: Solving irregular strip parking problems by hybridising simulated annealing and linear programming. European Journal of Operational Research 171, 811–829 (2006)
17. Leung, S.C.H., Lin, Y., Zhang, D.: Extended local search algorithm based on nonlinear programming for two-dimensional irregular strip packing problem. Computers & Operations Research 39, 678–686 (2012)
18. Sung, R., Ritchiea, J.M., Reab, H.J., Corney, J.: Automated design knowledge capture and representation in single-user CAD environments. Journal of Engineering Design 22(7), 487–503 (2011)
19. Davis, J., et al.: The HPU. In: IEEE Computer Vision and Pattern Recognition Workshop on Advancing Computer Vision with Human in the Loop (ACVHL) (June 2010)

Indexing for Image Retrieval:
A Machine Learning Based Approach

Santanu Chaudhury and Ehtesham Hassan

Department of Electrical Engineering, IIT Delhi, India
santanuc@ee.iitd.ac.in, hassan.ehtesham@gmail.com

Abstract. In this paper, we explore the use of machine learning for multimedia indexing and retrieval involving single/multiple features. Indexing of large image collection has been well researched problem. However, machine learning for combination of features in image indexing and retrieval framework is not explored. In this context, the paper presents novel formulation of multiple kernel learning in hashing for multimedia indexing. The framework learns combination of multiple features/ modalities for defining composite document indices in genetic algorithm based framework. We have demonstrated the evaluation of framework on dataset of handwritten digit images. Subsequently, the utility of the framework is explored for development for multi-modal retrieval of document images.

1 Introduction

Efficient indexing simplifies the management and preservation of large collection of multimedia documents by assigning unique index to documents having similar content, or expressing similar semantics. The existing multimedia document indexing methods generate the document indices using the extracted features characterizing the underlying content. Typical feature extraction methods exploit the low-level content attribute such as intensity, color and shape. Uniqueness of the information provided by different attributes contribute varying invariance and robustness to different feature sets. Feature based representation being the primary information channel for understanding the semantics of content, define the performance quality of multimedia retrieval systems. Also, the multiple modalities existing in documents provide the complementary information for improved understanding of the semantics of underlying content. Here, we concentrate on the application of information from multiple features and multiple modalities for retrieval of multimedia documents. We present novel framework for integrating multiple features for defining the composite/different indexing space by applying the concept of Multiple kernel learning (MKL). The framework provides logical platform for fusion of different information modalities for multimedia indexing and retrieval. The existing MKL algorithms developed for classification problems learn the combination of features while searching for maximum margin boundary planes by solving a joint optimization problem [1–3]. However, Multiple kernel

A. Agrawal et al. (Eds.): IITM 2013, CCIS 276, pp. 25–39, 2013.

learning for Indexing requires optimization of retrieval performance as the objective. In this paper, the distinct nature of indexing objective is addressed by defining a different MKL formulation. The retrieval performance based objective makes the conventional optimization techniques inapplicable. In this direction, we present application of Genetic algorithm (GA) for performing the optimization task in present MKL. The experimental evaluation of the framework is demonstrated on bench mark dataset of handwritten digit images. Subsequently, we apply the presented framework for developing multi-modal retrieval framework evaluated on sampled English magazine cover pages. The paper structure is as follows. The next section presents the literature review. Section 3 presents the proposed MKL framework for indexing with introduction to hashing based indexing, optimization problem formulation and initial evaluation. Application of proposed concept for multi-modal retrieval is demonstrated in section 4. The final section concludes the presented work with discussion on future scope.

2   Related Works

The following discussion presents the existing works related to proposed concepts which covers two major research problems 1). Hashing for indexing, and 2). Multiple feature based indexing and retrieval. The details are as follows.

2.1   Hashing Based Indexing Schemes

Traditionally, nearest neighbour search has been the most preferred retrieval algorithm because of its simplicity and robustness [4]. However the linear time search complexity ($O(n)$) is practically unacceptable in modern retrieval applications handling large amount of high dimensional multimedia data. The approximate nearest neighbour search methods give efficient solution to this problem. These algorithms achieve sub linear search complexity with trade off in terms of marginal decrease in accuracy [5]. Hashing based indexing for various applications is a popular research problem. The scheme generates object indices by projection on lower dimensional hash space. The process generates hash table containing multiple buckets. Each bucket represents group of objects corresponding to an unique index. The retrieval process includes query index generation by applying the same mapping function to query. The relevant documents are obtained by performing similarity search over the objects in bucket corresponding to query index. The work presented in [6] demonstrated one of the earliest application of Geometric hashing for handwritten document indexing. Locality sensitive hashing (LSH) introduced by Indyk and Motwani is state-of-the-art method for finding similar objects in large data collection [7]. The LSH solves approximate nearest neighbour search in $O(n^{1/1+\epsilon})$ for $\epsilon \geq 0$, by projecting the high dimensional data points to low dimensional hash space with high probability that similar points are mapped to same location. In recent years, many applications have applied LSH for performing similarity search in high dimensional spaces [8–11]. The LSH based indexing assumes the uniform distribution of objects in feature space for hashing. In this case, the retrieval success proba- bility is increased by generating multiple hash tables and collecting objects cor- responding to query buckets of all hash tables for similarity search. However, the generation of multiple hash tables increases space complexity of data structure containing the indexing information. Additionally, the assumption for uniform distribution does not satisfy for most of the practical applications. In recent effort towards reducing the size of LSH data structure, concept of Multi probe hashing has been proposed [12]. The multi-probing reduces the required number of hash tables by increasing the utilization of single hash table. The multi-probe hashing selects more than one bucket from each hash table for probing, therefore increasing the usability of hash tables. In this way, the multi-probing consider- ably reduces the number of hash tables required for high success probability. However the definition of locality sensitive hashing function requires informa- tion about object space. Distance based hashing (DBH) is a recent development in hashing methods which preserves the distance between objects in hashing space [13]. The DBH functions are defined over set of pivot objects using the line projection formula. The prerequisite for DBH is the availability of defined distance measure for object space.

2.2 Multiple Feature Based Retrieval

Use of multiple features for various indexing and retrieval applications is not uncommon. The concatenation of different features for document representation is the simplest approach. In this direction, one of the earliest work presented in [14] used concatenated texture features for image retrieval. In [15], combina- tion of color and texture features for image retrieval is done by concatenating the normalised features. The normalization is performed by feature dimension and standard deviation to reduce the effect of different feature dimensions and variances. In [16], image representation is defined by concatenating the bag-of- words histogram computed for different features. Bai *et al.* [17] concatenated a set of topological shape features for word shape coding for word based document retrieval. The concatenation increases the resulting feature dimension, thereby increasing the retrieval complexity. Additionally, the resulting feature set does not guarantee improved discriminative capability because the complementary information of different features are not optimally exploited. The linear combi- nation of descriptors present another simpler approach for feature combination. The preferred approach in this direction has been to create separate index struc- ture for different descriptors, and combine them at the time of query retrieval. In [18], color and texture features have been combined for image retrieval by adding the query distance to example images using both the features. The authors in [19] have shown improvement in retrieval results by considering the geometric mean of similarity measures computed with different features. In [20], heuristic based feature combination approach is defined for image retrieval which com- bines the similarity scores obtained for color, texture and edge histogram features by a non-linear function. Rath and Manmatha [21] applied linear combination approach for word based document retrieval by merging the feature sets with uniform weights. However the learning based methods for feature combination provide a more constructive approach than heuristic based methods. Learning based feature combination has shown improved results for various classification and recognition problems. Dasigi *et al.* [22] presented one of the earliest work on learning based feature combination for text classification. The neural network based supervised learning framework is defined for combining the low dimensional document representation obtained by Latent Semantic Analysis. Lin and Bhanu [23, 24] have explored the application of Genetic Programming for learning the combination of different features for object recognition problem. In [25], neural network learning is applied to perform non-linear dimensionality reduction over combination of pitch, timbre and rhythm features for music retrieval. In [26], feature combination at local neighbourhood level is performed for face image retrieval. The feature combination is learned as Genetic Algorithm based learning for local regions and user feedback based learning for region weights for confidence measurement. At this point, we briefly review the concept of MKL for classification. The recent research in kernel learning methods have shown that using multiple kernels instead of single kernel can improve the interpretation of decision function as well as classifier performance. This problem is solved in MKL framework, where the optimal kernel for classification is learned by combining set of base kernels through the process of learning. Additionally, the fact that typical learning problem often involves multiple, heterogeneous data source, the MKL provides a principled approach for combining information from such data sources. The most natural approach for MKL is considering linear combinations of kernels. The combination of kernels is defined as $K_c = \sum_{k=1}^{M} \eta_k K_k$, where η is defined as kernel weight parameters. In this context, considering unweighed base kernel set, i.e., direct addition of kernels is the simplest approach. In [27], Lazebnik *et al.* presented extensive discussion on different combinations of different features for texture analysis. However, unweighed addition gives equal preference to all kernels and which may not be optimal. Weighted combination of kernels present a more logical approach. The weights in this case define the importance of the kernels for discrimination. The MKL algorithm learns these weight parameters from the training data. Lanckriet *et al.* [3] have proposed conic combination of kernel matrices by formulating a quadratically constrained quadratic program. In [2], Sonnenburg *et al.* formulated the MKL problem as semi-infinite linear program. In [28], Gehler and Sebastian presented extensive evaluation of different kernel combination rules in MKL for object recognition. Campos *et al.* [29] have combined six different features using MKL for character recognition in natural images.

3   Multiple Kernel Learning for Indexing

3.1   Kernel Distance Based Hashing (KernelDBH)

Here, we begin the discussion with introduction to DBH in kernel space. In kernel based learning methods, the kernel matrix represents object similarities in high dimensional feature space. The transformation to higher dimensional space, i.e., kernel space, by *kernel trick* helps to extract the similarity information between high dimensional data points which otherwise is difficult to extract in input space. The application of kernel matrix has been the preferred data similarity measure for various computer vision problems. Here, we present extension of DBH to Kernel based DBH. The extension provides the platform to use kernel matrix as the distance measure for indexing. However, the fundamental property of DBH i.e. distance preservation in hash space is maintained. Considering $\mathcal{X}$ as Euclidean vector space and $\mathcal{D}$ Euclidean distance, the squared distance $\mathcal{D}^2(x_1, x_2)$ can be expanded as $x_1^T x_1 + x_2^T x_2 - 2x_1^T x_2$. Subsequently the line-projection defined in [13] is redefined as

$$F^{x_1, x_2}(x) = \frac{x_1^T x_1 - x_1^T x + x_2^T x - x_1^T x_2}{\sqrt{x_1^T x_1 - 2x_1^T x_2 + x_2^T x_2}} \tag{1}$$

The above expression represents the line projection computation using dot products. The kernel methods increase the computational power of linear learning algorithms by mapping the data to potentially higher dimensional feature space [30]. Let ϕ be the nonlinear mapping which does the transformation from input space $\mathcal{X}$ to high dimensional space (kernel space) $\mathcal{S}$, i.e., $\phi : \mathcal{X} \rightarrow \mathcal{S}$. The mapping defines dot product $x_1^T x_2$ in the kernel space as $\phi^T(x_1)\phi(x_2)$. The direct mapping to space $\mathcal{S}$ is implicitly performed by selecting a feature space which supports the direct computation of dot product using a nonlinear function in input space. The kernel function k which performs such a mapping is defined as

$$K(x, x') = \langle \phi(x), \phi(x') \rangle = \phi^T(x)\phi(x')$$

The expression shows that mapping to space S by function K happens implicitly without considering the actual form of ϕ. The kernel space equivalent of the squared distance $\mathcal{D}^2(x_1, x_2)$ is defined as $K(x_1, x_1) + K(x_2, x_2) - 2K(x_1, x_2)$. Therefore; kernel space representation of equation (1) is expressed as

$$F^{\phi(x_1), \phi(x_2)}(\phi(x)) = \frac{K(x_1, x_1) - K(x_1, x) + K(x_2, x) - K(x_1, x_2)}{\sqrt{K(x_1, x_1) - 2K(x_1, x_2) + K(x_2, x_2)}} \tag{2}$$

The above expression gives the formulation of line projection in kernel space defined by pivots $(\phi(x_1), \phi(x_2))$. We define the set of intervals $[t_1, t_2]$ for binarization of equation (2) as

$$V(\phi(x_1), \phi(x_2)) = \{[t_1, t_2] | \text{Pr}_{x \in \mathcal{X}}(F_{t_1, t_2}^{\phi(x_1), \phi(x_2)}(\phi(x)) = 0) = 0.5\} \tag{3}$$

The kernel distance based hash function family is defined as

$$\mathbb{H}_{\text{KDBH}} = \{F_{t_1, t_2}^{\phi(x_1), \phi(x_2)}(\phi(x)) | x_1, x_2 \in \mathcal{X}, [t_1, t_2] \in V(\phi(x_1), \phi(x_2))\} \tag{4}$$

An indexing and retrieval scheme can be formulated using the hash function family $\mathbb{H}_{\text{KDBH}}$ as discussed in [13]. The hash table parameters L and k have similar implication as in the indexing with traditional distance based hashing.

Equation (2) represents the line projection function in kernel space and defines the mapping function for Kernel DBH. The optimum kernel selection is an important task in kernel learning based methods. The MKL methods use set of kernels instead of selecting one specific kernel function for learning the decision boundary in kernel space. The learning process of the algorithm selects the optimum kernel as the combination of base kernels. The algorithm removes the dependency of kernel methods over cross-validation for optimal kernel search. Additionally, the selection of specific kernel may induce bias in the solution. In this case, the MKL based combination of kernels over single kernel gives more robust solution. In practice many vision problems involve multiple input features; MKL provides an efficient way to combine them as different features have different similarity measures. In the following discussion, we present novel concept of MKL in indexing applications, so as to apply multiple features to improve the indexing performance. Our framework uses Kernel DBH function for generating indexing data structure. In this section, we discuss the limitation of existing MKL schemes in the context of our problem and present a new GA based optimization framework which overcomes the limitations of the classical approach for indexing applications.

3.2   Optimization Problem Formulation

The proposed framework selects the kernel K for hashing in the equation (2) by defining a learning based framework. The composite kernel K is defined as the parametrized linear combination of n base kernels, i.e., $K(x_1, x_2) = \sum_{i=1}^{n} w_i K_i(x_1, x_2)$ with $w_i \geq 0$ $\forall i$. The non-negativity constraint enforces Mercer's condition on kernel K. The proposed learning framework intends to learn optimum hashing kernel for indexing; therefore, we define retrieval performance maximization as the optimization objective. The nature of optimization objective requires the learning to be performed in semi-supervised setting, which utilizes subset of training examples available with label information during training. The ideal case of Distance based hashing should generate a hash table assigning unique index to all the examples belonging to a category. However, feature similarity based hashing does not guarantee unique hash index for similar category objects because of the semantic gap between low level features and high level semantics. The category information available with an example represent significant amount of inbuilt semantics. Therefore, the utilization of category information available with the training examples in a semi-supervised framework enforces more realistic grouping of objects in hash space.

The limited amount of labelled data may create the condition of over fitting. Therefore, the optimization objective requires a regularizer term to ensure desirable indexing performance independent of the amount of labelled training data. We apply the maximum entropy principle based regularizer presented by Wang et al. [31]. The objective of the regularizer is to maximize the information provided by each function value $h(\cdot)$ in object index $g(\cdot)$. The regularizer is implemented by applying maximum entropy principle which assigns equal probability for function value $h(\cdot)$ to be 0 or 1; therefore, generating balanced partition of data in hash space. Following the result presented in [31], variance maximization of $h(X)$ satisfies the maximum entropy condition for function h. Therefore, the complete optimization objective for MKL problem is defined as:

$$\mathbf{w}^* = \mathrm{argmax}_{\mathbf{w}} \quad \mathbf{F}(X, X_v, \mathbf{w}) \qquad (5)$$
$$\mathbf{F} = \mathbf{J}(X_v, \mathbf{w}) + \lambda \mathbf{V}(X, \mathbf{w})$$

X represents the complete training set, X_v represents the subset of training examples assumed to be available with label information for which function $\mathbf{F}$ is evaluated for different weight parameter $\mathbf{w}$. λ represents the regularization parameter. Function $\mathbf{J}(X_v, \mathbf{w})$ represents the retrieval performance of KernelDBH computed over X_v and $\mathbf{w}$.

$$\mathbf{J}(X_v, \mathbf{w}) = \mathrm{mean} \left\{ \sum_{x_i \in X_v} \Delta(y_i, \hat{y}(x_i, \mathbf{w})) \right\}$$

$\hat{y}(x_i, \mathbf{w})$ represents the set of retrieved results for the validation query $x_i \in X_v$. y_i represents the actual label for the query and $\Delta(y_i, \hat{y}(x_i, \mathbf{w}))$ represents the computed retrieval score for x_i. Function $\mathbf{V}(X_v, \mathbf{w})$ represents regularizer term defined as the sum of variance of the hash values for all hash tables which is computed as

$$\mathbf{V}(X, \mathbf{w}) = \sum_{i=1}^{L} \sum_{j=1}^{k} \mathtt{Variance}\{h_{ij}(X, \mathbf{w})\}$$

3.3   Genetic Algorithm Based Optimization Framework for MKL

The kernel combination weights ($\mathbf{w}$) in equation (5) are the optimization parameter. The existing literature in MKL methods have various optimization problem formulations which define joint optimization task for decision boundary and optimal kernel learning. The optimization objective of these MKL formulations are continuous in nature and follow the conventional gradient based methods for solution. However, the proposed MKL formulation for indexing evolves as an unique class of optimization objective (Equation (5)). The current optimization function is discrete in nature whereas the optimization parameter space is continuous. The non-differentiable nature of the optimization function restricts the application of existing gradient based solutions for proposed MKL.

For such optimization tasks, meta-heuristic optimization algorithms provide efficient solution for searching large parameter spaces. The Genetic algorithm is class of Evolutionary algorithms which is extremely suitable for global optimal parameter search in complex spaces [32]. GA follows the fundamental of natural evolution to explore the large and complex parameter spaces, and performs intelligent random search to quickly identify the best solution. The primary advantage of GA based optimization comes from its parallel nature of parameter search. The GA process samples candidate solutions in different directions of parameter space and evaluates their suitability based on their fitness value. The iterative optimization proceeds the search direction towards the prominent candidate solutions; therefore, providing a robust and fast methodology to search through large parameter spaces. The multiple direction search also reduces the possibility of local optimas as the best solution. Considering the complex nature of parameter space, exhaustive search based solution for the current optimization problem is unacceptable. Therefore, we propose the MKL formulation for indexing in GA based optimization paradigm.

The parameter search is started by creating initial population as set of strings representing chromosomes. The population strings in GA represent the genetically encoded set of possible solutions. The search follows the evolutionary process defined by a set of genetic operations performed over population strings. The evolutionary process retains the potential strings and uses them for successive population generation. The selection of potential strings, i.e., candidate strings for successive regeneration, is based on their fitness values. The fitness value represents suitability of the population strings for the current problem. The fitness function in GA should be closely related to optimization objective. As maximization of retrieval performance defines the objective of learning problem, we define function $\mathbf{F}$ as the fitness function. The training data subset X_v available with label information is used as validation query set.

In the present GA optimization framework (Refer table 1), a population string represents the concatenation of genetic encoding of kernel weight parameters w_i. The genetic encoding of optimization parameters allows the application of different genetic operators to proceed the search process. The fitness evaluation for each population string is done by measuring the retrieval performance of indexing using X_v as the query set. Initial population strings are randomly generated. Tournament selection based approach is used for selection of potential strings for successive generation. Tournament selection is easier to implement and works efficiently on parallel and no-parallel architectures. Additionally, it provides a simple way control its performance by optimizing tournament size. The tournament selection method selects p individuals randomly from the population,

Table 1. Algorithm: GA for MKL

1	Population generation $\Rightarrow Pop = $ `Generate`$()$
2	Population initialization $\Rightarrow$ `Initialization`(Pop): `Evaluate`$(\mathbf{F})$ for each string in Pop
	For each i $<$ noIterations
3	Selection of individuals for successive population generation $\Rightarrow Pop_sub = $ `Selection`(Pop) using *Tournament Selection*
4	Offspring generation step 1 $\Rightarrow Pop_1 = $ `Crossover`(Pop) using *Single Point Crossover*
5	Offspring generation step 2 $\Rightarrow Pop_2 = $ `Mutation`(Pop_1) using *Uniform Mutation*
6	Evaluate Offspring $\Rightarrow$ `Evaluate`$(\mathbf{F})$ for each string in Pop_2
7	New population generation $\Rightarrow Pop_new = $ `Generate`(Pop, Pop_2) using *Elitist Selection*
	End

and the string with highest fitness in the selected p is placed in Mating pool. For a population vector having M strings, the process is repeated M times. The selected strings regarded as parents are subsequently used for generating the new population strings. Crossover and Mutation define to steps to generate new string for exploring the parameter space. We apply Single point crossover and Uniform mutation over the Mating pool for offspring generation. The Single point crossover selects a crossover point, and swaps the part of parent strings defined by crossover point position. Crossover operation is controlled by crossover probability p_c which defines the percentage of individual strings from the mating pool to be used for generation. It is normally selected from $0.6 \sim 0.9$, i.e., using most of the mating strings for generation. The generation strings are subsequently applied to mutation operator. Mutation helps to search the unexplored search space by enhancing the variability of reconstructed strings by generating new string by single parent. Here, we have applied uniform mutation over the strings generated by crossover operation. Uniform mutation inverts each bit of parent string with probability p_m defined as mutation probability. It is normally selected between $0.02 \sim 0.05$. Higher values of p_m deviates the algorithm from optimal search path, therefore terming it as random search process. The set of offspring obtained by crossover and mutation are further used to generate new population. New population is constructed by Elitist selection based strategy using the old population and offspring set. We use Elitist selection based strategy for constructing new population as it preserves the better individuals in the current population for successive evolution process from both the old and new population.

3.4   Preliminary Evaluation with MNIST Dataset

Initial evaluation of the proposed feature combination based indexing scheme is performed on MNIST dataset [33]. The experiment evaluates the Kernel DBH based indexing scheme by learning the optimal kernel by proposed MKL. MNIST dataset is a collection of handwritten digit images containing 60000 training and 10000 test images. Each dataset example represents 28×28 grayscale image displaying, an isolated digit between 0 to 9. In this experiment, we have considered grayscale pixel intensities as features, i.e., each image is represented by a 784-d vector.

The initial population in GA optimization framework consisted 40 strings. The crossover and mutation probabilities are selected as 0.8 and 0.05, respectively. The kernel weight parameter (w_i) is encoded by a 5-bit binary string. The regularization parameter λ is set as 0.25 for all the experiments discussed in this work. After learning the kernel weight vector ($\mathbf{w}$), the indexing and retrieval process follows the conventional DBH based indexing scheme. The parameter selection is an important issue in GA based optimization. GA approaches the best solution by adaptive operations on the population strings. The optimization convergence depends on the choice of adaptation strategy and parameters. Significant amount of research has gone into development and analysis of GA optimization, however, a general methodology for deciding GA parameters for any problem is unavailable [34, 35]. The basic GA parameters for experiments in this work have been selected following the recommendations in [35]. The random nature of GA requires sufficient number of function evaluations to arrive at the best solution. Here, total function evaluations are computed as product of the number of population strings to maximum generations. For a difficult function, more number of function evaluations are needed. The difficulty of the objective function is described in terms of multi-modality, deception, isolation and collateral noise in the search path [34]. The structure of the optimization objective (Equation (5)) is complex to describe, therefore the number of generations is finalized based on initial trials to ensure the convergence is achieved. Here, we present results of the experiment simulated for maximum of 100 for establishing the validity of GA based optimization.

The base kernel set for learning the optimum kernel for hashing included set of 10 Gaussian kernels having variances from 100 to 900 on a linear scale. For learning the $\mathbb{H}_{KDBH}$, the evaluation set X_v contains 1000 images selected by stratified sampling from the training images. The function generation is performed by stratified sampling of 1000 images from remaining training images (excluding the images selected in the evaluation set). The hash table generation is performed over 59000 training images. The ranking of retrieved results is an important performance measure for an indexing and retrieval scheme. The traditional retrieval measures, i.e., precision and recall are computed over unordered sets. However, Mean average precision (MAP) measure for query set X_v is computed over the ranked retrieval results [36]. In the present indexing scheme, average precision for query q is computed over the collection of neighbours obtained from L hash tables having indices $g_i(q)$ for $i = 1, ..., L$. The neighbour ranking is performed based on the Euclidean distance from the query.

For performance measurement, the hash function families $\mathbb{H}_{DBH}$ & $\mathbb{H}_{KDBH}$, have been generated by stratified sampling of 1000 images from complete set of training images. The complete test image set has been used for performance evaluation. The LSH based indexing results for the similar hashing parameters are also presented. To define LSH based indexing, random hyperplane based hashing functions have been applied [37]. We have considered three parameters: Precision, MAP and Average number of comparisons for performance measurement which have been commonly used for the evaluation of retrieval methods. The number of comparisons represent the retrieval time complexity. Precision and Recall represent the grouping property of indexing scheme in hash space, with precision being the probability of the relevance of retrieved results and recall being the probability of the retrieval of relevant results. It is always desired to have high values of both measures; however, independent consideration neglects the ranking information of retrieved results. In this context, MAP presents single point measure of ranked retrieval performance by computing the average precision over the complete recall scale. Therefore, MAP is adopted as the primary performance measure. The KernelDBH shows significant improvement in precision values over LSH and DBH with less number of comparisons. The experimental results for different hashing parameters are presented in

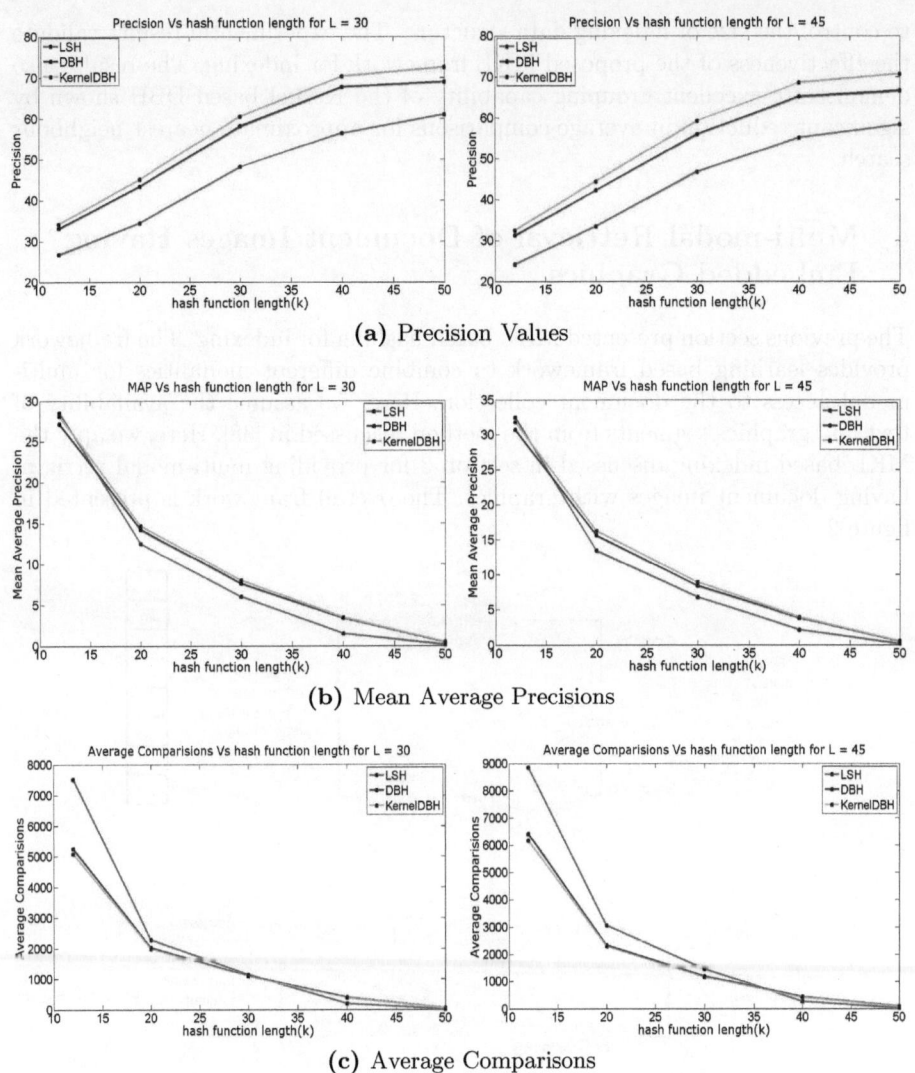

(a) Precision Values

(b) Mean Average Precisions

(c) Average Comparisons

Fig. 1. Results with MNIST dataset: 100 generations

figure 1. We have also simulated the similar experiment for 150 generations which yielded similar trend with $0.5 \sim 7\%$ of relative variation in observed parameters. For all the hashing methods, we observe sharp decrease in MAP score with increase in hash function length as the collision probability decreases exponentially with increase in k, resulting sharp decrease in recall. The KernelDBH and DBH achieved better precision and MAP values with LSH requiring less number of average computations for larger k. It is justified as the random hyperplane based projections are independent of data distribution; therefore, for smaller k, the hashing function g shows poor discriminative power. However, in practice, short hash functions are preferred at acceptable retrieval performance

to control the size of indexing data structure. The experimental results validate
the effectiveness of the proposed MKL framework for indexing. The results also
demonstrate excellent grouping capability of the Kernel based DBH shown by
significant reduction in average comparisons for approximate nearest neighbour
search.

4   Multi-modal Retrieval of Document Images Having Embedded Graphics

The previous section presented MKL based hashing for indexing. The framework
provides learning based framework to combine different modalities for multimodal access to the document collection. Here, we assume the availability of
text and graphics segments from the method discussed in [38]. Here, we aply the
MKL based indexing discussed in section 3 for providing multi-modal retrieval
having document images with graphics. The overall framework is presented in
figure 2.

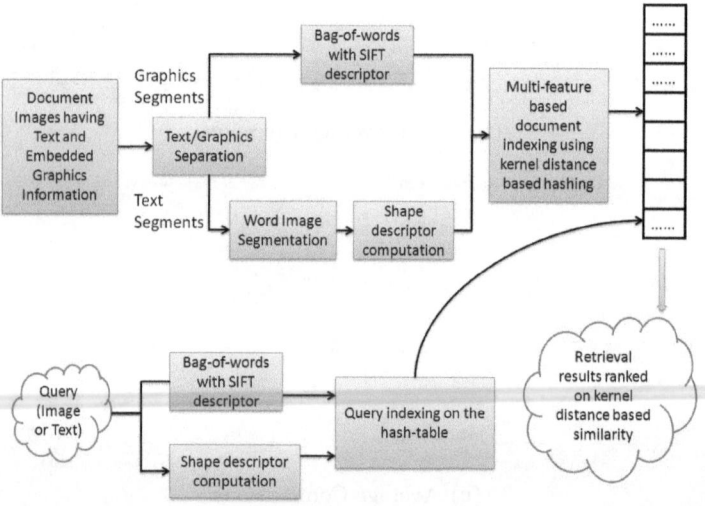

Fig. 2. Multi-modal retrieval for document images having text and graphics

The framework generates unique document index by kernel distance based
hashing, where optimal kernel for indexing is learned by combining kernels computed from text, and graphics features. The framework computes query (Text or
graphics) index on the hash table, and retrieves relevant documents by similarity
search. The initial evaluation of the framework is performed on English magazine
document collection having 192 scanned pages. After segmentation, the graphic
components which are smaller than $1/50^{th}$ of the page size are filtered out. The
segmentation process may generate noisy graphics regions. Therefore, bag-of-
words computed with SIFT feature is applied for robust graphics representation
(Refer [39] for details). A visual vocabulary of 50 words is selected, therefore,

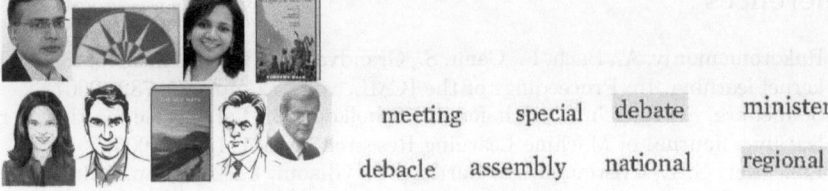

meeting   special   debate   minister

debacle   assembly   national   regional

Fig. 3. Examples from X_q

resulting 50-d bag-of-words representation for graphics segments. The word image segmentation and corresponding feature computation from text segments is performed as discussed in [40]. The complete segmentation process resulted in 367 graphics image and 18871 word images. The set of linear and Gaussian kernels is used for forming the base kernel set corresponding to both type of information. For the evaluation, graphic segments having subjects such as faces, natural scenes, and buildings are selected. The validation query set X_v consisted 117 queries having 103 word object and 14 graphics objects. Final evaluation of the indexing is performed with query set X_q having 91 word and 8 graphics objects (Sample examples of graphics segments and word images are shown in figure 3). The base kernel set included linear and set of Gaussian kernels having variances from 2^{-5} to 2^5 with incremental step of 0.5 at exponent. The word images are represented by shape descriptor computed with following parameters: $\{m = 38, n = 36, 1 \times 6 \text{ partition}\}$. The genetic algorithm optimization is simulated for 100 iterations. The similarity search is done based on the kernel distance K_{dis} computes as $\sum_{i=1}^{n} w_i K_i$. The retrieval for hashing parameters $\{L = 50, k = 12\}$ achieved MAP score of 23.45% with graphics based queries, 73.47% with text queries. The overall MAP score of 72.18% is achieved for query set X_q. The results establish that the segmentation approach can be successfully applied for developing a multi-modal content based retrieval framework for document images.

5   Conclusion

We have proposed novel extension of DBH to kernel space which provides the platform for MKL formulation in feature based indexing. The novel formulation provides an efficient and robust approach for application of multiple features in indexing problems by learning their optimal combination in kernel space. The proposed indexing scheme demonstrated novel application of Genetic algorithm for optimization task in MKL. The learning based feature combination for indexing provides a principled approach for fusion of multiple modalities existing in documents. Subsequently, we demonstrated the application of the framework for multi-modal retrieval of document images. Application of different performance measures, and exploration of ranking function learning in the current MKL formulation are the possible direction of future work.

References

1. Rakotomamonjy, A., Bach, F., Canu, S., Grandvalet, Y.: More efficiency in multiple kernel learning. In: Proceedings of the ICML, vol. 772, pp. 775–782 (2007)
2. Sonneburg, S., Ratsch, G., Schafer, C., Scholkopf, B.: Large scale multiple kernel learning. Journal of Machine Learning Research 7, 1531–1565 (2006)
3. Lanckriet, G.R., Cristianini, N., Bartlett, P., Ghaoui, L.E., Jordan, M.I.: Learning the kernel matrix with semi-definite programming. Journal of Machine Learning Research 4, 27–72 (2004)
4. Bhm, C., Berchtold, S., Keim, D.A.: Searching in high-dimensional spaces: Index structures for improving the performance of multimedia databases. ACM Computing Surveys 33(3) (2001)
5. Indyk, P., Motwani, R.: Approximate nearest neighbor - towards removing the curse of dimensionality. In: Proceedings of the 30th ACM Symposium on Theory of Computing, pp. 604–613 (1998)
6. Mehmod, T.S.: Indexing of handwritten document images. In: Proceedings of the 1997 Workshop on Document Image Analysis, pp. 66–73 (1997)
7. Andoni, A., Indyk, P.: Near optimal hashing algorithms for approximate nearest neighbor in high dimensions. Communications of the ACM 51(1), 117–122 (2008)
8. Haghani, P., Michel, S., Aberer, K.: Distributed similarity search in high dimensions using locality sensitive hashing. In: Proceedings of the 12th International Conference on Extending Database Technology, pp. 744–755 (2009)
9. Shen, H., Li, T., Schweiger, T.: An efficient similarity searching scheme in massive databases. In: Proceedings of the 3rd International Conference on Digital Telecommunications, pp. 47–52 (2008)
10. Weihong, W., Song, W.: A scalable content-based image retrieval scheme using locality-sensitive hashing. In: Proceedings of the International Conference on Computational Intelligence and Natural Computing, vol. 1, pp. 151–154 (2009)
11. Matei, B., Shan, Y., Sawhney, H.S., Tan, Y., Kumar, R., Huber, D., Hebert, M.: Rapid object indexing using locality sensitive hashing and joint 3d-signature space estimation. IEEE Transactions on PAMI 28(7), 1111–1126 (2006)
12. Lv, Q., Josephson, W., Wang, Z., Charikar, M., Li, K.: Multi-probe lsh: Efficient indexing for high-dimensional similarity search. In: Proceedings of the 33rd International Conference on Very Large Data Bases, pp. 950–961 (2007)
13. Vassilis, A., Michalis, P., Panagiotis, P., George, K.: Nearest neighbor retrieval using distance based hashing. In: Proceedings of the 24th International Conference on Data Engineering, pp. 327–336 (April 2008)
14. Chun, Y.D., Seo, S.Y., Kim, N.C.: Image retrieval using bdip and bvlc moments. IEEE Transactions on Circuits and Systems for Video Technology 13(9), 951–957 (2003)
15. Chun, Y.D., Kim, N.C., Jang, I.H.: Content-based image retrieval using multi-resolution colour and texture features. IEEE Transactions on Multimedia 10(6), 1073–1084 (2008)
16. Gosselin, P.H., Cord, M., Philipp-Foliguet, S.: Combining visual dictionary, kernel-based similarity and learning strategy for image category retrieval. Computer Vision and Image Understanding 110, 403–417 (2008)
17. Bai, S., Li, L., Tan, C.L.: Keyword spotting in document images through word shape coding. In: Proceedings of the 10th ICDAR, pp. 331–335 (2009)
18. Dorairaj, R., Namuduri, K.R.: Compact combination of mpeg-7 color and texture descriptors for image retrieval. In: Proceedings of the 38th Asilomar Conference on Signals, Systems and Computers, vol. 1, pp. 387–391 (2004)

19. Gagaudakis, G., Rosin, P.L.: Incorporating shape into histograms for cbir. Pattern Recognition 35, 81–91 (2002)
20. Qi, X., Han, Y.: A novel fusion approach to content-based image retrieval. Pattern Recognition (38), 2449–2465 (2005)
21. Rath, T.M., Manmatha, R.: Features for word spotting in historical manuscripts. In: Proceedings of the 7th ICDAR, vol. 1, pp. 218–222 (2003)
22. Dasigi, V., Mann, R.C., Protopopescu, V.A.: Information fusion for text classification - an experimental comparison. Pattern Recognition 34, 2413–2425 (2001)
23. Lin, Y., Bhanu, B.: Evolutionary feature synthesis for object recognition. IEEE Transactions on SMC-Part C: Applications and Reviews 35(2), 156–171 (2005)
24. Lin, Y., Bhanu, B.: Object detection via feature synthesis using mdl-based genetic programming. IEEE Transactions on SMC-Part B: Cybernetics 35(3), 538–547 (2005)
25. Shen, J., Shepherd, J., Ngu, A.H.H.: Towards effective content-based music retrieval with multiple acoustic feature combination. IEEE Transactions on Multimedia 8(6), 1179–1189 (2006)
26. Basak, J., Bhattacharya, K., Chaudhury, S.: Multiple exemplar-based facial image retrieval using independent component analysis. IEEE Transactions on Image Processing 15(12), 3773–3783 (2006)
27. Lazebnik, S., Schmid, C., Ponce, J.: A sparse texture representation using local affine regions. IEEE Transactions on PAMI 27(8), 1265–1278 (2005)
28. Gehler, P., Nowozin, S.: On feature combination for multiclass object classification. In: Proceedings of the IEEE ICCV, pp. 1–8 (2009)
29. de Campos, T.E., Babu, B.R., Varma, M.: Character recognition in natural images. In: Proceedings of International Conference on Computer Vision Theory and Applications (VISAPP) (February 2009)
30. Scholkopf, B., Smola, A.J.: Learning with Kernels: Support Vector Machines, Regularization, Optimization, and Beyond. The MIT Press (2006)
31. Wang, J., Kumar, S., Chang, S.F.: Sequential projection learning for hashing with compact codes. In: Proceedings of ICML, pp. 1127–1134 (2010)
32. Goldberg, D.E.: Genetic Algorithms in Search, Optimization and Machine Learning. Addison Wesley Longman (Singapore) Private Limited (2000)
33. Lecun, Y., Bottou, L., Bengio, Y., Haffner, P.: Gradient based learning applied to document recognition. The Proceedings of IEEE 86(11), 2278–2324 (1998)
34. Deb, K., Agrawal, S.: Understanding interactions among genetic algorithm parameters. In: Foundations of Genetic Algorithms 5, pp. 265–286. Morgan Kaufmann (1998)
35. Czarn, A., Macnish, C., Vijayan, K., Turlach, B.: Statistical exploratory analysis of genetic algorithms. IEEE Transactions on Evolutionary Computation 8 (2004)
36. Manning, C.D., Raghavan, P., Schtze, H.: An Introduction to Information Retrieval. Cambridge University Press, Cambridge (2009)
37. Charikar, M.S.: Similarity estimation techniques from rounding algorithms. In: Proceedings of the 34th ACM STOC, pp. 380–388 (2002)
38. Garg, R., Hassan, E., Chaudhury, S., Gopal, M.: A crf based scheme for overlapping multi-colored text graphics separation. In: ICDAR, pp. 1215–1219 (2011)
39. Lowe, D.G.: Object recognition from local scale-invariant features. In: Proceedings of the IEEE ICCV, vol. 2, pp. 1150–1157 (1999)
40. Hassan, E., Chaudhury, S., Gopal, M.: Word shape descriptor-based document image indexing: a new dbh-based approach. IJDAR, 1–20 (2012)

A Unifying Framework for Correspondence-Less Shape Alignment and Its Medical Applications

Zoltan Kato

Department of Image Processing and Computer Graphics,
University of Szeged, P.O. Box 652., 6701 Szeged, Hungary
kato@inf.u-szeged.hu

Abstract. We give an overview of our general framework for registering 2D and 3D objects without correspondences. Classical solutions consist in extracting landmarks, establishing correspondences and then the aligning transformation is obtained via a complex optimization procedure. In contrast, our framework works without landmark correspondences, is independent of the magnitude of transformation, easy to implement, and has a linear time complexity. The efficiency and robustness of the method has been demonstarted using various deformations models. Herein, we will focus on medical applications.

Keywords: Registration, Shape, 3D Object, Affine transformation, Thin plate splines, Bone Fracture, Prostate, MRI, TRUS.

1 Introduction

Registration is a crucial step when images of different views or sensors of an object need to be compared or combined. Application areas include visual inspection, target tracking in video sequences, super resolution, or medical image analysis. In a general setting, one is looking for a transformation which aligns two images such that one image (called the *observation*, or moving image) becomes similar to the second one (called the *template*, or model image). When registering an image pair, first we have to characterize the possible deformations. From this point of view, registration techniques can be classified into two main categories: physical model-based and parametric or functional representation [1]. Herein, we deal with the latter representation, which typically originate from interpolation and approximation theory.

From a methodological point of view, we can differentiate *feature-based* and *area-based* methods. *Feature-based* methods [2] aim at establishing point correspondences between two images. The main drawback of these methods is the assumption of a limited deformation and high computational cost. Their main advantage is that as long as a sufficient number of point matches are available, one can usually find an optimal aligning transformation implying that feature-based algorithms are less sensitive to occlusions. *Area-based* methods [3, 4] treat the problem without attempting to detect salient objects. The drawback of this family of methods is also the high computational cost and the restricted range

A. Agrawal et al. (Eds.): IITM 2013, CCIS 276, pp. 40–52, 2013.

of distortions. In many situations, the variability of image features is so complex (*e.g.* multimodal medical images) that it is more efficient to reduce them to a binary representation and solve the registration problem in that context. Therefore binary registration (*i.e.* shape alignment) is an important problem for many complex image analysis tasks. Herein, we will present our generic framework for recovering linear [5–8] and nonlinear [9–12] deformations of 2D and 3D objects without correspondences.

For example, spline-based deformations have been commonly used to register prostate images or volumes. The interpolating Thin-plate Splines (TPS) was originally proposed by [29], which relies on a set of point correspondences between the image pairs. However, these correspondences are prone to error in real applications and therefore [13] extended the bending energy of TPS to approximation and regularization by introducing the correspondence localization error. On the other hand, we [10] proposed a generic framework for non-rigid registration which does not require explicit point correspondences. In [14], this framework has been adopted to solve multimodal registration of MRI and TRUS prostate images.

Another prominent medical application is complex bone fracture reduction which frequently requires surgical care, especially when angulation or displacement of bone fragments are large. In such situations, computer aided surgical planning is done before the actual surgery takes place, which allows to gather more information about the dislocation of the fragments and to arrange and analyze the surgical implants to be inserted. A crucial part of such a system is the relocation of bone fragments to their original anatomic position. In [9], we applied our framework to reduce pelvic fractures using 3D rigid-body transformations. In cases of single side fractures, the *template* is simply obtained by mirroring intact bones of the patient.

2   Registration Framework

Let us denote the point coordinates of the *template* and *observation* by $\mathbf{x} \in \mathbb{R}^n$ and $\mathbf{y} \in \mathbb{R}^n$ respectively. Corresponding point pairs $(\mathbf{x}, \mathbf{y})$ are related by an unknown diffeomorphism $\phi : \mathbb{R}^n \to \mathbb{R}^n$ such that

$$\mathbf{y} = \phi(\mathbf{x}) \quad \Leftrightarrow \quad \mathbf{x} = \phi^{-1}(\mathbf{y}), \tag{1}$$

where $\phi^{-1} : \mathbb{R}^n \to \mathbb{R}^n$ is the corresponding inverse transformation. Note that ϕ^{-1} always exists since a diffeomorphism is a bijective function such that both the function and its inverse have continuous mixed partial derivatives. The goal of registration is to recover the aligning transformation ϕ.

Classical approaches would establish a set of point correspondences $\{(\mathbf{x}_i, \mathbf{y}_i)\}_{i=1}^N$ and, making use of Eq. (1), define a *similarity metric* $S(\{(\mathbf{x}_i, \mathbf{y}_i)\}, \hat{\phi})$ which characterizes the geometric alignment of the point pairs $\{(\mathbf{x}_i, \hat{\phi}(\mathbf{y}_i))\}$ achieved by a particular transformation $\hat{\phi}$. The solution is usually obtained via an iterative optimization procedure, where S is maximized (or equivalently, the *dissimilarity* is minimized). Such procedures require a good initialization (*i.e.* the transformation must be close to identity) and are computationally expensive as the evaluation of S requires the actual execution of each intermediate transformation. Furthermore, landmark extraction and correspondence implicitly assumes, that one can observe some image features (*e.g.* gray-level of pixels [15]) f and g that are *covariant* under the transformation

$$f(\mathbf{x}) = g(\phi(\mathbf{x})) = g(\mathbf{y}). \tag{2}$$

However, lack of characteristic features (*e.g.* binary images, printed art) or changes in features (*e.g.* illumination changes, mulimodality) make landmark extraction and matching unreliable in many cases. Segmentation of such images is often straightforward and is available as an intermediate step of a complex image analysis task. Herein, we will discuss a generic correspondence-less framework which works well in such situations.

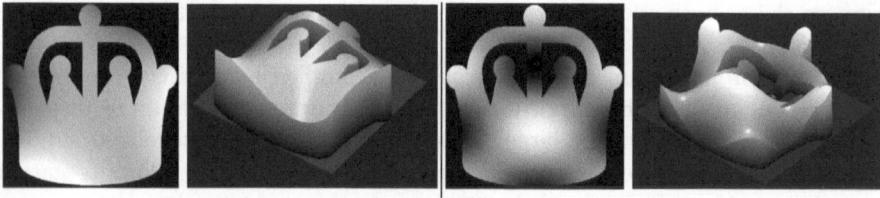

Fig. 1. The effect of applying a polynomial (left) and a trigonometric (right) ω function can be interpreted as a consistent colorization or as a volume

Since correspondences are not available, Eq. (1) cannot be used directly. However, individual point matches can be integrated out yielding the following integral equation:

$$\int_{\mathcal{D}} \mathbf{y} d\mathbf{y} = \int_{\phi(\mathcal{F})} \mathbf{z} d\mathbf{z}, \tag{3}$$

where $\mathcal{D}$ corresponds to the *observation* shape's domain and $\phi(\mathcal{F})$ is the transformed *template* shape's domain. Note that computing the latter integral involves the actual execution of the transformation ϕ on $\mathcal{F}$, which might be computationally unfavorable. Therefore, let us rewrite the above integrals over the *template*'s domain $\mathcal{F}$ and *observation*'s domain $\mathcal{D}$ by making use of the integral transformation $\mathbf{z} \mapsto \phi(\mathbf{x})$ and $d\mathbf{z} \mapsto |J_\phi(\mathbf{x})| d\mathbf{x}$:

$$\int_{\mathcal{D}} \mathbf{y} d\mathbf{y} = \int_{\mathcal{F}} \phi(\mathbf{x}) |J_\phi(\mathbf{x})| d\mathbf{x}, \tag{4}$$

where $|J_\phi(\mathbf{x})|$ is the Jacobian determinant of the transformation ϕ. Note that the above equation corresponds to a system of n equations, where n is the dimension of the shapes. Although the space of allowed deformations is low dimensional, determined by the number of free parameters k of the deformation ϕ, n is typically 2 (planar shapes) or 3 (3D objects), which is not sufficient to solve for all parameters of a real deformation. Therefore we need a general mechanism to construct new equations. Indeed, Eq. (1) remains valid when a function $\omega : \mathbb{R}^n \to \mathbb{R}$ is acting on both sides of the equation

$$\omega(\mathbf{y}) = \omega(\phi(\mathbf{x})), \tag{5}$$

and the integral equation of Eq. (4) becomes

$$\int_{\mathcal{D}} \omega(\mathbf{y}) d\mathbf{y} = \int_{\mathcal{F}} \omega(\phi(\mathbf{x})) |J_\phi(\mathbf{x})| d\mathbf{x}. \tag{6}$$

Adopting a set of nonlinear functions $\{\omega_i\}_{i=1}^{\ell}$, each ω_i generates a new equation yielding a system of ℓ independent equations. Hence we are able to generate sufficient number of equations by choosing $\ell \geq k$. Intuitively, each ω_i generates a consistent coloring of the shapes and the equations in Eq. (6) match the volume of the applied ω_i function over the shapes (see Fig. 1). The parameters of the aligning transformation ϕ are then simply obtained as the solution of the nonlinear system of equations Eq. (6). In practice, usually an overdetermined system is constructed (i.e. $\ell > k$), which is then solved in the *least squares sense* by minimizing the algebraic error. Hereafter, we will omit the integration domains from the equations.

Algorithm 1. Pseudo code of the registration algorithm

Require: *template* and *observation* objects
Ensure: The transformation parameters of ϕ
1: Choose a set of $\ell > k$ nonlinear functions $\{\omega_i\}_{i=1}^{\ell}$.
2: Compute the normalizing transformations which maps coordinates into $[-0.5, 0.5]$.
3: Construct the system of equations.
4: Find a least-squares solution of the system using the *Levenberg-Marquardt* algorithm. Use the identity transformation for initialization.
5: Unnormalizing the solution gives the parameters of the aligning transformation.

What kind of ω functions can be used to generate these independent equations? From a theoretical point of view, only trivial restrictions apply: the functions must be integrable and rich enough (i.e. generate a non-constant colorization). Furthermore, they have to be unbiased: each equation should have an equally balanced contribution to the algebraic error, which can be achieved by normalizing the images into the unit square (or cube in 3D) around the origin and the range of the ω functions should also be normalized [10]. From a practical point of view, we have to solve a system of integral equations meaning that intermediate deformations need to be evaluated hence complexity is highly dependent on image size. If we could get rid of the integration in the equations, then considerable speed-up could be achieved. Fortunately, the equation of Eq. (6) can be reduced to a plain polynomial system under the following conditions [5, 10]:

1. The deformation ϕ is given as a linear combination of basis functions. Note that the most common transformation groups, such as linear, polynomial and

thin plate spline deformations are of such form, while other diffeomorphisms can be approximated by their Taylor expansion.

2. The adopted set of nonlinear functions $\{\omega_i\}_{i=1}^{\ell}$ are polynomial.

Let us now briefly overview how to use our framework for various medical applications.

3   Medical Applications

3.1   Fusion of Hip Prosthesis X-Ray Images

Hip replacement [16, 17] is a surgical procedure in which the hip joint is replaced by a prosthetic implant. In the short post-operative time, infection is a major concern. An inflammatory process may cause bone resorption and subsequent loosening or fracture, often requiring revision surgery. In current practice, clinicians assess loosening by inspecting a number of post-operative X-ray images of the patient's hip joint, taken over a period of time. Obviously, such an analysis requires the registration of X-ray images. Even visual inspection can benefit from registration as clinically significant prosthesis movement can be very small.

There are two main challenges in registering hip X-ray images: One is the highly non-linear radiometric distortion [18] which makes any greylevel-based method unstable. Fortunately, the segmentation of the prosthetic implant is quite straightforward [19] so shape registration is a valid alternative here. The second problem is that the true transformation is a projective one which depends also on the position of the implant in 3D space. Indeed, there is a rigid-body transformation in 3D space between the implants, which becomes a projective mapping between the X-ray images. Fortunately, the affine assumption is a good approximation here, as the X-ray images are taken in a well defined *standard position* of the patient's leg. For diagnosis, the area around the implant (especially the bottom part of it) is the most important for the physician. It is where the registration must be the most precise. Based on such an alignment, we can *e.g.* visualize the fused follow-up images for evaluation by an expert (see Fig. 2).

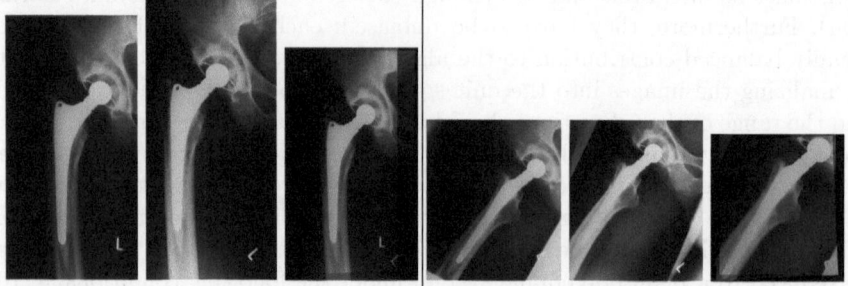

Fig. 2. Fusion of hip prosthesis X-ray image pairs by registering follow up images using a 2D affine transformation (typical CPU time is around 1 sec. in Matlab)

Our framework can be easily applied to register the segmented prosthesis shapes: the diffeomorphism ϕ becomes a non-singular linear transformation matrix $\mathbf{A}$ and the identity relation takes the following simple form:

$$\mathbf{A}\mathbf{x} = \mathbf{y} \quad \Leftrightarrow \quad \mathbf{x} = \mathbf{A}^{-1}\mathbf{y}. \tag{7}$$

Since the Jacobian is the determinant of $\mathbf{A}$, which can be computed as the ratio of the areas of the two planar shapes to be aligned, we can easily construct a system of polynomial equations [5, 6], which is straightforward to solve *e.g.* in Matlab [5] by a classical LSE solver like the *Levenberg-Marquardt* algorithm [7]. Some registration examples can be seen in Fig. 2, where hip prosthesis X-ray image pairs are aligned using a 2D affine transformation. Note that correspondence-based methods are challenged by lack of corner-like landmarks and the nonlinear radiometric distortion between follow-ups. In spite of the inherent modeling error (the physical transformation of the implant is a 3D rigid motion followed by a projection), our method was able to find a precise alignment.

3.2 Registration of Pelvic and Thoracic CT Volumes

The extension of the affine solution to 3D objects [6–8] is relatively straightforward. Typical medical applications include the alignment of pelvic and thoracic CT volumes based on segmented bony structures. Such alignments are important starting points for *e.g.* further elastic alignment of soft tissue organs.

Fig. 3. Superimposed registered 3D bones segmented from CT volumes. Perfect alignment is not possible on the thoracic CT image (last one) due to the relative movements of the bone structure, but affine alignment results are good starting point for *e.g.* lymph node detection.

3.3 Bone Fracture Reduction

Complex bone fracture reduction frequently requires surgical care, especially when angulation or displacement of bone fragments are large. Since the input data is typically a volume CT image, bone fragment repositioning has to be performed in 3D space which requires an expensive special 3D haptic device and quite a lot of manual work. Therefore automatic bone fracture reduction can save considerable time, providing experts with a rough alignment which can be manually fine-tuned according to anatomic requirements. Since surgical planning involves the biomechanical analysis of the bone with implants, only rigid-body transformations are allowed. In [20], a classical ICP algorithm is used to realign fractures. Winkelbach *et al.* [21] proposed an approach for estimating the relative transformations between fragments of a broken cylindrical structure by using well known surface registration techniques, like 2D depth correlation and the ICP algorithm. In [22], registration is solved by using quadrature filter phase difference to estimate local displacements.

In [9], we formulated the problem as an *affine puzzle*: Given a binary image of an object (the *template*) and another binary image (the *observation*) containing the fragments of the *template*, we want to reconstructs the complete *template* object from its parts. The overall distortion is a global nonlinear transformation with the following constraint [9]:

- the object parts are distinct (*i.e.* either disconnected or separated by seg-mentation),
- all fragments of the *template* are available, but
- each of them is subject to a different affine deformation, and the partitioning of the *template* object is unknown.

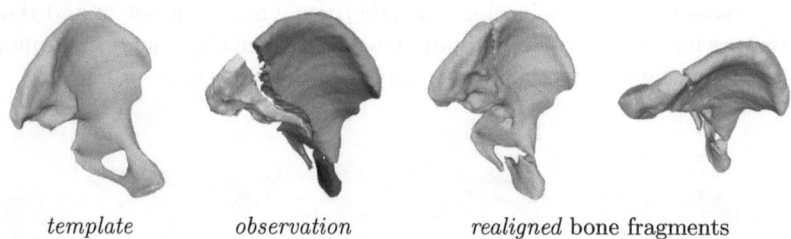

template   observation   *realigned* bone fragments

Fig. 4. Bone fracture reduction (CPU time in Matlab was 15 sec. for these 1 megavoxel CT volumes). The template is obtained by mirroring the intact bone.

The proposed solution [9] consists in constructing and solving a polynomial system of equations similar to the affine case, which provides all the unknown parameters of the alignment. We have quantitatively evaluated the proposed algorithm on a large synthetic dataset containing 2D and 3D images. The results show that the method performs well and robust against segmentation errors. In Fig. 4, we show a bone fracture reduction solution on a volumetric medical image.

3.4   Elastic Registration of Multimodal Prostate Images

Countries in Europe and USA have been following prostate cancer screening pro-grams since the last 15 years [23]. A patient with abnormal findings is generally advised for a prostate biopsy to diagnose the benign or malignant lesions. During needle biopsy, the most common appearance of malignant lesions in Transrec-tal Ultrasound (TRUS) is hypoechoic. The accuracy of sonographic finding of hypoechoic prostate cancer lesions is typically 43% [24]. In contrast, Magnetic Resonance Imaging (MRI) has a negative predictive value of 80% − 84% for significant cancer and the accuracy of MRI to diagnose prostate cancer is approximately 72% − 76% [25]. Therefore, MRI may serve as a triage test for men deemed to be at risk of prostate cancer and may reduce the number of re-biopsies while at the same time provide more useful information for those who are sent for biopsy. Consequently, fusion of pre-biopsy MR images onto interoperative TRUS images might increase the overall biopsy accuracy [26].

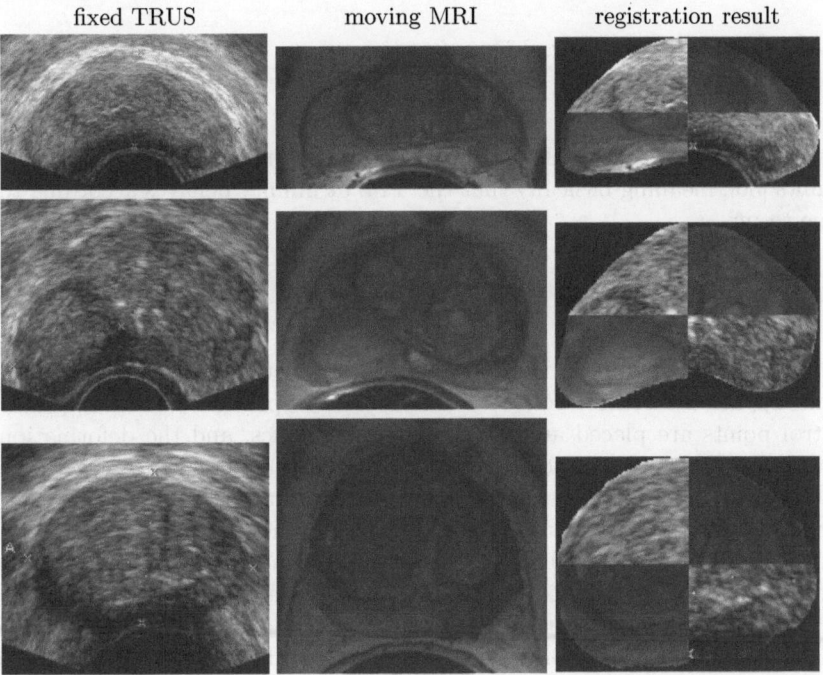

Fig. 5. MRI-TRUST multimodal prostate registration results. Registration result is shown as a checkerborard of TRUS and transformed MR images to show the alignment of the inner structures.

The registration of such prostate images requires a nonlinear deformation model. When ϕ is a nonlinear transformation, then the Jacobian $J_\phi(\mathbf{x})$ is not a constant anymore and thus Eq. (6) has to be used directly:

$$\int \omega_i(\mathbf{y})d\mathbf{y} = \int \omega_i(\phi(\mathbf{x}))|J_\phi(\mathbf{x})|d\mathbf{x}, \quad i = 1, \ldots, \ell \qquad (8)$$

From a practical point of view, this means that our method can be applied to any diffeomorpism ϕ for which one can compute its Jacobian $J_\phi(\mathbf{x})$. Of course, in order to obtain an overdetermined system, ℓ has to be larger than the number

of free parameters of ϕ. In nonlinear medical registration problems, a broadly
used class of parametric deformation models are splines, in particular thin plate
splines (TPS) [29, 30]. TPS models are quite useful whenever a parametric free-
form registration is required but the underlying physical model of the object
deformation is unknown or too complex. Given a set of control points $\mathbf{c}_k \in \mathbb{R}^2$
and associated mapping coefficients $a_{ij}, w_{ki} \in \mathbb{R}$ with $i = 1, 2$, $j = 1, 2, 3$ and
$k = 1, \ldots, K$, the TPS interpolating points $\mathbf{c}_k$ is given by [30]

$$\varphi_i(\mathbf{x}) = a_{i1}x_1 + a_{i2}x_2 + a_{i3} + \sum_{k=1}^{K} w_{ki}Q(||\mathbf{c}_k - \mathbf{x}||) , \tag{9}$$

where $Q : \mathbb{R} \to \mathbb{R}$ is the *radial basis function*

$$Q(r) = r^2 \log r^2 .$$

The local parameters are also required to satisfy the following additional constraints [30], meaning basically that the TPS at infinity behaves according to its
affine term:

$$\sum_{k=1}^{K} w_{ki} = 0 \quad \text{and} \quad \sum_{k=1}^{K} c_{kj}w_{ki} = 0, \quad i, j = 1, 2 . \tag{10}$$

Note that parameters include 6 global affine parameters a_{ij} and $2K$ local coefficients w_{ki} for the control points. In classical correspondence based approaches,
control points are placed at extracted point matches, and the deformation at
other positions is interpolated by the TPS. When correspondences are available,
the exact mapping of the control points are also known which, using Eq. (9),
provides constraints on the unknown parameters. Therefore in such cases, a TPS
can be regarded as an optimal *interpolating* function whose parameters are usually recovered via a complex optimization procedure [29, 30].

However, we are interested in solving the TPS registration problem without correspondences. Therefore in our approach, a TPS can be considered as a
parametric model to *approximate* the underlying deformation field [10]. Control
points (*i.e.* radial basis functions) can be placed *e.g.* on a uniform grid in order
to capture local deformations everywhere. Obviously, a finer grid would allow a
more refined approximation of the deformation field at the price of an increased
number of free parameters.

To construct our system of equations Eq. (8), we need the Jacobian $|J_\varphi(\mathbf{x})|$
of the transformation φ, which is composed of the following partial derivatives
$(i, j = 1, 2)$ [10]

$$\frac{\partial \varphi_i}{\partial x_j} = a_{ij} - \sum_{k=1}^{K} 2w_{ki}(c_{kj} - x_j)\big(1 + \log(||\mathbf{c}_k - \mathbf{x}||^2)\big) . \tag{11}$$

The system is then solved via *Levenberg-Marquardt* algorithm [10].

In [14], we have improved the generic non-linear registration framework of
[10] by establishing prostate-specific point correspondences and regularizing the

overall deformation. The point correspondences under the influence of which the thin-plate bends are established on the prostate contours by a method based on matching the shape-context ([2]) representations of contour points using Bhattacharyya distance ([27]). The approximation and regularization of the bending energy of the thin-plate splines are added to the set of non-linear TPS equations and are jointly minimized for a solution. Fig. 5 shows some registration results on multimodal prostate images.

3.5   Elastic Registration of 3D Lung CT Volumes

Lung alignment is a crucial task in lung cancer diagnosis [28]. During the treatment, changes in the tumor size are determined by comparing *follow-up* PET/CT scans which are taken at regular intervals depending on the treatment and the size of the tumor. Due to respiratory motion, the lung is subject to a nonlinear deformation between such *follow-ups*, hence it is hard to automatically find correspondences. A common practice is to determine corresponding regions by hand, but this makes the procedure time consuming and the obtained alignments may not be accurate enough for measuring changes.

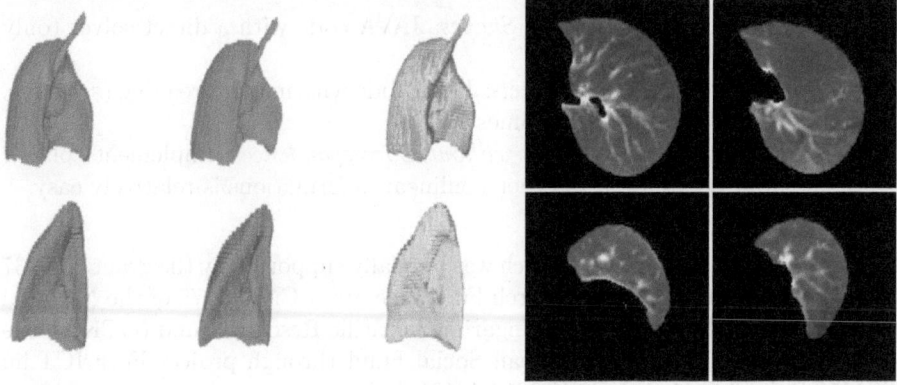

Fig. 6. Alignment of lung CT volumes and the combined slices of the original and the transformed images as an 8x8 checkerboard pattern. Segmented 3D lung images were generated by the *InterView Fusion software of Mediso Ltd.*.

Our algorithm has been successfully applied [11, 12] to align 3D lung CT scans. As usual in elastic medical imaging, the adopted parametric model is a 3D Thin plate splines (TPS) [29, 30] $\varsigma : \mathbb{R}^3 \to \mathbb{R}^3$ which can also be decomposed as three coordinate functions $\varsigma(\mathbf{x}) = [\varsigma_1(\mathbf{x}), \varsigma_2(\mathbf{x}), \varsigma_3(\mathbf{x})]^T$. Given a set of control points $c_k \in \mathbb{R}^3$ and associated mapping coefficients $a_{ij}, w_{ki} \in \mathbb{R}$ with $i = 1, \ldots, 3, j = 1, \ldots, 4$ and $k = 1, \ldots, K$, the TPS functions are

$$\varsigma_i(\mathbf{x}) = a_{i1}x_1 + a_{i2}x_2 + a_{i3}x_3 + a_{i4} + \sum_{k=1}^{K} w_{ki}Q(\|c_k - \mathbf{x}\|) \qquad (12)$$

where $Q : \mathbb{R} \to \mathbb{R}$ is the radial basis function, which has the following form in 3D [29]:

$$Q(r) = |r|.$$

The number of the necessary parameters are $N = 3(K+4)$ consisting of 12 affine parameters a_{ij} and 3 coefficients w_{ki} for each of the K control points c_k.

As for the prostate registration problem, we also included a bending energy regularization to ensure the proper alignment of the inner structures. Some registration results are presented in Fig. 6, where we also show the achieved alignment on grayscale slices of the original lung CT images. For these slices, the original and transformed images were combined as an 8×8 checkerboard pattern.

4   Conclusion

A unified framework for correspondence-less registration of 2D and 3D shapes has been presented. The method is applicable for various diffeomorphic deformations. In this paper, we have summarized our earlier results and persented different medical applications. Demo implementations of our method are also available from http://www.inf.u-szeged.hu/~kato/software/ as follows:

- *Affine Registration of Planar Shapes*: JAVA code with a direct solver (only runs under Windows).
- *Affine Registration of 3D Objects*: JAVA code with multi-threading ($\approx$ 0.2sec. CPU time for megavoxel volumes).
- *Nonlinear Shape Registration without Correspondences*: Implements planar homography, extension to other nonlinear deformations is relatively easy.

Acknowledgments. This research was partially supported by the grant K75637 of the Hungarian Scientific Research Fund; the grant CNK80370 of the National Innovation Office (NIH) & the Hungarian Scientific Research Fund (OTKA); the European Union and the European Social Fund through project FuturICT.hu (TAMOP-4.2.2.C-11/1/KONV-2012-0013).

The author gratefully acknowledges the contributions of Csaba Domokos, Zsolt Santa, Jozsef Nemeth, and Attila Tanács from University of Szeged, Hungary; Jhimli Mitra, Soumya Ghose, and Fabrice Meriaudeau from Le2i-UMR CNRS 6306, Université de Bourgogne, France.

The fractured bone CT images were obtained from the University of Szeged, Department of Trauma Surgery and were used with permission of Prof. Endre Varga, MD.

Pelvic CT studies and hip prosthesis Xray images were provided by Endre Szabó, Ádám Perényi, Ágnes Séllei and András Palkó from the Radiology Department of the University of Szeged.

Lung CT images were provided by László Papp from Mediso Ltd., Hungary.

References

1. Holden, M.: A review of geometric transformations for nonrigid body registration. IEEE Transactions on Pattern Analysis and Machine Intelligence 27, 111–128 (2008)
2. Belongie, S., Malik, J., Puzicha, J.: Shape matching and object recognition using shape context. IEEE Transactions on Pattern Analysis and Machine Intelligence 24, 509–522 (2002)
3. Heikkilä, J.: Pattern matching with affine moment descriptors. Pattern Recognition 37, 1825–1834 (2004)
4. Hagege, R., Francos, J.M.: Parametric estimation of multi-dimensional affine transformations:an exact linear solution. In: Proceedings of International Conference on Acoustics, Speech, and Signal Processing, Philadelphia, USA, vol. 2, pp. 861–864. IEEE (2005)
5. Domokos, C., Kato, Z.: Parametric estimation of affine deformations of planar shapes. Pattern Recognition 43, 569–578 (2010)
6. Tanács, A., Domokos, C., Sladoje, N., Lindblad, J., Kato, Z.: Recovering Affine Deformations of Fuzzy Shapes. In: Salberg, A.-B., Hardeberg, J.Y., Jenssen, R. (eds.) SCIA 2009. LNCS, vol. 5575, pp. 735–744. Springer, Heidelberg (2009)
7. Tanács, A., Sladoje, N., Lindblad, J., Kato, Z.: Estimation of linear deformations of 3D objects. In: Proceedings of International Conference on Image Processing, Hong Kong, China, pp. 153–156. IEEE (2010)
8. Tanacs, A., Kato, Z.: Fast linear registration of 3D objects segmented from medical images. In: Proceedings of International Conference on BioMedical Engineering and Informatics, Shanghai, China, pp. 299–303. IEEE (2011)
9. Domokos, C., Kato, Z.: Affine Puzzle: Realigning Deformed Object Fragments without Correspondences. In: Daniilidis, K., Maragos, P., Paragios, N. (eds.) ECCV 2010, Part II. LNCS, vol. 6312, pp. 777–790. Springer, Heidelberg (2010)
10. Domokos, C., Nemeth, J., Kato, Z.: Nonlinear shape registration without correspondences. IEEE Transactions on Pattern Analysis and Machine Intelligence 34, 943–958 (2012)
11. Santa, Z., Kato, Z.: Elastic registration of 3D deformable objects. In: Proceedings of International Conference on Digital Image Computing: Techniques and Applications, Fremantle, Australia. IEEE (2012)
12. Santa, Z., Kato, Z.: A unifying framework for non-linear registration of 3D objects. In: Proceedings of International Conference on Cognitive Infocommunications, Kassa, Slovakia, pp. 547–552. IEEE (2012)
13. Rohr, K., Stiehl, H.S., Sprengel, R., Buzug, T.M., Weese, J., Kuhn, M.H.: Landmark-based elastic registration using approximating thin-plate splines. IEEE Transactions on Pattern Analysis and Machine Intelligence 20, 526–534 (2001)
14. Mitra, J., Kato, Z., Marti, R., Oliver, A., Llado, X., Sidibe, D., Ghose, S., Vilanova, J.C., Comet, J., Meriaudeau, F.: A spline-based non-linear diffeomorphism for multimodal prostate registration. Medical Image Analysis 16, 1259–1279 (2012)
15. Hagege, R., Francos, J.M.: Parametric estimation of affine transformations: An exact linear solution. Journal of Mathematical Imaging and Vision 37, 1–16 (2010)
16. Downing, M., Undrill, P., Ashcroft, P., Hukins, D., Hutchison, J.: Automated femoral measurement in total hip replacement radiographs. In: Proceedings of International Conference on Image Processing and Its Applications, Dublin, Ireland, vol. 2, pp. 843–847. IEEE (1997)

17. Hardinge, K., Porter, M.L., Jones, P.R., Hukins, D.W.L., Taylor, C.J.: Measurement of hip prostheses using image analysis. the maxima hip technique. Journal of Bone and Joint Surgery 73-B, 724–728 (1991)
18. Florea, C., Vertan, C., Florea, L.: Logarithmic Model-Based Dynamic Range Enhancement of Hip X-Ray Images. In: Blanc-Talon, J., Philips, W., Popescu, D., Scheunders, P. (eds.) ACIVS 2007. LNCS, vol. 4678, pp. 587–596. Springer, Heidelberg (2007)
19. Oprea, A., Vertan, C.: A quantitative evaluation of the hip prosthesis segmentation quality in x-ray images. In: Proceedings of International Symposium on Signals, Circuits and Systems, Iasi, Romania, vol. 1, pp. 1–4. IEEE (2007)
20. Erdőhelyi, B., Varga, E.: Semi-automatic bone fracture reduction in surgical planning. In: Proceedings of the International Conference on Computer Assisted Radiology and Surgery. International Journal of Computer Assisted Radiology and Surgery, vol. 4, pp. S98–S99. Springer, Berlin (2009)
21. Winkelbach, S., Westphal, R., Goesling, T.: Pose Estimation of Cylindrical Fragments for Semi-automatic Bone Fracture Reduction. In: Michaelis, B., Krell, G. (eds.) DAGM 2003. LNCS, vol. 2781, pp. 566–573. Springer, Heidelberg (2003)
22. Pettersson, J., Knutsson, H., Borga, M.: Non-rigid registration for automatic fracture segmentation. In: Proceedings of International Conference on Image Processing, Atlanta, GA, USA, pp. 1185–1188. IEEE (2006)
23. Andriole, G.L., Crawford, E.D., Grubb, R.L., Buys, S.S., Chia, D., Church, T.R., Fouad, M.N., Gelmann, E.P., Reding, D.J., Weissfeld, J.L., Yokochi, L.A., O'Brien, B., Clapp, J.D., Rathmell, J.M., Riley, T.L., Hayes, R.B., Kramer, B.S., Izmirlian, G., Miller, A.B., Pinsky, P.F., Prorok, P.C., Gohagan, J.K., Berg, C.D.: Mortality results from a randomized prostate-cancer screening trial. The New England Journal of Medicine 360, 1310–1319 (2009)
24. Carroll, P., Shinohara, K.: Transrectal ultrasound guided prostate biopsy. Technical report, Department of Urology, University of California, San Francisco (2010), http://urology.ucsf.edu/patientGuides.html (accessed December 30, 2010)
25. Vilanova, J.C., Barceló-Vidal, C., Comet, J., Boada, M., Barceló, J., Ferrer, J., Albanell, J.: Usefulness of prebiopsy multi-functional and morphologic MRI combined with the free-to-total PSA ratio in the detection of prostate cancer. American Journal of Roentgenology 196, W715–W722 (2011)
26. Hu, Y., Ahmed, H.U., Taylor, Z., Allem, C., Emberton, M., Hawkes, D., Barratt, D.: MR to ultrasound registration for image-guided prostate interventions. Medical Image Analysis (2011) (in press), doi:10.1016/j.media.2010.11.003
27. Mitra, J., Srikantha, A., Sidibé, D., Martí, R., Oliver, A., Lladó, X., Vilanova, J.C., Meriaudeau, F.: A shape-based statistical method to retrieve 2D TRUS-MR slice correspondence for prostate biopsy. In: Proc. of SPIE Medical Imaging, San Diego, Calfornia, USA, vol. 8314, pp. 83143M-1–83143M-9 (2012)
28. Bryant, A.S., Cerfolio, R.J.: The maximum standardized uptake values on integrated FDG-PET/CT is useful in differentiating benign from malignant pulmonary nodules. The Annals of Thoracic Surgery 82, 1016–1020 (2006)
29. Bookstein, F.L.: Principal warps: Thin-Plate Splines and the Decomposition of deformations. IEEE Transactions on Pattern Analyis and Machine Intelligence 11, 567–585 (1989)
30. Zagorchev, L., Goshtasby, A.: A comparative study of transformation functions for nonrigid image registration. IEEE Transactions on Image Processing 15, 529–538 (2006)

Adaptive Hand Gesture Recognition System for Multiple Applications

Siddharth S. Rautaray and Anupam Agrawal

Indian Institute of Information Technology, Allahabad, U.P., India
{sr.rgpv,anupam69}@gmail.com

Abstract. With the increasing role of computing devices facilitating natural human computer interaction (HCI) will have a positive impact on their usage and acceptance as a whole. Techniques such as vision, sound, speech recognition allow for a much richer form of interaction between the user and machine. The emphasis is to provide a natural form of interface for interaction. As gesture commands are found to be natural for humans, the development of the gesture based system interface have become an important research area. One of the drawbacks of present gesture recognition systems is application dependent which makes it difficult to transfer one gesture control interface into multiple applications. This paper focuses on designing a hand gesture recognition system which is adaptable to multiple applications thus making the gesture recognition systems to be application adaptive. The designed system is comprised of the different processing steps like detection, segmentation, tracking, recognition etc. For making system application-adaptive different quantitative and qualitative parameters have been taken into consideration. The quantitative parameters include gesture recognition rate, features extracted and root mean square error of the system and the qualitative parameters include intuitiveness, accuracy, stress/comfort, computational efficiency, the user's tolerance, and real-time performance related to the proposed system. These parameters have a vital impact on the performance of the proposed application adaptive hand gesture recognition system.

Keywords: application-adaptive, gesture recognition, interface, qualitative, quantitative parameters.

1 Introduction

In the earlier years man to machine interaction was constrained by the techniques based on graphics display, keyboard, mouse, joystick etc. Recently this trend has been changed with the introduction of techniques based on recognition of vision, sound, speech, projective displays etc. which provides a much richer and natural mode of interaction between man and machine [1].

In the current day research scenarios the hand gesture recognition as input for man machine interface is being developed vigorously. The advantage of these techniques is that users can control devices without touching anything such as panel, keyboard, mouse etc. [2]. The user just needs to face the camera and raise his/her hands for

A. Agrawal et al. (Eds.): IITM 2013, CCIS 276, pp. 53–65, 2013.
© Springer-Verlag Berlin Heidelberg 2013

operational control. This provides a natural mode of interaction between user and machine with hand as input device. Hand gesture recognition systems provide users a high degree of freedom and intuitive feeling. This serves as a motivating force for research in modeling, analyzing and recognition of hand gestures. Meaningful hand gestures can be classified as static and dynamic gestures. Static gestures are defined as the orientation and position of hand in the space during an amount of time without any movement. A dynamic gesture is a series of posture over time span converted by motions. Hand postures appear statistically as a combination of different finger status, orientations and angles of finger joints [3]. Hand modeling is one of the most important task in recognizing postures, as fingers are usually articulated. Self occlusion makes detection and tracking local hand configuration challenging [15].

Today there are many different devices available for hand based HCI. Some examples like cybergloves, 3D mice, magnetic tracking devices etc. [4]. However they have certain drawbacks such as costly for general use, complex setup procedures and calibration and further lack the naturalness of gesture [5].

Figure 1 shows an overview of system setup for vision based hand gesture recognition for adaptive application. In the present setup a webcam is attached to the PC for capturing the gestures performed by the user (gesture creator). The gestures from a gesture set are processed and converted into meaningful commands. The list of these gestures is stored in the gesture set.

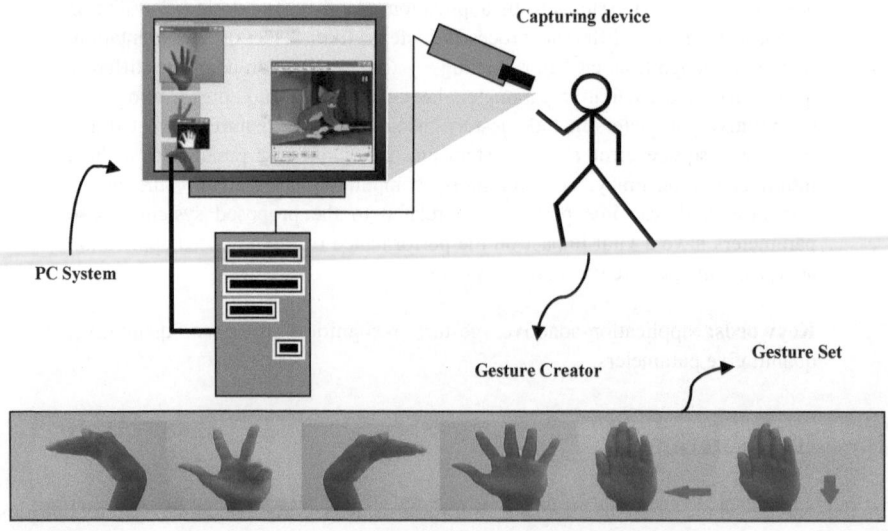

Fig. 1. Vision based hand gesture recognition system setup

In spatial gesture model there two main approaches: 3D hand model based and appearance based methods [15]. Appearance based systems have two categories: motion based and posture based recognition. Posture based recognition handles not only the location of hand, but also recognizes its characteristic features.

Motion-based systems make use of dynamic gestures, and the posture-based systems make use of static hand gestures [6]. The appearance-based methods can be divided into two groups, such as region-based and boundary-based methods. They include edge-based contours [7], [10], edges [8], [9], image moments [11], image eigenvectors [12], etc. Some other techniques use second order moments such as Zernike's methods [13] that are invariant to the rotation of the shape. Another method uses orientation histograms [14], which are invariant to lighting conditions and represent summarized information of small patch orientations over the hand image.

2   Application Adaptive Hand Gesture Recognition System: System Model

The aim of building a hand gesture recognition system application adaptive poses many design and implementation challenges. The issues and challenges involved include various parameters considering the needs of present day contact less human machine interfaces. Convergence technologies and advancements in machine architecture independence has made the application adaptive possible for the present day's computers and thus need for application adaptive man to machine interaction has come into picture. Applications may be numerous in number if we consider a set of applications as $A_{di} = (A_{d1}, A_{d2}, A_{d3} \dots\dots\dots\dots A_{dn})$ and the set of commands to map to hand gestures as $C_{A_{di}}^{j} = (C_{A_{d1}}^{1}, C_{A_{d2}}^{2}, C_{A_{d3}}^{3}, \dots\dots C_{A_{dn}}^{m})$, application adaptive hand gesture recognition system (H_{GRS}) needs to minimize the efforts $E_{f\ (H_{GRS})}$ required to map the set of commands associated with different application domains associated with the minimization function $\prod$:

$$ E_{f\ (H_{GRS})} \stackrel{\text{def}}{=} \prod_{i=1}^{n} \prod_{j=1}^{m} \left\{ \left(\sum_{j=1}^{m} C_{A_{di}}^{j} \right) \times \left(\sum_{i=1}^{n} A_{di} \right) \right\} \tag{1} $$

Now the efforts required to map the set of commands associated with different application domains are dependent on various the parameters of each and every step involved in the gesture recognition system. Let's have an insight of the step involved in gesture recognition system and various parameters associated with it. The hand gesture recognition basically includes four steps also referred to as the four major components of a hand gesture recognition system(H_{GRS}) : hand detection, hand segmentation, tracking and recognition. These four components of (H_{GRS}) consist of various processes as hand detection includes background subtraction, followed by skin segmentation and feature extraction to detect the user's hand in the input sequence. The performance of $P_{er}(AI(H_{GRS}))$ of application adaptive (i.e. independent) $AI\ (H_{GRS})$ interface depends on some quantitative parameters and some qualitative parameters.

Quantitative Parameters: The quantitative parameters are those parameters that may be quantified as numerical values for the recognition system that include the gesture recognition rate, features extracted and root mean square error of the system.

a) **Recognition Rate(R_r):** The recognition rate (R_r) is defined as the ratio of the number of correctly classified samples to the total sampling number, shown as Eq. (2)

$$R_r = \frac{R_c}{R_t} * 100 \tag{2}$$

Where: R_c = *Correctly recognized gestures*
R_t = *Total recognized gestures*

b) **Root mean square error(R_{mse}):** R_{mse} is calculating root mean square between the expected value and system output value for each and every iteration of gesture recognition. R_{MSE} can be calculated as:

$$R_{mse} = \sqrt{\sum_{i=1}^{n} \frac{(d_i - y_i)^2}{n}} \tag{3}$$

where: n = *the number of iterations*
d_i = *actual accurate value of gesture recognition*
y_i = *predicted accurate value of gesture recognition*

Qualitative Parameters: The qualitative parameters are those parameters that may be not be quantified as numerical values for the recognition system. These parameters include intuitiveness, accuracy, stress/comfort, computational efficiency, user's tolerance and real-time performance.

a) **Intuitiveness $I_{AI(H_{GRS})}$:** Intuitiveness is the naturalness of expressing a given command with a gesture. There are two types of intuitiveness, *direct* and *complementary*. For direct intuitiveness the value $I_d\left(C_{A_{di}}^j\right)$, represents the strength of association between command $C_{A_{di}}^j$ of the application domain A_{di} and its matched gesture G_s. Complementary intuitiveness, $I_c\left(C_{A_{di}}^j\right)$ gives the level of association of matching complementary gestures pairs (such as mirrored poses) to complementary command pairs (i, j) (semantically opposed). Total intuitiveness could be given by

$$I_{AI(H_{GRS})} = \sum_{j=1}^{n}\left[\sum_{j=1}^{n} I_d , \sum_{j=1}^{n} I_c\right]$$

$$= \sum_{j=1}^{n} \left[\sum_{j=1}^{n} I_d \left(C_{Adi}^j \right), \sum_{j=1}^{n} I_c \left(C_{Adi}^j \right) \right] \tag{4}$$

b) **Accuracy** $A_c\big(AI(H_{GRS})\big)$: Accuracy is a measure of how well a set of gestures can be recognized. To obtain an estimate of gesture accuracy, a set of sample gestures for each gesture in G_s is required to be tested on the implemented gesture recognition system. The numbers of gestures classified correctly are called $T_c\,(G_s)$ and misclassified gestures may be denoted as$T_e\,(G_s)$. The gesture recognition accuracy is denoted by

$$A_c\big(AI(H_{GRS})\big) = \frac{T_c\,(G_s) - T_e\,(G_s)}{T_c\,(G_s)} \times 100 \tag{5}$$

c) **Stress/comfort** $S_t\big(G_sAI(H_{GRS})\big)$: Stress/comfort is related to the effort needed to perform a gesture. Total stress is obtained by the stress index of a gesture, weighted by duration and frequency of use. The value $G_s(k \rightarrow l)$ represents the physical difficulty of a transition between gestures G_k to G_l, and $S_t(G_s)$ represents the stress of repeating the same gesture over an interval of time t. The duration to reconfigure the hand between gestures k and l is represented by$t_d\,\big(G_s(k \rightarrow l)\big)$. The symbol $F(G_s)$ stands for the average frequency of transition between commands j and $j+1$ for the task under consideration. The value K is a constant and is used to convert stress into its inverse measure, comfort.

$$S_t\big(G_sAI(H_{GRS})\big) =$$
$$K - \sum_{j=1}^{n} \big(G_s(k \rightarrow l), t_d\,\big(G_s(k \rightarrow l)\big), F(G_s)\,\big) \tag{6}$$

d) **Computational Efficiency**(C_e): Generally, Vision based interaction often requires real-time systems. The vision and learning techniques/algorithms used in Vision-based interaction should be effective as well as cost efficient.

e) **User's Tolerance**(U^t): The malfunctions or mistakes of Vision-based interaction should be tolerated. When a mistake is made, it should not incur much loss. Users can be asked to repeat some actions, instead of letting the computer make more wrong decisions.

f) **Real-Time Performance**(R^t): By real-time performance, the system must be able to consider, i.e. the image at the frame rate of the input video to give the user instant feedback of the recognized gesture.

The design issue for an application adaptive human computer interaction system $AI(H_{GRS})$ may be give as the :

Minimization function (Min) of

$$E_{f(H_{GRS})}, R_{mse(H_{GRS})}, C_{e(H_{GRS})}, S_t(G_s AI(H_{GRS}))$$

$$AI(H_{GRS}) Min \begin{pmatrix} E_{f(H_{GRS})}, R_{mse(H_{GRS})}, C_{e(H_{GRS})}, \\ S_t(G_s AI(H_{GRS})) \end{pmatrix} \tag{7}$$

and maximization function

$$(Max) of\ R_{r(H_{GRS})}, R_{o(H_{GRS})}, I_{AI(H_{GRS})}, \ A_c(AI(H_{GRS})), U^t{}_{(H_{GRS})}, R^t{}_{(H_{GRS})}$$
i.e.

$$AI(H_{GRS}) = Max\ (R_{r(H_{GRS})}, R_{o(H_{GRS})}, I_{AI(H_{GRS})}, \\ A_c(AI(H_{GRS})), U^t{}_{(H_{GRS})}, R^t{}_{(H_{GRS})}) \tag{8}$$

Performance of an application adaptive hand gesture recognition system $AI(H_{GRS})$ could be given as:

$$P_{er}(AI(H_{GRS})) = \bigcup \Big\{ Min\ \big(E_{f(H_{GRS})}, R_{mse(H_{GRS})}, \quad C_{e(H_{GRS})}, S_t(G_s AI(H_{GRS})) \big)$$

$$\&\&$$

$$Max\ \begin{pmatrix} R_{r(H_{GRS})}, R_{o(H_{GRS})}, I_{AI(H_{GRS})}, A_c(AI(H_{GRS})), \\ U^t{}_{(H_{GRS})}, R^t{}_{(H_{GRS})} \end{pmatrix} \Big\} \tag{9}$$

3   Architecture Design

The application The system designed recognizes 10 static gesture classes in real time as shown in figure 2. The modules in the proposed application adaptive hand gesture recognition system can be broadly categorized as detection, segmentation, tracking, recognition etc.

Through this setup the camera grabs the projected background image from a major sub region of the recognition area and other minor part of the image (information area) can be used to display the state of the recognition process e.g. pictogram of the detected gesture class. This configuration setup applies only a minimal and cost efficient configuration with general devices. The system applies a boundary based method to recognize poses of static hand gestures. The detected hand gesture and position can be used for navigating menus and for the manipulation of different software objects. Controlling by gestures is based on both the localization and the meaning of the command. It is fundamental to use a relatively small and simple gesture set instead of large and complex sign languages because the main point of our user interface is that any non trainer users should be able to learn the gesture vocabulary and the controlling rules.

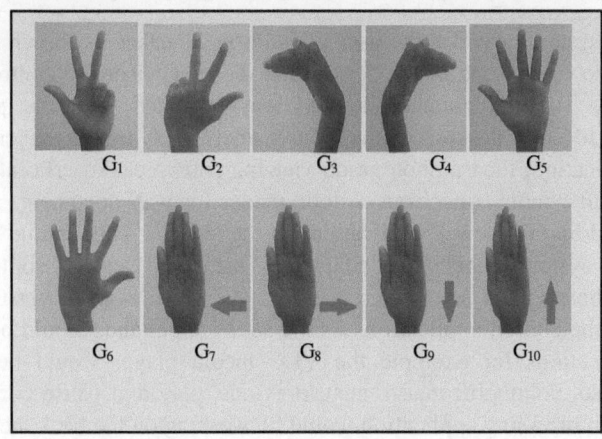

Fig. 2. Vocabulary Database (An incorporated set of gestures $G_s = \{G_1, G_2, G_3 \ldots \ldots \ldots G_{10}\}$)

The proposed system consists of five processing stages detailed as follows:

Background Subtraction

Background subtraction is the part of initial processing required to be done in the proposed system. In this step, we compute the absolute difference between frame and background to form the background subtracted image.

Segmentation

After the background subtracted image is lead towards skin segmentation so that the skin segments of the image could be differentiated from rest of the image.

Feature Extraction

While designing efficient gesture recognition system is an important issue to decide which features to be extracted from hand to generate a unique identity for each command.

Tracking

Tracking means to locate the object and report its changes in position over time. It can be considered as a repeated frame-by-frame object detection, which usually implies more than discontinuous processing.

Gesture Recognition

Hand gesture recognition involves the construction of a model for each gesture to be recognized. This usually proceeds by collecting a number of examples of the gesture, computing the mean gesture and quantifying the variance seen in these examples.

3.1   Application Adaptive Hand Gesture Recognition System $AI(H_{GRS})$

The proposed system provides the user with a user interface as shown in figure 3 (a) for the selection of any one of the application the user wishes to control through the hand gestures. The implemented system was provided with the provisions for selection five different desktop applications namely VLC media player, Firefox web browsing application, Picasa photograph viewing software, PowerPoint presentations of the Microsoft windows package, Adobe reader for web document, and a custom interface for adding up newer applications to the system. This unique feature makes the proposed system application adaptive. Once the desired application to be controlled is chosen the system enters the next phase of assigning gestures to various commands of the chosen application. As the set of commands would be different for multiple applications for example the VLC media player would be working for volume increase, volume decrease, next, previous, play and pause commands while the Firefox web browsing application would be working on the back, next, homepage, zoom in and zoom out commands, on the other hand if we talk of Picasa photo viewing software it would take different set of commands comprising of next, previous, rotate clockwise ,rotate anti-clockwise zoom in and zoom out.

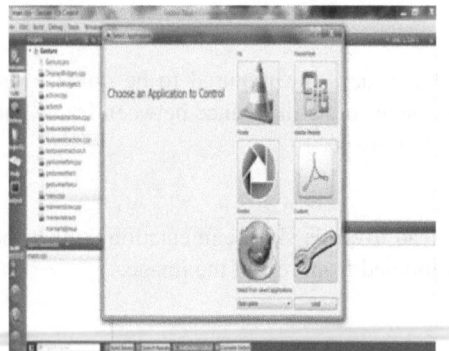 

(a)Application adaptive gesture interface   (b) Mapping of hand gestures

Fig. 3. Gesture recognition process

   To make the mapping of these variations in a set of commands for different application we associated the gestures with keyboard strokes and provided the user interface for selection of gestures to be associated with the command of the specific application as the figure 3 (b) depicts association of gesture to keyboard events and commands for VLC media player application. The system implemented has been made robust having the provisions for adding of more gestures to the gesture vocabulary set G_s and applications set A_s.

Process Flow: *Application Adaptive hand gesture recognition system*

    Input: U_i (Window)   // User Interface Window//

    Qtoolbutton   // mouse and keyboard events//

    Qpushbutton   // Gesture for gesture vocabulary set//

    Qcombobox   // Drop down menu box //

    Setup: U_i {Label 1:= "Application 1" $\in A_{di}$

    Label 2:= "Application 2" $\in A_{di}$

....   **Label** n:= "Application n" $\in A_{di}$ **}**

    Qtoolbutton: { Btn 1:= "mouseevent1/ keyboard event 1" $\in C_{A_{di}}^{j}$

    Btn 2:= "mouseevent2/ keyboard event 2" $\in C_{A_{di}}^{j}$

......   **Btn** n: = "mouse event n/ keyboard event n" $\in C_{A_{di}}^{j}$ **}**

    Functions: Connect (Btn , U_i, Signal) // Connects the Application to the event//

//For the gesture vocabulary Invocation//

    Gesture Setter (U_i, Qtoolbutton, Qlabel, Qmsgbox , Qsettings)

    Qlabel // Addition of new application $\notin A_{di}$//

    Qmsgbox // Informative messages //

    Output : Qsettings { G_i:= "Gesture 1" $\in G_S$

                         G_2:= "Gesture 2" $\in G_S$

                        .... G_n:= "Gesture   n" $\in G_S$ **}**

To make the proposed application adaptive hand gesture recognition system we had to implement a dedicated module with special features of being application adaptive. This special module was incorporated within the hand gesture recognition system to make it adaptive of any particular application's set of commands. We take user interface window (Ui) as the input to this application adaptive module. This user interface window (Ui) is responsible for making the proposed system application adaptive and interactive as it allows the user to select one of the applications out of the list incorporated to be operated upon by the hand gesture recognition system. The setup of the user interface window (Ui) includes various labels corresponding to different applications along with a specific provision for the user to add up any new application dynamically at the real time. Through the Qtoolbutton label of the setup different keyboard button and mouse events are mapped to various gestures incorporated in the gesture vocabulary set G_S. Before mapping to the hand gesture posed by user these keyboard button and mouse events are converted to their universal hexadecimal codes used by operating systems for their recognition. This provides the user flexibility to associate different gestures or a set of gestures to a different set of keyboard button and mouse events. This application adaptive module also has Qmsgbox component that provides informative messages related to the proposed system to the user. These informative messages make the system more user-friendly and add up to the intuitiveness of the system with additional accuracy and lesser user stress. These informative messages act as a user manual for the proposed system. Qsettings within the setup is responsible for gesture vocabulary setup and updating of the already existing gesture definitions within the gesture vocabulary set G_S .The *Gesture Setter* function of the module is responsible for mapping of user posed gestures to the gestures defined in the gesture vocabulary set G_S and in turn to the set of commands of the user selected applications.

4   Results and Analysis

Performance analysis based on the accuracy and recognition rate accuracy was experimented for all the ten gestures incorporated in the proposed gesture vocabulary set G_S for different laboratory conditions like different illuminating conditions, background and for the set of applications incorporated A_s. Though the results are obtained under the laboratory conditions they may vary with the real time applications still the system has been built for adaptability, scalability and accuracy of real time applications but the results may be different. Figure 4 shows the recognition and accuracy in percentage for the vision based application adaptive gesture recognition system.

In general it was observed that G_1 has the highest accuracy which was 85%. G_2 presented the accuracy of 80% which is due to some inaccuracy in exact calculations of orientation of the hand. G_3 depicted 80% accuracy because of the number of defects (being 1 for this gesture recognition which is more prone to false detection of defect. Gesture G_4 also had 75% accuracy since the number of defects is 1that is more prone to false detection of defect as is the case with G_3 that also depends on the right orientation which further decreases its accuracy. G_5 provided the results of 82% accuracy as the number of defects associated with this gesture is 5 and so it is less probable to detect all the defects. G_6 depicted a lesser accuracy than G_5 of 78% accuracy as the number of defects is 5 and it is less probable to detect all the defects and also right orientation associated with the $G_6$is problem. Gesture G_7, G_8, G_9 posed 72% accuracy as all these gestures are movement based dynamic gestures and these types of gestures are observed to give less accuracy. G_{10} has the lowest accuracy in our proposed system that is 70%. This is because when the user opens the hand the center of hand shift upward and it is confused with upward movement of the hand.

The proposed application adaptive gesture recognition system was tested for the overall performance parameters defined in previous sections. The proposed system was tested to obtain its performance for the quantitative parameters with the help of multiple iterations of the system with variations in experimental conditions and tested by different number of users to obtain the accurate results.

For testing the root mean square error R_{mse} of the proposed system the system was tested for ten numbers of iterations with the recognition of each and every gesture in the used gesture vocabulary set G_s. The results obtained for R_{mse} are compared with the average root mean square percentage between the expected value and system output value of various iterations of the gesture recognition. Figure 5 presents the comparative mean square error percentage for different number of iterations of the proposed application adaptive hand gesture recognition system for various gestures belonging to the gesture vocabulary set G_s.

Gesture (Gs)	Accuracy (%)	Recognition rate (%)
G_1	85	82
G_2	80	86
G_3	80	77
G_4	75	75
G_5	82	95
G_6	78	65
G_7	72	90
G_8	72	77
G_9	72	82
G_{10}	70	95

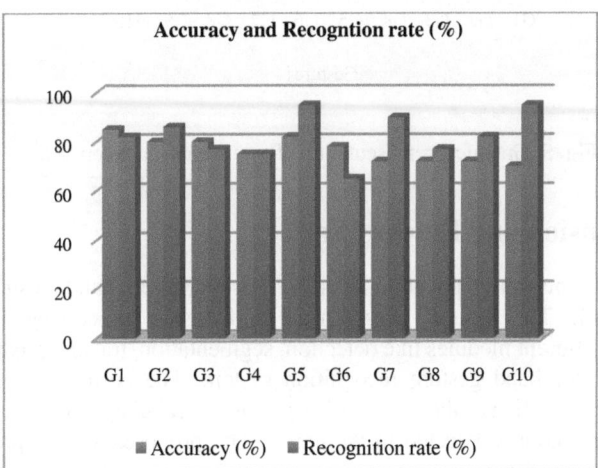

Fig. 4. Tabular and graphical representation of recognition and accuracy of system

The R_{mse} percentage for gesture G_1 has been maximum reaching to 90% in the case of 30 iterations while the minimum R_{mse} was reported for G_5 for all the iterations from 10 to 20 to 30 iterations. Hence we can conclude that the gesture G_5 could be used for more complicated and robust system while gesture G_1 should be avoided for such applications because of its higher root mean square error rate. Other preferred gestures for real time complex applications of the current application adaptive hand gesture recognition system could be gestures G_3, G_4, G_6, G_8, G_9, G_{10} they have lesser root mean square error rate. As per experiments gesture G_1 again gives a minimum stress level results which makes this gesture more user adaptive and its higher accuracy adds up to this. While gesture G_2 provides the maximum stress level hence gesture G_2 would be lesser preferred gesture by the users as it also has lower accuracy and lower intuitiveness. We have tested our system on our defined set of gestures within the laboratory conditions though the results may variant with other set of gestures and environmental conditions along with a different arbitrary quantification methodology adoption.

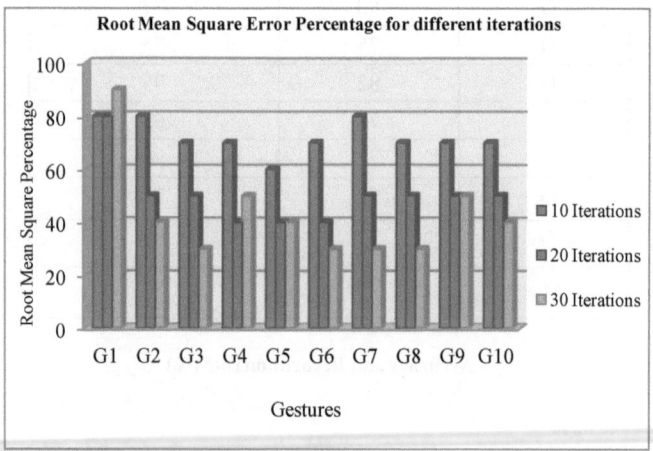

Fig. 5. Graphical representation of root mean square error R_{mse}

5   Conclusion and Future Work

This paper presents an application adaptive vision based hand gesture recognition system$AI(H_{GRS})$. The system uses image and vision processing techniques for implementing different modules like detection, segmentation, tracking, feature extraction, recognition etc for hand gesture recognition system. The gestures recognized by the system are then identified as the p   art of a gesture vocabulary set G_s with the help of number of defect counts detected in the hand. The proposed system provides the end user ability to control the applications incorporated in the set of applications A_s as the software's like VLC, FIREFOX, PICASA, POWERPOINT and ADOBE READER with the help of gestures incorporated in the gesture vocabulary set G_s.

The future directions of the research in progress of the proposed application and user adaptive hand gesture recognition system includes the robustness to be added to the system in the terms of variations in illumination conditions, changes in background, distance of hand and angle of camera. Also the system could be made scalable to higher number of applications with a larger probable database of gesture vocabulary incorporated.

References

1. Hardenberg, C., Bérard, F.: Bare-Hand Human-Computer Interaction. In: PUI 2001, Orlando, FL, USA, pp. 1–8 (2001)
2. Hsieh, C., Liou, D., Lee, D.: A Real Time Hand Gesture Recognition System Using Motion History Image. In: 2nd International Conference on Signal Processing Systems (ICSPS), pp. 394–439 (2010)
3. Wu, Y., Huang, T.S.: Hand Modeling, Analysis and Recognition. IEEE Signal Processing Magazine 18(3), 51–60 (2001)
4. Ren, Z., Meng, J., Yuan, J.: Depth Camera Based Hand Gesture Recognition and its Applications in Human-Computer-Interaction. In: 8th International Conference on Information, Communications and Signal Processing (ICICS), Singapore, pp. 1–6 (2011)
5. Kim, D., Song, J., Kim, D.: Simultaneous gesture segmentation and recognition based on forward spotting accumulative HMMs. Pattern Recognition 40, 3012–3026 (2007)
6. Freeman, W.T., Tanaka, K., Kyuma, K.: Computer vision for computer games. In: International Conference on Aut. Face and Gesture Recogition, Vermont, USA, pp. 100–105 (1996)
7. Shahrary, B., Anderson, D.J.: Optimal estimation of contour properties by cross validated regularization. IEEE Tran. Pattern Anal. Mach. Intell. 11(6), 600–610 (1989)
8. Moghadam, B., Pentland, A.: Probabilistic Visual Learning for Object Detection, Tech. Rep., MIT media lab., TR-326 (1995)
9. Bowden, R., Mitchell, T.A., Sarhadi, M.: Reconstructing 3d pose and motion from a single camera view. In: BMVC, Southampton, UK, pp. 904–913 (1998)
10. Ng, C.W., Ranganath, S.: Real-time gesture recognition system and application. Image and Vision Computing 20, 993–1007 (2002)
11. Athitsos, V., Sclaroff, S.: An Appearance-based Framework for 3D Hand Shape Classification and Camera Viewpoint Estimation. In: IEEE International Conference on Automatic Face and Gesture Recognition, pp. 45–50 (2002)
12. Imagawa, K., Taniguchi, R., Arita, D., Matsuo, H., Lu, S., Igi, S.: Appearance-based Recognition of Hand Shapes for Sign Language in Low Resolution Image. In: 4th Asian Conference on Computer Vision, pp. 943–948 (2000)
13. Schlenzig, J., Hunter, E., Jain, R.: Vision-based hand gesture interpretation using recursive estimation. In: 28th Asilomar Conference Signals, Systems, and Computer, pp. 1267–1271 (1994)
14. Freeman, W.T., Roth, M.: Orientation Histograms for Hand Gesture Recognition. In: International Workshop on Automatic Face and Gesture Recognition, Zurich, pp. 296–301 (1995)
15. Rautaray, S.S., Agrawal, A.: Vision based Hand Gesture Recognition for Human Computer Interaction: A Survey. Journal of Artificial Intelligence Review, 1–54 (2012)

Enhancement of High Dynamic Range Dark Images Using Internal Noise in DWT Domain

Nidhi Gupta[1] and Rajib Jha[2]

[1] Computer Science and Engineering
[2] Electronics and Communication Engineeing
IIIT Design and Manufacturing Jabalpur, 482005, India
{nidhi180,jharajib}@gmail.com

Abstract. Among the various existing techniques for the enhancement of dark images, it has been observed that if the images have certain bright area, then it becomes more bright after application of those techniques. The idea has emerged from this existing drawback. In this paper we have changed the parameter used earlier. In aspect of the visual performance the proposed algorithm emerges as quite easy and efficient with keeping concentration on the bright area that should not to be degraded. The decomposition of areas has been done on the basis of entropy of the image. Dynamic SR has been applied in iterative manner and the optimum output response is ensured by the various parameter metrics of the image. Parameter ensures the optimality via statistical and quantitative analysis of the result obtained. The proposed approach is compared with other existing techniques and it has been found that since number of iterations has been reduced drastically, hence the total consumed time. The rate of accuracy is highly increased and no information loss in the output. Also the color quality is maintained and sharpness has been enhanced as well.

1   Introduction

High Dynamic Range (HDR) image represents more accurately the range of intensity levels found at real scenes. HDR image allows real time visualization that is not possible with any other imaging modality. In real world we capture the scenes, but due to poor illumination or sometimes due to handling with wrong angle by photographer, it becomes unable to capture the entire range. Therefore, there is need for contrast enhancement and reconstruction of area which gets distorted. The entire process should be done keeping in mind that without any information loss the outcomes are projecting [11].

However, noise is not always deleterious to a system. The addition of noise of the system sometimes improves its ability to transfer information reliably. Sometimes the optimal noise enhances the degree of order in a system. Here comes the idea of Stochastic Resonance. Stochastic Resonance is one of the most significant examples of type of dynamical systems. Generally noise is unwanted signal that is related to term hindrance. When noise is used to enhance the signal in non-linear dynamic system, the phenomenon called Stochastic Resonance. The notion of SR determines

A. Agrawal et al. (Eds.): IITM 2013, CCIS 276, pp. 66–74, 2013.

the group of phenomenon wherein the response of the system to a weak input signal can be significantly increased with appropriate tuning of noise intensity. SR includes three basic components i.e.

(1) Non-linear system,

(2) Source of noise and

(3) Weak coherent input, described by [4][6]. The paper has been organized as following. Section II describes the mathematical concept behind the stochastic resonance that how it works and able to enhance the image. Further Section III contains the detail theory about the threshold selection for the decomposition of the area using entropy. Section IV is all about the proposed algorithm for the enhancement. Section V and VI compares the results from others and shows the computational results done in different images. Section VII and VIII describes the role of internal noise and reason for selection of color model respectively. Finally section IX describes the brief conclusion of the paper.

2   Mathematical Concept of DSR

Mathematically it has been proven that maximizing the Signal -to- Noise Ratio (SNR) enhances the signal. For the reconstruction of the signal, inherent noise has been used. The most common quantifier of stochastic resonance is signal-to-noise ratio. Benzi's double well theory suggests two states of image contrast, i.e; low and high and the particles are analogous to state of coefficient magnitude [1][2]. So in this bistable system, particle's oscillation corresponds to no. of iteration applied on DSR equation described following,

$$X(n + 1) = X(n) + \Delta t [aX(n) - b^3 X(n) + Input]$$

Here input is defined by $B \sin(\omega t) + \sqrt{D} \xi(t)$ and parameters is defined by $a = 2\sigma^2$ and $b < (4a3)/27$. σ is standard deviation of the image. Maximizing the signal-to-noise ratio (SNR) we enhance the image quality. The equation is basically maintained by these parameters. The values of a and b are obtained by differentiating the maximization of SNR signal, as described by [6].

3   Role of Entropy

In the information theory, entropy is a measure of uncertainty associated with a random variable. Statistically it is a measure of randomness that can be used to characterize the texture of the input image. It is defined as,

$$\text{Entropy} = \Sigma(p * \log(p))   (1)$$

Where p is histogram count returned from imhist function applied on the image. It quantifies the expected value contained in the image. Since the predictability is inversely proportional to the entropy, so subtraction by entropy from its pixel value increases the predictness. We become able to predict more accurately the illumination of the image.

In the information sense, it is the measure of unpredictability. Basically the entropy describes the business of the image. Low entropy image such that lots of blue sky having little contrast and large runs of pixels. The perfectly flat image has entropy zero. Because there prediction may be easily happened. On the other hand, high entropy image such as an image having cratered areas on moon have a great deal of contrast from one pixel to next and consequently cannot be compressed due to low entropy image.[12] The entropy is given as uncertainty associated with random variable. These variables in our approach are quantitative measure of the pixel. The measures could be-

1. Color
2. Luminance
3. Saturation
4. Location

Maximum contrast of the image is the contrast ratio or dynamic range. Contrast is the difference between color and shadings of the printed material on any document and background on which it is printed. Luminance is a only useful measurement for implementation of the proposed algorithm. Location is most useless, not important for our approach. Here we have used luminance to achieve the accuracy. Idea behind conversion of color model from RGB to HSV is same as above.

4   Proposed Algorithm

The proposed DSR based technique has been applied on HDR images. In our approach the enhancement has been done only to the required dark areas of the images. This makes algorithm more specific. The simulation steps are following-

A. Selection of Area
Since the entire image need not to be enhanced. Because there are certain areas already constructed and bright enough. Due to less light some area are not visible and need to be enhanced. To separate bright and dark area, compare each pixel value whether it is less than maximum pixel value deducted by twice of the entropy of the image. For the decomposition of the area we have define the threshold using entropy of the image. Entropy plays a major role in decomposition of the area. Deduction by entropy of image by pixel value ensures that unpredictability has been somewhat reduced. In other words, uncertainty of the pixels are reduced at certain limit. Therefore lesser the value than above said threshold, area taken as dark and rest as bright area. Our main focus is on dark area only onwards, to recover all hidden information which becomes invisible due to the darkness. We get the two separated area after applying the decomposition technique discussed earlier.

B. Color Model Conversion and DWT Decomposition
The input images are High Dynamic Range (HDR) dark images. Convert the RGB color model into HSV model on the dark area and apply discrete wavelet transform on the v vector value. V vector determines the illumination of the image. 1-level

decomposition gives the coefficient values as, detailed and approximation. Bi-orthogonal spline wavelet bank having 9X7 filter coefficient has been used here.

C. Separately Application of DSR

After the DWT application, we get coefficients; detailed and approximate both. The iterative equation of DSR has been applied on these, assuming the constants as following stated below-

$$\Delta t = 0.06 \text{ for required area}$$

Our algorithm is concentrated on dark area enhancement without any information loss. The no. of iteration has been estimated by parameters described by [9][4]. The parameter metrics F, PQM and CEF makes the algorithm adaptive. The parametric metrics are Color Enhancement Factor (F), Contrast Enhancement Factor (CEF) and Perceptual Quality Measure (PQM) described by [4].

These parameters measures the statistical as well as quantitative, from both aspects of the image. This all parameters not only ensures that output produced is of good quality but have better visual perception. These all parameter are calculated for each output we get after each iterations. All parameters are evaluated each time of the iteration. At best visual perception the outcome is estimated.

D. Parameter Optimization and Selection

Experimental results shows that for the enhancement of the images, the parameters applied on the DSR equation plays a major role. They helps in controlling the no. of iteration. The estimated parameters are evaluated and displayed in table (1). This experimental data for figure (1) is

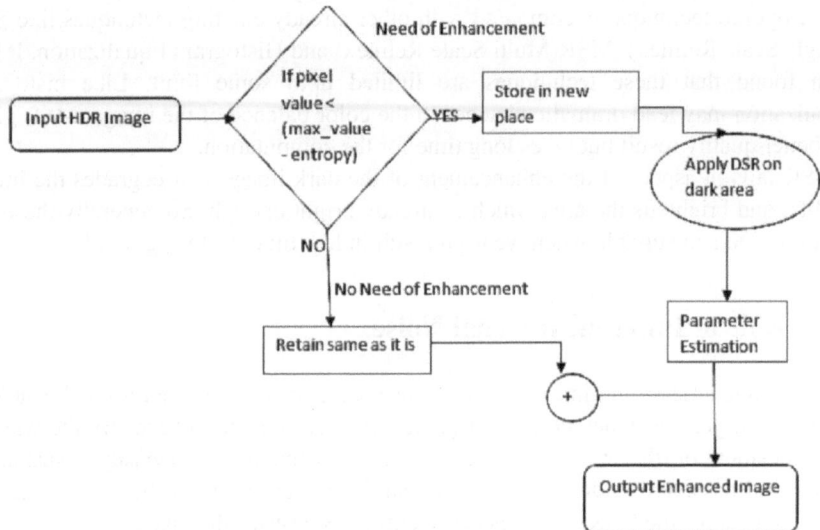

Fig. 1. Computational Sequence Chart for Enhancement of the Image

5   Observations by Experiments

It has been observed that pixels which are distributed previously in random order and not in proper way, gets redistributed so that the output image is reconstructed by the intensity value enhancement with the help of inherent noise. The no. of iteration depends on the parameter's value and visual perception estimation. These are displayed in terms of histogram construction.

The parameters values we get are estimated by visual perception. The image quality is determined by both quantitative as well as qualitative approach. By our experiments, we come to the conclusion that quantitative parameters F and CEF, would also be small as much as possible. The summation of both parameters should be around 1. The result denotes that when value of PQM is around 10, then the outcomes are better. PQM is a statistical measurement of the reconstruction which gives the perceptual quality measure. Table (1) is for comparative study from other existing techniques.

Table 1. Comparative Study by Experiments

Methods	F	CEF	PQM
Proposed Algorithm	3.532	1.67	10.2
MSR	2.052	3.87	17.3
SSR	1.637	2.3	14.3
Histogram Equalization	4.982	3.48	18.4

6   Comparison by Other Existing Techniques

The proposed technique is compared with other already existing techniques like SSR (Single Scale Retinex), MSR(Multi Scale Retinex) and Histogram Equalization. It has been found that these techniques are limited upto some limit. Like histogram equalization may lead dramatic changes in the color balance of the image. MSR gives the better quality result but takes long time for the computation.

SSR fails in aspect of the enhancement of the dark images. It degrades the image quality, and brightens the area which is already bright enough. So generally these are not preferred and suitable when we need result in less time. Refer figure (4).

7   Role of Inherent Internal Noise

However due to less light intensity, we visualizes the poor image contrast and unable to see the dark portion. Inherent noise degrades the quality of the image. By the wavelet decomposition of the wavelet the coefficients resembles the intensity distribution. Because of the noisy nature of frequency transform coefficients of the dark image, we preferred to apply the DSR on these coefficients to reconstruct the image.

Fig. 2. Input images and their enhanced output images respectively

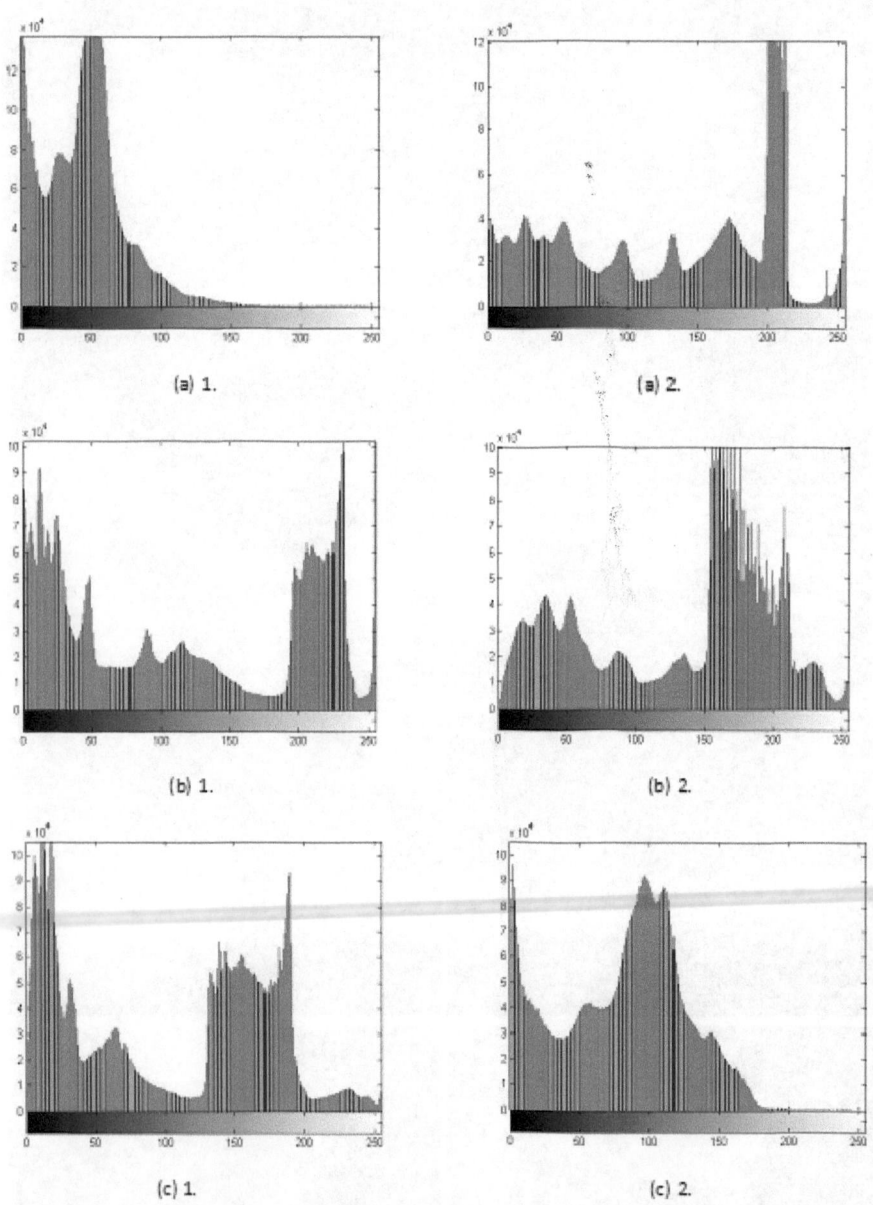

Fig. 3. Histogram construction of input images after application of proposed algorithm

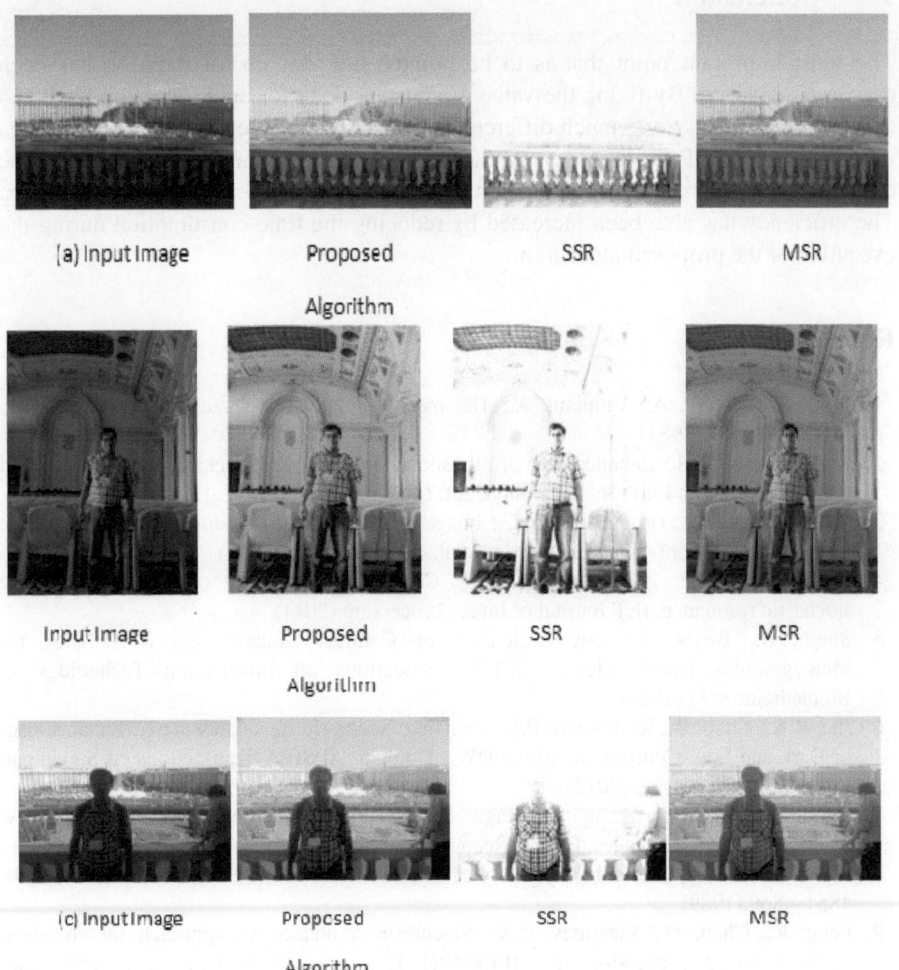

Fig. 4. Comparison by other existing techniques

8   Role of Color Model

For the image reconstruction the color model measurement is important. HSV color model preserves the color after no. of iteration. Non-linearity of the system is increased by mean, variance and entropy. The point to be noted here that output of our proposed approach has no blocking artifacts, also no color degradation. But other techniques have loss of color in their enhanced images. HSV color model provides more stability of colors. The application of algorithm in HSV model doesn't disturb color channel properties.

9   Conclusion

The most important point that is to be pointed out that no. of iteration has been drastically reduced. By fixing the value of constant delta for area separately and then application of DSR, gives much different and better result. We focus on the dark area rather than bright. The proposed approach is well adaptive and time consuming. The qualitative and statistically comparison denotes the effectiveness of the algorithm. The efficiency has also been increased by reducing the time consumption during the execution of the proposed algorithm.

References

1. Benzi, R., Sutera, A., Vulpiani, A.: The mechanism of Stochastic Resonance. J. Phys. A. 14, 453–457 (1981)
2. Rallamandi, V.P.S.: Enhancement of ultrasound images using stochastic resonance based wavelet transform. In: Proc. IEEE Int. Conf. Image Processing, vol. 1, pp. 263–266 (2004)
3. Ye, Q., Huang, H., He, X., Zhang, C.: Image enhancement using stochastic resonance. In: Proc. IEEE Int. Conf. Image Processing, vol. 1, pp. 263–266 (2004)
4. Jha, R.K., Biswas, P.K., Chatterji, B.N.: Contrast Enhancement of dark images using stochastic resonance. IET Journal of Image Processing (2011)
5. Singh, S., Bovis, K.: An Evaluation of Contrast Enhancement Techniques for Mamographics Breast Masses. IEEE Transactions on Information Technology in Biomedicine 9(1) (2005)
6. Jha, R.K., Chouhan, R., Biswas, P.K.: Dynamic Sochastic Resonance-based Enhancement of Dark and Low Contrast Images in DWT Domain. APSIPA Transactions on Signal and Information Processing (2012)
7. Choonwoo, R., Kong Scong, G., Hakil, K.: Enhancement of feature extraction for low quality fingure print images. Pattern Recognition Letters 32, 107–113 (2011)
8. McNamara, B., Wiesenfeld, K.: Theory of stochastic resonance. Physical Review A 39(9), 4854–4869 (1989)
9. Peng, R., Chen, H., Varshney, P.K.: Stochastic resonance:An approach for enhanced medical image processing. In: IEEE/NIH Life Science Systems and Application Workshop, vol. 1, pp. 253–256 (2007)
10. Gonzalez, R.C., Woods, R.E.: Digital Image Processing, 2nd edn. Prentice Hall (2002)
11. High dynamic range imaging, http://en.wikipedia.org/wiki/Highdynamicrangeimaging
12. Entropy information theory, http://en.wikipedia.org/wiki/Entropyinformationtheory

Identification of Title for Natural Languages Using Resource Description Framework and Anaphoric Reference Resolution

Madhuri A. Tayal[1], Mukesh Raghuwanshi[2], and Latesh Malik[1]

[1] G.H.Raisoni College of Engineering, Nagpur,
Maharashtra, India
madhuri.tayal@gmail.com,
latesh.malik@raisoni.net

[2] Rajiv Gandhi College of Engineering and Research, Nagpur,
Maharashtra, India
m_raghuwanshi@rediffmail.com

Abstract. In the today's era of growing information it is very difficult to go through the actual contents of a text-document. Title of a text-document is a collection of meaningful words that signify the content at a glance. This paper presents the method for identifying a title for a text-document using elements of language specific grammar structure i.e. Subject, verb and objects. Ordered this grammar structure is called as RDF (Resource Description Framework). Thismethod firstly, selects certain sentences in the current document. Then it parses them into RDF. Using search engine it retrieves matched documents for the RDF's. Finally it adopts the title of the best retrieved document as the new title of the current document. This approach works well for any domain related text-documents. The use of Anaphoric reference resolution of discourse processing has further enhanced the result of title identification.

Keywords: Text document, Chen's Algorithm, RDF(Resource Description Framework), Anaphoric resolution, Discourse processing.

1   Introduction

WWW (World Wide Web) is the largest and most useful Knowledge base for users with huge amount of information. The other sources of information are newspapers, magazines, textbooks etc. WWW consists of billions of text documents and everyday many new documents are added to it. Most of the documents are marked by their titles. The title of a text-document can help people in searching relevant documents. Title always gives information about the content of the document. Identifying title for a text-document may be useful for several purposes. It can be useful for data analysis, information clustering, text categorization etc. Title identification is a relatively new issue in information retrieval (IR) technology.

Various techniques for information retrieval have been received escalating attention since their introduction in 1998. Many earlier works have been verified that,

A. Agrawal et al. (Eds.): IITM 2013, CCIS 276, pp. 75–88, 2013.

they are well suited to topic identification [3],[7] using data mining and clustering respectively. Researchers have investigated that finding title for a given text document is not an easy task as text document may contains multiple topics. The most important restrictions for identifying title are: Firstly, most of the techniques are language dependent as they use tools like POS tagger, parser [13-14] which are available in English language only. Secondly, most of the techniques are corpus based. In addition length of a text-document is another hurdle to find title of the text-document. If a sentence in a text document uses a pronoun that refers to an entity in a previous sentence then that sentence does not meaningfully contributes for its potential use. So, these types of references have been resolved through previous named entities in the sentence using anaphoric reference resolution. Resolving pronominal references is essential in applications like information extraction and text summarization. Hence anaphoric reference resolution has improved the performance of the proposed algorithm.

This paper proposes the algorithm TIDA (Title Identification Algorithm) to identify a title for a text-document automatically and it consists of four steps.

1. It takes the text-document and finds the length of that text-document. After checking length of text-document, it collects the important statements from text-document.
2. It collects the RDF's (Subject, Verb, and Object) triple for every statement in the corresponding text-document using POStagger [14].A.D.Acierno[11] have defined the RDF representation for a sentence as a triple $\sigma = <s, T, \omega>$, s is the original sentence, T the relative RDF-triple describing the semantic content of s in terms of subject, predicate and Object and ω an identifier related to the page source containing s. From this model only term for the semantic content of a sentence is used, that is obtained using POS tagger [14].
3. It selects the utmost matched appropriate text-document for every RDF using search engine.
4. Finally it matches these text-documents RDF's with the original, entered query text-document to identify title of the text-document.

This algorithm has some similarities with [2] algorithm.

The paper is organized as: Section 2 contains various methods which are available for topic identification of text-document. Section 3 describes disadvantages of the earlier methods; Section 4 proposes the title identification algorithm using Natural Language Processing. This section, also describes how it removes various disadvantages of various methods. Section 5 describes the experimental results aimed to measure the effectiveness of proposed approach for identifying the title of text-document in comparison with other methods. At the end we conclude this study in conclusion and future work.

2   Literature Survey

Attempts have been made to develop title identification systems with various approaches [1], [3],[6-9] and for Hindi language[12] (as headline generation).

Majority of approaches for title identification are based on clustering algorithms. Cluster examination or simply clustering is the assignment of a set of observations into subsets (called clusters) so that observations in the same cluster are similar in some logic. They have intend to extract a stream of terms fallen in a most prior cluster by their algorithms. Most modern approaches mostly rely on exploiting semantics of keywords present in the text-document. Chen [5] has proposed corpus based approach on topic identification based on two types of grammatical pairs: noun-noun and noun-verb. To select these pairs, they have determined the importance of each noun and verb by Inverse Text document Frequency (IDF).

$$IDF (W) = \log ((P - O (W)) / O (W)) + c \qquad (1)$$

Where, P is the number of text-documents in Corpus, i.e., 500, O (W) is the number of text-documents with word W and c are threshold value. The threshold value for nouns is 0.77 and for verbs are 2.46. These values are used to characterize the unimportant words by rearranging negative IDF values to zero, and then calculate the strength of each pair. The strength of one occurrence of a verb-noun pair or a noun-noun pair is computed by the importance of the words and their distances, equation (2) and (3) reveal how these values are calculated.

$$SNV (N, V) = IDF (N).IDF (V) / D (N, V) \qquad (2)$$

$$SNV (N, N) = IDF (N).IDF (N) / D (N, N) \qquad (3)$$

D is the distance and it is measured by the difference between cardinal numbers of two words. Chen assigned a cardinal number to each verb and noun in sentences. The cardinal numbers are reserved continuous across sentences in the same paragraph. The strongest pair can be considered as a title for each paragraph or entire text-document. Chen achieved to obtain around 80% precision (both total and partial matching) in identifying the discourse title. The disadvantages of this method are:

1. It is corpus based method.
2. It uses LOB Corpus set of (1989) British English texts; therefore results are based on the corpus. If the corpus get altered, then the values SNV (N, V), SNV (N, N) would be altered, and it may affect the final results of the algorithm.
3. It has overhead of calculation for the weight of a few unimportant terms.

Hossein [2] have recommended algorithm to find the topic of text document. This algorithm works in five Steps as follows:

Step-1 Split the text into sentences.

Step-2 Parse the sentences to find (n, v) (Using Stanford Parser).

Step-3 Choose the candidate Parts. (NP's and VP's).

Step-4 Compute   the weight for each Candidate title (Using Chen's IDF & SNV).

Step-5 Select the final title.

This algorithm has some similarities to Chen's Algorithm in terms of steps; however, some basic parts like selected parts in each sentence and calculation formula have been changed to equation (4).

$$SNV (NP, head (VP)) = IDF (NP). IDF (head (VP)) / D (NP, head (VP)) \qquad (4)$$

The disadvantages of this method are as follows:

1. If the sentence get complex then it is difficult to get the important candidate parts.
2. It uses LOB Corpus collection of (1989) British English texts. So results will be based on the corpus.
3. It is more language dependent as it uses POS tagger as well as Stanford Parser both.

Krishnan Ramanathan[4] have proposed subsequent algorithm to find the title of text document. This method is language independent method. They have mapped document sentences to semantic concepts in Wikipedia. Bipartite Graph has been used to find the title and summary of text-document. The steps for this algorithm are as follows.

Step-1 It maps individual sentences in the text-document to Wikipedia concepts.

Step-2 The entire Wikipedia corpus is indexed using the Lucene engine.

Step-3 The sentence is then input as a query to the Lucene engine.

Step-4 The titles of the Wikipedia text-documents are extracted from the results to the query.

The disadvantages of this method are:

1. A sentence could get chosen in the title identification by virtue of getting mapped to only one concept.
2. If length of the text-document increases bipartite graph gets complicated to find the accurate results.

All these methods with respective drawbacks have been mentioned in the next section.

3   Disadvantages of Earlier Methods

In proposed algorithm the disadvantages of earlier methods have been removed.

If length of the document increases, calculations overhead will be on higher side for Chen's method. Hossein's Method is having less calculation overhead as compared to Chen's method. If Length of the document increases bipartite graph gets complicated to find exact results in case of Krishnan's method. The proposed algorithm can handle maximum length paragraph. Both Chen's and Hossein's method are corpus based.

Table 1. Disadvantage of Various Methods

Sr. No.	Factors	Disadvant-age for Chen's Method	Disadvantage for Hossein Method	Disadvantage for Krishnan Method	TIDA (Title Identification Algorithm)
1.	Length	If length of the document increases, calculations overhead will be on higher side.	If length of the documentincr eases, calculations will be comparatively less as compared to Chen'sMetho d.	If length of the document Increases, the bipartite graph will be complex to find exact results.	It can handle maximum length paragraph.
2.	Depend ency	On corpus: LOB corpus collection of present day (1989) British English texts. So results would be based on the corpus.	On corpus: LOB corpus collection of present day (1989) British English texts. So results would be based on the corpus.	On NLP tools: Dependency of language is higher using the Stanford parser and POS tagger.	On NLP tool: It avoids the use of Stanford parser.
3.	Comple xity/ Overhe ad	It has the overhead of calculation for the weight of some unimportant terms.	If the sentence gets complex then it would be difficult to get the important candidate parts.	A sentence could get chosen in the topic identification by virtue of getting mapped to only one concept.	It would never get mapped to only one concept.

Krishnan's method is unable to produce results for long length text-document. The cause for this, bipartite graph became complicated to give right answers. This drawback has been removed through the concept of short length and long length document. For short length, ten sentence to be chosen and for long length of document 20% sentences to be chosen for further processing from the original text-document. Another drawback for Krishnan's method is that a sentence could get chosen in the title identification by virtue of getting mapped to only one concept. This drawback has been removed through web, because sentences get mapped for a variety of concepts. This method uses linguistic tools like POS tagger and POS Parser etc. TIDA uses only POS tagger.

The drawbacks like length of a document, Language dependency and complexity from Krishnan's method have been removed in TIDA and are elaborated in the next section.

4 Title Identification Algorithm (TIDA)

As it has been investigated in literature review, there are many approaches to identify a document's main topic. TIDA is closely similar to Krishnan's method. In comparison with the Krishnan's method Carrot2 Search engine is used for searching the required text-documents in concerned with the corresponding RDF (Resource Description Framework). The steps for the algorithm are as follows.

1. Enter the Query text-document for which the title has to be identified.
2. Find the length of this text-document. (In terms of number of sentences)
3. If length of text-document is less than 100 Sentences then it is a Short length text document and goes to Step-4,else long length text-document and go to Step-5.
4. Collect first five and last five sentences from the text-document.
5. Collect 20% sentences from the start and 20% sentences from the endof the text document.
6. Convert all these statements to RDF sentence form using POS Tagger. (For example in case of short length text-document, 10 RDF's have been made for corresponding ten sentences.)
7. For (i=RDF (1); i<=RDF (10); i++)

   a. Find the corresponding matched (n) number of text-documents from Search engine (Carrot2).
   b. Collect the first 10 text-documents from these n documents.
   c. Convert all these 10 documents to RDF using step-2, 3, 4, 5 and 6.
   d. Compare the RDF (i) of original document with the RDF of 10 text documents one by one. (Comparison is in between Subject of RDF (1) with Subjects of these ten documents RDF sentence by sentence and similarly for verb and object. The total ([S] [V] [O]) will be called as Match-Value of that Text-document.)
   e. Find the document, out of these 10 text-documents for which match value (MatchValue) is maximum.
   f. (At the end of this step, ten best matched text-documents are there for corresponding ten RDF's of original entered text-document.)

8. Consider these ten text-documents for matching with the original entered text-document's RDF on the whole.
   For (i=text-document (1); i<=text-document (10); i++)

   a. Compare the RDF of text-document (1) with the RDF of Query text-documentsentence by sentence.
   b. Find the text-document out of these ten text-documents for which big match value(BigMatchValue) will be maximum.

9. Display the corresponding title of text-document for which this Big Match Value is maximum.

Similar Procedure will be followed for long length document.

This algorithm initially checks the length of the entered query text-document in terms of number of sentences. If the query text-document having greater than 100 sentences, then it's a long length text-document else it is short length text-document. 20% sentences from the start and 20% sentences from the end of the text-document to be selected for further processing, if the text-document is long length. Otherwise (for short length text-document) first and last five sentences to be selected. The reason for choosing 20% of the sentences is that, if this percentage is increased from 20% to 30% the searching process gets complicated and it affects the efficiency of TIDA (in terms of "No output"). Similarly if this percentage is reduced to 10% then it also affects the efficiency (in terms of "No matching"). The types of output mentioned above can be verified through the sample sets attached at the end of this paper. After selecting these sentences convert them in RDF form triple i.e. Subject verb and Object form. This tagging of subject-verb- object is done using POS Tagger[14].Then find the corresponding matched text-documents for every RDF using Carrot2 search engine. Select top ten text-documents out of these n numbers of text-documents. Convert all these ten documents in the RDF form. Compare the first RDF of query text document with current ten text documents RDF one by one. Comparison is in between Subject of first RDF with Subjects of these ten documents RDF sentence by sentence. Same procedure is carried out for verb and object also. The total ([S] [V] [O]) is called as Match Value of that text-document. Select a document, out of these ten text-documents for which, the match value (Match Value) is maximum. At the end of this, ten best matched text-documents are available corresponding to ten RDF's of original entered text-document. Now, consider these ten text-documents for matching with the original entered text-document's RDF on the whole. Compare the RDF of first text-document with the RDF of query text-document sentence by sentence, and the BigMatchValue is calculated. The title of corresponding text-document has been selected, for which BigMatchValue is maximum.

5   Performance Evaluation

To check performance of TIDA the sample sets have been prepared. Efficiency of the algorithm can be checked with how successfully the title matches with actual title of a text document. Two criteria's can be there weather they are perfectly matched or partially matched. To check the accuracy of proposed system the list of actual title and the title proposed by TIDA have been prepared. [2], [10] had taken sample sets as HTML web pages from different categories and Wikipedia pages respectively. After implementing TIDA, the results have been tested for two categories. First category contains four different sample-sets of diverse fields and second category contains text document related two different domains (as "Computer" and "Language"). For the experimentation of diverse field sample sets have chosen, each holds 25 random text-documents with corresponding titles. The corresponding results for those samples are shown in Table 2. For the domain related experimentation sample sets have chosen, each holds 50 random text-documents with corresponding titles. They are arbitrarily selected from Wikipedia and howstuffworks.com. The text-documents chosen are flexible enough from diverse fields taking into view that proposed algorithm would be in a position to produce the results for any text-document, and not for specific domain related text-document. The corresponding results for those samples are shown in Table 3. From total hundred samples, 74 topics are getting matched totally with original titles for the text-document, 5 are getting partially matched with the original titles and for 21 samples are not matching with actual titles. The success rate of TIDA for these samples is 74%.

Table 2. Experimental Results of TIDA

Sample-SETS (Short Length)	No Matching	Partial Matching	Total Matching
Set-1 (25-Samples)	8	-	17
Set-2 (25-Samples)	4	-	21
Set-3 (25-Samples)	5	2	18
Set-4 (25-Samples)	4	3	18
Total= 100- Samples	21	05	74

Table 3. Experimental Results TIDA (Domain related experimentation)

Sr. no.	Domain-Name (Each includes 50 text samples)	No Matching	Partial Matching	Total Matching	No-out put	Success Rate	Average Success Rate
1.	Computer	9	5	36	0	82%	81%
2.	Language	7	5	35	3	80%	

5.1 Performance Improvement for Title Identification Algorithmthrough Reference Resolution of Discourse Processing

According to the definition quoted byTanveerSiddiqui and U.S. Tiwary[15], a discourse is most commonly described as the language above the sentence level. In order to make meaningful representation of a text-document, it should have the related sentences. The phenomena that operate at discourse level include Cohesion and Coherence. Cohesion is a textual phenomenon whereas coherence is a mental phenomenon. A text is cohesive if its elements link together and coherent if it makes sense. Cohesiveness can be further subdivided as Reference cohesion, Ellipsis cohesion, and lexical cohesion. Reference is a means to link a referring expression to another referring expression in the surrounding text, as shown in the following example.

Peter helps her mummy. He is a good boy.

Here, 'He' refers to a person named Peter. Such a reference is called as anaphoric reference. These type of anaphoric references can be resolved by replacing the pronouns like, "he", "she", "her", "his", "him", "it", "this", "His", "me", "He", "they", "you", "these", "that", "my", "your", "our", "mine", "yours", "those" with the subject of a previous statement for improvement of title identification algorithm. The results of TIDA are enhanced by 6% after anaphoric reference resolution as shown in table 4.

Table 4. Success Rate of TIDA after Anaphoric Reference resolution

Text-Document SETS	No Matching (1)	Partial Matching (2)	Total Matching (3)	Output After Anaphoric Reference Resolution (4)	Success Rate% (3)+(4)
Set-1 (25-Samples)	8	-	17	3	20
Set-2 (25-Samples)	4	-	21	NIL	21
Set-3 (25-Samples)	5	2	18	2	20
Set-4 (25-Samples)	4	3	18	1	19
Total=100-Samples	21	05	74	6	80%

As far as sentence construction is concerned, there are many types of sentences for Subject, Verb and Object combination. Some combinations like object is nowhere in the sentence like: "She laughed." "We do." "I left." etc., these statements have been made by using subject and verbs only. Objects are missing in these sentences. Take another example, where subject is nowhere in the sentence like: "Collect the samples.", "Leave the campus.", etc., So, in the text-documents for which the title has to be identified, and the objects are missing in some case, subjects are missing in some cases, then does that affects the results. Wren and Martin[16] have been quoted that, the main ingredients for English language are Subject, Verb and Object. Each one has their importance in the sentence. To check their importance in the absence of another will certainly play some role while finding the title of the text-document. To answer this question, parametric analyses have been done on the availability of Subject, Verb and Object. The analysis is shown in the Table 5. (For this huge analysis of Subject, Object and Verb, ten random samples have been experimented.)

Here, Subject, Verb and Object represent the availability of corresponding inputs. (If SVO equals to 100, as mentioned in case-5, only subject is kept as it is and rest of the values of verb and objects are made zero for text-document samples.

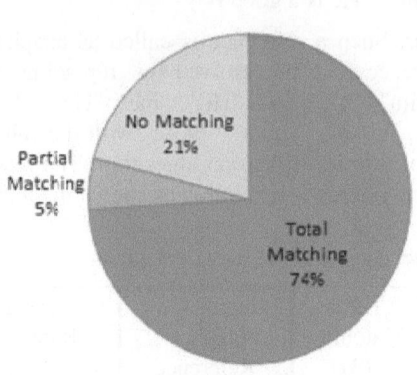

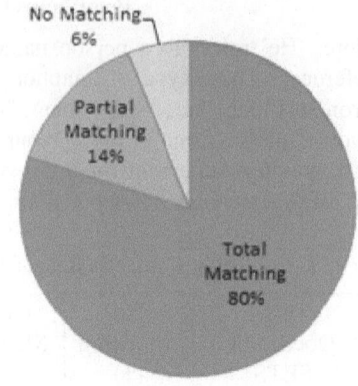

Fig. 1. Results for TIDA   **Fig. 2.** Results for TIDA after Anaphoric Reference Resolution

Table 5. Parametric Analysis

Cases	Subject	Verb	Object	Total Success Rate for TIDA	Remarks
Case-1	0	0	0	----	Invalid Combination of sentences. Only exclamatory sentences are possible without S, V, O.
Case-2	0	0	1	60%	-
Case-3	0	1	0	----	Insufficient Information: No results. Only action statements are possible.
Case-4	0	1	1	70%	--
Case-5	1	0	0	70%	--
Case-6	1	0	1	65%	--
Case-7	1	1	0	60%	--
Case-8	1	1	1	85%	--

6   Comparison with Other Methods

The test data suite used for Chen's method [5] was LOB corpus. LOB Corpus is a million-word collection of present-day British English texts. It contains 500 texts of approximately 2,000 words distributed over 15 text categories. These categories include reportage, editorial, reviews, religion, skills, trades, popular, biography, essays, learned and scientific writings, fictions, adventure and western fiction, love story, etc. [2] had taken Wikipedia as suit dataset for the evaluation of the title. Wikipedia is an online encyclopedia with their pages is entitled exactly by their titles. The Wikipedia page's titles can be considered as their titles. To achieve this purpose, they had taken a set of 200 random pages with their titles. The result of their experiment is drawn as a pie chart in Figure 3. The result of proposed experiment is drawn in comparison in Figure 4.

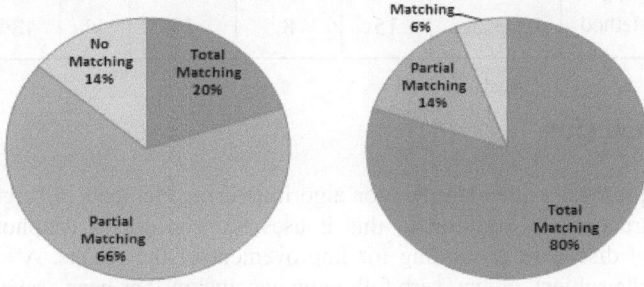

Fig. 3. Results for Automatic Title Identification [2]. **Success Rate:-86%.**

Fig. 4. Results for TIDA after Reference Resolution. **Success Rate:-94%.**

(Success Rate= % Sum of total matching and Partial Matching)

Experimentation is done for text documents related to domains having categories (i.e. for Computers and Language) each contains fifty text documents as samples. The corresponding results for those samples are shown in Table 6. After the comprehensive experimentation it is found that TIDA produces 81% results as compared to Krishnan's method for the domains "Computers" and "Language". Krishnan method produced 51% results for the same sample text documents for the mentioned categories.

Table 6. Success Rate of TIDA in comparison with Krishnan's method for same dataset.

Sr. no	Method to be used	Domain name (Each includes 50 text samples)	No Match-ing	Partial Match-ing	Total Match-ing	No-out put	Success Rate	Avg.Success Rate
1.	TIDA	Computer	9	5	36	0	82%	81%
2.		Language	7	5	35	3	80%	
3.	Krishnan's Method	Computer	15	6	21	8	54%	51%
4.		Language	15	8	16	11	48%	

7   Conclusion

This paper presents a title identification algorithm using elements of language specific grammar structure. In addition to this it uses the concept of anaphoric reference resolution of discourse processing for improvement of the results. After parametric analysis of the subject, object, verb following conclusions has been drawn.

1. Using this algorithm, the titles can be found for utmost length of a document.
2. Reference resolution increases the performance of algorithm by 6%. Also it alters status of performance from partial results to Matched results for some cases.
3. Verbs are solely not important for sentence construction. Wren and Martin [16]have been quoted that, for this combination of (010) only action statements are possible. (i.e. Go, Eat, and Come). etc.
4. Without subject, verb and object sentences are not possible. Wren and Martin[16] have been quoted that, for this combination of (000) only exclamatory statements are possible (i.e. Oh! Ha Ha!). etc.
5. If length of the document goes for higher Side, then in a few cases the reference resolution increases the performance of the algorithm.

Some of the restrictions for this algorithm are as follows. Firstly, this algorithm is web reliant, so each time the outcomes will not be the similar (Search Engine). The current version of TIDA carries out the experiment with English pages only. This inadequacy is emerged from POS Tagger that is one of the NLP tools which is capable to process only English texts. In future, some more types of reference can be resolved for improvement of title identification algorithm. The performance can be enhanced with diverse parameters like synonyms homonyms, polysemy using word net.

References

1. Clifton, C., Cooley, R., Rennie, J.: Data Mining for Topic Identification in a Text Corpus. IEEE TOPCAT (2004)
2. Baghdadi, H.S., Ranaivo-Malançon, B.: An Automatic Topic Identification Algorithm. Journal of Computer Science 7(9), 1363–1367 (2011)
3. Jayabharathy, J., Kanmani, S., Ayeshaa Parvee, A.: Document Clustering and Topic Discovery based on Semantic Similarity in Scientific Literature, 425–429. IEEE (2011)
4. Ramanathan, K., Subramaniam, Y.S., Mathur, N., Gupta, A.: Document summarization using Wikipedia. In: HPL. Springer (2009)
5. Chen, K.-H.: Topic Identification in Discourse. In: Proceedings of the 7th Conference on European Chapter of the Association for Computational Linguistics, ECACL (1995)
6. Aery, M., Ramamurthy, N., Alp Aslandogan, Y.: Topic Identification of Textual Data. Technical Report CSE (2003)
7. Aharaon, M., Cohen, I., Itskovitch, A., Marhaim, I., Banner, R.: The PARIS Algorithm for Determining Latent Topics. IEEE (2010)
8. Capasso, P., Cesarano, C., Picariello, A., Sansone, L.: A Semantic Topic Identification System for Text-document Retrieval on the Web. First Appeared in International Journal of Computer Science and Network Security 6(5B) (2006)
9. Tiun, S., Abdullah, R., Kong, T.E.: Automatic Topic Identification Using Ontology Hierarchy. Computer and Internet: Security and Encryption
10. Adaikkalavan, R., Elkhalifa, L., Alp Aslandogan, Y.: Topic Identification through Ontology based concept Generalization. Technical Report CSE (2003)
11. Acierno, A.D., Moscato, V., Persia, F., Picariello, A., Penta, A.: Semantic Summarization of Web Documents. In: IEEE Fourth International Conference on Semantic Computing (2010)
12. Dorr, B., Zajic, D.: Cross-Language Headline Generation for Hindi. ACM Transaction on Asian Language Information Processing 2(3), 270–289 (2003)
13. STANFORD PARSER, http://nlp.stanford.edu/software/lex-parser.shtml
14. STANFORD POS TAGGER, http://nlp.stanford.edu/software/tagger.shtml
15. Siddiqui, T., Tiwari, U.S.: Natural language Processing and Information Retrieval. Oxford University Press
16. Wren, Martin: English Grammar and Composition. S. Chand & Company LTD.

SAMPLE

Sample: Text-Document with Original Title and Generated Title by TIDA.

Text-document with Title	TIDA –Output (Title)
Stacks In computer science, a stack is a last in, first out (LIFO) abstract data type and linear data structure. A stack can have any abstract data type as an element, but is characterized by only three fundamental operations: push, pop and stack top. The push operation adds a new item to the top of the stack, or initializes the stack if it is empty. If the stack is full and does not contain enough space to accept the given item, the stack is then considered to be in an overflow state. The pop operation removes an item from the top of the stack. A pop either reveals previously concealed items, or results in an empty stack, but if the stack is empty then it goes into underflow state (It means no items are present in stack to be removed). The stack top operation gets the data from the top-most position and returns it to the user without deleting it. The same underflow state can also occur in stack top operation if stack is empty. A stack is a restricted data structure, because only a small number of operations are performed on it. The nature of the pop and push operations also mean that stack elements have a natural order. Elements are removed from the stack in the reverse order to the order of their addition: therefore, the lower elements are those that have been on the stack the longest.	Stack (abstract data type) - Wikipedia, the free encyclopedia

Facilitating Social Interaction in Public Space

Nishtha Mehrotra[1] and Pradeep Yammiyavar[2]

[1] Department of Design, Indian Institute of Technology Guwahati, Assam, India
nishtha@iitg.ernet.in
[2] Centre for Educational Technology, Indian Institute of Technology Guwahati, Assam, India
pradeep@iitg.ernet.in

Abstract. Social capital is about the value of social networks, bonding similar people and bridging between diverse people, with norms of reciprocity. Social capital is fundamentally about how people interact with each other[24]. Public Spaces can provide an ideal location for building social capital. We outline our design approach, which involved conducting a user perception study of interaction in private public spaces. Based on the study, a framework of relationship - patterns was developed. We have further identified key components of social interaction installations and common interaction design modalities. The study reported in this paper will be used to develop a design that aims to foster community bonding in a city environment through socialization and play. The possibility of adopting digital technologies in giving a new meaning to public space has been explored.

Keywords: Social Capital, Interaction Design, Public space, Digital Bonding.

1 Introduction

In its simplest and most concise form, the term social capital refers to the connections between divergent groups in heterogeneous societies that lead to the sustaining operations of a country or society[1]. Social capital builds socio-cultural bonds that cultivate good will, fellowship, sympathy and social intercourse in a community. Public space, regardless of ownership, provides an opportunity of shared use and activity, meeting and exchange for people[2]. This interaction gives public spaces the ethical and aesthetic power to build social capital that underscores the stability of society, its common threads and interests, increases reciprocity and trustworthiness, thereby establishing the foundations of cohesiveness among those that make up a social unit.

Digital technology based mobile and ubiquitous systems are offering new opportunities for interaction in these public spaces. We present the concept of using emerging interaction design technologies in public spaces to build social capital through increased interactions. Ground level 'user' based data collection to understand user perception of public space is reported. The collected data has been analyzed by drawing upon theories of sociology. These findings are supplemented by analyzing different examples of human technology interactions in public spaces to come up with a design proposal that focuses on building collective user experience in such interactions.

A. Agrawal et al. (Eds.): IITM 2013, CCIS 276, pp. 89–101, 2013.
© Springer-Verlag Berlin Heidelberg 2013

2   Motivation: Outlining the Importance of Social Capital

Social capital refers to a stock of active connections that build trust, appreciation for different perspectives, needs, and shared values. It is those shared values that bind human networks and communities to a society making cooperative action possible[1].

There are several benefits from a rich reservoir of social capital. First, social capital allows citizens to resolve collective problems more easily through cooperation. Second, social capital greases the wheels that allow communities to advance smoothly, where people are trusting and trustworthy, and where they are subject to repeated interactions with fellow citizens, everyday business and social transactions are less costly. The third way, in which social capital improves alot, is by widening our awareness of the many ways in which our fates are linked. When people lack connection with others, they are unable to test the veracity of their own views, whether in the give or take of casual conversation or in more formal deliberation. Without such an opportunity, people are more likely to be swayed by their worse impulses [3].

One of the many ways in which social capital can be built, is by encouraging community interaction and bonding in common spaces. It is to this effect that the next section focuses on defining the shifting paradigms, implemented and mental models of public space- where we intend to build our premise.

3   Shopping Mall as an Interaction Space

In the past, public space has often been relegated to open grounds, parks, pavements, playgrounds, central squares, market places, libraries, religious gathering places like temples, churches, mosques etc. In an idealistic view, most people would expect that a public space provides relative openness of access to most members of society, allows them to use that space without other restrictions than those dictated by broadly accepted social norms of behavior, and guarantees them some say over key decisions regarding the running of the space [4]. While these attributes are important in their own right, the primary defining factor that makes a space "public" is the attitude of society towards it. Public spaces are participatory landscapes. Through human action, visual involvement and the attachment of values, people create their own spaces. Thus, public space can be said to be a publically perceived, valued and acclaimed landscape[5].

Accordingly, in recent times Urban India has catapulted shopping malls as the most ubiquitous and frequently visited places. With the advent of FDI in Retail, this trend- in all likelihood- will see further exponential growth. People visit mallsfor shopping, leisure, recreation, experience or to simply spend excess time. Now, the new shopping malls are designed to encourage flânerie and "hanging out." The combination of ambience, space and convenience is a big attraction for atime strapped city dweller.

By virtue of being privately owned, even though technically shopping malls may not be public spaces, the mental model of urban Indian community considers them so. Therefore, for the purpose of this paper, we concentrated on using the space available in such shopping malls for our intended interaction. We believe that while on one hand spontaneous interaction between people previously unknown to each other will strengthen the societal fabric, it will also prove beneficial for private owners of such space by increasing the dwell time of users.

4   User Study

A survey was carried out to understand how people perceive, experience and respond to spaces within a shopping mall. Data was collected using an extensive questionnaire containing 89 items. The questionnaire was constructed using Likert's Scale, Discrete Visual Analog Scale and Scenario Evaluation. The total sample was 44 respondents, of which 20 were based in Guwahati, Assam. 24 of the 44 respondents were spread across India and were contacted online. The remaining respondents were surveyed in person across 3 different malls in Guwahati city. The questionnaire consisted of questions that were related to ambience of a mall, perception of space, state of mind, peer group, attitude towards social interaction, and their impression of gaming inside malls.

5   Results

5.1   Ambience of a Mall

For most respondents, the decision to go to a mall is based on its ambience. They're sensitive to difference in ambience of different malls and give factorial importance to it for experience enhancement. Interior Design of a mall along with details of color, texture, furnishings are also highly noticeable.

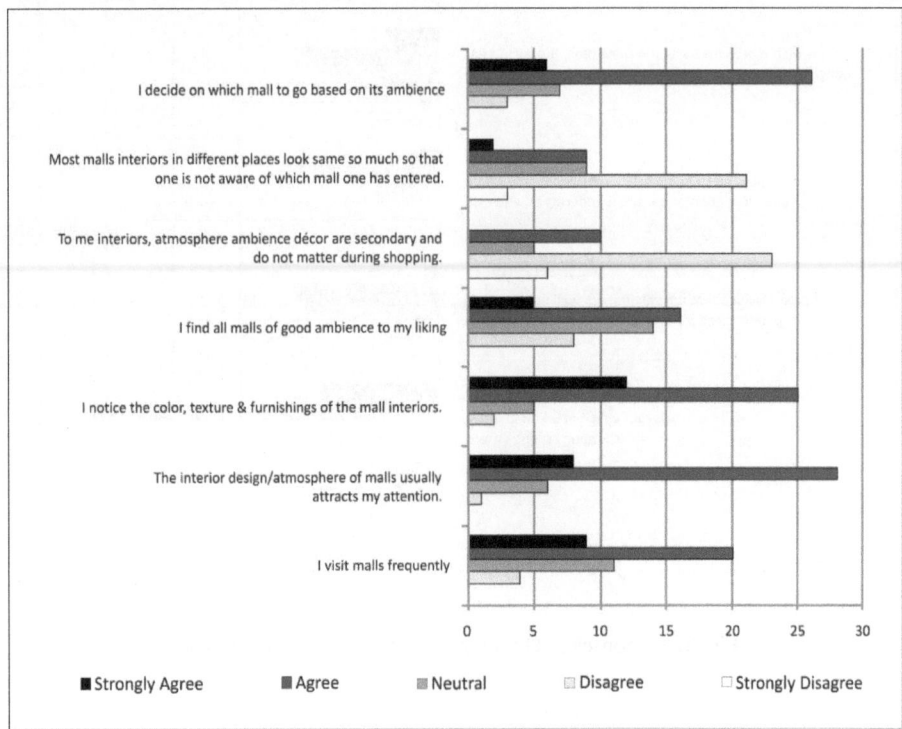

Fig. 1. Responses of Questions based on Ambience

These findings establish a user-environment relationship where the experience of the user is directly proportional to perceived aesthetics of the environment. McCarthy and Wright describe this approach as dialogical which draws attention to anticipation of experience, reflection on experience, and the dynamic relations between user and space including a possibility of reflection influencing anticipation and vice versa[6].

5.2   Perception of Space

Respondents liked consistency in layout of spaces and were confident of their ability to quickly find exit directions. They would prefer wide-open spaces on entering the mall and around shops in general.   This need for open space not only represents a metaphysical bond with evolution but also suffices a pragmatic need of providing for recreation and emotional nourishment. Such open spaces provide an ideal location structure for setting up an installation that will open up abstract possibilities for interaction. The underlying assumption is that the spatial properties of an environment can be designed to influence the way people act in and use that environment.

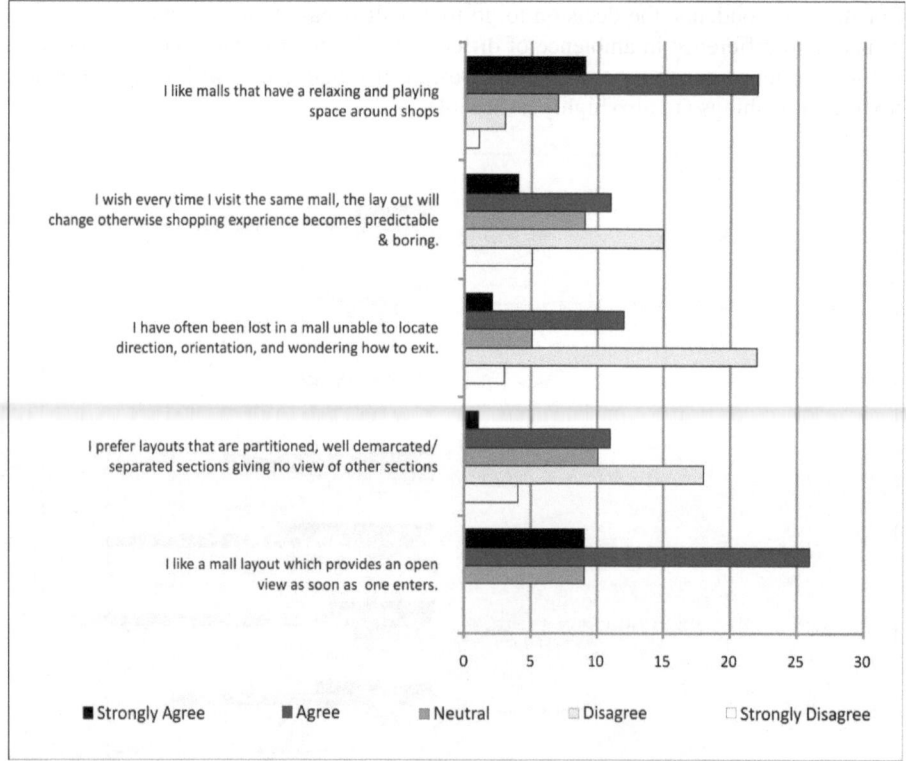

Fig. 2. Responses of Questions based on Perception of Space

5.3   State of Mind

Respondents said that they are usually in a good amicable mood while visiting malls, feel safe inside its vicinity, relaxed after visits and prefer to pass time there. They also think that they spend a good amount of window-shopping. These factors indicate the presence of essential pre-requisites for people to engage in any form of interaction.

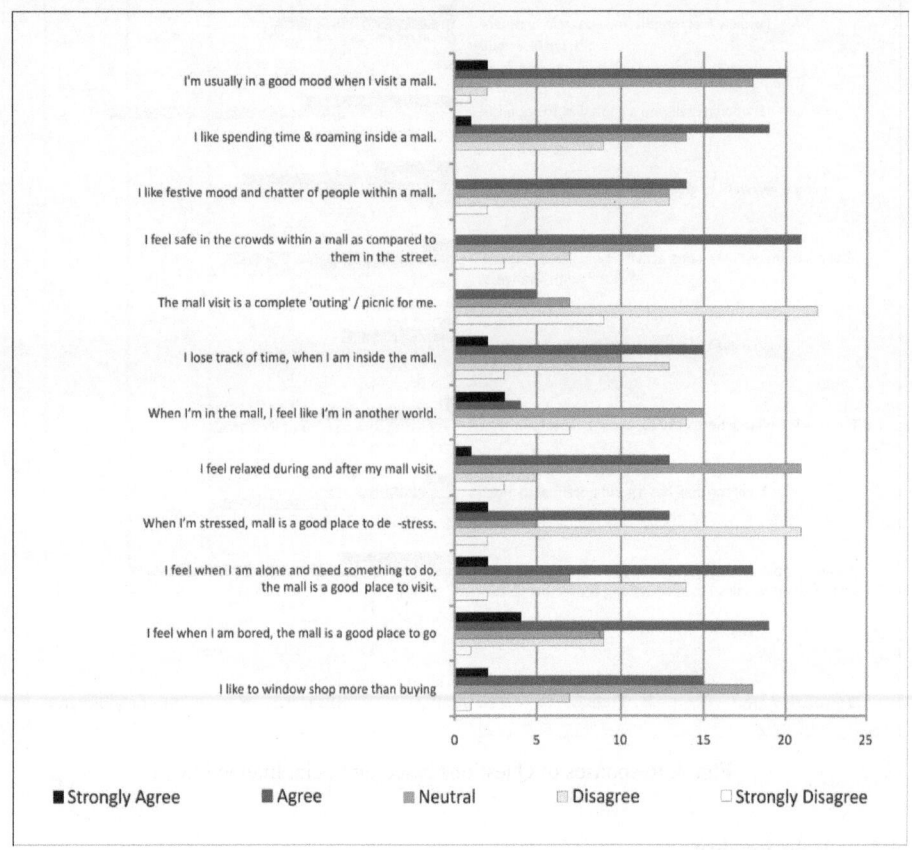

Fig. 3. Responses of Questions based on Perception of Space

5.4   Social Interaction

These set of questions were the most important aspect of this survey. Most respondents believed, that the malls have replaced older public spaces for socializing. While people were apprehensive about initiating talks with strangers, they were more willing to do so given a mutually interesting activity. They are curious to examine crowd-gathering activities and are more willing to help acquaintances rather than complete strangers in case of an emergency.

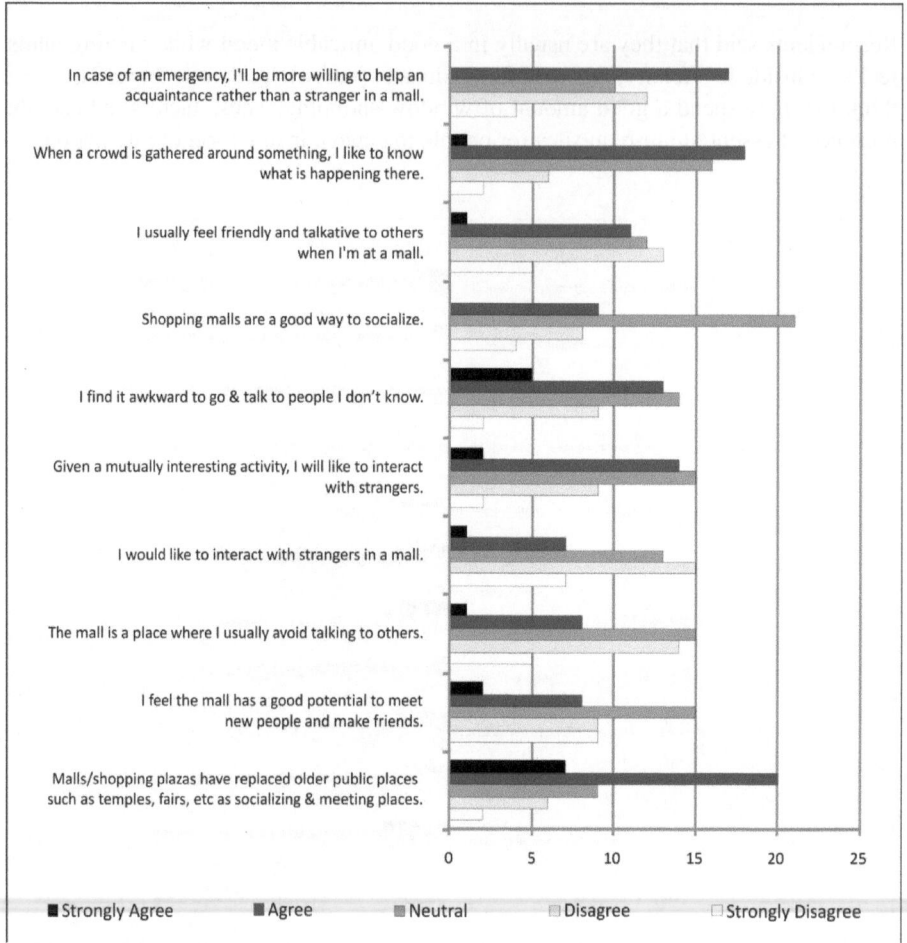

Fig. 4. Responses of Questions based on Social Interaction

5.5   Relationships

Respondents preferred going to a mall with friends and family. The survey also showed that malls have become a popular spot for meeting up with friends. Study of Relationship pattern of users is necessary for effective design solutions. These patterns will be discussed in detail in the next section.

These results correlate with our basic premise of using the mental model of users as a guiding force deciding the location of space. These findings also fit the conceptual framework [7] of stages of social interaction namely: distributed focus, shared attention, dialogue and collective action. We will further use this framework for analyzing concepts and case studies.

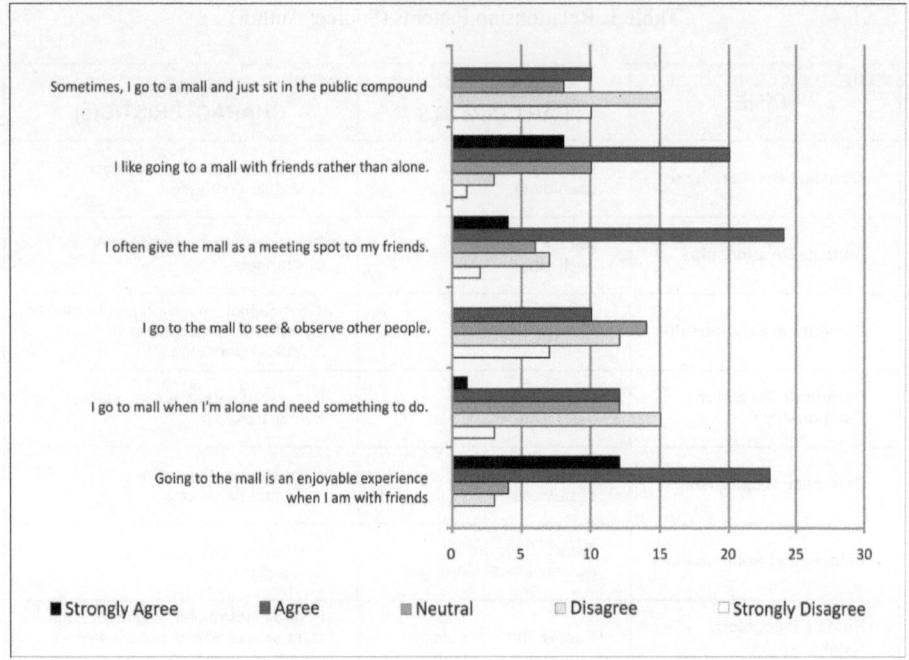

Sometimes, I go to a mall and just sit in the public compound

I like going to a mall with friends rather than alone.

I often give the mall as a meeting spot to my friends.

I go to the mall to see & observe other people.

I go to mall when I'm alone and need something to do.

Going to the mall is an enjoyable experience when I am with friends

0   5   10   15   20   25   30

■ Strongly Agree   ■ Agree   ■ Neutral   □ Disagree   □ Strongly Disagree

Fig. 5. Responses of Questions based on Relationships

6   Relationship Patterns

Based on primary user observation, certain relationship patterns that exist in the chosen space were identified. On further analysis of the patterns, the authors assigned labels as follows:

6.1   Transient Relationships

These relationships occur between people who are completely unknown to each other. They are characterized by brief non-verbal interactions. For example, strangers who take the same escalator, people encountered while entry/exit in a mall, standing in a queue or looking for a place to sit in the central atrium. Goffman refers to such behavior as "unfocussed interactions." [8,9] Strangers in co-present situations are aware of the actions of other(s) but remain publicly inattentive to them- they are accessible but not necessarily available.

6.2   Amiable Relationships

These relationships occur between people who are completely unknown to each other. However, most often they are characterized by friendly verbal/ non-verbal interactions that may span for a very short period of time. For example, discussing an art installation inside a mall, suggesting an ice cream flavor, commenting on goods bought while standing in billing queue or holding open a door for someone to pass through. Such interactions help create social goodwill in a community.

Table 1. Relationship Patterns (Source: Author)

NAME	PRIMARY PARTICIPANTS	MAIN CHARACTERISTIC(s)
Transient Relationships	People Unknown to each other	1. Brief non verbal interactions 2. Mutual ignorance
Amiable Relationships	People Unknown to each other	Brief friendly acknowledgment of strangers.
Perceptible Relationships	Familiar Strangers	1. Frequency, repetition and familiarity 2. Brief non verbal interactions 3. Mutual ignorance
Performer Spectator Relationships	People Unknown to each other	Being center of attraction affects normal behavior
Pragmatic Relationships	Provider and receiver of services	1. Professional in nature 2. Formal Behaviour
Established Relationships	Family/ Peer group/ Acquaintance/ Colleague	1. Informal communication 2. Comfort zone
Human Technology Relationships	People and Technology	Portable, distributed and embedded technologies affects experience of place

6.3   Perceptible Relationships

These are relationships with individuals that we regularly observe but do not interact with. The key here is frequency, repetition and familiarity. For example, frequent visitors of a local shopping mall may encounter familiar faces. This relationship is marked by an absence of Verbal/non verbal interaction where both parties agree to ignore each other. This social phenomenon was first addressed by the psychologist Stanley Milgram in his 1972 essay and is referred to as "Familiar Strangers" [10].Paulos and Goodman adopted the concept as part of research program titled Familiar Stranger Project[11].

6.4   Performer Spectator Relationships

These relationships derive their name from research put forth by Dalsgaard and Hansen in 2008 [12].There are certain incidences when people stand out in a crowd, are observed but there is a stark absence of direct interaction. A central facet of this relationship is rooted in the stranger's knowledge of being the "center of attraction" which affects his behavior. Goffman would term it under focused interaction. For example, kids who play in the central atrium of a mall, may exhibit exaggerated reactions knowing that they are being watched by others. This relationship will be of central importance in interaction design for experience-oriented uses of technology. The visitors will always be constantly aware of the fact that if they were to interact with the façade/other design, they would be under the scrutiny of other visitors.

6.5   Pragmatic Relationships

These relationships develop due to practical needs. They are mostly professional in nature. The extent and type of communication is context based. Also, these interactions are more formal with well-defined roles and boundaries. For example, the waiter-customer or salesman-buyer relationships.

6.6   Established Relationships

These relationships exist between known groups of people like family/ peer group/ acquaintance/ colleagues and are characterized by informal communication and the presence of inherent comfort zones. It is gathered from the user study that most people prefer going to a shopping mall with friends or family. Additionally, they frequently have chance encounters with acquaintances in such places. All such interactions come under the umbrella of Established Relationships. Emotional features like ego, intimacy, love, fear, anger, respect, concern, humor prominently affect relationship dynamics.

6.7   Human Technology Relationships

Some of the most important relationships that were observed in the space were human technology relationships. These may be planned, routine or incidental interactions. When the technologies of interest are portable, distributed and embedded in our physical and social environment, people's experience of place and its mediation by technology becomes central. Experience involves acting and being acted upon, sensing and feeling both, and transforming them into an emotional and intellectual sense. A question for Interaction Design then is how ubiquitous and portable computing and communications technologies can be used to enrich these experiences.

7   Framework of Social Interaction

Ludvigsen[7] has proposed a framework of social Interaction. The responses of the conducted user study co relate well with this framework. As a result, this has been used to further guide the design direction. The conceptual framework is structured along a scale of engagement into the social situation. The first level is Distributed Attention where people co-present in the same space have different attention foci. The second level of Shared Focus involves people being co-present with directed attention. At the third level called Dialogue level each participant is engaging in a shared activity that requires some form of situated engagement with a counterpart and accessibility to the counterparts participation. The last level of the framework, Collective Action denotes the type of activity that occurs when participants are working together towards a shared goal engaged in, on the overall level, the same activity.

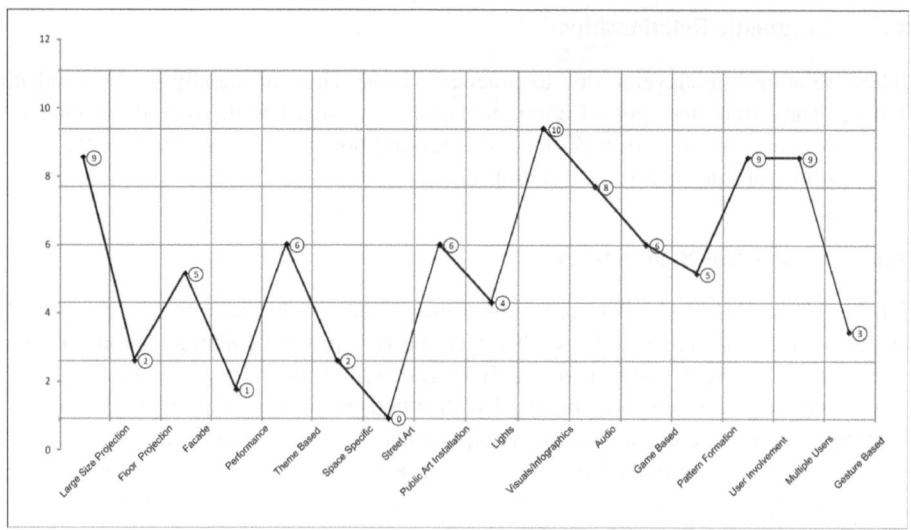

Fig. 6. Component Analysis of Installations

8   Component Analysis in Contemporary Public Space Games and Installations

In this section, we have tried to evaluate what are the various components present in contemporary Public Space games and Installations across the world. The 10 examples [13-22] have been selected on the basis of their scale, content, public involvement, use of technology and broad adherence to the above-mentioned framework.

Lozano-Hemmer's "Body Movies" [19] explores alien presence and embodied relationships. Thousands of pre-clicked portraits taken in the host city are projected on a wall at a scale of 400-1800m^2. These portraits appear inside projected shadows of passers creating a sense of intimacy, intrigue and collaboration. "Night Lights" by Yes Yes No [13] encourages viewers to become performers by capturing their body movements and amplifying them 5 stories tall. "Hidden Fields" [14] explores dance Spectroscopy technology to convert performing dancers into real-time energy fields. The invisible beauty of everyday movements and social interactions is made accessible in the form of visual and self-composing soundscapes.

9   Modalities in HCI

Based on the above-mentioned analysis of examples and literature review, we have come up with a comprehensive aggregation of various modalities that can be used while designing interactions. These can be listed as:

Visual-Based. Facial Expression Analysis, Body Movement Tracking (Large-scale), Gesture Recognition, Gaze Detection (Eyes Movement Tracking)

Audio-Based. Speech Recognition, Speaker Recognition, Auditory Emotion Analysis, Human-Made Noise/Sign Detections (Gasp, Sigh, Laugh, Cry, etc.), Musical Interaction

Sensor- Based. Pen-Based Interaction, Mouse & Keyboard, Joysticks, Motion Tracking Sensors and Digitizers, Haptic Sensors, Pressure Sensors, Taste/Smell Sensors.
    These modalities can be further combined to form multimodal interactions.

10   Technology Exploration

We have explored some of the promising digital technologies that have potential to enhance public space interaction - We plan to use Camera's, Projectors and Embedded Pressure Sensitive Sensors as the primary technology. Audio and Visual Output will ensue. This will result in a multimodal system.
    Infrared beams, microcontrollers, RFID bands, motion detection technology like Kinect, accelerometers and gyroscopes are some other technologies that we are exploring. Each of them can be used in context specific situations that are especially suitable in the Indian scenario.

10.1   Case I: Digitizing "Kite Flying"

A threedimensional screen is put up. Threads used as sensors are attached to the screen. As players play with threads, they manipulate virtual on screen kites in real time. The 3 dimensionality of the screen allows users to move in space for added challenge. The last remaining player in the kite fight wins an offer coupon from the shopping mall.

10.2   Case II: Mirror on the Wall

The shopping arcade has a huge projection that is perceived to be a mirror by passersby. This is achieved by capturing and projecting real time videos of the space. As the viewer comes near the mirror, the perceived reflection is transformed to a silhouette that then projects the image of another person present in the same vicinity. Cameras mounted on the mirror capture this image. The challenge is for both the person to find each other and present the captured picture to avail an offer coupon of one of the shops in the mall.
    The above mentioned are some scenarios that are currently being explored by the authors. Further work is being conducted in developing prototypes to test the above.

11   Conclusion and Future Work

In this paper, we have defined a need for developing social capital. Following this, we have justified the use of space in a shopping mall for building upon interactions that lead to community bonding. We have conducted primary user survey and identified key areas of interest. Based on this, we have developed Relationship Patterns that occur in such a space. Following a conceptual framework for social interaction, we have analyzed components from installation case studies. Additionally, we have identified a series of modalities that can be used while developing design proposals.

We have also given a design proposal based upon the above-mentioned research. There are several issues to tackle with this work in the future. We are finishing the implementation of first version and will begin alpha testing with student participants. However, evaluation of the user experience and usability is the biggest issue to concentrate on. This requires real users in real settings. We will deploy the design to an appropriate spot and will conduct large-scale user tests and queries. The third and perhaps the most challenging part of the work,is to evaluate whether the use of this system actually leads to the development of community bonds.

References

1. Ijla, A.M.: Does public space create social capital? International Journal of Sociology and Anthropology 4(2), 48–53 (2012)
2. Worpole & Knox, p. 4 (2007)
3. Robert, P., Bowling, A.: The collapse and revival of American community, pp. 288–290. Simon and Schuster, New York (2000)
4. Tridib, B.: The Future of Public Space: Beyond Invented Streets and Reinvented Places. Journal of the American Planning Association 67(1), 9–24 (2012)
5. Altman, I., Zube, E.H.: Public Places and Spaces, vol. 10, p. 148. Basic Books (1989)
6. McCarthy, J., Wright, P.: Technology in Place: Dialogics of Technology, Place and Self. In: Costabile, M.F., Patern\'{o}, F. (eds.) INTERACT 2005. LNCS, vol. 3585, pp. 914–926. Springer, Heidelberg (2005)
7. Martin, L.: Designing for social interaction- Physical, Co-located Social Computing. Center for Interactive Spaces, ISIS Katrinebjerg, Aarhus School of Architecture, Denmark (2006)
8. Erving, G.: Behavior in Public Places; Notes on the Social Organization of Gatherings. Free Press of Glencoe, New York (1966)
9. Miller, D.E.: University of Dayton, Late at night contemplating Erving Goffman as a Perceptual Control Theorist. Annual meeting: Society for the Study of Symbolic Interaction, Chicago (2002)
10. Milgram, S.: The familiar stranger: An aspect of urban anonymity. Division 8, Newsletter (1972)
11. Eric, P., Elizabeth, G.: The Familiar Stranger: Anxiety, Comfort, and Play in Public Places. CHI, Vienna (2004)
12. Dalsgaard, P., Hansen, L.K.: Performing perception—staging aesthetics of interaction. ACM Trans. Comput.-Hum. Interact. (2008)
13. Creation of engaging, magical installations, http://yesyesno.com/night-lights
14. Part video game, part science visualization, http://danceroom-spec.com/
15. Interactive puppetry experiencehttp, http://design-io.com/site_docs/work.php?id=15
16. Devloping games, http://www.kma.co.uk/work/great-street-games/

17. Interactive aquarium,
    http://vanderlin.cc/projects/carnival-interactive-aquarium
18. Interactive kinetic light, http://www.kma.co.uk/work/congregation/
19. Interective movies, http://www.lozano-hemmer.com/body_movies.php
20. Interactive kinetic art video, http://www.funnyordie.com/videos/
    6eda0c22c3/xbox-kinect-interactive-art-installation
21. Interactive jump, http://joexpo.wordpress.com/2009/09/27/jump-v-2-2
    /#more-716
22. Karray, F., Alemzadeh, M., AbouSaleh, J., Arab, M.N.: Human-Computer Interaction:
    Overview on State of the Art. International Journal on Smart Sensing and Intelligent Sys-
    tems 1(1) (2008)
23. Dekker, P., Uslaner, E.M.: Introduction. In: Uslaner, E.M. (ed.) Social Capital and Partici-
    pation in Everyday Life, p. 2. Routledge, London (2001)

Testing the Effectiveness of Named Entities in Aligning Comparable English-Bengali Document Pair

Rajdeep Gupta and Sivaji Bandyopadhyay

Dept. of Computer Science, Jadavpur University, Kolkata, India
rajdeepgupta20@gmail.com, sivaji_cse_ju@yahoo.com

Abstract. Named entities (NEs) play an important role in Cross Lingual Information Retrieval (CLIR). To verify whether documents in two different languages share information about same things, we may check if those two documents have fair number of NEs in common. Comparable documents generally share many named entities. In the present work, we test the effectiveness of named entities in aligning English-Bengali comparable document pairs. We develop an aligned corpus of English-Bengali document pairs using Wikipedia. We crawl English-Bengali document pairs by visiting the cross-lingual links found in the documents on Wikipedia. These document pairs are assumed to be comparable. To find the effectiveness of NE in aligning English-Bengali document pair, each English document is compared with all the other Bengali documents and the most similar Bengali document in terms of NE similarity is found. And then it is verified whether it is aligned successfully (since we already know the correct alignment). Rule based transliteration module is used to transliterate English named entities into Bengali named entities. Since, transliteration modules may not always produce exact transliterations; textual properties like longest common subsequence and minimum edit distance are adopted to check whether two Bengali words can be considered as alignment of each other. Our system achieved an accuracy of 45% for 100 English-Bengali document pairs.

Keywords: Cross lingual information retrieval, Named entity, Document similarity, Comparable Documents.

1   Introduction

Recently comparable corpora have got great attention in the field of NLP. Comparable corpus is particularly useful for extracting parallel fragments of texts which in turn facilitates training of machine translation systems [4]. For this purpose, it is necessary to collect comparable document pairs. One resource for comparable documents is obviously the Internet. But in this process; to identify comparable document pairs we need some mechanism to align the relevant documents.

Named entities are very important in computing document similarity [6]. Also, in cross lingual setup we deal with named entities in different languages. So, we cannot merely look into dictionary to search for proper translations of a named entity because

A. Agrawal et al. (Eds.): IITM 2013, CCIS 276, pp. 102–110, 2013.
© Springer-Verlag Berlin Heidelberg 2013

in most cases named entities are "out of vocabulary words" (OOV). So, this poses a challenging task to align named entities in different languages. In the present work, we try to experiment with the effectiveness of named entities in aligning an English-Bengali comparable document pair. We have worked with Wikipedia documents. We first collect an English document from Wikipedia and then follow the inter-language link to find the same document in Bengali (obviously, if such a link exists). In this way, we create a small corpus. We assume that such English-Bengali document pairs from Wikipedia are already comparable since they talk about the same entity. To test the effectiveness of named entities in aligning English-Bengali document pair, we find out the most similar Bengali document corresponding to each English document in terms of NE similarity. To be more precise, let us assume that E is a Wikipedia English document and B is the corresponding Bengali version of E. Now we try to find the most similar Bengali document B' corresponding to the English document E in terms of NE similarity. If B=B' then we say that we successfully aligned E with its correct Bengali version.

Also, due to lack of good NE extractor for Bengali language, we do not identify named entities in Bengali documents. The challenge was that each word in a Bengali document could be a possible match for an English named entity. To handle this situation we transliterate the English named entities and search for their alignments in Bengali documents. However, our system does not require heavy language specific resources like bilingual dictionary. So, this system could be modified for other language pairs.

Named entities have already been exploited in cross lingual information retrieval. Mandl and Womser-Hacker (2005) studied the influence of named entities on the retrieval performance of the systems submitted in Cross Language Evaluation Forum (CLEF) campaign. Braschler and Scäuble (1998) presented a method for computing document level similarity written in different languages. They used a set of indicators to find the similarity between multilingual documents. Such indicators include presence of common proper nouns, numbers, dates etc. Named entities have also been proved important in machine translation. Pal, Naskar, Pecina, Bandyopadhyay and Way (2010) showed improvements in English-Bengali machine translation by proper handling of named entities.

The rest of the paper is organized as follows: Section 2 describes the resource preparation. The detail of the system architecture is described in section 3. Section 4 describes the result of our experiment and section 5 discusses the future work.

2   Resource Preparation

We have worked with Wikipedia documents. To collect comparable English-Bengali document pairs we designed a crawler. The crawler first visits an English page, saves the raw text (in HTML format), and then finds the cross-lingual link (if exists) to find the corresponding Bengali document. Thus, we get one English-Bengali document pair. Moreover, the crawler visits the links found in each document and repeats the process. In this way, we develop a small aligned corpus of English-Bengali comparable document pairs. We retain only the textual information and all the other details are discarded. We experimented with different number of document pairs. We found that in our corpus Bengali documents are usually less informative than the corresponding English documents. Some statistics of the corpus can be found in Table-1.

Table 1. Statistics of the Corpus

Total Number of Document Pairs in Corpus	Total Number of Sentences in Corpus		Total Number of Tokens in Corpus	
	English	Bengali	English	Bengali
100	10647	4852	230662	65627
200	21467	9680	455595	130618
300	43982	12384	951933	164126
400	64926	14581	1409591	191330
500	78334	16842	1696306	220316

2.1   System Framework

We try to measure how effective named entities are in aligning comparable English-Bengali document pairs. Therefore, we use only named entities to align the English-Bengali document pairs. For each English document, we try to find the most similar Bengali document in terms of NE similarity and then we check whether the output document is same as the original Wikipedia Bengali document. To be more precise, if E is an English document and B is its Bengali version (which is found by inter-language link) we find out the most similar Bengali document B' to E, in terms of NE similarity. If B=B', then we say E is successfully aligned with its correct Bengali version.

2.1.1   Similarity Measure

We use overlap in named entities between an English document and a Bengali document as the similarity measure. We define $SIM(E,B)$, the similarity between English document E and Bengali document B as follows:

$SIM(E,B)$ = Number of English named entities (which would be transliterated into Bengali) in E for which an alignment in Bengali would be found in B.

2.1.2   System Architecture

To find the similarity between an English document E and a Bengali document B, we first extract the single token named entities in E using Stanford CoreNLP NER[1]. We do not extract the named entities in a Bengali document due to the lack of good quality Bengali NER.

In order to find Bengali alignments of the English named entities; we transliterate the English named entities into Bengali. We use rule based transliteration module[2]. We consider all the alternative transliterations for an English NE. We then compute SIM(E,B) In this way, E is compared with all the Bengali documents in the corpus and the most similar Bengali document to E is found. The alignment for English document E is denoted by MATCH(E) and is defined as follows:

$$MATCH(E) = argmax_{B \in S} SIM(E,B)$$

where S is the set of all Bengali documents in the corpus considered. Figure 1 shows the system architecture.

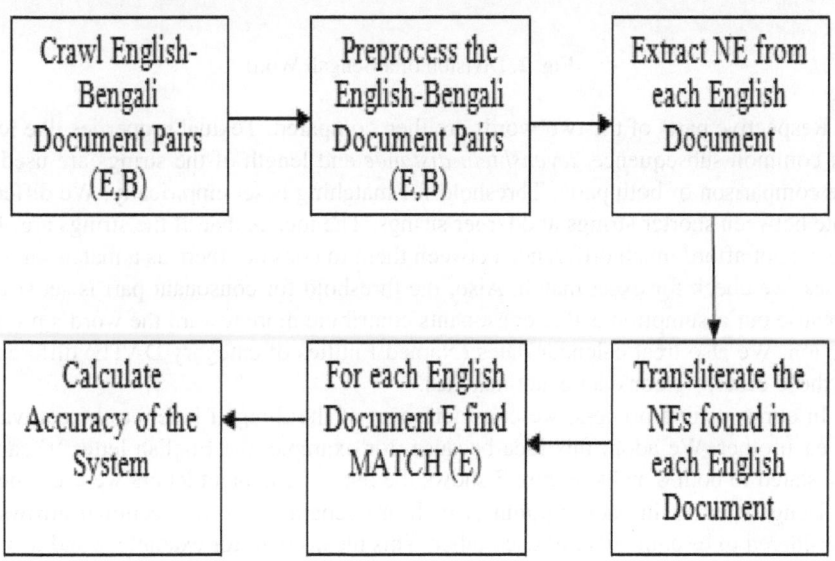

Fig. 1. Overview of System Architecture

---

[1] http://nlp.stanford.edu/software/corenlp.shtml
[2] http://tdil-dc.in/index.php?option=com_vertical&parentid=72

106   R. Gupta and and S. Bandyopadhyay

Aligning Named Entities

As mentioned already, we do not locate Bengali named entities. In our system, each word in a Bengali document could be a possible match for an English named entity. So, we need to consider each word in a Bengali document to try to find the possible match for an English named entity. It is to be noted that the transliteration module doesn't produce exact transliterations most of the times. So, we should not rely on exact match to find the overlap in named entities. To be more precise, if *bt* is a named entity found after transliteration of English named entity *e*, we may not find *bt* in the Bengali document most of the times. Instead, we may find another word *b* which is very close to *bt*. In that case, we will consider *b* to be an alignment for *bt* (i.e. *e*).

For our purpose, we first divide the two words into their *matra* (vowel modifiers) part and consonant part keeping the relative orders of characters in each part same. For example, Figure 2 shows the division of the word কলকাতা.

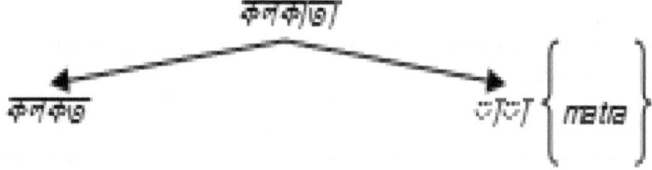

Fig. 2. Division of a Bengali Word

Respective parts of the two words are then compared. Textual properties like longest common subsequence, *levenshtein distance* and length of the strings are used for the comparison of both parts. Threshold for matching is set empirically. We differentiate between shorter strings and larger strings. The idea is that, if the strings are short we cannot afford much difference between them to consider them as a match. In those cases, we check for exact match. Also, the threshold for consonant part is set stricter because our assumption is that consonants contribute more toward the word's pronunciation. We also treat calendar dates (Named Entities of category DATE) differently. In those cases, we consider exact matches.

In our matching process, we consider some of the Bengali letters to be equivalent of each other. We adopt this idea because, for example, the English letter '*t*' can be translated to both ত and ট. Figure 3 shows the list of equivalent letters we use. The set of Bengali letters in each column (which are separated by bidirectional arrows) is considered to be equivalent of each other. This means that, for example, ন and ড, স and শ, ত and ট etc. Are treated as equivalent of each other.

Table 2 shows some examples of alignments that our system found; where the 1st column contains the English NE, the 2nd column contains the transliterated English NE and the 3rd column contains the Bengali alignment found.

As it has already been told, we see from Table 2 that transliteration module does not always produce exact transliteration. The last two rows are example of cases where we find exact matches.

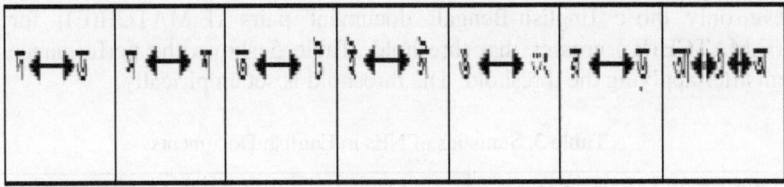

Fig. 3. List of Equivalent Bengali Letters

Table 2. Some Examples of Alignment

English NE	Transliteration	Found Bengali Alignment
Mumbai	মুম্বি	মুম্বই
Hindustan	হিন্দুস্তান	হিন্দুস্তান
Kolkata	কল্কটা	কলকাতা
Rabindranath	রবিন্দরনথ	রবীন্দ্রনাথ
Bartaman	বরটমন	বর্তমান
East	ইস্ট	ইস্ট
2001	২০০১	২০০১

3   Result and Observation

We have experimented with different number of documents pairs. It is found that, although the total number of named entities in the English documents in our corpora is quite large, the standard deviation of their number of occurrences in different documents is high. So, the number of named entities in different English documents is quite varying. Total number of distinct named entities is quite less than the total number of named entities. This indicates that there is fair amount of overlapping of named entities between the English documents. Also, as the number of documents increases in the corpus, the standard deviation tends to increase. Table 3 shows some statistics of the English documents.

Table 4 shows the number of documents that are correctly aligned using our system. It is identified that most of the documents that are correctly aligned had comparatively larger number of named entities than others. So, we define a threshold to retrieve only those English-Bengali document pairs (E,MATCH(E)) for which SIM(E,MATCH(E)) crosses that threshold. Table 5 shows the performance of our system after applying the threshold. The threshold is set empirically.

Table 3. Statistics of NEs in English Documents

Number of Document Pairs in Corpus	Total Number of NE in English Docs	Average Number of NE in English Docs	Total Number of Distinct NE in English Docs	Standard Deviation of NE in English Docs
100	22590	225.90	10224	216.51
200	42921	214.60	16965	190.19
300	82900	276.33	30647	251.73
400	120522	301.30	40642	270.15
500	144617	289.23	46675	266.98

Table 4. Accuracy of the System without any Threshold

Number of Document Pairs in Corpus	Number of Document Pairs Correctly Aligned	Percentage of Document Pairs Correctly Aligned
100	45	45.00
200	65	32.50
300	95	31.66
400	111	27.75
500	122	24.40

Table 5. Accuracy of the System after Applying Threshold

Number of Document Pairs in Corpus	Precision (%)	Recall (%)	F-Score (%)	Number of False Positive	Number of False Negative
100	63.26	31.00	41.61	18	14
200	53.84	24.50	33.67	42	16
300	55.47	23.66	33.17	57	24
400	50.00	20.50	29.07	82	29
500	46.11	17.80	25.68	104	33

4   Conclusion and Future Work

This is an initial attempt towards measuring the effectiveness of named entities in aligning English-Bengali document pairs. Since, there is considerable amount of overlapping of named entities between the English documents; we think that our result is encouraging. In order to improve accuracy we intend to include multi-word NEs and incorporate a weighting scheme where the contribution of an NE towards a document is weighted. The disambiguation technique of named entities could also be incorporated in order to align named entities unambiguously. Also, this system can be easily modified to cluster similar English-Bengali document pairs.

The future work consists of identifying comparable fragments from the already aligned document pairs. Also, extracting parallel sentences (translations of each other) or parallel phrases or parallel tokens from those fragments would be of great importance because this may greatly enrich the bilingual dictionary and the existing machine translation systems. This might need the clubbing of some other similarity features with our existing system.

References

1. Mandl, T., Womser-Hacker, C.: The effect of named entities on effectiveness in cross-language information retrieval evaluation. In: Proceedings of the 2005 ACM Symposium on Applied Computing, pp. 1059–1064. ACM (March 2005)
2. Braschler, M., Schäuble, P.: Multilingual Information Retrieval Based on Document Alignment Techniques. In: Nikolaou, C., Stephanidis, C. (eds.) ECDL 1998. LNCS, vol. 1513, pp. 183–197. Springer, Heidelberg (1998)
3. Jagarlamudi, J., Daumé III, H.: Extracting Multilingual Topics from Unaligned Comparable Corpora. In: Gurrin, C., He, Y., Kazai, G., Kruschwitz, U., Little, S., Roelleke, T., Rüger, S., van Rijsbergen, K. (eds.) ECIR 2010. LNCS, vol. 5993, pp. 444–456. Springer, Heidelberg (2010)
4. Hewavitharana, S., Vogel, S.: Extracting parallel phrases from comparable data. In: Proceedings of the 4th Workshop on Building and Using Comparable Corpora: Comparable Corpora and the Web, pp. 61–68. Association for Computational Linguistics (June 2011)
5. Munteanu, D.S., Marcu, D.: Extracting parallel sub-sentential fragments from non-parallel corpora. In: Annual Meeting-Association for Computational Linguistics, vol. 44(1), p. 81 (July 2006)
6. Kumaran, G., Allan, J.: Text classification and named entities for new event detection. In: Proceedings of the 27th Annual International ACM SIGIR Conference on Research and Development in Information Retrieval, pp. 297–304. ACM (July 2004)
7. Pal, S., Kumar Naskar, S., Pecina, P., Bandyopadhyay, S., Way, A.: Handling named entities and compound verbs in phrase-based statistical machine translation. Association for Computational Linguistics (2010)

Self-embedding Pixel Wise Fragile Watermarking Scheme for Image Authentication

Durgesh Singh, Shivendra Shivani, and Suneeta Agarwal

Department of Computer Science and Engineering
Motilal Nehru National Institute of Technology Allahabad-211004, India
{Durgeshcse,shivendrashivani}@gmail.com, suneeta@mnnit.ac.in

Abstract. This paper presents an effective self-embedding pixel wise fragile watermarking scheme for image content authentication along with tampered region localization capability. In this approach the watermark is generated from the five most significant bits (MSBs) of each pixel using three different algorithms and embedded into the three least significant bits (LSBs) of the corresponding pixel in the host image. At the receiver side by comparing the recalculated and extracted LSBs, one can easily identify the tampered pixels of the watermarked image. Results of experiments demonstrate that the proposed scheme has very high fragility and fidelity.

Keywords: Fragile Watermarking, Tamper Detection, Self-embedding.

1   Introduction

Due to the increasing requirements of multimedia technology, the security of multimedia information like video, audio, image and text have become a key concern. Integrity of image content is vital especially when this is used for authentication e.g. court evidence or medical diagnosis. Hence watermarking technique is highly required. These techniques are generally classified into three different categories as robust, semi fragile, and fragile watermarking. To confirm the data integrity and legitimacy, the idea of fragile watermarking technique came in picture. A fragile watermark is a mark that is readily destroyed when the watermarked image is altered through a nonlinear or linear transformation [9] [10]. The sensitivity of fragile watermark to modification leads to their use in image authentication. Fragile watermarking is categorized into two major classes pixel-wise fragile watermarking [1] [5] [8] [12] [13] and block-wise fragile watermarking [2] [3] [4] [7] [14]. The main idea of the block-wise fragile watermarking is that the host image is divided into non overlapping blocks and each block has its own watermark information. This watermark may be any function which is based on extensive content of the host image. If image is tampered unintentionally or intentionally, the altered block and watermark available in that block will not match. A block-wise mechanism for tampered area detection and a pixel-wise mechanism for original content recovery was proposed by X. Zhang et al.[14]. In this scheme, permute the image pixels based on a secret key and then permuted pixels are divided into a series of pixel-pairs.

A. Agrawal et al. (Eds.): IITM 2013, CCIS 276, pp. 111–122, 2013.

The recovery data generated by exclusive-OR operation on the original MSBs and authentication data derived from MSBs and recovery data are embedded into the three LSB planes. At receiver side, after identifying the tampered blocks using authentication data, recovery data extracted from other regions and the spatial correlation are exploited to recover the principal content in the tampered area in a pixel-by-pixel manner. In block-wise fragile watermarking, a single block will contain many pixels. So within altered block some pixels are truly altered but some may be unaltered, which causes problem when we require accurate location of modification with high precision. This negative feature of block-wise fragile watermarking can be abated by pixel-wise fragile watermarking.

In pixel-wise fragile watermarking technique, watermark is embedded into LSBs of each pixels of host image. If gray scale value of any pixel is modified then embedded watermark corresponding to that pixel will also be changed hence altered pixels can easily be localized. If the watermark is calculated by host image itself then this procedure is called self embedding. A pixel-wise fragile watermarking scheme is proposed by *Y Lim et al.*[8]. According to this technique seven Most Significant Bits (MSBs) of a pixel are given as an input to the hash function. Using a secret key and hash value, we calculate a single value either 0 or 1 for each pixel and this value is embedded in the LSBs of corresponding pixel. If any modification is done with any pixel, on the receiver end, calculated hash value and extracted hash value from LSB will mismatch hence tampered pixel can be identified.

Similarly *X Zhang and S Wang* have proposed a new fragile watermarking scheme based on hierarchical mechanism [13]. In this scheme block-wise and pixel-wise watermark, which are derived from MSBs are used to directly substitute all the LSBs of a host image. On the receiver end, after spotted the blocks containing altered content, the watermark data hidden in the rest of the blocks are exploited to accurately find the tampered pixels.

Our approach is based on a self-embedding pixel-wise fragile watermarking scheme. In this scheme, watermark is generated by three different mechanisms and embedded into three LSBs of each pixel of host image.

The remaining paper is organized as follows: the proposed scheme is given in section 2 and in section 3, the experimental results are shown. The paper is concluded in section 4 followed by the references.

2   Proposed Algorithm

In our proposed scheme, the five most significant bits (MSBs) of all pixels in the host image are kept unchanged, and the three least significant bits (LSBs) of all pixels are replaced with watermark data that is determined by the MSBs of that pixel itself. These three bits Watermark data of each pixel of host image are called as authentication bit.

Consider a gray scale host image I having number of rows and columns as N_1 and N_2. Then N represent the number of pixels ($N=N_1 \times N_2$). So the intensities range of each pixel of the image is denoted by $P_n \in [0,255]$ where $n =1, 2, 3, ..., N$. Here, we assume that N_1 and N_2 are multiples of 2. Each P_n can be represented by eight bits, $b_{n,8}, b_{n,7}, ..., b_{n,1}$, where

$$b_{n,m} = \left\lfloor \frac{P_n}{2^{m-1}} \right\rfloor \bmod 2, m = 1,2,3,...,8 \qquad (1)$$

2.1   Watermark Embedding Procedure

In our proposed technique we are calculating the three authentication bits for each pixel of host image by three different methods.

2.1.1   Authentication Bit₁ Generation

Consider any pixel of I as P_n. So we take only five MSBs of P_n represented as $b_{n,m}$ where $m \in (4...8)$. Block Diagram for Authentication bit₁ generation shown in Fig. 1.

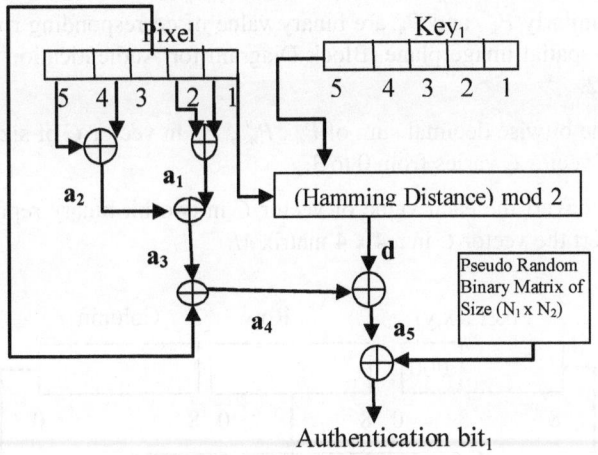

Fig. 1. Block Diagram of Authentication bit₁ Generation

Step 1. Calculate the Authentication bit1 as following:

$$a_1 = b_{n,4} \oplus b_{n,5}$$
$$a_2 = b_{n,7} \oplus b_{n,8}$$
$$a_3 = a_1 \oplus a_2$$
$$a_4 = b_{n,6} \oplus a_3 \qquad (2)$$

Step2. Now calculate the hamming distance d between MSBs of each pixel and a secret key Key_1.

$$k_1 = Key_1 \bmod 32 \tag{3}$$
$$d = (HammingDistance(b_{n,m}, k_1)) \bmod 2 \tag{4}$$
$$a_5 = a_4 \oplus d \tag{5}$$

Step 3. *Take a pseudo random binary matrix B having the size same as of the host image, based on a secret key.*

$$A_{b1} = a_5 \oplus B_n \tag{6}$$

Where A_{b1} is the Authentication bit$_1$, and B_n is value of corresponding pixel location of P_n in pseudo random binary matrix B.

2.1.2 Authentication Bit$_2$ Generation

Consider any pixel of I as P_n. Now three LSBs of P_n set zero and five MSBs remain unchanged. Similarly $P_n^{\ r}$ and $P_n^{\ c}$ are binary value of corresponding row and column value of P_n in spatial image plane. Block Diagram for Authentication bit$_2$ generation shown in Fig. 2.

Step1. Take the bitwise decimal sum of P_n, $P_n^{\ r}$, $P_n^{\ c}$ in vector C of size 1 x 8. So the value range of vector C varies from 0 to 3.

Step 2. Now convert the each value of vector C in two bit binary representation and further reconvert the vector C in a 4 x 4 matrix M.

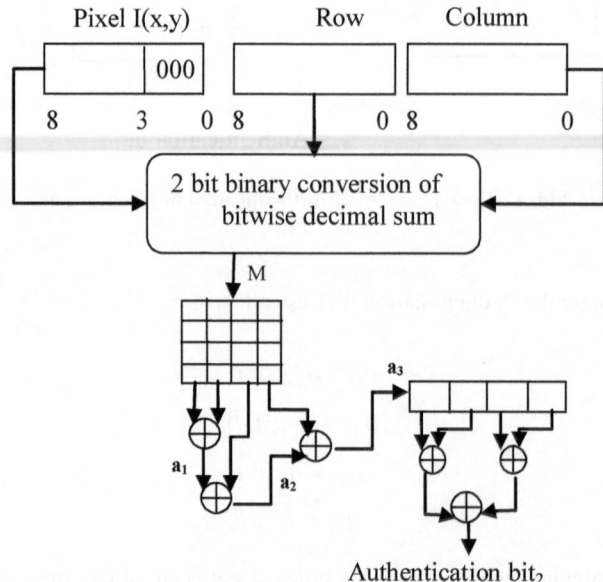

Fig. 2. Block Diagram of Authentication bit$_2$ Generation

Step 3. Take column wise X-OR operation of matrix M as

$$a_1 = M_1 \oplus M_2$$
$$a_2 = a_1 \oplus M_3$$
$$a_3 = a_2 \oplus M_4 \tag{7}$$

where M_1, M_2 M_3, M_4 are column vector of matrix M *and* a_1, a_2, a_3 are 4 x 1 column vector.

Step 4. Now take the bitwise X-OR within vector a_3 as shown in Fig. 2 and get the Authentication bit$_2$.

2.1.3   Authentication Bit$_3$ Generation

In case of Authentication bit$_3$ generation process first of all we discard the three LSBs from each pixel of host image and called the resulting image as content image I_c. Consider any pixel of I_c as P_i. So five binary bits of P_i are represented as b_a where a ∈ (1..5). Let us consider that pixel P_i having coordinate value x and y. Now there will be four diagonal neighbors as shown in Fig. 3. Now we will calculate the Authentication bit$_3$ by following method.

Step 1. Calculate x=x-1 and y=y-1 repeat until x=0 or y= 0
        if x=0 then P_{D1} = C else P_{D1} = R.
Where R and C are the corresponding row and column value which range from 0 to N_1 -1 and 0 to N_2 -1 respectively.

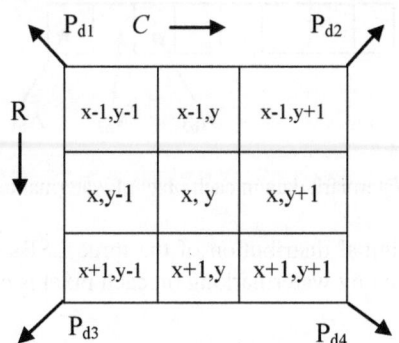

Fig. 3. Block Diagram of Diagonal neighbors of a pixel

Step 2. Calculate x=x-1 and y=y+1 repeat until x=0 or y= N_2-1
        if y= N_2-1 then P_{D2} = R else P_{D2}= C.

Step 3. Calculate x=x+1 and y=y-1 repeat until x=N1 -1 or y= 0
        if x=N_1 -1 then P_{D3} = C else P_{D3} = r

Step 4. Calculate x=x+1 and y=y+1 repeat until x=N_1-1 or y= N_2-1
        if x=N_1-1 then P_{D4} = C else P_{D4}= R

Step 5. Now convert the P_{D1}, P_{D2}, P_{D3} and P_{D4} into 8 bit binary format and discard the three MSBs then five LSBs denoted by $b_i(P_{D1})$, $b_i(P_{D2})$, $b_i(P_{D3})$ and $b_i(P_{D4})$ respectively.

Step 6. Now calculate the following

$$B_1 = (b_i(\mathrm{P_{D1}})) \oplus b_a$$
$$B_2 = (b_i(\mathrm{P_{D2}})) \oplus (onebitRightShift\,(b_a))$$
$$B_3 = (b_i(\mathrm{P_{D3}})) \oplus (twobitRightShift\,(b_a))$$
$$B_4 = (b_i(\mathrm{P_{D4}})) \oplus (threebitRightShift\,(b_a))$$
$$B_{12} = B_1 \oplus B_2$$
$$B_{34} = B_3 \oplus B_4$$

$$A_{b3} = \left(\sum_{j=1..5} (B_{12} \wedge B_{34}) \right) \bmod 2 \qquad (8)$$

Where A_{b3} is the Authentication bit$_3$.

Finally we get three Authentication bits which are called watermark data for that image. The watermark is embedded in the three LSBs of each pixel and five MSBs of host image are kept unchanged as shown in Figure 4 and got the watermarked image.

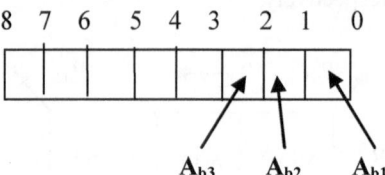

Fig. 4. Watermark data in each pixel of watermarked Image

Assuming that the original distribution of the three LSBs is uniform, the average energy of distortion caused by watermarking on each pixel is calculated as

$$MSE = \frac{1}{N_1 \times N_2} \sum_{i=0}^{N_1-1} \sum_{j=0}^{N_2-1} (I(i,j) - D(i,j))^2 \qquad (9)$$

where MSE is Mean Square Error which is for $N_1 \times N_2$ two monochrome images I and D in which one of the image is original host image and another one is watermarked image. Now the PSNR is defined as

$$PSNR = 10 \log_{10} \frac{\max^2}{MSE} \qquad (10)$$

here, *max* is the highest pixel intensity value of the image.

2.2   Watermark Detection Procedure

At the receiver end, we need to check the integrity of watermarked image. Suppose an attacker has changed the image intentionally or unintentionally without changing the image size then it will be our prime task to identify that whether the image is authentic or not. For unauthentic image we have to exactly locate the tampered region. Hence the tamper detection algorithm is as follows:

Step 1.   Generate a pseudo random binary matrix having dimension $N_1 x N_2$ with the same secret key which was used for embedding.

Step 2.   Enter the secret key Key_1 which is used for embedding.

Step 3.   For each pixel of tampered image calculate the Authentication bit_1 discussed in subsection 2.1.1, then extract first LSB of all pixels of tampered image. Compare the Authentication bit_1 with the extracted first LSB of corresponding pixel of tampered image. If there is mismatch, we mark those pixels as altered one.

Step 4.   This step is carried out for those pixels which have first LSB is matched with extracted Authentication bit_1. Calculate the Authentication bit_2 discussed in subsection 2.1.2, then extract second LSB of all pixels of tampered image. Compare the Authentication bit_2 with the extracted second LSB of corresponding pixel of tampered image. If there is mismatch then those pixels will be marked as altered pixel.

Step 5.   This last step is carried out for those pixels which have passed the test of Step 3, and Step 4 i.e. if no mismatch detected. Calculate the Authentication bit_3 discussed in subsection 2.1.3, then extract third LSB of all pixels of tampered image. Compare the Authentication bit_3 with the extracted third LSB of corresponding pixel of tampered image. If there is mismatch then those pixels will be marked as altered pixel.

If there will be no mismatch, it means those pixels are not altered during any attack or intensity value of altered pixel and original pixel is same.

3   Experimental Results

The accuracy and effectiveness of the proposed approach can be demonstrated by experimental results and its analysis. Experiments have been performed on many host

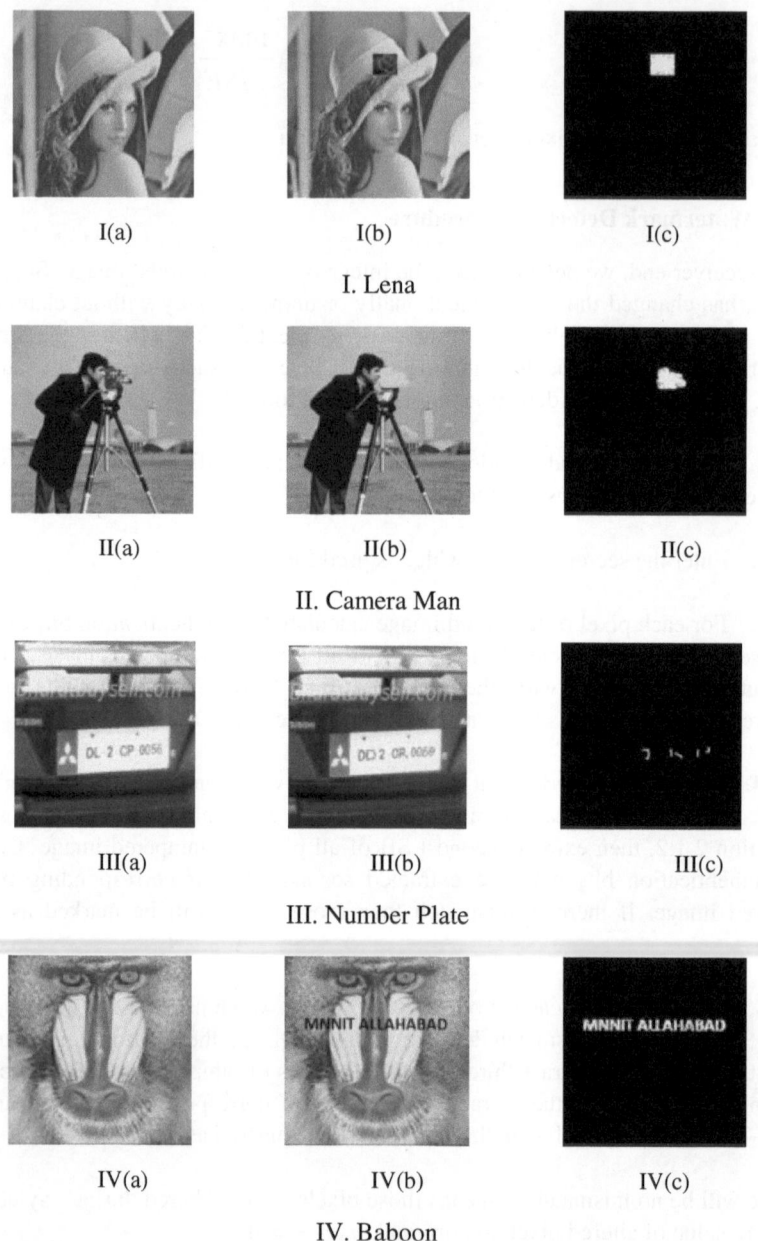

I(a)   I(b)   I(c)

I. Lena

II(a)   II(b)   II(c)

II. Camera Man

III(a)   III(b)   III(c)

III. Number Plate

IV(a)   IV(b)   IV(c)

IV. Baboon

Fig. 5. (a) Watermarked (b) Altered Watermarked (c) Tamper Detected Image

images of size 256 x 256. We have got very satisfactory results during embedding with high level PSNR value as well as good tamper detection. Here we have done some major attack on image which can alter the valuable extensive content of image as shown in Fig. 5. Many images have been taken from standard database for verifying the proposed approach. Series (c) of all figures having black region shows the unaltered pixel whereas white region shows altered one. The first attack is object addition which is done on Lena image in which an attacker adds some additional object on image. By the help of our algorithm we can effectively locate the region of alteration. The second type of attack is object removal which is done on Camera Man image. Third type of attack is very sensitive attack because some time number plate is only evidence for court and it is owner's responsibility to keep the integrity of that evidence. Similarly fourth attack is text addition, by the help of experimental view we can see the efficiency of our approach.

The summary of the experimental results are shown in Table 1 in which we can see the altered number of pixels for various images along with their detection rate and PSNR value. The PSNR value can be calculated using equation 9 and 10. High PSNR value shows the efficiency and noise resistance property of our algorithm.

Table 1. Essential information observed during watermark embedding

Host Image	PSNR (Embedding)	No. of Altered Pixel	Detected (%)
Lena	40.40 dB	1050	94 %
Camera Man	40.07 dB	900	97%
Baboon	40.52 dB	1600	97%
Number Plate	40.72 dB	130	99%

Here in order to estimate the imperceptibility property of the suggested watermarking approach, histogram disparity is compared between the original cover image and the watermarked image. In performed experiments, we have found reasonably high *PSNR* value (i.e. 40.40 dB). Fig. 6, shows that the constructed histogram of the original cover image is almost similar to the histogram of watermarked image which is verified by the correlation coefficient that is almost equal to 1. So another way it shows that the proposed approach is reasonably imperceptible.

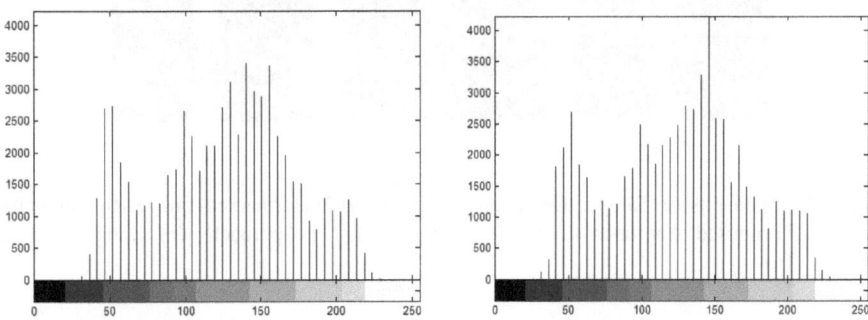

Fig. 6. Histogram of (a) Lena Original Image (b) Watermarked Image of Lena

Fig. 7 shows the accuracy of proposed algorithm's result that is alteration detection which is done on large set of database. We can see that it is an approximate identity curve which shows the accuracy of tamper detection.

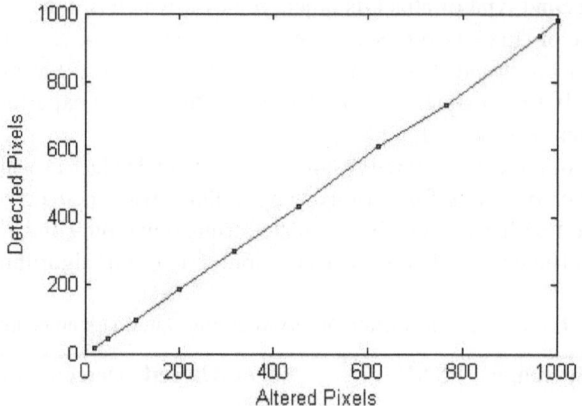

Fig. 7. Test results for altered and detected pixels

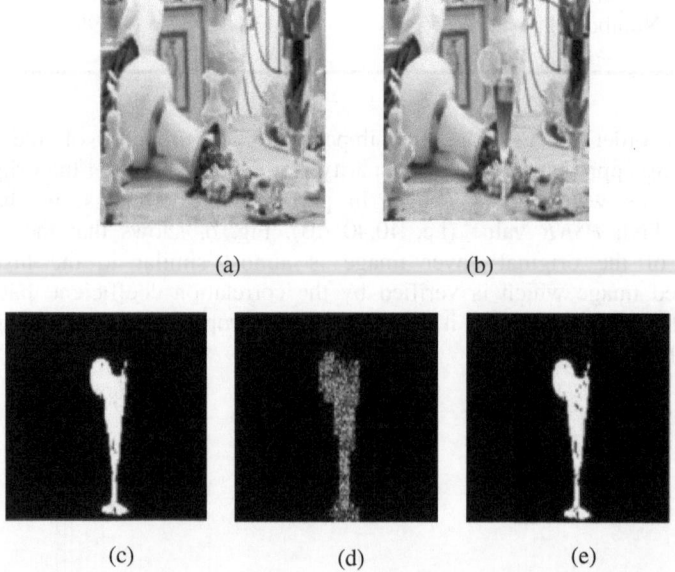

Fig. 8. Comparisons of Tamper Detection Accuracy (a) Watermarked Image (b) Tampered Image (c) Proposed Approach (d) P. W. Wong et al.[11] Approach (e) Hong Jie et al. Approach [6]

Wong's[11] LSB-modification scheme from the literature, embed the watermark derived from a block into the LSB of the same block. Similarly Hong Jie[6] embed the watermark into the each pixel. Thus, in Wong's approach no matter where the tampering is done on image contents, the alternations shown in the final image are still confined in that whole block. Using the same cover image and the same alteration we have checked proposed approach with respect to Wong's and Hong jie approaches. Comparison is shown in figure 8 and table 2. We have analyzed that the tamper detection rate and fidelity of proposed approach is good enough.

Table 2. Essential information observed during the comparison among various approaches

Approach	Altered Pixels	Tamper Detected (%)	PSNR
P. W. Wong et al.	3800	54.23 %	30 dB
Hong Jie et al.	3800	96.45%	41 dB
Proposed Approach	3800	98.21%	40.8 dB

4   Conclusions

This paper proposes an efficient pixel-wise fragile watermarking scheme capable of exactly localizing the pixels that are tampered intentionally or unintentionally. The proposed scheme generates three bits using three different methods and these three bits will be replaced by the three original least significant bits of the host image. The experiments have been performed on the wide set of standard image data set and different kinds of attacks. The rate of detection of altered pixels is very high. Also the average perceptual quality of the tampered image is near to 41 dB. Thus the proposed technique provides a good solution to the tamper localization without affecting the perceptual quality. In the future some issues require further exploration, as capability of pixel restoration. If extensive content of an image is tampered then it must be perfectly recovered as its original value.

References

1. Che, S., Ma, B., Che, Z.: An adaptive and fragile image watermarking algorithm based on composite chaotic iterative dynamic system. In: Intelligent Information Hiding and Multimedia Signal Processing, IIHMSP 2008, pp. 159–162. IEEE (2008)
2. Fridrich, J., Goljan, M.: Images with self-correcting capabilities. In: Proceedings of International Conference on Image Processing, ICIP 1999, vol. 3, pp. 792–796 (1999)
3. He, H., Zhang, J., Chen, F.: Block-wise Fragile Watermarking Scheme Based on Scramble Encryption. In: Bio-Inspired Computing: Theories and Applications, BIC-TA 2007, pp. 216–220, 14–17 (2007)
4. Hernandez, J.R., Amado, M., Perez-Gonzalez, F.: DCT-domain watermarking techniques for still images: detector performance analysis and a new structure. IEEE Transactionson Image Processing 9(1), 55–68 (2000)

5. He, Y.Z., Han, Z.: A fragile watermarking scheme with pixel-wise alteration localization. In: 9th International Conference on Signal Processing, ICSP 2008, pp. 2201–2204, 26–29 (2008)
6. He, H.-J., Zhang, J.-S., Tai, H.-M.: A Wavelet-Based Fragile Watermarking Scheme for Secure Image Authentication. In: Shi, Y.Q., Jeon, B. (eds.) IWDW 2006. LNCS, vol. 4283, pp. 422–432. Springer, Heidelberg (2006)
7. Ho, A.T.S., Zhu, X., Shen, J., Marziliano, P.: Fragile Watermarking Based on Encoding of the Zeroes of the z-Transform. IEEE Transactions on Information Forensics and Security 3(3), 567–569 (2008)
8. Lim, Y., Xu, C., Feng, D.D.: Web based Image Authentication Using Invisible Fragile Watermark. Australian Computer Society, Inc. (2002)
9. Lin, E.T., Delp, E.J.: A review of Fragile Watermarking. Center for Education and Research in Information Assurance and Security. Purdue University, West Lafayette, IN 47907-2086
10. Shivani, S., Patel, A.K., Kamble, S., Agarwal, S.: An effective pixel-wise fragile watermarking scheme based on ARA bits. In: International Conference on Communication, Computing & Security (ICCCS 2011), pp. 221–226. ACM, New York (2011)
11. Wong, P.W., Memon, N.: Secret and Public Key Image Watermarking Schemes for Image Authentication and Ownership Verification. IEEE Transactions on Image Processing 10(10) (2001)
12. Zhang, X., Wang, S.: Statistical fragile watermarking capable of locating individual tampered pixels. IEEE Signal Processing Letters 14(10), 727–730 (2007)
13. Zhang, X., Wang, S.: Fragile watermarking scheme using a hierarchical mechanism. Signal Processing 89(4), 675–679 (2008), doi:10.1016/j.sigpro.2008.10.001
14. Zhang, X., Wang, S., Qian, Z., Feng, G.: Self-embedding watermark with flexible restoration Quality. Journal Multimedia Tools and Applications 54, 385–395 (2010)

CUDA Based Interactive Volume Rendering
of 3D Medical Data

Piyush Kumar and Anupam Agrawal

Information Technology Department
Indian Institute of Information Technology, Allahabad
{rs109,anupam}@iiita.ac.in

Abstract. Improving the image quality and the rendering speed have always been a challenge to the programmers involved in large scale volume rendering especially in the field of medical image processing. The paper aims to perform volume rendering using the GPU, in which, with its massively parallel capability has the potential to revolutionize this field. The final results would allow the doctors to diagnose and analyze the 2D CT-scan data using three dimensional visualization techniques. The system is used in two types of data, one is human abdomen (45 MB) and colon_phantom8 (300MB) volume data. Further, the use of CUDA framework, a low learning curve technology, for such purpose would greatly reduce the cost involved in CT scan analysis; hence bring it to the common masses. The volume rendering has been done on Nvidia Tesla C1060 card and its performance has also been benchmarked.

1   Introduction

Since ancient times vision has been an important part of how a human perceives the environment around him. Vision is responsible for providing inputs upon which necessary action is performed. Then came the advent of television when the world around was projected on a screen having only two dimensions. However, long before that various other forms of projection on two dimensions have been in use. A point in this case is the painting by the ancient artists which have depth in them. Soon, it was realized that if the data by other senses can also be projected in a form which is visible, then, new information can be extracted out of that.

The term visualization means the construction of a visual image in the mind. Scientific visualization is an important part of 3D computer graphics. Volume data is used for visualizing purpose. A typical 3D volumetric data set is a group of 2D slice images acquired by CT, MRI machines or 3D scanners. 3D MRI or CT data reconstruction is a complicated and challenging problem with high computing density and also a time consuming process. Volume rendering is a method which is used to visualize this type of dataset. This is also called direct volume rendering. It is a set of techniques used to display a 2D projection of a 3D discretely sampled data set.

The complicated and challenging problems are now easier due to the fast development of the parallelism technique in parallel computing. Especially thankful to multi-core CPU and CUDA on GPU making fast 3D reconstruction practically possible [1]. The 3D volume data would be reconstructed and rendered in just a few

A. Agrawal et al. (Eds.): IITM 2013, CCIS 276, pp. 123–132, 2013.

seconds after scanning by the scanner. This is very helpful in the field of medical operations/ surgeries and online inspection. Here, it can be easier to run complex filtering and segmentation based techniques in real-time. With the development of APIs just like CUDA and OpenCL, the flexibility for scientific visualization programming has achieved new heights [2].

This paper will go through some literature review of the volume rendering in scientific visualization in next section. The third section explains the proposed methodology and its implementation in CUDA on GPU. A few interactive result snapshots and performance analysis results are summarized in fourth section. Finally we have concluded these entire things with the future work in the end of the fifth section.

2   Literature Review

Ray casting algorithm for volume rendering was first introduced by Kajiya [3]. The ray casting algorithm is an important approach for volume visualization. This has mainly come through two phase process. One is CPU-based and the other is GPU-based. Here, it would explore the method with the help of graphical model and the CUDA model [1].

During rendering, optical properties are accumulated along each viewing ray to form an image of the data. Here, an optical model was used to map data values to optical properties. The role of optical model is to describe that how particles in the volume interact with light. Optical parameters are specified by the data values directly, or they are computed from applying one or more transfer functions to the data [4]. The transfer functions can either be applied before the interpolation from the surrounding scalar values (pre-classification) and interpolating the resulting RGBA values, or after the interpolation of post-classification [4]. The most commonly used algorithms are summarized here which were: splatting, shear-warp, texture mapping, and ray casting under Direct Volume Rendering. But the ray casting is the most popular method for volume rendering [4].

Generally the same process is used to do this for all rendering techniques as [4]:

- **Splatting method:** It is a technique, where every volume element is splatted on the projection plane in a systematically back to front order. These splats are rendered with various attributes depending on the volume density and the transfer function.
- **Shear-Warp method:** It is a factorization technique, where the viewing transformation is used. The faces of the volume become axis aligned with image plane and voxels (volume element) to pixels scale is fixed. If all slices have been rendered, the buffer is warped into the desired orientation.
- **Texture mapping:** This approach is based on blending of textured slices. Volume is stored on the GPU in three sets of 2D textures. One set of 2D texture for each dimension. These textures are rendered using alpha blending. The second possibility is to store volume in one 3D texture and then render polygons using alpha blending.

- **Volume Ray Casting:** It is a basic technique for volume visualization. In our research work, initially we will concentrate on this technique of direct volume rendering for a large scale dataset. The GPU-based volume ray-casting technique provides high-quality result at interactive frame rates [3].

2.1   Volume Ray Casting Approach

General ray casting is based on the idea of shooting rays, which originate in the user's eye, through an object, thus computing the colours of the pixels passed by the rays. For ray casting through volumetric data, each ray is traversed from the location of the eye until it leaves the dataset [4] [13].

Direct volume rendering methods are used to generate 3D volumetric data visualization without extracting the surface geometry from the data [12]. The basic idea is to accumulate the optical properties such as color and opacity as we travel along the ray emanating from each pixel of the screen.

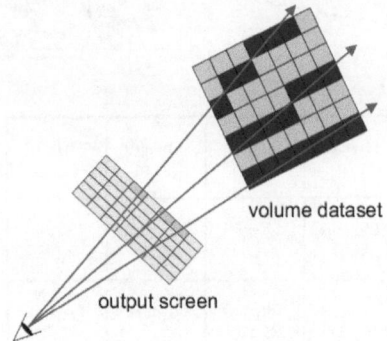

volume dataset

output screen

Fig. 1. Casting Rays through an Object [4]

Fig.1. illustrates how the rays are cast from the eye through the screen and the object: dark blue voxels in the volume object are the voxels that are traversed by the algorithm. The light navy blue pixels on the output screen represent the pixels that are involved. Images are created by sampling the volume along all viewing rays and accumulating the resulting optical properties [6].

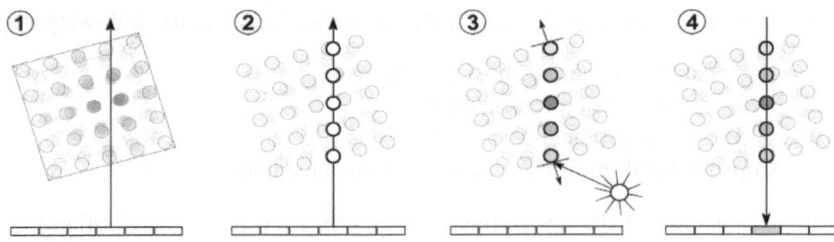

Fig. 2. Four basic steps of volume ray casting: (1) Ray Casting (2) Sampling (3) Shading (4) Compositing Rays [5]

The basic four steps are used in the method of volume ray casting algorithm which are shown in above Fig.2. which are: ray casting , sampling, shading, and compositing rays.

2.2   CUDA Based Architecture

The hardware has been designed to support lightweight driver and runtime layers, resulting in high performance. The structure of the CUDA (Compute Unified Device Architecture) device has described in the form of threads, blocks, and grid [9]. This is shown in Fig.3.

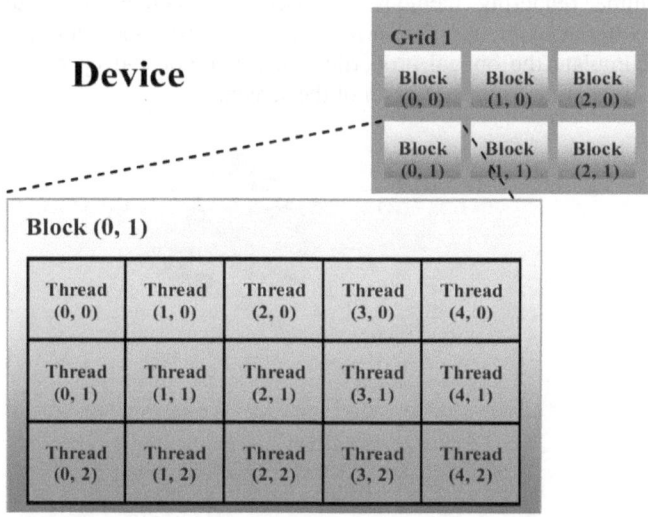

Fig. 3. Showing the distribution threads in CUDA [9] [14]

In the above figure the minimal execution unit is thread. The GPU is a device which computes several numbers of threads at a time. The CUDA API defines each thread according to its thread id and the batch of threads is organized as a block. Each block has its own block id. The batch of blocks is then organized as a grid [14]. One thread block can synchronize and efficiently shared through shared memory.

Systematically Processing flow on CUDA, as shown in Fig.4., has following steps:

1. Copy data from main memory to GPU memory.
2. CPU instructs the process to GPU.
3. GPU execute parallel in each core.
4. Copy the result from GPU memory to main memory.

The implementation of the ray casting architectures of volume visualization [4] [8] and ray casting method using CUDA can be observed from [7] [10] [11]. Changgong et. al [4] proposed a volume ray casting method which performs sampling within a ray segment using B-spline.

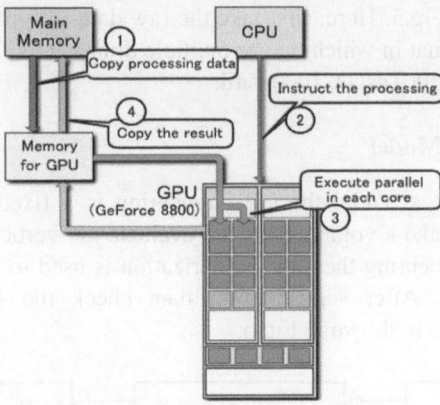

Fig. 4. Processing Flow on CUDA [9]

3   Proposed Methodology

Direct volume rendering or volume rendering method is used to generate 3D volume data visualization without extracting the surface geometry from the sampled data.

The basic idea is to accumulate the optical properties such as color and opacity as we travel along the ray emanating from each pixel of the screen. We have used a form of direct rendering approach called the Ray casting. It's a form of image rendering approach based on volume rendering. The whole procedure is defined as a block

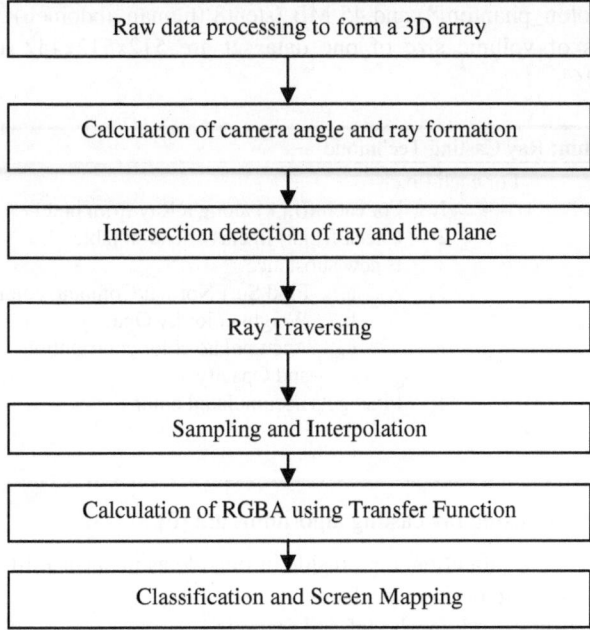

Fig. 5. Block Diagram of Proposed Methodology

diagram as shown in Fig.5. Here, first take the raw data for processing to form a 3D array. Raw data is format in which two or multiple dimensions. The volume rendering would be done on Nvidia Tesla C1060 card.

3.1   The Graphics Model

In the graphical process model the GPU rendering is a fixed pipeline mode. The approach would first take a volume data and evaluate the vertices. Then rasterization is applied for the segmenting the data. Rasterization is used to defining the data in a sequential grid form. After segmentation then check the frame cache for the segmented voxels. This is shown in Fig.6.

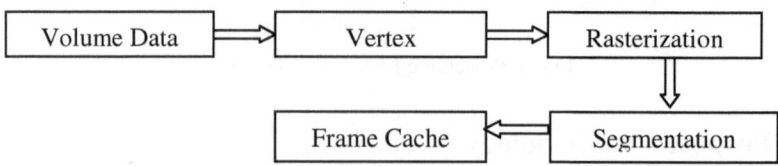

Fig. 6. Block Diagram of Rendering Pipeline

3.2   Ray Casting Implementation Using CUDA

Volume rendering is used for describing the visualization of 3D data. This visualizes the sampled functions of all three spatial dimensions by evaluating of the 2D projections. The volume rendering has been performed using two type of datasets of size 300 MB (colon_phantom8) and 45 MB (stent8 (human abdomen)) using CUDA. The dimensions of volume size of one data set are 512x512x442 and another is 512x512x128 [16].

Algorithm: Ray Casting Technique

For each Pixel
1.   For each f(i,j,k) along a Ray from pixel
2.   Check f(i,j,k) in classification tables
3.   If new substance
        a.   Find Surf Normal/Compute color
        b.   Weight color by Opacity
        c.   Accumulate color contribution
            and Opacity
4.   Pixel gets accumulated color

The advantages of using ray casting algorithms are [6]:

- No binary classification, e.g., inside or outside as in surface fitting methods
- Shows structure between surfaces
- Displays small and poorly defined features
- Readily parallelizes

Algorithm: CUDA-based Volume Rendering with Ray Casting Technique

---

(Each Block executes the following in parallel on GPU)

1. Render image using CUDA
   map backbuffer to get CUDA device pointer
       cutilSafeCall(cudaGraphicsMapResources());
       cutilSafeCall(cudaMemset());
   call CUDA kernel, writing results to backbuffer
       render_kernel(gridSize, blockSize, d_output, width,
       height, density, brightness, transferOffset,
       transferScale);
   Display results using OpenGL (called by GLUT)
   Now encode for performing the operations
       gridSize=dim3((width, blockSize. x), (height,
       blockSize. y));

2. Load raw data from disk
   void *loadRawFile()
   if (check fps limit) CUDA device with highest Gflops/s
   else (First initialize OpenGL context, so we can properly
       set the GL for CUDA then use command-line
       specified CUDA device, otherwise use device with
       highest Gflops/s)
   Then load volume data and synchronize
       cudaThreadSynchronize();
       calculate new grid size
       gridSize = dim3((width, blockSize.x), (height,
       blockSize.y));
   call CUDA kernel, writing results to Buffer
       copyInvViewMatrix(invViewMatrix,
       sizeof(float4)*3);
   Start timer 0 and process n plane loops on the GPU

3. Then free CUDA Buffer Memory
       freeCudaBuffers();

This system is doing by a single CUDA kernel. Conventional ray casting algorithms specify the ray attributes through the volume rendering of the volume dataset. In this algorithm, the opacity required for the changing the sampling rate globally or locally will be evaluated by equation 1:

$$\alpha_{corrected} = 1 - (1 - \alpha_{stored})^n \qquad (1)$$

Where, $\alpha_{corrected}$ is adjusted opacity and α_{stored} is opacity stored in transfer function. Transfer functions shows variation between opacity and scalar values. Now the whole algorithm is given below:

4   Experimental Results

We have implemented the ray casting based volume rendering using CUDA and tested it on a datasets of size 300 MB and 45 MB. The colon_phantom8 (512x512x442) and human abdomen (512x512x128) datasets can be downloaded from http://www.gris.uni-tuebingen.de/edu/areas/scivis/volren/datasets/new.html [16]. Skin transparency based on density achieved along with the ability to rotate camera. This is shown in Fig.7. and Fig.8.

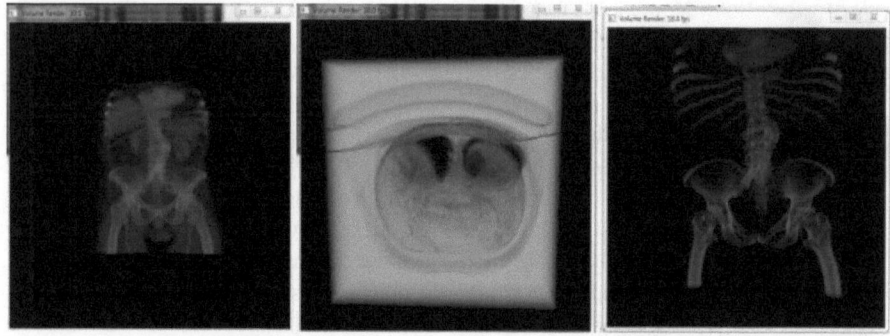

Fig. 7. Results from 45 MB dataset of human abdomen

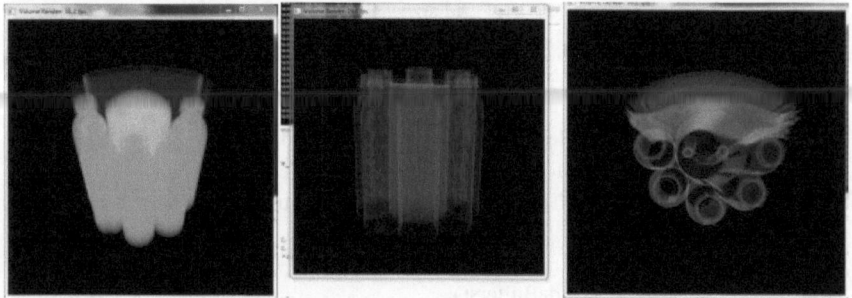

Fig. 8. Results including transparency from a 300MB dataset

The volume size of one data set is 512x512x442 and another is 512x512x128. These data sets give better result which is visualized with the help of ray casting algorithm using OpenGL in CUDA.

The above Table 1 and Fig.9 are showing the result analysis on two types of volume data sets. This shows that if use data of 512x512x442 in CPU the result would be problem in execution. But for another dataset CPU is given 10 fps which is less

Table 1. Comparison Results of performance on a NVIDIA Tesla C1060 GPU

Data Set Name	Volume Size Dimension	Rendering speed (FPS)	
		CPU	GPU(CUDA)
colon_phantom8	512x512x442	--	30
(300 MB)			
stent8 (human abdomen	512x512x128	10	40
45 MB)			

than as compared to GPU's result. Both data sets give almost 30 and 40 frames per second result with CUDA based rendering on GPU. The volume rendering has be done on a system equipped with Nvidia Tesla C1060 card with Nvidia GeForce 9500 GT. CUDA toolkit 4.0 is used in i7 950 CPU.

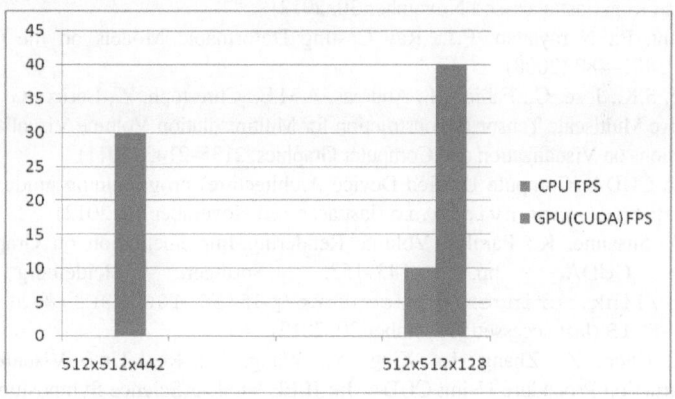

Fig. 9. Graph shows difference in CPU fps and GPU fps

5   Conclusion and Future Work

The advent of GPU's is changing the way complex computations were done till now. We envisaged that it would play a major role in the medical domain where doctors would be able to diagnose and analyze results provided by CT scans and MRI scans. The computational ability provided by the modern GPU's has enabled us to produce a three dimension interactive virtual human form.

To prototype the potential of CUDA in volume rendering, we used a data set of 300 MB through which we can zoom inside to get a better view or rotate to see the figure from a different angle. Further, through transparency change different organs hidden by layers of skin would also be visible.

The CUDA based code can be made to run on huge data sets of the order of giga bytes as explored in [15]. Currently a lot of research is going on in this front.

References

1. 1. Bi, W., Chen, Z., Zhang, L., Xing, Y., Wang, Y.: Real-Time Visualize the 3D Reconstruction Procedure Using CUDA. In: IEEE Nuclear Science Symposium Conference Record, pp. 883–886 (2009)
2. Zwecke, Eduard, Markus, Katja, Wien: GPU-based Multi-Volume Rendering of Complex Data in Neuroscience and Neurosurgery. PhD Thesis. Eurographics Digital Library Vienna University of Technology (2009), http://www.cg.tuwien.ac.at/research/publications/2009/beyer-2009-gpu/
3. James, K.T.: Ray Tracing Volume Densities. In: Proc. SIGGRAPH ACM, pp. 165–174 (1984)
4. Zhang, C., Xi, P., Zhang, C.: CUDA-based Volume Ray-Casting Using Cubic B-spline. In: IEEE International Conference on Virtual Reality and Visualization, pp. 84–88 (2011)
5. Wikipedia: Volume Ray Casting (last accessed November 10, 2012)
6. John, P.: Volume Visualization with Ray casting (1997), http://web.cs.wpi.edu/~matt/courses/cs563/talks/powwie/p1/ray-cast.htm (last accessed November 30, 2012)
7. Suryakant, P., Narayanan, P.J.: Ray Casting Deformable Models on the GPU. IEEE ICVGIP, 481–488 (2008)
8. Susanne, S.K., Jose, G., Fabio, M., Andreas, A.M.E., Chrestoph, Z., Enrico, G., Renato, P.: Interactive Multiscale Tensor Reconstruction for Multiresolution Volume Visualization. IEEE Transactions on Visualization and Computer Graphics, 2135–2143 (2011)
9. NVIDIA CUDA (Compute Unified Device Architecture) programming guide version 1.0 (2007), http://www.nvidia.in (last accessed November 26, 2012)
10. Jens, F., Susanne, K.: Parallel Volume Rendering Implementation on Graphics Cards Using CUDA, pp. 143–153. Springer, Heidelberg (2010), http://link.springer.com/content/pdf/10.1007%2F978-3-642-16233-6_15 (last accessed November 30, 2012)
11. Bi, W., Chen, Z., Zhang, L., Xing, Y., Wang, Y.: Real-Time Visualize the 3D Reconstruction Procedure Using CUDA. In: IEEE Nuclear Science Symposium Conf., pp. 883–886 (2009)
12. Milan, I., Joe, K., Aaron, L., Charles, H.: Volume Rendering Techniques. Book Randima Fernando. GPU Gems NVIDIA, pp. 667–672 (2004), http://http.developer.nvidia.com/GPUGems/gpugems_ch39.html (last accessed November 15, 2012)
13. Philipp, S., Maxim, M., Renato, P.: Extinction-based Shading and Illumination in GPU Volume Ray-Casting. IEEE Transactions on Visualization and Computer Graphics, 1795–1802 (2011)
14. Zhao, Y., Cui, X., Cheng, Y.: High-Performance and Real-Time Volume Rendering in CUDA. In: IEEE International Conference on Biomedical Engineering and Informatics China, pp. 1–4 (2009)
15. Agrawal, A., Josef, K., Gordon, C.J., Nigel, M.J., Feng, D., Marco, V., Fulvia, T., Debora, T.: Enabling the interactive display of large medical volume datasets by multiresolution bricking. ACM The Journal of Supercomputing, 3–19 (2010)
16. New Real World Medical Datasets, http://www.gris.uni-tuebingen.de/edu/areas/scivis/volren/datasets/new.html (last accessed December 20, 2012)

Enhancement of Screen Film Mammogram Up to a Level of Digital Mammogram

Aparna Bhale and Manish Joshi

School of Computer Sciences, North Maharashtra University, Jalgaon, India
{aparnakulkarnibhale,joshmanish}@gmail.com

Abstract. Breast cancer is one of the major causes of death among women. If a cancer can be detected early, the options of treatment and the chances of total recovery will increase. From a woman's point of view, the procedure practiced (compression of breasts to record an image) to obtain a digital mammogram (DM) is exactly the same that is used to obtain a screen film mammogram (SFM). The quality of DM is undoubtedly better than SFM.

However, obtaining DM is costlier and very few institutions can afford DM machines. According to the National Cancer Institute 92% of breast imaging centers in India do not have digital mammography machines [14] and they depend on the conventional SFM.

Hence in this context, one should answer 'Can SFM be enhanced up to a level of DM?' In this paper we discuss, our experimental analysis in this regard. We applied elementary image enhancement techniques to obtain enhanced SFM. We performed the quality analysis of digital mammogram and enhanced SFM using standard metrics like PSNR and RMSE on more than 350 mammograms. The results showed that the clarity of processed SFM is as good as digital mammogram.

Keywords: Mammogram, SFM, histogram, PSNR, RMSE.

1 Introduction

Breast cancer is the second largest, most common and deadly of all cancers, occurring in nearly one in ten women. Early detection is the key to improve diagnosis of breast cancer. The most efficient method for breast cancer early detection is mammography. A mammogram is an x-ray of a breast that is used to detect abnormalities in a breast, particularly breast cancer. But it is difficult to analyze mammograms manually due to the lack of clarity, two dimensional views, and complexities associated with the images. All women at risk go through mammography screening procedures for early detection and diagnosis of tumor. Analysis of mammograms is considered as one of the important tests in breast cancer detection. The efficiency and the precision of the analysis of mammograms is a key factor in such tests. An unambiguous and good quality image would be the best for analysis.

A. Agrawal et al. (Eds.): IITM 2013, CCIS 276, pp. 133–142, 2013.

Screen Film Mammogram (traditional mammograms) is produced on film, and a radiologist examines the developed image on a light box. Screen Film Mammography (SFM) or analogue mammograms have been used for more than 35 years and is still considered to be very good at detecting breast abnormalities at early stage. This technology has been used in detecting breast cancers, but it is not perfect. About 20% of breast cancers are missed by conventional mammography

Digital mammography is already available in many major cities, but may not be found everywhere just yet due to its cost constraint. Digital mammography systems cost about 1.5 to 4 times more than film systems. As far as accuracy is concerned both the methods have similar level of accuracy that is 92 % at ruling out breast cancer and the percentage of false positive were same for both the methods [11]. Although digital mammography has many potential advantages over traditional film mammography, clinical trials show that [10] the overall diagnostic accuracy levels of current digital and film mammography are similar when used in breast cancer screening.

In India, the incidences of breast cancer is increasing, with an estimated 80,000 new cases diagnosed annually [15]. Moreover, survey shows that 92% of breast imaging centers in India lack digital mammogram and are using SFM [14]. In spite of the considerable research being carried out on mammography and related technologies there is no conclusive work/method available which will focus on comparative study of traditional mammogram and digital mammogram. In this context, we decided to determine if quality of SFM can be enhanced up to a level of DM. The goal of this study is to compare the results of digital mammography system to a conventional screen film mammography system. We collected 450 digital mammogram images from Hedgewar hospital, Aurangabad, Maharashtra and 350 Screen film mammogram from Kodlikeri Hospital, Aurangabad, Maharashtra, India. We have a collection of both SFM and DM of approximately of 800 patients.

The remaining paper is organized as follows. Other researchers' work related to SFM, DM and enhancements of SFM for various applications are reviewed in Section 2. Section 3 outlines the image enhancement techniques used to transform raw SFM into an enhanced SFM. The details of approach used for comparative analysis followed by experimental analysis and observations are also presented in different subsection of section 3. Conclusions are put forth in section 4.

2   Related Work

Lot of research work have been carried out in the field of medical image processing and particularly in mammographic images. Both types of SFM and DM iamges are used for processing. The comparisons of SFM and DM are done using various other perspectives as discussed below.

Manish Joshi et al. [9] discussed various application areas that works with mammogram such as CAD, Image compression applications, Content based

Image Retrieval (CBIR) etc. in detail. Using screen-film mammography and soft-copy digital mammography Eric A. Berns et al. [1] compared the acquisition time and interpretation times and observed that the use of digital mammography for screening examinations significantly shortened acquisition time but significantly increased interpretation time.

A comparative study on SFM and digital mammography was done [1] [5] [3] [13] and John D. Keen [3] found that almost all (91%) digital mammography facilities in the United States use computer aided detection, compared with 49% for film screening facilities. Kerlikowske [6] shown evidence that benefits outweigh the harms before the medical community adopts new technologies, specifically regarding computer-aided detection. Wagner Iared et al. [13] focus was on the comparison of the performance of digital mammography and film mammography in terms of cancer detection rates, patient recall rates and characteristics of the tumors detected. Karla Kerlikowske et al. [4] found that the proportion of cancer cases diagnosed at an early stage varies due to the sensitivity and specificity of each modality by age, tumor characteristics, breast density, and menopausal status. The studies to date do not support the advantage of DM over SFM when used for diagnostic mammography [7] [12].

Sara Dehghani and et al. [2] suggested a method to improve the background as mammography images have dark background, these parts are not important in processing of mammography images. Three steps were used to achieve this. By the usage of the pixels brightness the excessive image parts which are in the two sides of the image are omitted in the first phase. In the second phase the distinction of the breast direction is done by using threshold limit of gray level of the two halves of the image and put all images in one direction. The third phase is the breast region segmentation from the background, they do this work by the usage of series of point operations and the growing region method.

Marcia Koomen et al. [8] discussed the use of newer versions of mammography, such as digital mammography, with tomosynthesis and digital subtraction mammography with different tools for women at high risk and also the use of tools that might be useful for less invasive therapy of breast cancer with imaging to monitor the efficacy of the therapy.

The details of experimental analysis are explained in the next section.

3   Experimental Analysis

In order to determine the fate of analogue mammography machines after the emergence and influence of digital mammography systems, we are testing if enhanced SFM image can be as satisfactory as a DM? We have decided to perform comparative analysis of enhanced SFM and DM. The experiments are carried out in two phases. Firstly, applying preliminary image enhancement techniques to obtain enhanced SFM images. Secondly, obtain comparative analysis between enhanced SFM and DM. The following subsections elaborate image enhancement, our approach for comparative analysis and the comparative results thereof.

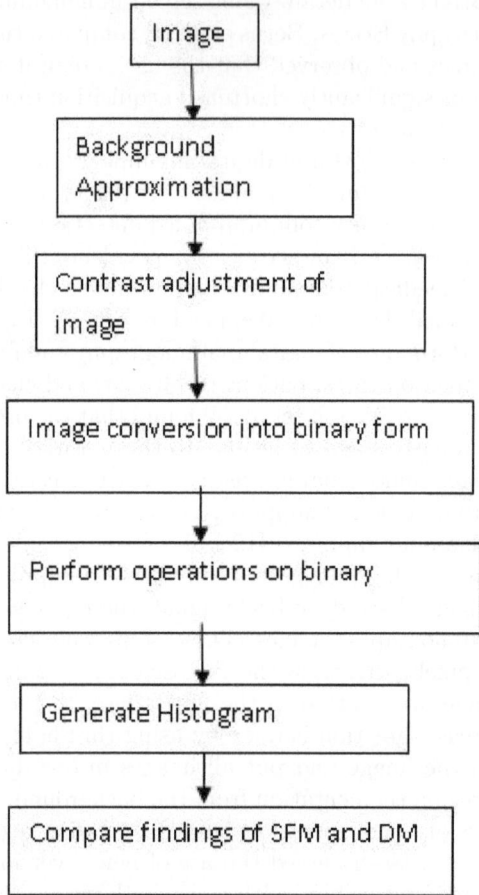

Fig. 1. Procedure for enhancement of SFM

3.1 Enhancement of SFM

Original and unprocessed mammographic images are not suitable for medical prognosis. These images warrant a preprocessing phase in order to reveal explicit features/information that helps in critical decision making. Image enhancement and feature extraction are two distinctive aspects of preprocessing. We have implemented preprocessing steps on the screen film mammograms to enhance the original SFMs.

In order to compare the enhanced SFM with DM the first step is of image enhancement. We applied a series of image enhancement techniques on a raw SFM as depicted in Figure 1. The steps shown pictorially are described in detail as follows.

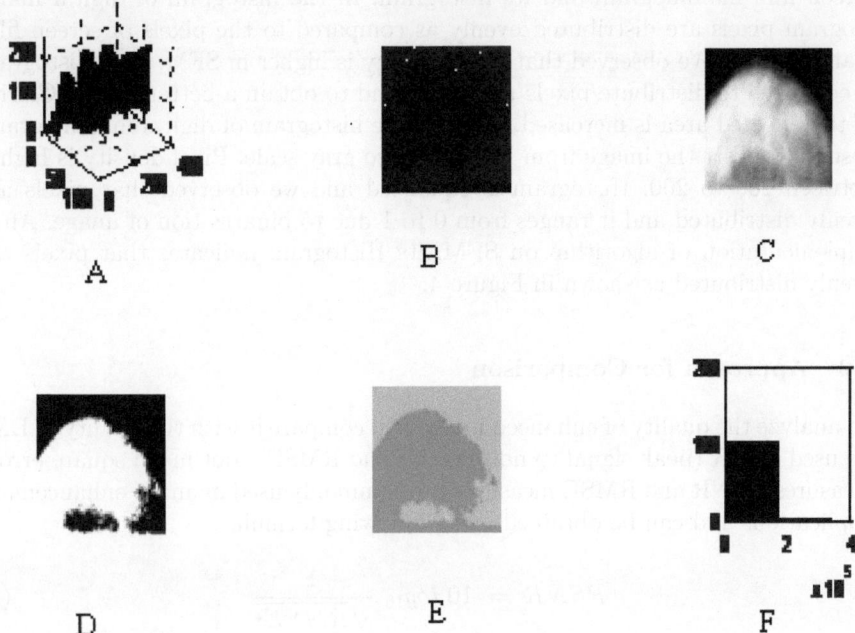

Fig. 2. Intermediate images obtained during SFM Image enhancement

1. **Image Reading:** Read a SFM image from a dataset and next step is to work upon an uneven background of a mammogram.
2. **Background Approximation:** Sara Dehghani and et al.[14] suggested a method to improve the background of mammographic images as these images have dark background. Hence, we performed background approximation as illustrate in following two sub steps.
   (a) We observe background illumination is brighter in the center of the image than at the bottom as observed in Figure 2A.
   (b) Figure 2B shows that background is approximated to reduce the noise.
3. **Contrast stretching:** Pixels are adjusted uniformly to enhance the clarity of a image by contrast stretching method and Figure 2C represents the same.
4. **Binary Image:** The next step is to convert the contrast stretched image into binary form as shown in Figure 2D.
5. **RGB Image:** Once image is converted into binary form, we obtain RGB labeled image. Three distinct parts of mammogram namely malignant, benign and normal parts can be represented using RGB labeled image as shown in Figure 2E.
6. **Histogram of Processed SFM:** Due to binarisation of an image, pixels of image are distributed uniformly in the range of 0 to 1 as shown in Figure 2F.

We have implemented above stated steps for all the images and few sample images are as shown in Figures (2 and 3). An upper section of Figure 3 represents digital mammogram and its histogram. Lower section of Figure 3 shows screen film mammogram and its histogram. In the histogram of digital mammogram pixels are distributed evenly as compared to the pixels of screen film mammogram. We observed that pixel density is higher in SFM. This histogram is equalized to distribute pixels uniformly and to obtain a better image. Clarity of the affected area is increased. To generate histogram of digital mammogram, first we convert the image from RGB scale to gray scale. Pixel density is higher between 100 to 200. Histogram is equalized and we observed that pixels are evenly distributed and it ranges from 0 to 1 due to binarization of image. After implementation of algorithm on SFM, its Histogram indicates that pixels are evenly distributed as shown in Figure 4.

3.2   Approach for Comparison

To analyze the quality of enhanced image and compare it with the quality of DM, we used PSNR (peak signal to noise ratio) and RMSE (root mean square error) measures. PSNR and RMSE measures are commonly used in image enhancement applications and can be obtained using following formulas.

$$PSNR = 10 \, log_{10} \, \frac{1}{\sqrt{RMSE^2}} \tag{1}$$

$$RMSE = \sqrt{\frac{\sum [f(i,j) - F(i,j)]^2}{MN}} \tag{2}$$

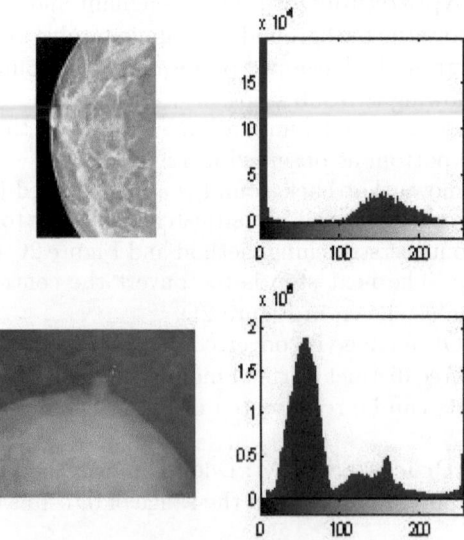

Fig. 3. Images of DM and SFM with their corresponding histograms

Here, f (i, j) is a noisy image, F (i, j) is an enhanced image and M stands for rows and N for columns of an image. If the value of RMSE is low and the value of PSNR is also low then the enhancement approach is better.

In order to compare quality of enhanced SFM and DM, we have to adopt an indirect method. Because of the excessive pains involved due to compression of breasts we could not insist for SFM as well as DM of a same patient. Hence, we do not have SFM and DM of the same breasts. Its a typical case of shortage of sample cases for experimentation. We therefore have to follow and indirect method to obtain comparative analysis between enhanced SFM and DM images.

We have decided to overcome the problem of non-availability of same patient's SFM and DM for comparison using following approach. We have identified a DM that has similar orientation as most of the SFMs that we have as a 'Reference DM'. We used this 'Reference DM' for comparative analysis purpose. The comparative analysis is obtained in two steps.

1. We compared 'Reference DM' with original SFMs and enhanced SFMs. Average PSNR and RMSE values are obtained. We labeled these calculated values as $PSNR_{SfmDm}, RMSE_{SfmDm}$ and $PSNR_{EnSfmDm}, RMSE_{EnSfmDm}$ respectively.
2. We obtain PSNR and RMSE values among a few DMs and the average PSNR and RMSE values obtained are labeled as $PSNR_{DM}$ and $RMSE_{DM}$ respectively.

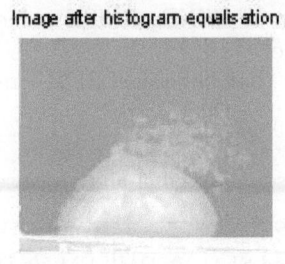

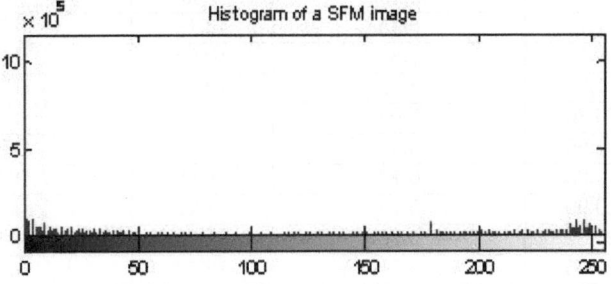

Fig. 4. Processed SFM and its histogram

Lower the PSNR and RMSE values, better the enhancement. The difference between average PSNR, RMSE values among the three types of images helped us to draw some observations.

The details of our results and the observations are presented in the next subsection.

3.3   Comparative Analysis

We have implemented algorithm on more than 350 images and obtained the values of PSNR and RMSE. Out of 350 examples few are listed in Table 1.

Table 1 indicates the values of $PSNR_{EnSfmDm}, RMSE_{EnSfmDm}$ (11.67, 0.53) of enhanced SFM when compared with DM are low as compare to the values of $PSNR_{SfmDm}, RMSE_{SfmDm}$ (-21.28, 5.56). It clearly indicates that if we compare the image clarity of original SFM with digital mammogram, digital mammograms' clarity is more. When the original SFM image is enhanced the enhanced SFM can meet the standard of digital mammogram very well.

When we observe the average PSNR and RMSE values we can conclude that:

1. As the $PSNR_{EnSfmDm}, RMSE_{EnSfmDm}$ values are considerably smaller than the values of $PSNR_{SfmDm}, RMSE_{SfmDm}$ we can say that enhanced SFM are qualitatively more superior than original SFM and relatively more similar to DM.
2. Even the average $PSNR_{DM}$ and $RMSE_{DM}$ among a few DM (8.33, 0.38) is very close to the average values of $PSNR_{EnSfmDm}, RMSE_{EnSfmDm}$ that is (11.67, 0.53). We can observe that PSNR, RMSE values between an enhanced SFM are similar to that of PSNR, RMSE values when any two DMs are compared with each other.

   Hence, we can conclude that enhanced SFM can be improved upto a level that of DM.

Table 1. Comparison of original and processed SFM with DM

Sr. No.	PSNR		PSNR	
	SFM Vs DM	Enhanced SFM Vs DM	SFM Vs DM	Enhanced SFM Vs DM
1	-19.17	5.19	9.09	0.54
2	-21.71	5.35	12.18	0.53
3	-20.52	5.80	10.62	0.51
4	-21.91	5.71	12.46	0.51
5	-20.86	5.03	11.04	0.56
6	-22.66	3.35	13.58	0.67
7	-19.93	6.17	9.92	0.49
8	-20.99	5.15	11.21	0.55
9	-20.89	6.76	11.09	0.45
10	-22.75	4.11	13.72	0.62
11	-22.67	6.95	13.61	0.44
12	-21.24	7.12	11.54	0.44
Avg.	-21.28	5.56	11.67	0.53

Table 2. Comparison among digital mammograms

Sr. No.	Comparing DM	PSNR	RMSE
1	D1 Vs D2	10.34	0.30
2	D2 Vs D3	8.07	0.39
3	D3 Vs D4	7.62	0.41
4	D4 Vs D5	8.63	0.37
5	D5 Vs D6	9.76	0.32
6	D6 Vs D7	7.80	0.40
7	D7 Vs D8	7.13	0.43
8	D8 Vs D9	7.63	0.41
9	D9 Vs D10	8.17	0.39
10	D10 Vs D1	8.16	0.39
Avg.		**8.33**	**0.38**

4   Conclusions

A vast research is being carried out on mammography. Still there is a huge scope for research which will help medical experts for better diagnosis. This may help to reduce mortality rate due to breast cancer.

In this paper we obtained comparative analysis of SFM and DM to determine that whether SFMs can still be used in the era of Digital Mammography systems. We compare the features of digital mammograms with the features of SFM in order to analyze their significance. Various image enhancement techniques applied on the SFM. After the implementations of preprocessing methods, performed qualitative analysis by using PSNR and RMSE techniques and observed that the both the values are low indicating enhancement approach is better. Result showed that the clarity of processed SFM is as good as digital mammogram. We conclude here that due to cost constraint use of traditional mammogram machine (SFM) is more in India. So we can apply appropriate image enhancement techniques to SFMs to obtain the clarity of digital mammograms.

Acknowledgment. The authors wish to thank Dr. U. V. Takalkar [M.S. (Gen.Surg.) M.E.D.S FUICC (SWITZERLAND) FAIS, MSSAT (USA), Cancer, General & Endoscopic Surgeon Fellow Johns Hopkins (USA) Chairman, Kodlikeri Memorial Hospital] for their support and valuable guidance. Images were provided by Kodlikeri memorial Hospital, Aurangabad and Hedgewar Hospital, Aurangabad, Maharashtra, India.

References

1. Berns, E.A., Edward Hendrick, R., et al.: Digital and Screen- Film Mammography: Comparison of Image Acquisition and Interpretation Times. American Journal of Radiology/org/cgi (2006)

2. Dehghani, S., et al.: A Method For Improve Preprocessing Images Mammography. International Journal of Information and Education Technology 1(1) (April 2011) ISSN: 2010-3689

3. Keen, J.D.: MBA Stroger Hospital of Cook County Chicago, IL 60612, Annals of Internal Medicine 248, American College of Physicians (2012)

4. Kerlikowske, K., et al.: Comparative Effectiveness of Digital Versus Film-Screen Mammography in Community Practice in the United States - A Cohort Study. Ann. Intern. Med. 155, 493–502 (2011)

5. Kerlikowske, K., Hubbard, R.A., Miglioretti, D.L., Geller, B.M., Yankaskas, B.C., Lehman, C.D., et al.: Breast Cancer Surveillance Consortium. Comparative effectiveness of digital versus film-screen mammography in community practice in the United States: a cohort study. Ann. Intern. Med. 155, 493–502 (2011) (PMID: 22007043)

6. Kerlikowske, K.: A call for evidence of benefits outweighing harms before implementing new technologies: comment on Diffusion of computer-aided mammography after mandated Medicare coverage. Arch. Intern. Med. 170, 990–991 (2010) (PMID: 20548014)

7. Kim, H.H., Pisano, E.D., Cole, E.B., et al.: Comparison of calcication specicity in digital mammography using soft-copy display versus screen-lm mammography. Am. J. Roentgenol. 187, 47–50 (2006)

8. Koomen, M., Pisano, E.D., et al.: Future Directions in Breast Imaging. J. Clin. Oncol. 23, 1674–1677 (2005)

9. Joshi, M., Bhale, A.K.: Computational Unfoldment of Mammograms. In: Proceedings of PRIME 2012, March 21-23. IEEE Xplore, Salem (2012)

10. Pisano, E.D., Gatsonis, C., Hendrick, E., Yaffe, M., Baum, J., Acharyya, S., Conant, E., Fajardo, L., Bassett, L., DOrsi, C., Jong, R., Rebner, M.: Diagnostic performance of digital versus film mammography for breast cancer screening. New England J. Med. 353(17), 1773–1783 (2005)

11. Stephan, P.: Digital Mammography Compares Well With Film Mammography New and Old Machines Equally Accurate - Younger Women Benefit Most, About.com Guide (updated June 15, 2010)

12. Tice, J.A., Feldman, M.: Full-eld digital mammography compared with screen-lm mammography in the detection of breast cancer: rays of light through DMIST or more fog? Breast Cancer Res. Treat. (March 22, 2007), doi:10.1007/s10549-007-9545-4

13. Iared, W., et al.: Comparative evaluation of digital mammography and film mammography: systematic review and meta-analysis. Sao Paulo Med. J. 129(4), 250–260 (2011); Med. 155, 493–502 (2011); Annals of Internal Medicine 155(8), W–155 (2011)

14. http://healthcarehacks.com/are-digital-mammograms-worth-theextra-cost

15. http://nitawriter.wordpress.com/2007/04/26/india-has-one-of-the-highest-cancer-rates-in-the-world

An Object Separability Based No-Reference Image Quality Measure Using Statistical Properties of Objects

De Kanjar and V. Masilamani

Indian Institute of Information Technology Design & Manufacturing
Kancheepuram Chennai-600127, India
kanjar.de@gmail.com

Abstract. In many modern image processing applications determining quality of the image is one of the most challenging tasks. Researchers working in the field of image quality assessment design algorithms for measuring and quantifying image quality. The human eye can identify the difference between a good quality image and a noisy image by simply looking at the image, but designing a computer algorithm to automatically determine the quality of an image is a very challenging task. In this paper we propose an image quality measure using the concept of object separability. We define object separability using variance. Two objects are very well separated if variance of individual object is less and mean pixel values of neighboring objects are very different.

Keywords: Image Quality, No-Reference image quality, Object separability.

1 Introduction

Determination of quality of a given image is extremely useful in certain applications of image processing, for example in medical images noisy images may lead to improper diagnosis. Most of the basic techniques to find quality of images require the use of reference images of the same scene to determine the quality of the test image. These techniques are known as full-reference image quality assessment (FR-IQA) techniques. The image quality measures which need a references image of the same scene are Peak Signal to Noise ratio(PSNR)[3], Structural Similarity Index Measure(SSIM)[4], Visual Information fidelity (VIF)[2].

The next class of image quality assessment algorithms also needs a reference image of the same scene but instead of using the full reference image they use only certain features of the reference image and with those features they determine the image quality measure of the given test image, these techniques are known as Reduced reference image quality assessment (RR-IQA) techniques. One of the examples of latest Reduced Reference Image Quality Assessment is RRED [12].

The next class of image quality assessment techniques does not require any reference image for calculating image quality measure and these techniques are known as No-Reference image quality assessment techniques (NR-IQA) [5]. Some of the latest

A. Agrawal et al. (Eds.): IITM 2013, CCIS 276, pp. 143–153, 2013.

No-reference image quality techniques are DIVINE [6], Blinds2 [7], using visual codebooks [14] and BRISQUE [8] [9]. Few of the no-reference techniques are distortion-specific for example, for JPEG image compression there are spe- cific techniques mentioned in [10],[11]. The goal of this paper is to quantify the quality of a given image without the use of reference images and the measure value must be able to convey whether the image is good or noisy and to what extent the image is noisy.

The basis for our measure is that the pixels in a particular segment have values closer to each other and two different segments must be well separated in a good quality image. Based on these two ideas we come up with a measure which consists of a vector which has two terms, one on each of the concepts explained above. In Section 2 we will provide the theoretical concept on which our model is based. In Section 3, we will provide our measure and in Section 4 we will present the results and finally we conclude with brief concluding remarks in section 5.

2   Preliminaries

Object in an image is nothing but a segment where the pixel values are close to one another [1]. An object may differ from its surroundings in shape, size, texture, color etc. An object is said to be well separated from the surroundings when the difference between the pixel values in the object are very small and the difference between the pixel values of the object and surrounding is considerably high. In human perception the quality is good when the object is well discriminated from its immediate surroundings [1]. We calculate certain spatial domain statistical properties to determine how close the pixel values object segment are and how well separated the object is from its immediate surroundings. In noisy images the discrimination between object and its immediate surroundings is less accurate as compared to good images. Our image quality measure is based on object separability. The concept of object separability is explained by the example in figure 1, there are four regions marked and we consider each region as a separate object and in a good image each object must be distinct and easily differentiable from other objects. The measure we propose in this paper is a vector with two components, W and B. The component W measures the closeness of the pixel values within an object. The variance within a segment should be very less. We compute variance within each individual segment and sum up for all the segments in the image. The other component B measures how well separated objects are from its surroundings, to compute we consider the difference between average pixel values between adjacent segments, and we take sum of these difference for all pairs of adjacent segments. For example, in figure 1 we compute W by taking variance from all the four individual objects multiplying the variance with probability of the segment and finally summing up for all the four segments. We compute B by considering adjacent segment pairs (1,2),(1,3),(2,3),(3,4),(2,4) and for each pair we find the difference of means of adjacent segments multiplied with their corresponding probabilities and finally summing up the products from all adjacent pairs. We multiply the probability of segment terms in both *W* and *B* components to find the contribution of the particular segment to the quality measure. For instance a larger object must have more influence on the quality measure than a smaller object, the probability terms in the components are for this purpose only.

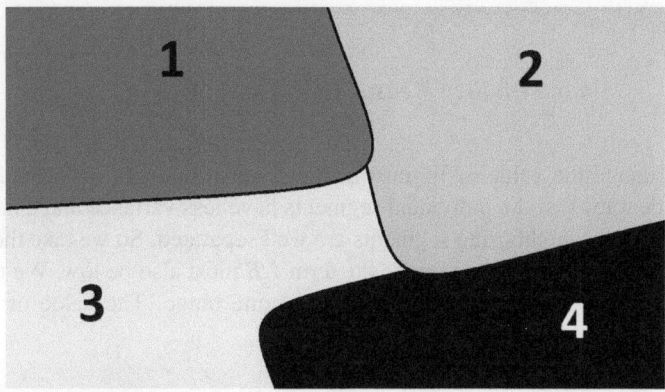

Fig. 1. Image as component of different segments

3   Proposed Image Quality Measure

Let us consider an Image *I*, we are proposing a measure which is a vector *(W, B)*. *W* denotes the measure computed within the segments and B denotes the measure computed between the adjacent segments.

Calculation of W:
Let *N* = number of segments in the image *I*.
Let T_N = Total number of pixels in the image *I*.
Let μ_i = mean pixel value in the ith segment, where i = *1, 2... N*
Let σ_i = variance of pixel values in the ith segment, where i = *1, 2... N*
Let T_i be the number of pixels in i^{th} segment, where *i = 1, 2... N*.
Let p_i be the probability of pixels in the ith segment where *i=1, 2 ...N*.

$$p_i = \frac{T_i}{T_N} \tag{1}$$

$$W = \sum_{i=1}^{N} p_i \times \sigma_i \tag{2}$$

Calculation of B:
Let p_i and p_j be the probability of pixels in the ith segment and j^{th} segment respectively, where *i, j=1, 2, ...N*. and $i \neq j$ and *i, j* are adjacent segments

Let μ_i and μ_j be the mean of pixels in the ith segment and j^{th} segment respectively where $i, j=1, 2, ...N.$ and $i \neq j$ and i, j are adjacent segments.
Let M be a pair of adjacent segments.

$$B = \sum_{k=1}^{M} p_i \times p_j \times \left(\mu_i - \mu_j\right)^2 \tag{3}$$

$$Image\ Quality\ Measure(QM) = W + \frac{1}{k \times B} \tag{4}$$

For a good image the value of W must be small and value of B must be high. Small value of W denotes that the individual segments have less variance and a high value of B denotes that two neighboring segments are well separated. So we take the inverse of B component so that for a good image the term $1/B$ must also be low. We need a multiplying factor k to make two components in same range. The value of k has been experimentally found to be 10000.

4   Results

We have used the Berkeley Segmentation (BSD500) dataset [13] for our analysis purpose as our algorithm requires segmented images and since Berkeley BSD500 data set provides us with segmented images for our analysis. We have tested our algorithm with images distorted with Salt pepper, speckle and Gaussian noise and we present our results.

We have considered three types of noise for our analysis purpose. Firstly we consider salt-pepper noise, we run our algorithm and compute image quality measure (QM) for all images of the dataset, then we introduce salt-pepper noise with noise density d and we increase d gradually and compute the quality measure. We observe that as noise density increases the quality measure (QM) increases which means higher the value of quality measure QM, the lower is the quality of image. Next we consider images distorted with speckle noise, we run the algorithm for different variances of speckle noise for the same images and we observe the similar increasing trend as we observed with salt-pepper noise. Finally we do our analysis with images distorted with gaussian noise with zero mean and we vary the variance and we observe that when the noise in the image increases the quality measure gives a higher value, from which we can infer that the quality of the image is poor.

We observe the trend in all the images of the Berkeley (BSD500) dataset. We consider the image shown in figure 2 and we represent graphically the trends shown by our algorithm and one of the latest state of the art no-reference image quality assessment technique BRISQUE and also PSNR on this image in figures 3-5 respectively.

We observe both BRISQUE and our image quality measure (QM) show an increasing trend when noise in the image increases we get a higher value as quality measure. The trend shown by our image quality measure (QM) is almost linearly proportional to the increase in noise. This particular trend is not only specific to this particular example but all the images of the BSD500 dataset. PSNR measure shows a decreasing trend which means a higher value of the PSNR refers to a better quality of image and as the image becomes noisier the corresponding PSNR value decreases.

Next we explain one of the applications of our algorithm with example, let us consider images in figure 6 degraded with salt and pepper noise, now do median filtering to remove noise from the image. We observe that our algorithm gives a better quality measure when the image is filtered by 7×7 in comparison with 5×5 or 3×3 median filter.

(a) Image with no noise

(b) Image with Salt-Pepper Noise with noise density 0.05

(c) Image with Speckle Noise with variance 0.05

(d) Image with Gaussian Noise with zero mean and variance 0.05

Fig. 2. Example of original and noisy images

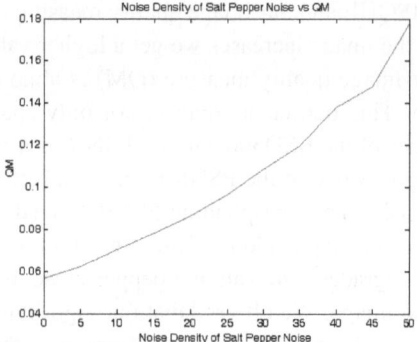

(a) Proposed Image Quality Measure (QM) vs. Noise Density of Salt-Pepper Noise

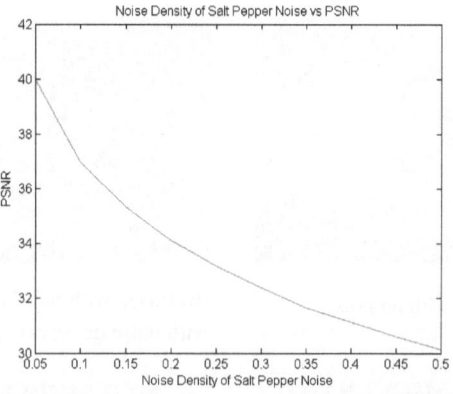

(b) PSNR vs. Noise Density of Salt-Pepper Noise

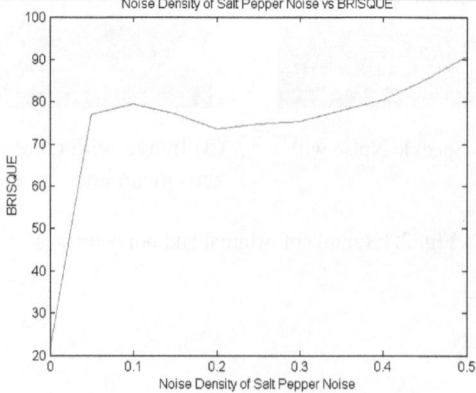

(c) BRISQUE vs. Noise Density of Salt-Pepper Noise

Fig. 3. Image Quality measures for varying salt-pepper Noise

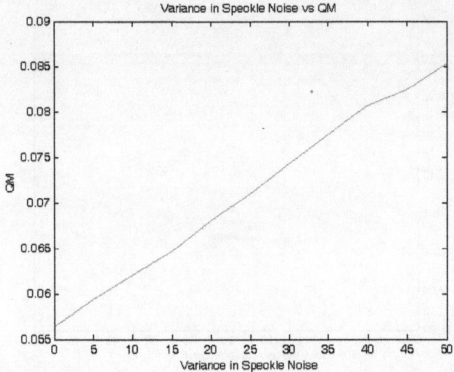

(a) Proposed Image Quality Measure (QM) vs. Vari-ance in Speckle Noise

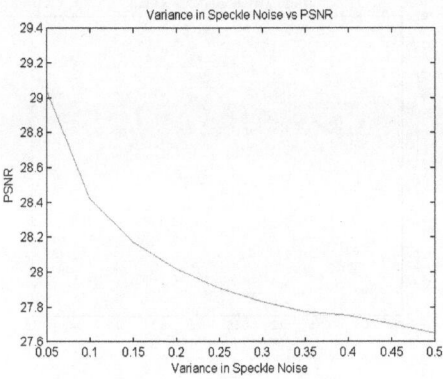

(b) PSNR vs. Variance in Speckle Noise

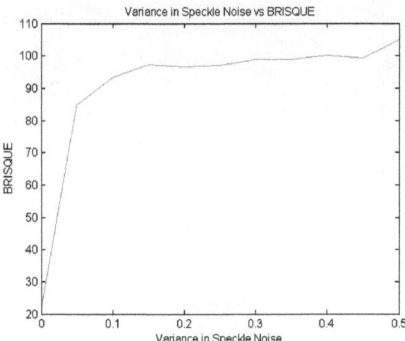

(c) BRISQUE vs. Variance in Speckle Noise

Fig. 4. Image Quality measures for varying speckle Noise

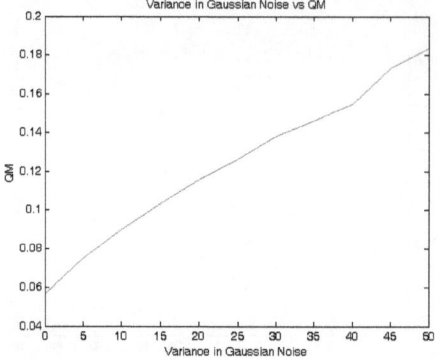

(a) Proposed Image Quality Measure (QM) vs. vs.Variance in Gaussian Noise

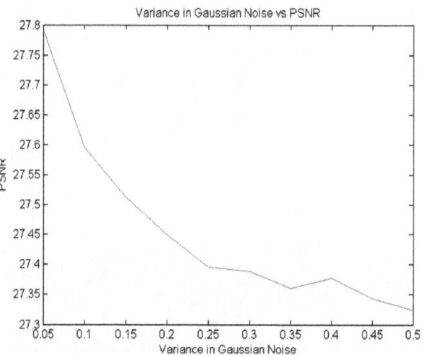

(b) PSNR vs. Variance of Gaussian Noise

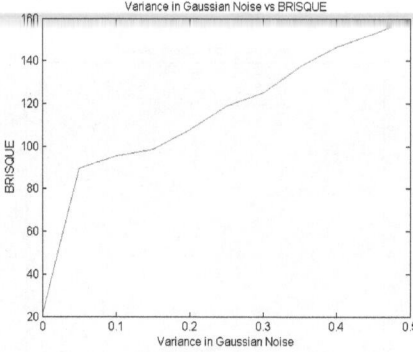

(c) BRISQUE vs. Variance of Gaussian Noise

Fig. 5. Image Quality measures for varying Gaussian Noise

(a) Image with Salt-Pepper Noise with noise density 0.05 QM = 0.0594

(b) Image denoised with 3 × 3 median filter QM= 0.0465

(c) Image denoised with 5 × 5 median filter QM= 0.0421

(d) Image denoised with 7 × 7 median filter QM= 0.0409

Fig. 6. Quality Measure behavior after denoising the image

5   Conclusion

Currently the proposed image quality measure works only for grayscale images. This measure is heavily dependent on the quality of segmentation algorithm which is one of the limitations of this measure. For our experimental results we have used Berkeley segmentation (BSD500) dataset where the dataset is already segmented manually. The efficiency of our proposed measure is dependent on the efficiency of the image segmentation algorithm. Our image quality measure fails to give the quality of the measure in case of blurred images. The advantage of our technique is that there is no requirement of a reference image of the same scene. Currently work is going onto improve our image quality measure to incorporate blurred images also. Another advantage is that our image quality measure values increase almost linearly when noise increases linearly for salt-pepper and Gaussian noise, where as standard NR-IQA algorithms like BRISQUE does not show linear trend for all images.

References

1. Blake, R., Sekuler, R.: Perception. McGraw-Hill Higher Education (2006)
2. Sheikh, H.R., Bovik, A.C.: Image Information and Visual Quality. IEEE Transactions on Image Processing 15(2), 430–444 (2006)
3. Eskicioglu, A.M., Fishers, P.S.: Image Quality Measures and their Performance. IEEE Transactions on Communications 43(12), 2959–2965 (1995)
4. Wang, Z., Bovik, A.C., Sheikh, H.R., Simoncelli, E.P.: Image Quality Assessment: From Error Visibility to Structural Similarity. IEEE Transactions on Image Processing 13(4), 735–759 (2004)
5. Wang, Z., Bovik, A.C.: Modern Image Quality Assessment. Morgan and Claypool, San Rafael (2006)
6. Moorthy, A.K., Bovik, A.C.: Blind Image Quality Assessment: From Natural Scene Statistics to Perceptual Quality. IEEE Transactions on Image Processing 20(12), 3350–3364 (2011)
7. Saad, M.A., Bovik, A.C.: Blind Image Quality Assessment: A Natural Scene Statistics Approach in the DCT Domain. IEEE Transactions on Image Processing 21(8), 3339–3352 (2012)
8. Mittal, A., Moorthy, A.K., Bovik, A.C.: Referenceless Image Spatial Quality Evaluation Engine. In: 45th Asilomar Conference on Signals, Systems and Computers (November 2011)
9. Mittal, A., Moorthy, A.K., Bovik, A.C.: No-Reference Image Quality Assessment in the Spatial Domain. IEEE Transactions on Image Processing (2012) (to appear)
10. Wang, Z., Sheikh, H.R., Bovik, A.C.: No-reference perceptual quality assess ment of JPEG compressed images. In: IEEE International Conference on Image Processing, vol. 1, pp. I-477–I-480 (September 2002)
11. Wang, Z., Bovik, A.C., Evans, B.I.: Blind measurement of Blocking artifact in images. In: Proceedings of IEEE International Conference of Acoustics, Speech and Signal Processing, pp. 3.977–3.980 (September 2000)

12. Soundararajan, R., Bovik, A.C.: RRED Indices: Reduced Reference Entropic Differencing for Image Quality Assessment. IEEE Transactions on Image Processing 21(2), 517–526 (2012)
13. Martin, D., Fowlkes, C., Tal, D., Malik, J.: A database of human segmented natural images and its application to evaluating segmentation algorithms and measuring ecological statistics. In: 8th International Conference on Computer Vision, vol. 2, pp. 416–423 (2001)
14. Ye, P., Dorman, D.: No-Reference Image Quality Assessment using Visual Codebooks. IEEE Transactions on Image Processing 21(7), 3129–3138 (2012)

Generation of Future Image Frames
for an Image Sequence

Nishchal K. Verma[1], Ankan Bansal[1], and Shikha Singh[2]

[1] Indian Institute of Technology Kanpur, Kanpur, India
[2] Banasthali University, Rajasthan, India

Abstract. A way of generating the future frames of an image sequence is presented. In this paper first we present a way of predicting the future positions of rigid moving objects in a given sequence of images from a static camera.The moving object is first extracted from the images and its centroid is found as a measure of its position. These positions are used to find the future positions of the object using Artificial Neural Network models. This approach is found to predict the positions with very good accuracy. Next we give an algorithm for generating complete future image frames. The optical flow of the images is calculated to find the velocity of each pixel. Time series of the velocities are constructed for each pixel for both dimensions. A separate neural network model is used to predict the future velocities of each pixel and the pixels are then mapped to their new positions. Two different types of neural network models(sigmoidal function networks and radial basis function networks) have been used.

1 Introduction

The concept of future image generation can be very helpful in defence applications like early prediction of target trajectory, in robot motion and in numerous other fields of commercial and strategic interests. Appropriate actions can be taken based on these images. This work focuses on finding a technique to predict the images in advance to assist in such actions. Attempts have been made at generating future images of cyclones using fuzzy models [1] [10] and artificial neural networks [2] [11]. For early knowledge of the future images, information present in the given image sequence has to be exploited. This work relates to image prediction that is very important for day-to-day and strategic application. This approach makes use of the artificial neural network models' ability to predict the values in a time series. Many earlier attempts have successfully made use of artificial neural networks for time series prediction [3] [4].

For the first part of this work, the moving object is to be extracted from the images. For this, background is removed from each frame and then the centroid of the moving object is found and used as a measure of its position. Thus a time series of the object positions is created. This is used to predict the future positions of the object. This work would be helpful to improve the position

A. Agrawal et al. (Eds.): IITM 2013, CCIS 276, pp. 154–162, 2013.

prediction of moving objects and to plan and execute actions based on these predictions.

Next we propose methods of generating complete future image frames of the given sequence of images. Optical flow [8] techniques have been used to find the velocity of each pixel in both x and y directions. Thus, two time series are obtained for each pixel. Neural network models are trained on these time series and the future velocities are predicted. Using these predicted velocities the pixel are mapped to their future values and frames are generated.

The rest of the paper is arranged as follows: Sect. 2 explains the formulation of artificial neural networks for the prediction of time series. In Sect. 3, the extraction of the moving objects from the image sequence and the formation of time series is discussed. Section 4 explains the estimation of optical flow. The step-wise algorithm for the second part of the paper is given in Sect. 5. Section 6 presents the results obtained and finally, conclusions are drawn in Sect. 7.

2   Artificial Neural Network Model

Neural Networks have been widely used as time series forecasters. Typically this approach has been used for market predictions [5] [9], and meteorological forecasting [6].

The problem of forecasting time series with ANN is considered as modeling the relationship of the value of the element at time "t" and the values of the previous elements of the time series $(t\text{-}1,t\text{-}2,...,t\text{-}k)$ to obtain a function as it is shown:

$$a_t = f(a_{t-1}, a_{t-2}, ...a_{t-k}) \tag{1}$$

The standard neural network method of performing time series prediction is to induce the function f using a feedforward function approximating neural network architecture, using a set of k-tuples as inputs and a single output as the target value of the network. This method is called the *sliding window technique* as the k-tuple input slides over the full training set. Figure 1 gives the basic architecture.

2.1   Sigmoidal Function Networks

Each neuron in a sigmoidal function network has the sigmoid function, $b(x) = \frac{1}{1+e^{-x}}$, as its activation function. Hence this technique can be seen as an extension of auto-regression time series modelling, in which the function f is supposed to be a linear combination of a fixed number of previous series values. Such a restriction does not apply with the non-linear neural network approach as such networks are general function approximators.

2.2   Radial Basis Function Networks

A radial basis function network is an artificial neural network that uses radial basis functions as activation functions. The output of the network is

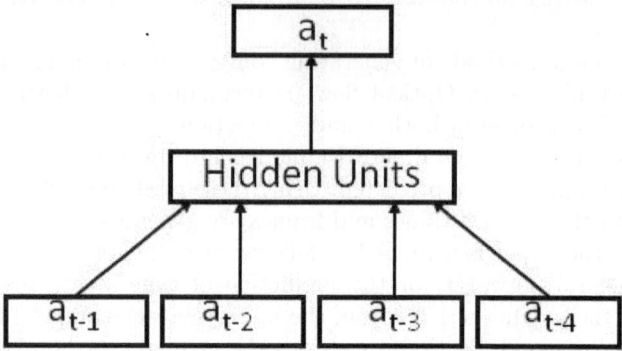

Fig. 1. The method of performing time series prediction using a sliding window of four time steps

$\psi(\mathbf{x}) = \sum_{i=1}^{N} a_i \rho(||\mathbf{x} - \mathbf{c}_i||)$, where N is the number of neurons in the hidden layer, $\mathbf{c}_i$ is the center vector for neuron i, and a_i are the weights of the linear output neuron.

For the prediction of future positions, the $X(t)$ time series was normalised by dividing every element of the series by the width of the image and the $Y(t)$ series was normalised by diving each element by the height of the image. Two separate neural network models were created, one for each the series. These models were then trained with the values of the centroids obtained from the given sequence of images. Here we have used four input neurons for both the models i.e. the last four coordinates are used to determine the next coordinate of the position of the object. After training the models, the last four coordinates of the given data were used as input to the networks and the new positions were predicted. And then using these more future positions were predicted.

For the second part, the optical flow V_t between all pairs of consecutive images were calculated. This gave the velocities of all pixels, (X, Y), as $u_t(X, Y)$ and $v_t(X, Y)$, $t = 1,....K$, for x and y directions respectively. Two separate neural networks for each pixel were then created and trained using the time series of the velocities. These trained networks were then used to predict the future velocities of each pixel and the pixels were moved to their new locations according to the velocities obtained and thus the frames were generated.

3   Extracting the Moving Object from the Given Image Sequence

For prediction of the position of the object, first the object is extracted from the given sequence. Let us consider an image sequence $f(t)$, $t = 1,....,K$. Assume that the the first frame $f(1)$ gives the background and the moving object enters the frames after it. The moving object is extracted by subtracting the background from each of the frames

$$g(t) = |f(t) - f(1)| \tag{2}$$

where $g(t)$, $t = 1,....,K$ represent the subtracted images which contain the moving object. The subtracted frames are then converted into binary images by applying a suitable threshold such that only the moving object remains. Let $C(t)$, $t = 1,....,K$, be the set containing the non zero pixels in $g(t)$ such that it represents the moving object. We define the position of the moving object as the centroid of $C(t)$.
i.e.

$$(X(t), Y(t)) = \left(\frac{\sum x_{C(t)}}{N}, \frac{\sum y_{C(t)}}{N}\right) \tag{3}$$

$t = 1,....,K$, where $(x_{C(t)}, y_{C(t)}) \in C(t)$, N is the total number of points in $C(t)$ and $(X(t), Y(t))$ represents the centroid of the moving object in the tth frame. Thus a time series is obtained for both x and y dimensions.

4 Estimation of Optical Flow

We have used the Horn-Schunck method [7] for estimating the optical flow. This introduces a global constraint of smoothness to solve the aperture problem. The flow is formulated as a global energy function and is sought to be minimized. The energy function for two-dimensional image stream is given as:

$$E = \iint [(I_x u + I_y v + I_t)^2 + \alpha^2 (\nabla u^2 + \nabla v^2)] \mathrm{d}x \mathrm{d}y \tag{4}$$

where I_x, I_y and I_t are the derivatives of the image intensity along the x ,y and time dimensions respectively, $V = [u(x,y), v(x,y)]^T$ is the optical flow vector, and the parameter α is a regularisation constant. In each image sequence I_x, I_y and I_t can be calculated for each pixel as:

$$I_x = \frac{1}{4}[I_{x,y+1,t} - I_{x,y,t} + I_{x+1,y+1,t} - I_{x+1,y,t} + I_{x,y+1,t+1} - I_{x,y,t+1} \\ + I_{x+1,y+1,t+1} - I_{x+1,y,t+1}] \tag{5}$$

$$I_y = \frac{1}{4}[I_{x+1,y,t} - I_{x,y,t} + I_{x+1,y+1,t} - I_{x,y+1,t} + I_{x+1,y,t+1} - I_{x,y,t+1} \\ + I_{x+1,y+1,t+1} - I_{x,y+1,t+1}] \tag{6}$$

$$I_t = \frac{1}{4}[I_{x,y,t+1} - I_{x,y,t} + I_{x+1,y,t+1} - I_{x+1,y,t} + I_{x,y+1,t+1} - I_{x,y+1,t} \\ + I_{x+1,y+1,t+1} - I_{x+1,y+1,t}] \tag{7}$$

The energy function can be minimized by solving the following Euler-Lagrange equations:

$$\frac{\partial L}{\partial u} - \frac{\partial}{\partial x}\frac{\partial L}{\partial u_x} - \frac{\partial}{\partial y}\frac{\partial L}{\partial u_y} = 0 \tag{8}$$

$$\frac{\partial L}{\partial v} - \frac{\partial}{\partial x}\frac{\partial L}{\partial v_x} - \frac{\partial}{\partial y}\frac{\partial L}{\partial v_y} = 0 \tag{9}$$

where L is the integrand in 4. Thus,

$$I_x(I_x u + I_y v + I_t) - \alpha^2 \Delta u = 0 \tag{10}$$

and

$$I_y(I_x u + I_y v + I_t) - \alpha^2 \Delta v = 0 \tag{11}$$

where $\Delta = \frac{\partial^2}{\partial x^2} + \frac{\partial^2}{\partial y^2}$ is the Laplace operator.

Approximating the Laplacian using finite differences, $\Delta u(x,y) = \bar{u}(x,y) - u(x,y)$ where $\bar{u}(x,y)$ is a weighted average of u calculated in the neighbourhood of (x,y). Thus 10 and 11 can be written as:

$$(I_x^2 + \alpha^2)u + I_x I_y v = \alpha^2 \bar{u} - I_x I_t \tag{12}$$

$$I_x I_y u + (I_y^2 + \alpha^2)v = \alpha^2 \bar{v} - I_y I_t \tag{13}$$

This is linear in u and v and may be solved for each pixel in the image.

5   Algorithm for Predicting the Future Images Using Optical Flow

The algorithm for predicting the future images of an image sequence can be summarised as:

Step 1: Represent the given images as a sequence *f(t)*.

Step 2: Calculate the optical flow between all pairs of consecutive images. (Sect. 4). Create two time series for the x and y velocities for each pixel.

Step 3: Create an ANN model for both the dimensions for each pixel and train them separately using the time series obtained from the previous step.(Sect. 2)

Step 4: Using these neural networks predict the future velocities of the pixels and map them to their new positions.

6   Results

For experimental validation, an image sequence of a person moving from one side of the frame to the other is considered. The sequence consists of 115 images out of which the first 105 image frames are used for obtaining the articifial neural network models and the next 10 image frames are used as test images in order to validate the model.

Note that the training and the test images correspond to two non-interesting time intervals. As discussed in the algorithm, four input variables *X(t-4)*, *X(t-3)*, *X(t-2)* and *X(t-1)* and one output variable i.e. *X(t)* are chosen for the first model. Similarly, for the second model, input variables, $Y(t-4)$, $Y(t-3)$, $Y(t-2)$ and $Y(t-1)$, and output variable $Y(t)$ are chosen.

We present the results in the following figures. Figs. 2, 4, and 6 are the images obtained by mapping the object to the predicted coordinates and Figs. 3, 5, and 7 are the corresponding test images.

For the next part, an image sequence of a jet plane flying over the sea is considered. The original images were resized to 100x100 pixels and converted to grayscale. 180 images were used for training the neural networks for both the sigmoidal networks and the RBF networks and the next 10 images were attempted to be predicted. Figs. 8 and 10 are the first and third predicted images using sigmoidal networks and Figs. 9 and 11 are the corresponding test images. Figs. 12, 14 and 16 are the first, third and fifth predicted images using RBF networks and Figs. 13, 15 and 17 are the corresponding test images.

Fig. 2. First predicted image

Fig. 3. First test image

Fig. 4. Fifth predicted image

Fig. 5. Fifth test image

Fig. 6. Tenth predicted image

Fig. 7. Tenth test image

Table 1. Test and Predicted Coordinates(Part 1)

Predicted x-coordinates	Test x-coordinates	Predicted y-coordinates	Test y-coordinates
63.4879	60.1116	101.5572	96.8796
59.873	56.1488	99.13	96.837
56.8699	52.9692	101.299	97.7244
52.5735	48.8562	98.9101	99.6603
48.8699	44.409	101.299	101.4554
44.5735	40.8842	98.9101	102.5616
40.8699	37.6833	101.299	103.4775
36.5735	34.1634	98.9101	103.8521
32.8699	31.0437	101.299	103.4424
29.2438	27.4441	99.5502	102.795

Fig. 8. First predicted image

Fig. 9. First test image

Fig. 10. Third predicted image

Fig. 11. Third test image

Fig. 12. First predicted image

Fig. 13. First test image

Fig. 14. Third predicted image

Fig. 15. Third test image

Fig. 16. Fifth predicted image

Fig. 17. Fifth test image

7   Conclusions

In this paper, future positions of a moving object have been predicted using an Artificial Neural Network model. Separate time series of both x and y coordinates was created using the given sequence of images and then the neural networks were trained using these time series. Future positions of the object were predicted using these trained neural networks. On comparing the first ten predicted values with test values we found that the mean absolute diference in the predicted and the real x and y coordinates was just 3.2091 and 0.6522 respectively. This revealed a good similarity between the predicted and the test values.

Also complete future images of sequences having moving objects were generated in the second part of the research. Optical flow of each pixel was calculated and neural networks were trained for velocities in both directions of each pixel. These were trained using separate neural networks and the future velocities of each pixel were predicted. The results show that the RBF networks approach is better than the sigmoidal networks approach for predicting the future images. The results were quite encouraging for us. This area holds a lot of scope for future research for still better predictions.

Acknowledgments. The proposed research presented in this paper is a part of Sponsored Research Project (DRDO/EE/20110037) funded by Defense Research and Development Organization, Ministry of Defense, Govt. of India and the research work has been carried out in the Department of Electrical Engineering, IIT Kanpur, India.

References

1. Verma, N.K., Pal, N.R.: Prediction of satellite images using fuzzy rule based Gaussian regression. In: 2010 IEEE 39th Applied Imagery Pattern Recognition Workshop (AIPR), pp. 1–8 (October 2010)
2. Verma, N.K., Tamrakar, P., Agrawal, S.: Generating Future Satellite Image Frame using Artificial Neural Network. In: International Conference on Image and Video Processing and Computer Vision (IVPCV 2010), pp. 158–164 (July 2010)
3. Edwards, T., Tansley, D.S.W., Davey, N., Frank, R.J.: Traffic Trends Analysis using Neural Networks. In: Proceedings of the International Workshop on Applications of Neural Networks to Telecommunications 3 (1997)
4. Dorffner, G.: Neural Networks for Time Series Processing. Neural Network World (1996)
5. White, H.: Economic Prediction using Neural Networks: the case of IBM daily stock returns. In: Proceedings of IEEE International Conference on Neural Networks, San Diego, Calif, USA (1998)
6. Paras, S.M., Kumar, A., Chandra, M.: A Feature Based Neural Network Model for Weather Forecasting. In: World Academy of Science, Engineering and Technology (2007)
7. Horn, B.K.P., Schunck, B.G.: Determining optical flow. Artificial Intelligence 17, 185–203 (1981)
8. Gibson, J.J.: The Perception of the Visual World. Houghton Miffin (1950)
9. Ma, L.L., Xu, X.S.: RBF Network-Based Chaotic Time Series Prediction and its Application in Foreign Exchange Market. In: Proceedings of the International Conference on Intelligent Systems and Knowledge Engineering (ISKE), Chengdu, China (2007)
10. Verma, N.K., Shimaila: Generation of Future Image Frames using Adaptive network based fuzzy Inference System on Spatiotemporal Framework. Accepted in Applied Imagery Pattern Recognition Workshop, AIPR (2012)
11. Verma, N.K.: Future Image Generation Using Artificial Neural Network with Selected Features. Accepted in Applied Imagery Pattern Recognition Workshop, AIPR (2011)

Solving a Maze: Experimental Exploration on Wayfinding Behavior for Cognitively Enhanced Collaborative Control

Adity Saikia and Shyamanta M. Hazarika

Biomimetic and Cognitive Robotics Lab,
Dept. of Computer Science and Engineering, School of Engineering, Tezpur University
{adity10,smh}@tezu.ernet.in

Abstract. The work described in this paper stems from the Cognitive Wheelchair Project - an effort to build a cognitively enhanced collaborative control architecture for an intelligent wheelchair. A number of challenges arises when developing such a system including ensuring indiscernibility of assistance provided by the system i.e., user unable to realize so easily that he is getting help. In this paper, our focus is primarily on design of such a reactive navigator for collaborative control of an intelligent wheelchair. Under conditions attuned to replicate the scenarios available to the wheelchair, we conducted a series of maze solving experiments. A set of design elements were extracted from the wayfinding experiment leading to the finite state machine (FSM) characterizing the reactive navigator. The FSM arrived at through such an exercise is expected to emulate the cognitive processes of human wayfinding under environment conditions as perceivable to an intelligent wheelchair and ensure indiscernibility of assistance.

Keywords: Cognitive modelling, Collaborative control.

1   Introduction

Moving around the environment is one of the primary tasks which human being and animals accomplish equally well. Mobility is vital to accomplishment of activities of daily living (ADL). Research within rehabilitation robotics have focused on intelligent wheelchairs to assist persons with physical and / or cognitive disability. An important criteria in design of any such intelligent assistive system is customization. User capabilities vary with their health condition. To keep individuals active and prevent them from residual skills loss, it is medically advisable that assistance must be provided on need basis [8]. Therefore, for an assistive system such as a wheelchair, an intelligent one, it is important that control is distributed between system and user. System must take full advantage of user's potential abilities. Under such a requirement, collaborative control has been explored [6].

Collaborative control involves both man and the machine working in tandem; approaches include a. safeguarded operation and b. shared control. Safeguarded

A. Agrawal et al. (Eds.): IITM 2013, CCIS 276, pp. 163–177, 2013.
© Springer-Verlag Berlin Heidelberg 2013

operation involves the machine taking over only in situations of imminent danger, with the man in control at all other times. Shared control is designed to assist the man in difficult situations; with machine coming into assistance either through manual selection or by event-oriented triggering. Number of smart wheelchairs - MAID, NavChair, TinMan and SmartChair use shared control [13]; differing only in how behaviors are implemented. A common problem is that the man and the machine do not contribute to control simultaneously. Though see [16]; wherein this is overcome using a purely reactive navigation system [2]. Urdialest et. al. [16] report detailed clinical trails of their collaborative system based on reactive navigation. Our research is largely motivated on their following observation.

> In order to improve acceptance, we would need the robot to mimic the driver up to a point, so that users do not realize so easily that they are getting help. In cases where persons present very severe cognitive problems, the proposed reactive layer can be integrated into a hybrid control architecture and use a deliberative planner to set destinations for them, according to their ADL agenda.

Urdialest et. al. [16, Page 190]

To improve collaboration between the wheelchair and the user, we exploit results from the area of Human Robot Interaction (HRI). For effective collaboration, the wheelchair must be cognitively enhanced. This is based on Alan C. Schultz's concrete illustration on why a cognitively enhanced artificial system is important for HRI [12]: 1. Embedded cognitive models can enhance the human system interface by allowing more common ground in the form of cognitively plausible representations and qualitative reasoning and 2. Incorporating cognitive models ensures systems, whose behavior is more compatible with human team members.

The work described in this paper stems from the Cognitive Wheelchair Project - an effort to build a cognitively enhanced collaborative control architecture for an intelligent wheelchair. A number of challenges arises when developing such a system including ensuring indiscernibility of assistance provided by the system i.e., user unable to realize so easily that he is getting help. In this paper, our focus is primarily on design of such a reactive navigator for collaborative control of an intelligent wheelchair.

2   Cognitively Enhanced Collaborative Control

The cognitively enhanced collaborative control architecture (shown in Figure 1) is adapted from well establish cognitive architecture ACT-R [1]. The architecture is three layered with a. User Interface Layer (UIL) b. Superior Control Layer (SCL) and c. Local Control Layer (LCL). Interaction with the user is through UIL. SCL effects collaboration through two main modules: the reactive module and the reactive navigator. The reactive module evaluates the user capability based on multi-modal interaction through UIL; produce a metric, based on which processes are distributed across modules of SCL. Reactive navigator contributes to the navigation plan based on the perceived environment. LCL take responsibilities of the low level control of the system hardware.

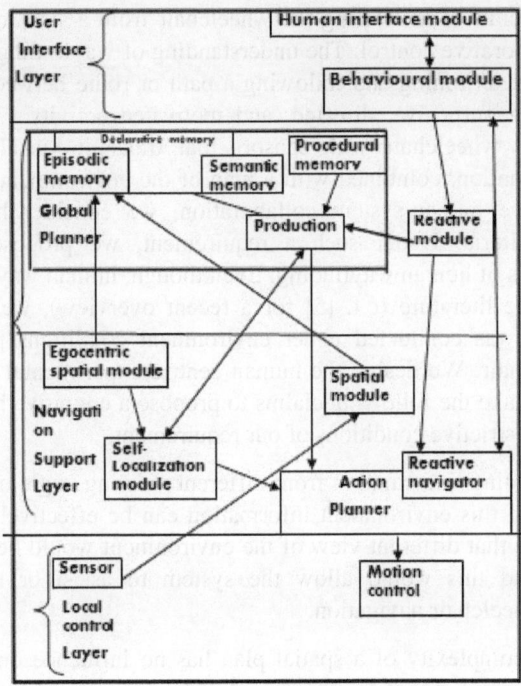

Fig. 1. Cognitively enhanced collaborative control architecture for intelligent wheelchair. The cognitive architecture is an adaptation of ACT-R.

The above architecture is not a simple reactive system; immediate reaction to the sensor information is not enough. A more evolved system with sense of sequence and context is required. Finite State Machine (FSM) [9] based approaches are useful as the system can be described as a sequence of states or context changes, taking into account sensor inputs that allows change from one state to another one, and also defining for each state a specific motor action associated to it. This ensures that each has an internal state and depending on the state will select actions that would lead to other states. Behaviour could be modeled by planning on the corresponding state-graph. Within such a cognitively enhanced collaborative framework, wayfinding would be achieved not only by exploiting one's own cognitive map[1], but with assistance from the reactive navigator. However, any assistance received by the user would not be discernable as the wayfinding FSM of the reactive navigator is expected to be no different from a human.

3   Reactive Navigator

The reactive navigator is engaged in navigation. Even though navigation and wayfinding have been used synonymously, we make a subtle distinction. Navigation

---

[1] Here the term cognitive map refers to the human mental representations of space.

is what the user achieves in steering the wheelchair from a start to the goal location albeit under collaborative control. The understanding of wayfinding as we understand is the process of determining and following a path or route between an origin and a destination. It is a purposive, directed, and motivated activity [7]. We consider a setting where the wheelchair with sensors that transmit visual information and localization information, combined with a map of the environment is expected to be used. For effective human-system collaboration, we consider human factor and human centric criteria. Under such a requirement, we propose to emulate the cognitive processes of human wayfinding. Even though, human wayfinding have been well studied in the literature (c.f. [5] for a recent overview), we were not able to identify any that was conducted under environment conditions perceivable by an intelligent wheelchair. We design the human centric experimental setting to explore wayfinding. We make the following claims to propose a cognitive human wayfinding model under the restrictive conditions of our requirement.

Claim1: In wayfinding, information from different viewing angle of the environment differs and each of this environment information can be effectively used. Claim1 is guided by the idea that different view of the environment would be perceived by on-board cameras and this would allow the system to assist or make use of this information for wheelchair navigation.

Claim 2: Spatial complexity of a spatial plan has no influence on wayfinding. The justification for Claim2 is that to reproduce human action, system usability must be independent of complexity of a spatial plan.

Claim 3: Wayfinding is simplified (by the way-finder) by switching between different strategies. Claim 3 guided is by the understanding that to coordinate the activities, the system should show flexibility of adopting different wayfinding strategies to reproduce human behaviour. Under the above claims, we set to explore human wayfinding by solving a maze. Claims 1 through 3 lead to the Hypothesis 1 through 6. To address these questions, wayfinding was analysed, as explained in Section 4.

Hypothesis 1(H_1^0): Wayfinding is not influenced by prior exocentric environment information.

Hypothesis 2(H_2^0): If multiple views of an environment is experienced, wayfinding in mirrored view of environment do not bring any difference in performance.

Hypothesis 3(H_3^0): Way-finder's view-specific effect of an environment does not decrease with increased exposure to the environment.

Hypothesis 4(H_4^0): Wayfinding does not differ with change in viewing angle of prior viewed environment.

Hypothesis 5(H_5^0): Complexity of spatial plan impact wayfinding.

Hypothesis 6(H_6^0): Way-finder does not switch between combinations of strategies to simplify wayfinding.

4   Experimental Exploration

4.1   Materials and Methods

For experimentation, a virtual maze environment was used. Virtual maze offers the opportunity of studying fairly realistic navigation traits; and obtained results are able to portray a conclusion that can be approved to human wayfinding.

Subjects: The experiment was conducted on 23 subjects. Four participants give up after playing the first game. 19 subjects (mean age = 25.32, S.D = 3.23) completed all eight games. Participants were naive to the purpose of the experiment and none of them was suffering from any perceptual, spatial or motor deficiency. Maze Design: Participant had to reach the target location in two different virtual mazes under different conditions. The mazes incorporated 3-D characteristics to give the sense of a real maze. Both mazes were constructed in such a way that when the participant maneuvered through the mazes, participants encounter many route intersections which required taking a decision of route selection (i.e., decision points). The two mazes were different in structuring of spaces, while keeping position of start and target locations constant. Participant have to solve the mazes from up start location to down direction of the target. Details of the two mazes are given in Table 1; including a list of geometrical structures that are used to generate our mazes. Maze2 was comparatively simpler than Maze1 (Plan complexity is according to [10]). Within the mazes, there were no landmark cues. However, it is pertinent to mention that Cheng and Newcombe [3], focused on two categories of cues to spatial orientation: geometric and featured cues. Geometric cues are provided by environmental surfaces (for example, shapes formed by walls of a room). Non-geometrical properties such as colours and textures which cannot be expressed in geometric terms solely are categorized as featured cues. Our experimental mazes contained components such as T-junctions that can be categorized as geometrical cue. Even though our experimental mazes are without any landmarks, environmental shapes may be interpreted as cues. Under such context our experiments can be generalized to scenarios where landmarks would be available. First, we varied each maze in two different viewing conditions. Next we simply flipped starting and target location of the mazes by 90 degree (array rotated mazes). Participants completed four different instances for each of the possible combinations of conditions (2 viewing angle X 2 different starting and target location pair = 4). Eight possible com- binations of mazes (2 viewing angle X 2 different target location X 2 maze) has to be solved. The mazes were administered on the HP computer equipped with 1GB of RAM and an 18.5-inch monitor. Participants were seated in a normal chair in a comfortable position at a distance about 50cm in front of the screen. The center of the computer screen located 15 to 20 degrees below horizontal eye level. Maneuver through mazes was controlled by the subjects using arrow keys on standard 101 computer key board. Each movement through the maze was recorded by screen casting CamStudio open source software.

Table 1. Structural details of Maze1 and Maze2

Maze	Number of decision points in maze	Geometrical structures (for both mazes)
Maze1	14	Dead end, Straight, L-shaped
Maze2	7	Cross intersection, T-intersection

Experimental Protocol and Overview

The experimental protocol is a sequence of four different tasks with intertask periods ranging between 30 seconds to 60 seconds.

Training Phase MO: In M0, participants were provided with instructions which explained the experimental modalities and highlighted the task they had to perform. Subjects were familiarized with arrow keys to maneuver through maze. The participant carried out practices with 5-7 mazes from the practice pool. Each participant was required to respond to the practice session correctly before beginning the next sequence of task. Subjects were given enough training time to practice.

Relax Phase M1: Subjects were asked to relax. During this phase computer screen remained blank and experimenter recorded participant age and gender. Participant have to choose one of the options ranging from "I have never played computer games" to "I play computer game every day".

Maze Solving Phase M2: An audio cue marked the start of the maze solving phase. Four different views were presented for Maze1 (respectively for Maze2). Each solving phase started by asking the participant if he was ready to start.

Phase11 (respectively Phase21): Participants were presented a exo- centric view of Maze1 (respectively Maze2). In these phases, participants were asked to imagine themselves as standing above the maze from where he could physically view the entire maze. With this we biased participants towards an exo-centric interaction with the environment to find a solution.

Phase12 (respectively Phase22): Partially egocentric view of Maze1 (respectively Maze2) were presented. Here participants were asked to imagine[2] themselves to be physically on the maze. We biased participants towards an egocentric interaction with the environment.

Phase13 (respectively Phase23): Participants were solving array rotated partially egocentric view of Maze1 (respectively Maze2).

Phase14 (respectively Phase24): Participants were presented an array rotated exo-centric view of Maze1 (respectively Maze2).

Participant Feedback Phase: After the experiments participants were instructed to fill up a questionnaire that highlighted the factors that they have taken into account during the solution of mazes. They were also instructed to give a rating with regards to solving difficulties of the mazes.

Overview of Experimental Design

Wayfinding in Phase11 (as well as Phase21) take place in an unfamiliar environment (with only knowledge of the relative position to the target). In Phase21, maze environment was comparatively simpler than in Phase11. Phase12 (respectively

---

[2] When mazes were presented to participants, they were asked to describe view of the environment. Few of participants spontaneously describe view of the environment. These imaginations were checked through participants mention of situation in their linguistic report; how they themselves related to presented environment view.

Phase22) quantified how well viewing angle effect prior knowledge of structure of Maze1 (respectively Maze2). Presented mazes in experiment Phase13 (respectively Phase23) were mirrored configuration of starting and target location of Maze1 (respectively Maze2) in Phase11 (respectively Phase21). We named these configuration as rotated array mazes. These experimental phases were designed to address impact of mirroring on orientation behavior. Experiment Phase14 (as well as Phase24) were designed for investigating subjects retention of original wayfinding strategy (if any) with change in viewing angle.

Performance Metrics of Interest

Participant performance were categorized in three levels [11].

Level-1: Wayfinding performance Level Participants' wayfinding performance was based on Navigation time: Measure how fast participant is able to reach the target. Impact of array rotation on wayfinding performance of maze solving phase 13 and 23 were analyzed by navigation time.

Level-2: Wayfinding Behavior Level Wayfinding behaviour was based on Response time: participant spent time before traversing a maze. As, Maze1 was comparatively complex plan than Maze2, reaction times of first trial of both mazes i.e. in Phase11 and 21 was considered specially important. Result would give us the impact of complexity of the spatial plan on way-finder response for a new environment.

Level-3: Rationale Level Our focus was on rationalized behavioural and task performance aspects of wayfinding, and were based on the metrics derived out of the written report. Participant's strategic focus was accessed through their written linguistic pattern. To identify used strategies, we limited ourselves to three wayfinding strategies: a. Least angle strategy [4] - Participants choose routes which are most in line to target location; b. Central point strategy [14] - When participant walk back to well known part of maze; c. Trajectory based strategy [15]- Conceptualize a route by positioning at a particular part of the maze, in or- der to avoid detours from trajectory; and d. Summary scanning strategy [15] - Participants find a way to target by conceptualizing the whole maze. We used linguistic keywords that serve as indicator of each of the strategy [14].

4.2   Experimental Result

Spearman's rank order correlation was run to determine the relationship between familiarity with computer games and participants self-rating on solving difficulties of mazes. Spearman's correlation coefficient is 0.159 (p= 0.516), which is statistically insignificant. Participant's familiarity with computer games did not signify that better they performed in the experimental mazes.

Analysis of Behavioural data

Table 2 provides descriptive statistics for the measured values of participant navigation time and reaction time. The table is categorized by the solving phases.

Table 2. Mean and standard errors of participant navigation time and reaction time

Maze1	Phase 11	Phase12	Phase13	Phase14
Navigation time	578.64(83.03)	465.5(87.58)	510.6(170.40)	304.42(95.51)
Reaction time	72.5(21.50)	27(8.38)	98(31.11)	27 (15.04)
Maze2	Phase 21	Phase22	Phase23	Phase24
Navigation time	172.21(20.89)	125.42(21.72)	142.89(22.36)	110.57(11.86)
Reaction time	31.92(11.01)	18.31(5.03)	37.92(16.65)	14.42 (4.80)

Null Hypothesis (H_1^0): Wayfinding is not influenced by prior exo-centric information of environment.

Alternative Hypothesis (H_1^a): Wayfinding is influenced by prior exo-centric information of environment.

To analyze the influence of environment information, participant navigation time in exo-centric and partially egocentric phase of Maze 1 (respectively of Maze2) were recorded. A paired sample t-test[3] was used to analyze the statistical significance in navigation time between Phase11 vs. 12 (respectively Phase 21 vs. 22). The paired sample t-test results are reported in Table 3. For Maze1, navigation time between solving phases: Phase11 to 12 (t(18)=2.345, p= 0.033) and for Maze2, Phase21 to 22 (t(18)=2.2217, p= 0.039) were statistically significant at the p=0.05 level. Thus, null hypothesis was (H_1^0) reject.

Table 3. Paired sample t-test results for H_1^0 **Table 4.** Paired sample t-test results for H_2^0

Maze	Solving Phases	t	df	Level of significance
Maze1	11 vs. 12	2.34	18	0.033
Maze2	21 vs. 22	2.21	18	0.039

Maze	Solving Phases	t	df	Level of significance
Maze1	112 vs. 13	-1.26	18	0.22
Maze2	212 vs. 23	0.376	18	0.711

Null Hypothesis (H_2^0): If multiple views[4] of an environment is experienced, wayfinding in mirrored view of environment do not bring any difference in performance.

Alternative Hypothesis (H_2^a): Experience of multiple views of an environment, leads to better wayfinding performance in mirrored view of the environment as well.

Wayfinding performance was analyzed in terms of navigation time. We computed mean navigation time of Phase11 and 12 (henceforth Phase112) (respectively Phase21 and 22; henceforth Phase212). We compared it with Phase13 (re- spectively Phase23),

---

[3] Paired t- test was used rather than 2x2 ANOVA since we were interested to know whether these different structure influence way-finding and how much; not the interaction of these two mazes' influence on wayfinding.

[4] The term 'multiple views' refers to solving experience of exo-centric as well as ego-centric view of same mazes.

which was just exo-centric view of rotated array of Maze1 (respectively Maze2). A paired sample t-test was conducted. It was found that difference was not statistically significant: for Maze1 between Phase112 and 13 (t(18)= -1.268, p= .228), and Maze2, Phase212 and 23 (t(18)= 0.376, p= 0.711) (as reported in Table 4). Thus, null hypothesis (H_2^0) was accepted. Comparison of the t-test value between Maze1 and Maze2, gives us an impression that there exists a performance difference with the two different mazes. One possibility of this result is that although mirrored view of an environment do not bring any difference to wayfinding performance, but performance shows strong association to spatial plan of the mazes and correspondingly to the environment. We made this assumption as Maze 2 was comparatively simpler in structure than Maze1.

Null Hypothesis (H_3^0): Way finder view-specific effect[5] of an environment does not decrease with increased exposure to the environment.

Alternative Hypothesis (H_3^a): Way finder view-specific effect of an environment decreases with increases exposure to the environment.

Table 5. Paired sample t-test results for H_3^0 **Table 6.** Paired sample t-test results for H_4^0

Maze	Solving Phases	t	df	Level of significance	Maze	Solving Phases	t	df	Level of significance
					Maze1	11 vs. 12	2.551	18	0.020
						13 vs. 14	2.183	18	0.042
Maze1	11 vs. 14	3.395	18	0.004	Maze2	21 vs. 22	2.30	18	0.033
						23 vs. 24	1.589	18	0.129
Maze2	21 vs. 24	3.29	18	0.004					

Here wayfinding was reviewed through navigation time between Phase 11 and 14 of Maze1 (respectively Phase 21 and 24 of Maze2). In solving Phase 11 and 21 participants do not have previously experienced knowledge of the environment; whereas Phase 14 (respectively Phase 24) was performed after extensive experience of Maze1 (respectively Maze2). Table 5 summarize the paired t-test results. Thus, the null hypothesis (H_3^0) was rejected.

Null Hypothesis (H_4^0): Wayfinding does not differ with change in viewing an- gle of prior viewed environment.

Alternative Hypothesis (H_4^a): Wayfinding differed with change in viewing angle of prior viewed environment.

Wayfinding was judged in terms of response time. Paired t-test was conducted to examine null hypothesis. The t-test revealed that the change in viewing angle between phases were significant at the p=.05 level (as reported in Table 6). Thus the null hypothesis (H_4^0) was rejected. In examining t-test results of Table 6, we note a

---

[5] Here the term view specific effect is used to mean appearance of environment (maze) under specific viewing (angle) condition.

differing result. The result could be due to the fact once the environment views are learned, change in viewing angle of prior viewed environment no longer influence wayfinding. This might be explained by the assumption that after wayfinding experienced through the array rotational view of Maze1,the learned experience of this kind of environment view serve as retrieval cue to solve the array rotational view of Maze2. Consequently, solving Phase 23 and 24 is not statistically significant.

Null Hypothesis (H_5^0): Complexity of spatial plan impact wayfinding.

Alternative Hypothesis (H_5^a): There is no impact of complexity of spatial plan on wayfinding.

Impact of plan complexity on response time is evaluated by comparing response time in solving Phase 11 and 21. The strength of the association between the solving Phase 11 and 21 was analyzed by Pearson correlation test. It was found that after traversing a complex plan in phase11, when comparatively simpler exo-centric information was presented in phase 21 participants, response time exhibited strong positive correlation with reaction time of presented complex exo-centric environment information, which was statistically significant (Pearson correlation, r (19)=0.559,p =0.012, df = 17), thus null hypothesis (H_5^0) is rejected. From this results we can conclude with 95 percent confidence that irrespective of spatial plan, possibility of a wayfinder spent time before traversing a plan remain same.

Analysis of Linguistic data

Specific Question Q_3 intended to highlight what a particular person would do to find his way around the maze. Question Q_4 intended to focus on how a person accessed his current wayfinding experience to develop a hypothetic user perceptive. Participant answers to question Q_3 was usually expressed in first person form, I.

Examples: 1. I make a virtual way to reach the target in my mind.
        2. When I got stuck, I retrace my path .....

Answer to question Q_4 was represented in second person form, you, referred to a hypothetical user navigating through and perceiving the maze.

Examples: 3. First you see which the options in hand to take turn are
        4. ... where there is more than one path take your decision carefully
It was also clear from these examples that the perspective they impose on the hypothetical user was egocentric. Furthermore, their answer to question Q_4, as expected, hypothetical user conceptualized on the basis of participant current experienced knowledge of the maze. It was typically a survey perspective experienced in which hypothetical user is supposed to have exo-centric information of the environment.

Examples: 5. Before starting, solve it once in your mind
        6. If you can't find way then try to find the possible path visually
Our analysis of linguistic reports provided the evidence that each form of environment information can be used in wayfinding and how participant related themselves to that environment view. With participant's conceptualization of hypothetical user with exo-centric representation of maze, we can draw a conclusion that exo-centric information aid to improved wayfinding.

Null Hypothesis (H_6^0): Way finder does not switch between different strategies to simplify wayfinding.

Alternative Hypothesis (H_6^a): Way finder switches between different strategies to simplify wayfinding.

We analyze the written data for strategic description. We limit ourselves to four wayfinding strategies. In our experimental scenario, we can imagine the following scenario: A way-finder walks through an unfamiliar environment and tries to navigate towards the target - a salient landmark. At intersection, way-finder can perceive the outgoing routes and the salient landmark. Under such scenario, if we assume that movement pattern would show a tendency to minimize the travel distance by choosing route which was least deviated from direction target the least angle strategy should result. The participant who used this strategy relied strongly on their movement in direction to target the refection of this concept is given by the following example:

Example: 8. ... direction that lead towards destination.

This example explicitly reflected least angle strategy as speaker referred to direction to the reach the target. In our experimental scenario, we can also imagine the following situation: to find a way to the destination, you were start to orient towards particular part of the maze or route, and trying to find a way to the destination from there. Such type of movement pattern where someone plan a route to a particular access point and then plan the next part of your plan there- the central point strategy should result. The refection of this concept be understood by the following example:

Example: 9. Try to set a point at junction ...

Here the participant described about how he mark place at a certain place of the maze and gradually exploring the maze from there. Other than these strategies, we also include strategy where participant mentally visualized the trajectory as part of a inspection process, as in example of following :

Example: 10. ... opted for no dead-end path.

There were indications in the data that some of participant conceptualized the maze as a whole, as in example of following:

Example: 11. ... memorized the view.

The above example can be interpreted as part of summary scanning strategy that the participant gradually developed.

Strategic description were analyzed with the following steps.

Step 1: Identify *bag of words* in relation to *strategies*. Construct wayfinding propositions.

Step 2: Re-write each report in propositional format.

Step 3: Select information items i.e., proposition that were either relevant to wayfinding related consideration or to action during wayfinding.

Step 4: Select process propositions: Minimum set of proposition that reflect the concept of wayfinding; as shown in Table 7.

Step 5: Reconstruction: Each report reconstructed with process proposition.

Table 7. Process propositions

label	Process proposition	examples of information unit	label	Process proposition	examples of information unit
a	Avoid detour	check dead end	b	Estimate the path length	Shortest path to target
c	Follow path		d	Solve in mind	Recall way
e	Visualizing the whole view	Remember turn	f	Backtrack to point	Retrace path to start
g	Move along the border		h	Possible movement from a point	Choose a check point at diversion
i	Path leads toward the goal	Follow direction towards the goal			

Step 6: Process descriptions: Process proposition categorized into four groups; as listed in Table 8.

Table 8. Processes description (PD)

label	group	label	group	label	group	label	group
a,b	route status	i	direction	f,h	mark	d,e	retention

Step 7 : Proposition mapping: Process descriptions mapped to strategies; as shown in Figure 2.

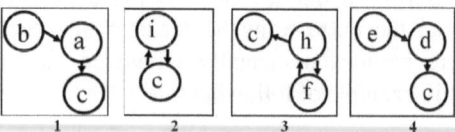

Fig. 2. Proposition mapping; 1- PD to trajectory based strategy ; 2- PD to least angle strategy; 3-PD to central point strategy; 4-PD to summary scanning strategy

Step 8 : Review participant's reconstructed report with proposition mapping to find out participant strategic description.

We found that only 26.31% (5 out of 19) participant's reconstructed report produced single strategic description; while 73.68% (14 out of 19) repots revealed combination of strategies and was statistically significant ($z=-3.472$, $p< 0.001$). Thus, there was sufficient evidence to reject the null hypothesis (H_6^0). Figure 3 shows the participant percentage who used combination of strategies. Majority of participant lexical choice reflecting the combination of trajectory based strategy and least angle strategy (5 out of 14); whereas 2 out of 14 combined trajectory based strategy and central point based strategy. As observed, least angle is combined with summary scanning by 2 out of 14 participants; central point strategy is combined with summary scanning strategy by 3 out of 14.

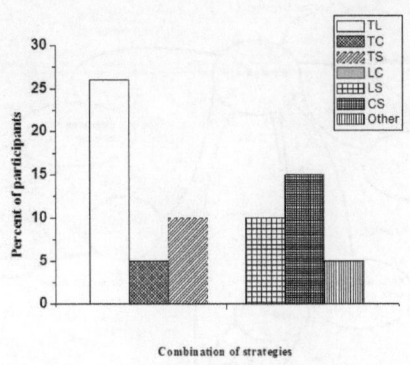

Fig. 3. Participant percentage with combination of strategies; T stands for trajectory based strategy; L stands for least angle strategy; C stands for central point strategy; S stands for summary scanning strategy

5   Discussion

The experimental result suggested that wayfinding performance is positively influenced by exo-centric environment information of environment. Moreover, our results show that view specific effect of the environment decrease with increased exposure. Interestingly, we showed that mirrored view of an environment do not bring any difference in wayfinding performance level. The result seems to confirm that an environmental configuration acts independently from one's wayfinding behaviour. Furthermore, retrospective written report indicates participant's mixed use of wayfinding strategies.

Table 9. Process description of reactive navigator

Strategy	Decision making criteria	Information received	Action taken
Least angle strategy	Direction to goal	Door is at left	Take based strategy turn at left
Trajectory based strategy	Route selection	There is an obstacle	1. Avoid the obstacle and move 2. Calculate the distance to object
Central point strategy	Select a check point	Your are at an intersection	1. Ask for help 2. Start to follow the path
Summary scanning strategy	Check the position	You are at room number x	Recall the way

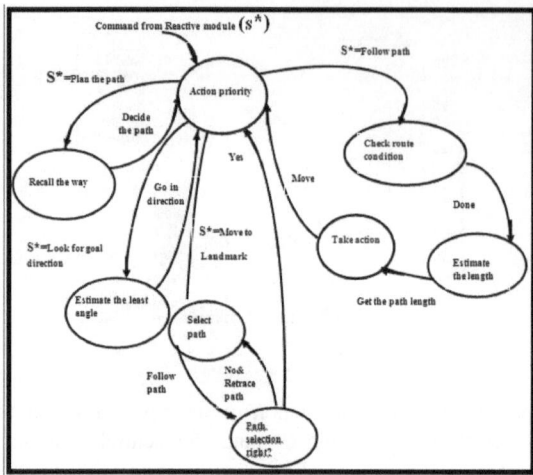

Fig. 4. Finite state machine of reactive navigator

Reactive Navigator–Revisited: Above findings have important practical significance in design of reactive navigator of the cognitively enhanced collaborative control architecture. Following are the set of design element extracted from the current wayfinding experiment.

1. Performance of wayfinding is improved by exo-centric as well as egocentric environment information; thus an effective navigator need to incorporate apparatus to exploit both.
2. Wayfinding need not be tuned to an established view of the environment; navigator can be made to plan on the available view.
3. On available information, wayfinding process must switch between different strategies to improve performance.

The process description for design of finite state machine (FSM) of the reactive navigator is in Table 9; the resulting FSM is shown in Figure 4.

6   Final Comments

Intelligent wheelchair system under the context of cognitively enhanced collaborative control demands understanding of human cognitive processes. Collaborative control system that is designed without knowledge of the cognitive processes of the human will miss its goal. This paper presents wayfinding exploration in an attempt to design system that takes into account human wayfinding process. We find out how participants find their way to reach the goal in a maze under environment conditions as would be perceivable to an intelligent wheelchair. Thereafter the knowledge is used for design of the reactive navigator. It is difficult to empirically evaluate how effective such a navigator would be in ensuring indiscernibility of assistance provided by it within collaborative control. Success of a human centric design for the reactive navigator can only be established once the cognitively enhanced collaborative control is put to practice and detailed clinical trials on the lines reported in [16] is conducted. This is part of ongoing research.

Acknowledgments. We are grateful to Pritom Rajkhowa, Computer Centre, Tezpur University for providing the 3-D maze models used in the experiment. We also thank the participants for their time and support. Adity Saikia acknowledges CSIR, India for financial support under the research grant CSIR-SRF-09/796/ (0039)/2012/EMR–I. ,

References

1. Anderson, J., Lebierel, C.: The newell test for a theory of cognition. Behav. Brain Sci. 26, 587–637 (2003)
2. Brooks, R.: A robust layered control system for a mobile robot. IEEE J. Robot. Autom. 2(1), 14–23 (1986)
3. Cheng, K., Newcombe, N.: Is there a geometric module for spatial orientation? squaring theory and evidence. Psychon. B. Rev. 12(1), 1–23 (2005)
4. Dalton, R.C.: The secret is to follow your nose:route path selection and angularity. Environ. Behav. 35(1), 107–131 (2003)
5. Farr, A.C., Kleinschmidt, T., Yarlagadda, P., Mengersen, K.: Wayfinding: A simple concept, a complex process. Transport Rev. 32(6), 715–743 (2012)
6. Fong, T.: Collaborative Control: A Robot-Centric Model for Vehicle Teleoperation. Ph.D Thesis, Carnegie Mellon University, Pittsburgh, Pennsylvania, USA (2001)
7. Golledge, R.G.: Human wayfinding and cognitive maps. In: Golledge, R.C. (ed.) Wayfinding Behavior: Cognitive Mapping and Other Spatial Process, pp. 5–45. The John Hopkins University Press (1999)
8. Gresham, G.E., Alexander, D., Bishop, D.S., Giuliani, C., Goldberg, G., Holland, A., Kelly-Hayes, M., Linn, R., Roth, E.J., Stason, W.B., Trombly, C.A.: Prevention and rehabilitation of stroke. Stroke 28(7), 1522–1526 (1997)
9. Hopcroft, J.E., Ullman, J.D.: Introduction to Automata Theory, Languages and Computation. Addison - Wesley (1979)
10. Raubal, M., Egenhofer, M.: Comparing the complexity of wayfinding tasks in built environments. Environmental Psychology B 25(6), 895–913 (1998)
11. Ruddle, R.A., Lessels, S.: Three levels of metric for evaluating wayfinding. Presence-Teleop Virt. 15(6), 637–654 (2006)
12. Schultz, A.C.: Using computational cognitive models to build better human-robot interaction. In: NAE US FOE Symposium
13. Simpson, R.: Smart wheelchairs: A literature review. J. Rehabil. Res. Dev. 42(4), 423–436 (2005)
14. Tenbrink, T., Bergmann, E., Konieczny, L.: Wayfinding and description strategies in an unfamiliar complex building. In: Proc. of the CogSci 2011 (2011)
15. Tenbrink, T., Seifert, I.: Conceptual layers and strategies in tour planning. Cogn. Process. 12(1), 109–125 (2011)
16. Urdiales, C., Fernnńdez-Carmona, M., Peula, J., Corteés, U., Annichiaricco, R., Calta-girone, C., Hernaéndezl, F.S.: Wheelchair collaborative control for disabled users navigating indoors. Artif. Intell. Med. 52, 177–191 (2011)

Semantic Annotation of Web Documents
for Efficient Information Retrieval

Rashmi Chauhan and Rayan H. Goudar

Department of Computer Science and Engineering
rashmi06cs@gmail.com
rhgoudar@gmail.com

Abstract. Searching the vast and distributed structure of the web requires the efficient search schemes. Semantic annotation is used to associate the meaningful tags with a document to perform semantic search. This paper puts forward an automatic approach for annotating web documents for efficient information retrieval. The proposed algorithm for semantic annotation constitutes five rules based on ontology and provides the semantic tags along with the degree of correlation between a tag and the consequent web document. As the annotation would be done automatically, the results obtained for a query would always be relevant and thus the improved precision and recall.

Keywords: ontology, semantic information retrieval, semantic annotation, Ranking, semantic index.

1   Introduction

In recent years, the World Wide Web has become the most significopant source to publish as well as retrieve the personal, social and commercial information. Finding relevant information from the web which has a vast and distributed structure requires efficient search schemes. Semantic search provides the most relevant information by considering the actual user's intent as the underlying information should be in a structured form as RDF (Resource Description Framework). Semantic Web documents are differentiated by semantic annotation and meaningful relation to other documents. Semantic annotation is the process of adding some meta-tags that are related to the corresponding web documents so that if any of the term occurs in user query, the associated web document would be retrieved. Tagging is a method by which anyone associates the terms to any content such as documents, Web pages, pictures and videos to describe, find and organize content. As the conventional search engines do not lead these features, a semantic search engine should be customized. The attainment of metadata for the web documents would permit various applications in semantic web to appear and put on broad recognition. Such applications would present new access techniques of information retrieval based on the linked metadata. Presently, there exist various Information Extraction approaches that provide meaningful terms within the document text, and the relations between them which are obtained with the help of Ontology.

A. Agrawal et al. (Eds.): IITM 2013, CCIS 276, pp. 178–185, 2013.

Ontology is an explicit specification of a conceptualization [4]. Ontology defines the various entities, events and relationships among them of a particular domain, in the form of Classes, Individuals and Properties. The existing approaches for semantic annotation [1] [2] are mostly manual or semi-automatic [7] based on the mapping of semantic terms between the documents and the consequent domain ontology. In some manual approaches the irrelevant terms may be associated with the documents due to which the results would be retrieved for dissimilar and unrelated queries as well [3]. To overcome this pitfall automatic annotation should be performed [6].

This paper puts forward an algorithm for annotating web documents followed by five rules. As rules are based on the frequency of a particular term in a document as well as on mapping the term with domain ontology, the tags thus obtained would always be semantic and somehow related with the corresponding documents.

The rest of the paper is organized as: section 2 presents the related work for semantic information retrieval, semantic annotation and semantic indexing. In section 3 the proposed architecture of semantic information retrieval is presented. The technique of semantic annotation and the proposed rules have been described. Section 4 draws the conclusions and some future directions for the proposed scheme.

2   Related Work

This paper is motivated by the important need for adding metadata to the existing web pages in an efficient and flexible manner that utilizes the advantages offered by RDF (Resource Description Framework) and ontology [4]. In recent years Information extraction and annotation through the web has been an active research area. Several researchers have presented their own techniques and systems to annotate the web pages and performing semantic information retrieval.

Yiyao Lu (2011) [1] presented an automatic annotation approach that first aligns the data units into several groups having the same semantic data and then for each group annotation is performed from different aspects and the different annotations are aggregated. An automatic annotation wrapper is constructed for the search sites. David Sánchez (2011) [2] introduced a technique to moderately annotate textual web content in an automatic and unsupervised way that uses various learning techniques and heuristics to ascertain relevant terms in text and to correlate them to the classes of ontology through linguistic patterns. In [3] the analysis of various problems and precision in the information retrieval has been performed according to the experimental data such as image retrieval with different retrieval terms and a search engine is constructed. To improve the precision of the search systems various recommendations have been suggested such as correcting keywords, building and enhancement of knowledge documentation, reasonable definition of features vectors, information matching and filtering, and increasing the intelligentization for spider, indexer and searcher.

Thomas R. Gruber [4] has given the formal description of the ontology and described the role of ontologies in various information sharing actions, and the guidelines for the development of ontologies have been presented. Engineering mathematics and bibliographic data was taken into consideration for the development and testing the ontology. In [6] an approach to resolve the problem of text categorization over a corpus of newspaper articles has been presented followed by the annotation. Lemmatization, a combination of Support Vector Machines (SVM), ontologies and heuristics has been applied to deduce the semantic tags for the annotation.

A semi-automatic annotation system is proposed in [7] that comprises an automatic annotator with a manual annotator. The manual annotator annotates the textual web data using the Knuth-Morris-Pratt (KMP) algorithm, and the automatic annooptator allows a user to use the terms to annotate metaphors with high conception. The technique proposed in [8] combines the lexical and semantic relationship to analyze user's query. A modulative method is proposed for result ranking based on the predictability of the results for users.

In [9] a technique for semantic annotation of web docments with individuals of ontology is proposed that recognizes the related individuals and marks them as role instances within OWL (Web Ontology Language) ontology by considering the tree structure of a web page and the semantics of the information it contains. FF-ICF algorithm has been modified by [10] for ranking and scoring semantic document annotation based on document richness. The modified algorithm has been applied into a retrieval engine, PicoDoc, to measure its performance in ranking and scoring documents annotation. The OntoGram-approach proposed in [11] performs indexing on texts by their conceptual content through ontologies along with syntactic grammars and lexico- syntactic information that is transformed into concept feature structures and mapped into concepts in a generative ontology. In [12] a framework for Cognitive Linguistics theories is proposed that is based on Construction Grammar (CxG). RDF (Resource Description Framework) has been used in the domain ontology to build constructions and a set of rules based on linguistic typology have been presented to deduce the semantics and syntax of the constructions.

3   Proposed Idea

In this paper, the architecture of semantic information retrieval and a technique of annotating web pages and ranking have been proposed. As in manual annotation there is a possibility to have some irrelevant tags with corresponding document; automatic annotation is being taken into consideration.

3.1   Overall Architecture

The overall architecture for the proposed system is given in Fig. 1. According to this architecture a semantic index is created with the help of semantic tags in annotated web pages and the degree of correlation between these tags and the documents.

The Web crawler collects the web documents through the web and submits it to the document manager. The proposed algorithm for annotating web pages is performed by the document manager by interacting the Rule Store and Ontology Knowledge Base (OKB). The Rule Store contains the rules proposed for annotation and ranking, described in further section. Ontology describes a particular domain in a structured form. The ontology knowledge base (OKB) is created in the form of classes/concepts, individuals/instances and various properties/relationships among them in a hierarchical manner. Ontology for a specific domain is created by an ontology toolbox as we have created it for e-shopping (electronic shopping) domain by Protégé Fig. 2.

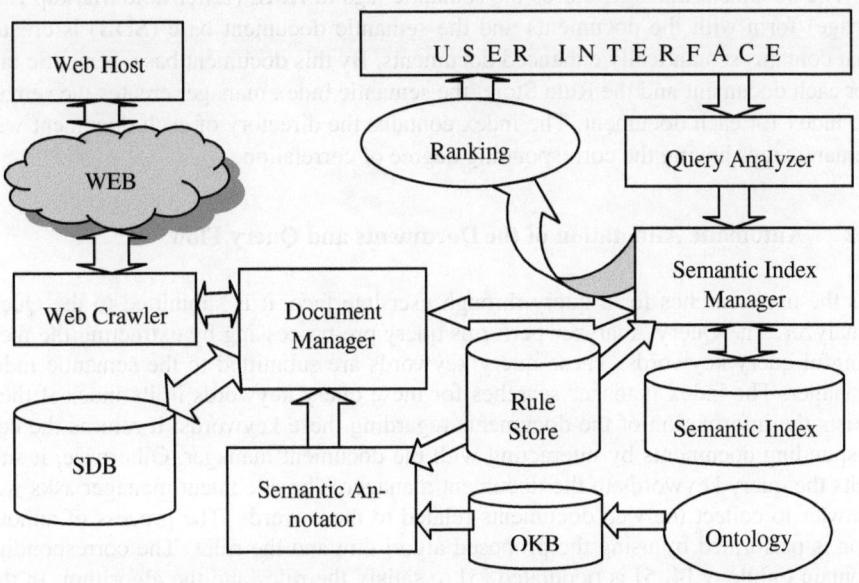

Fig. 1. Overall System Architecture

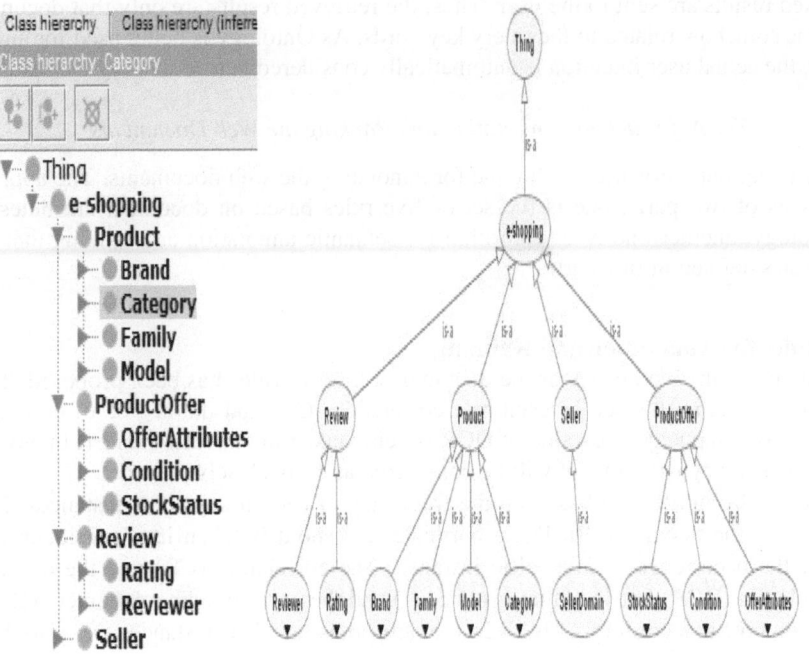

Fig. 2. Ontology constructed for e-shopping domain in Protégé

The document manager stores the semantic tags in XML (Extensible Markup Language) form with the documents and the semantic document base (SDB) is created that contains semantically enhanced documents. By this document base, semantic tags for each document and the Rule Store, the semantic index manager creates the semantic index for each document. The index contains the directory of each document with semantic tags having the corresponding degree of correlation.

3.2   Automatic Annotation of the Documents and Query Flow

As the user searches for a query through user interface, it is submitted to the Query Analyzer. The Query Analyzer performs query pre-processing by extracting the meaningful query keywords. These query keywords are submitted to the semantic index manager. The index manager searches for these query keywords in its index if there exists the information of the documents regarding these keywords; it returns the corresponding documents by interacting with the document manager. Otherwise, it submits the query keywords to the document manager. The document manager asks web crawler to collect the web documents related to these words. The process of annotation is performed by using the proposed algori thm and the rules. The corresponding domain ontology [4, 5] is populated [5] to satisfy the rules and the algorithm. In this way, the semantic annotation would be performed automatically.

The documents are then submitted to the ranker and after performing ranking the ranked results are sent to the user. Thus, the retrieved results are only that documents that is somehow related to the query keywords. As Ontology is being used for annotation, the actual user intention is automatically considered before sending the results.

The Approach for Annotating and Ranking the Web Documents

This paper puts forward a technique for annotating the web documents. The approach consists of two parts; one is the set of five rules based on document attributes and Ontology; another one is an algorithm for semantic annotation and ranking that uses the rules defined in first part.

1. Rules for Annotation and Ranking

To annotate the web pages or the documents, a set of rules has been proposed. There are five rules in this set. In each rule correlation (CR) and the degree of correlation (DCR) is computed. The value of DCR is being taken in between 0 and 1. In any case if it goes to beyond 1 then it will be considered as 1 i.e. closely related.

Rules R1 and R2 are based on the frequency of certain keywords/instances (I) occurred in the document. In R1, a particular threshold is taken into consideration to limit the occurrence of a specific instance. The correlation (CR) and the degree of correlation (DCR) between that instance (I) and the corresponding document (D) will be computed accordingly. In R2, the attributes of that instance are also being considered.

In case of R3 and R5, Ontology, is considered to obtain more effective correlation between the instance and the document considering the properties of that instance.

The rule R4 is the ideal case that if an instance belongs to the title of the content in the document, that it is closely related to the corresponding document having the degree of correlation (DCR) equal to 1.

R1: if (freq(I_i) > Th) then
CR (I_i, D_i) = TRUE
DCR (I_i, D_i) = freq (I_i) * |I_i| / TW (D_i) .... (1)
Where, freq(I_i) is the frequency of the Instance I_i , Th is the threshold, CR(I_i, D_i) is the correlation of I_i with D_i and DCR(I_i, D_i)   is the Degree of correlation between I_i and D_i.
If (DCR > 1) then Set DCR = 1

R2: if freq ((I_i + $\sum$(AT (I_i)) > Th)
Then
CR (I_i, D_i) = TRUE
And [CR (I_i, D_i)$\rightarrow$R2] > [CR (I_i, D_i)$\rightarrow$R1]
DCR (I_i, D_i) = (freq(I_i) + freq ($\sum$(AT(I_i)) * |I_i| / TW (D_i) + m ....(2)
Where, At[I_i] is the attribute of I_i m is the number of attributes of I_i presented in the document D_i
If (DCR > 1) then Set DCR = 1

R3: if ((I_i $\in$ O && D_i) && ($\sum P_j$(I_i) $\in$ D_i)
Then
CR (I_i, D_i) = TRUE
And [CR (I_i, D_i)$\rightarrow$R3] > [CR (I_i, D_i)$\rightarrow$R1, CR (I_i, D_i)$\rightarrow$R2] DCR (I_i, D_i) = $\sum$freq (P_j) * |I_i| / (TW (D_i) + n) .... (3)
Where, O is the domain ontology, P_j is the Property of I_i and n is the number of properties of I_i presented in the D_i
If (DCR > 1) then Set DCR = 1

R4: if (I_i $\in$ Title (D_i)
Then CR (I_i, D_i) = TRUE And
[CR (I_i, D_i)$\rightarrow$R3] = Highest
DCR (I_i, D_i) = 1 .... (4)

R5: if (I_i $\in$ O) && (ObjP$_j$ (I_i) $\in$ D_i))
Then
 CR (I_i, D_i) = TRUE
And [CR (I_i, D_i)$\rightarrow$R5] > [CR (I_i, D_i) $\rightarrow$R1, CR (I_i, D_i)$\rightarrow$R2]
DCR (I_i, D_i) = (freq (I_i) + freq (ObjP$_j$ (I_i) * |I_i|) / (TW (D_i) + n) ....(5)
Where, O is the domain ontology, P_j is the Property of I_i and n is the number of properties of I_i presented in the document D_i
If (DCR > 1) then Set DCR = 1

2. The Procedure for Algorithm

The web pages/documents contain the meaningful information with some extra links, advertisements etc. The unnecessary things need to be removed so that the purified web pages would be obtained. These purified web pages (PWP) are the input for the algorithm. As the output of this algorithm, the semantically enhanced web pages will be obtained having some semantic tags with the corresponding degree of correlation.

Algorithm

Input: Purified WebPages *(PWP)*

Output: Semantically enhanced Documents/WebPages

1.   *foreach PWP(i) do*
2.   *find $D_{id}(i)$ [w_i], $D_{t}(i)$ [w_i], T_i [w_i], URL_i [w_i]*
3.   *AT [w_i] = $D_{id}(i)$ [w_i] + $D_{t}(i)$ [w_i] + T_i [w_i] + URL_i [w_i]*
4.   *Store AT[w_i] into XML form*
5.   *Store all the text content of the webpage w_i into XML form in tag <text>*
6.   *Perform stemming on the text to obtain semantic keywords*
7.   *SKW [w_i] = [STEM→ Text (w_i)]*
8.   *Foreach instance I_j of SKW[w_i] do*
9.   *Apply Rn from the set of rules*
10.   *If (CR (I_j, D_j) = TRUE) then*
11.   *IN = IN + I_j*
12.   *Foreach instance I_k in O do*
13.   *if (I_j = I_k) then do*
14.   *ST = ST + I_j*
15.   *End for*
16. *SMT = IN U ST*
17.   *End for*
18.   *Store the keywords of SMT in XML form as semantic tags for annotating w_i*
19.   *Apply Rn from the set of rules*
20. *Add degree of correlation to w_i for each semantic tag according to DCR(I_i, D_i)*
21.   *End for*

The algorithm is defined by various steps as defined above. In step 2, attributes of a web page (w) such as Document id (Did), title (T), time of post (Dt), and URL (Uniform Resource Locator) etc. need to be extracted and stored in XML (Extensible Markup Language) form. The text content of the corresponding web page is stored in <text> tag of XML format. Stemming is the process of removing the stop/raw words to obtain meaningful keywords such as is, are, they, what, how, why etc. Stemming (STEM) is being performed on text content and meaningful keywords are being identified in set SKW (semantic keywords). Using set SKW, semantic tags are obtained by two ways: firstly, by applying rules from the set of rules in set IN (Instances) and secondly, using domain ontology (O) in set ST (semantic tag).

Finally, these two sets are combined into SMT (semantic tag) and stored in XML form for annotating the corresponding web page. The rules are also applied with the degree of correlation (DCR) for ranking purpose accordingly. If a user enters a query that is consisting any of these keywords, the web document would be automatically ranked according to DCR value associated with it and then it would be provided to the user. Thus, as output of this algorithm, semantically rich WebPages would be obtained with degree of correlation.

4   Conclusion

The proposed architecture provides the vision of semantic web. As in manually annotating the documents, there are the possibilities to add some irrelevant tags that are generally entered by the user; such documents would be displayed on the top and thus provides poor precision and recall. The proposed approach of automatic semantic annotation and ontology overcome this limitation and ensure that the annotated tags would always be semantic and thus more accurate results.

References

1. Lu, Y., He, H., Zhao, H., Meng, W., Yu, C.: Annotating Search Results From Web Databases. IEEE Transactions on Knowledge and Data Engineering (2011)
2. Sánchez, D., Isern, D., Millan, M.: Content annotation for the semantic web: an automatic Web Based Approach. Knowl Inf. Syst. 27, 393–418 (2011)
3. Wang, L., Hou, J., Xie, Z., Wang, X., Qu, C., Li, H.: Problems and Solutions of Web Search Engines. In: 2011 International Conference on Consumer Electronics, Communications and Networks (CECNet), April 16-18, pp. 5134–5137 (2011)
4. Gruber, T.R.: Toward Principles for the Design of Ontologies Used for Knowledge Sharing. In: International Workshop on Formal Ontology, Padova, Italy (March 1993/1995)
5. Missikoff, M., Navigli, R., Velardi, P.: The Usable Ontology: An Environment for Building and Assessing a Domain Ontology. In: Horrocks, I., Hendler, J. (eds.) ISWC 2002. LNCS, vol. 2342, p. 39. Springer, Heidelberg (2002)
6. Garrid, A.L., G'omez, O., Ilarri, S., Mena, E.: NASS: News Annotation Semantic System. In: 2011 23rd IEEE International Conference on Tools with Artificial Intelligence (2011)
7. Liu, C.-H., Chen, H.-C., Jain, J.-L., Chen, J.-Y.: Semi-automatic Annotation System for OWL-based Semantic Search. In: International Conference on Complex, Intelligent and Software Intensive Systems (2009)
8. Ma, B., Yang, Y., Zhou, X., Zhou, J.: An Ontology-based Semantic Retrieval Model for Uyghur Search Engine. IEEE (2010) 978-1-4244-6359
9. Tenier, S., Toussaint, Y., Napoli, A., Polanco, X.: Instantiation of relations for semantic annotation. In: International Conference on Web Intelligence. IEEE (2006)
10. Rahayu, S.B., Noah, S.A., Wardhana, A.A.: Ranking and Scoring Semantic Document Annotation. In: International Conference on Science and Social Research. IEEE (2010)
11. Andreasen, T., Bulskov, H., Jensen, P.A., Lassen, T.: The On-toGram-Approach to Text Processing and Semantic Relation Spotting for Indexing. In: International Conference on Fuzzy Systems and Knowledge Discovery (FSKD). IEEE (2011)

Intelligent Interactive Tutor
for Rural Indian Education System

Omna Toshniwal[1] and Pradeep Yammiyavar[2]

[1]Department of Design, Indian Institute of Technology Guwahati, Assam, India
omna@iitg.ernet.in
[2]Centre for Educational Technology, Indian Institute of Technology Guwahati, Assam, India
pradeep@iitg.ernet.in

Abstract. Rapid advancement in technology calls for efficient applications for empowering the rural population. Education is one of the fields holding innumerable developmental opportunities in rural India and with growing educational research, the challenges faced in the rural education system can be met. Concerns surrounding the Learner, Teacher and Infrastructure can be catered by introducing an intelligent interactive tutor in rural areas. This paper looks at the potential applications supported by the recent developments in Learning Technologies, which can be implemented in the context of Rural India. We also propose a model which uses the Problem Based Learning (PBL) approach to develop conceptual, practical and strategic knowledge of the learners and allow better transferability. Cognitive Load Theory and Learner Models provide the Instruction Design guidelines for the proposed tutoring system. The testing for effectiveness of the conceptual model of this tutor is under progress.

Keywords: Adaptive and Adaptable Scaffolding, Transferability, Problem Based Learning, Instruction Design, Learner Models.

1   Introduction

The advances in e-learning technologies and educational research have been tremendous in the recent years. This growth and the ubiquity of these technologies facilitate their application for furthering the reach of literacy. In terms of literacy, Rural India faces problems like lack of well- qualified teachers, poor teacher-student ratio, poor infrastructure, low motivation and lack of well-developed curriculum. Communication in learner's language and challenge-based or game-based curriculum to hold their attention could be some ways to solve these problems.[22] Although, the bigger questions of how to provide them with individualized one-on-one tutoring and how to make them realize the importance and need of learning still stay hanging.

The priority of a rural student is to survive for the day rather than look and work for a better future. [22] Designing their curriculum based on its relevance and familiarity to them and making contextual problem-solving the learning objective must prove beneficial to the rural students. Students are diverse in terms of knowledge, skills, interests, learning styles and the development of their expertise. To empower

A. Agrawal et al. (Eds.): IITM 2013, CCIS 276, pp. 186–199, 2013.

the diverse rural population with individualized tutoring, we propose a learner-adaptable and adaptive model of an Intelligent Interactive Tutor for helping them develop transferable conceptual, strategic and practical knowledge. The Instruction Design guidelines for the tutor are derived from the Cognitive Load Theory, Adaptive and Adaptable Scaffolding. We use the T-Matrix method, which offers consistent qualitative patterns of asymmetric transfer, for defining the curriculum sequence, which also depends on the student's previous actions and performance. We will be discussing these topics more in the following sections.

2   Background

2.1   Problem Based Learning (PBL)

For rural students, the priority is to survive for the day and solve problems to which they come across in the daily course of life. Making smart, meaningful decisions for effective solutions require knowledge, experience and reasoning abilities. Our aim is to help them develop relevant skills and become self-sufficient.

Students cannot learn how to solve problems by learning about problem-solving. They must engage with problems, make mistakes, conjecture about solutions, and argue for the best solution. Problem-based learning assumes that students will master content while solving a meaningful problem. [17] Learning to solve these problems is an effective method to develop decision-making skills. The problem to be solved should be engaging, but should also address the curricular issues required by the curriculum. [17]

Problem Characteristics

Eleven problem characteristics were identified by Schmidt in 2011 based on students' perceptions. They were 1) the extent to which the problem leads to the intended learning issues, 2) interest triggered by the problem, 3) format of the problem, 4) the extent to which the problem stimulated critical reasoning, 5) the extent to which the problem promoted self-directed learning, 6) clarity of the problem, 7) difficulty of the problem, 8) the extent to which the problem is relevant; that is applicable and useful, 9) the extent to which the problem relates to the student's prior knowledge, 10) the extent to which the problem stimulates elaboration, and 11) the extent to which the problem promotes teamwork. [30] Additionally, an increasing number of instructional theories view rich, real-life learning tasks as a basis for complex learning [24].

We will discuss about instructional theories later in this paper. These problem characteristics and factors affecting problem-solving are in mind while designing the curriculum to be taught by this tutor.

T-Matrix Method

Achieving transfer- the ability to apply acquired skills in contexts different from those contexts the skills were mastered in is arguably the sine qua non of education. [37] If the model does not provide practice with transfer in mind, it is unlikely that long term-learning will be strong. [29] An educational software system needs a model that is clever enough to see not only the effect of practice on repetition, but also see the effect of practice on transfer. [37]

Many approaches have been attempted over the years to handle transfer; the Q-matrix method of assigning latent knowledge components (KCs) to particular problems or problem steps has begun to have a large following. [19] In contrast, a newer "T-matrix" method assumes learning is less abstract by not describing latent variables, but rather looking at the transfer effects with a question by question matrix where each question causes learning that effects other questions directly [28] In the T-matrix method, there is no sharing of latent, instead it's a more complex method that specifies each directional pairwise relationship between a transferred-from item and a transferred-to item individually. T-matrix offers more interpretable learning transfer and is consistent in qualitative patterns of asymmetric transfer. [37]

Scaffolding for PBL

Scaffolds, which refer to supports provided so that the learner can engage in activities that would otherwise be beyond their abilities [16], include strategies for constructing strong problem schemas using analogical encoding, explicating or mapping causal relationships, argumentation, question prompts, problem modeling activities, and metacognitive self-regulation.

Cognitive scaffolds focus student attention on important relationships among the elements in the problem as well as between problems. For PBL, these include studying worked examples, structural analogues, case studies, prior experiences, alternative perspectives and simulations in relation to the problem. [17] Such scaffolds are included as tools, tasks and clues in the tutor.

2.2   Intelligent Tutoring Systems (ITSs)

Research has shown that one-on-one tutoring from an expert tutor has given better results than traditional group-based instruction [8]. Achieving a similar degree of individualization has been a key interest among developers of interactive learning environments and Intelligent Tutoring Systems (ITSs). To achieve one-on-one instruction, targeted and appropriate adaptation is required, which in turn requires accurate assessment of learners. [14] [15] For designing adaptive tutoring systems which match the diverse rural students' learning styles and pace of developing expertise, we studied various learner models, skill modeling approaches, and adaptive and adaptable scaffolding techniques.

Learner Models and Skill Modeling

The two problems addressed in Intelligent Tutoring Systems are (i) Student Modeling, which infers students' learning by observing student performance [12] and (ii) Cognitive Modeling, which factorizes problem solving steps into the latent set of skills required to perform them. [11] The tutor's ability to diagnose what a student knows and does not know, and the ability to select relevant interventions given this diagnosis, is pivotal to good tutoring. Another key feature is tutors' ability to infer, from the student's problem solving actions and answers, what is likely well understood or mastered, and what is not, from only a few observations , and to move on in the curriculum at the right pace for that specific student. [14] [15] Other requirements for learner models may be, if we want to know whether the student is bored or frustrated, what is the appropriate moment to switch from drill and practice to explanations and theoretical material, etc. [20]

We use problem solving, solution analysis [9] and curriculum sequencing tutoring approaches combined with Bayesian Knowledge-Tracing (BKT) approach for our model. The former tutors wil support highly specific, immediate, and effective feedback during problem solving and the ability to structure the learning path according to the individual skill profile of each student. BKT is essentially a model for determining if and when the learning of a skill (or other type or knowledge component) occurs during a specific problem-solving step. Assuming that each step of each learning exercise calls for a given single skill, an opportunity to demonstrate (and learn) that skill occurs and the student can either succeed or fail the task.

A sequence of actions can indicate mastery of a skill or a misconception. [14] [15] The occurrence of slips, when a student accidently (or due to carelessness) fails a known item, and guesses, when the student correctly answers an item by chance, are important sources of uncertainty [4] [5]. Uncertainty is particularly important for transfer models when the goal is to build global assessment from indirect evidence. Whereas the success of problem solving and solution analysis tutors rely on the ability to provide just-in-time remedial feedback and decide when to move on to a new topic, the success of curriculum sequencing lies in tailoring the learning content based on an accurate assessment of a large array of skills with the least possible amount of evidence . This requires a model that can build links among skills, such as prerequisites [14] [15]. Recent work in extending BKT has introduced a number of advances, such as the contextualization of estimates of guessing and slipping parameters [4] [5], estimates of the probability of transition from use of help features [6], and estimates of the initial probability that the student knows the skill [26] [27].

Researchers have begun to consider how to model key aspects of students' meta-cognition, motivation, and affect, towards providing adaptive scaffolding which can address individual differences in these areas. Arroyo have created a relatively inexpensive suite of sensors (webcam, conductance bracelet, pressure mouse, posture analysis seat), and have succeeded in deploying detectors of confidence, frustration, excitement, and interest to entire classrooms at one time. [1]

Detectors of off-task behavior [2] [13] have also been developed and validated. Biswas et al. (2010) developed a self-regulated learning model that can identify a range of behaviors in the space of self-regulated learning/ meta-cognition, including monitoring through explanation, self-assessment, and setting learning goals. [7] Recent advances increasingly allow the tutors to adapt not just based on which skills students know, but also based on assessments of complex meta-cognitive, motivational, and affective constructs.

Adaptive and Adaptable Scaffolding

Building scaffolding into software offers the opportunity to support diversity- through individualized support that accommodates learners of different skills, backgrounds, and learning styles, and growth- through options that provide more powerful functionality as the learner develops expertise. A critical component of scaffolding is therefore that it is capable of fading- as the learner's understanding and abilities improve, the computer, much like a human autonomy, fewer hints, etc. The potential advantages of tools with fade able layers of scaffolding are to provide learners with differentiable support that meets their changing needs.

In Guided Learner-Adaptable Scaffolding, learner will be in control of the changing and fading of scaffolding. Scaffolding is categorized into three types, (i) Supportive scaffolding, support for doing the task with a goal for the learner to have internalized the procedures and concepts which had been scaffolded, e.g. demonstrative examples, coaching, and modeling, (ii) Reflective scaffolding is support for thinking about the task by planning, making predictions, evaluation and reflecting about what the learner is doing, if it is working, what his goals are, etc. The mode of comparison and contrast, of thought, of decision-making, are essential for learning. (iii) Intrinsic scaffolding are the supports that change the task itself, by reducing the complexity of the task and focusing the learner's attention, e.g., maps and models for visualization) [16]

Adaptive Scaffolding varies the coaching and critiquing advice, or the problem proposed, based on an evaluation of the learner's understanding. [16]. The user model determines the amount of help or level of problem initially offered to the student, and in turn, the student's reaction is used to adjust the user model.

Adaptable Scaffolding is implemented through giving the learner options to choose a level of scaffolding. Adaptable scaffolding fits well with learner-centered pedagogy, and offers advantages for students' development of autonomous and reflective learning and thinking skills. Allowing students to choose the options they want to use will help them tailor the interface in ways that make more sense to them. [16]

Natural Language Interfaces
Natural Language Interfaces is a type of interface that allows the user to speak or type in their normal everyday language in order to interact with the computer. As communication in learner's language is a major issue in the Rural Indian Education System, a tutoring system in Natural Language Interface would be a comfortable solution.

2.3   Cognitive Load Theory

Cognitive Load Theory (CLT) uses interactions between information structures and knowledge of human cognition to determine instructional design. Designs interact with the characteristics of the information and tasks that learners are dealing with and with the characteristics of the learners themselves. [36]

Expertise develops as learners mindfully combine simple ideas into more complex ones. [36] Well-designed instruction should not only encourage schema construction but also schema automation for those aspects of a task that are consistent across problems. [33] Novel information must be processed in working memory in order to construct schemata in long-term memory. The ease with which information may be processed in working memory is a focus of CLT. The working memory load may be affected either by the intrinsic nature of the learning tasks themselves (intrinsic cognitive load) or by the manner in which the tasks are presented (extraneous cognitive load). If intrinsic load is high, extraneous cognitive load must be lowered; if intrinsic load is low, a high extraneous cognitive load due to an inadequate instructional design may not be harmful because the total cognitive load is within working memory load.

Extraneous Cognitive Load

Extraneous cognitive load may be imposed. [36] The written material can be presented in spoken form, to enable some of the cognitive load of visual processor to be shifted to the auditory processor. [25] Some of the major effects that yield better schema construction and higher transfer performance and that may be attributed to a decrease in extraneous cognitive load are goal-free effect, worked example, completion problem effect, split attention, modality, and redundancy effect. [36] They reduce the extraneous cognitive load by focusing learner's attention on problem states, available operators and useful solution steps, by reducing the size of problem space and integrating the information sources, using multimodal presentations thereby distributing the load on different processors and by reducing redundant information presentation to one source of information. [36]

Intrinsic Cognitive Load

Instructional methods that affect intrinsic and so-called germane cognitive load rather than extraneous load are examined. These methods deal with changes from (i) simple to complex learning, (ii) short experiments to lengthy training programs, and (iii) preplanned instruction to adaptive learning. [36]

Simple to Complex Learning

Complex learning aims at the integration of knowledge, skills, and attitudes; the coordination of qualitatively different constituent skills and the transfer of what are learned to daily life or work settings. [34] [35] In conceptual domains, many interacting knowledge structures must be processed simultaneously in working memory to be understood. In skill domains, many interacting constituent skills must be coordinated in working memory for a coherent performance. Such instruction positively affects learning and transfer performance for complex materials with a high level of element interactivity. [10] [21] [31] [32]

The progressive method of presenting information in isolated phases to reduce intrinsic load is an appropriate technique to use for novice learners who are confronted with highly complex materials but who lack the rudimentary schemata for dealing with those materials. [36] Rich learning tasks often require problem solving and reasoning skills. [18] Therefore, the interaction elements must be designed such that they support the working memory in coordinating the acquisition of knowledge, skills and attitudes.

Short Experiments to Lengthy Training Programs

Variability of problem situations encourage learners to construct cognitive schemata because variability increases the probability that similar features can be identified and that relevant features can be distinguished from irrelevant ones. [36] It is well documented that variability of practice may result in beneficial effects on schema construction and transfer of training [23] High variability also increases cognitive load during practice but yield better schema construction and transfer of learning as indicated by a better ability to solve problems that were not solved before. The increase in cognitive load was due to processes directly relevant to learning (schema construction and automation) instead of processes that resulted in extraneous cognitive load. Instructional manipulations to improve learning by diminishing extraneous cognitive load and by freeing cognitive resources is only effective if students are motivated and are willing to invest mental effort in learning processes that use the freed resources.

Preplanned instruction to adaptive learning
Adaptive e-Learning is a straightforward two-step cycle: (1) assessment of a learner's expertise, and (2) the dynamic selection of the next learning task. With regard to the on-going assessment of expertise, a learner who must work laboriously to attain a certain performance level is differentiated from a learner who attains the same performance level with little mental effort. Only the secondlearner who solved the problem with minimal mental effort should be presented with a more complex learning task. With regard to task selection, given the learner's expertise, one might select tasks that are less, equally, or more difficult than the previous task; one might vary the format of the task (e.g., worked examples, completion problems, or conventional problems), or one might vary the amount of problem-solving support that is given to the learner. [36]We use these methods as instructional design guidelines for our tutoring system model.

3   Model of Intelligent Interactive Tutor

We focus on the problems of lack of well-developed and one-on-one tutoring, lack of infrastructure, a good quality curriculum, and low motivational states of rural students. Considering their priority to survive over working for a better future, we choose the learning objective of our tutor as developing the abilities and skills to problem-solving in contexts and situations which make sense to the learners. The goal of this tutor is to teach them not only the knowledge which would define them as "literates" but to go beyond that level and make them self-sufficient to solve real-life problems. We also aim to make this tutor adaptive enough so that they develop a liking towards learning and understand its importance and the need to learn. We propose a model for an Intelligent Interactive Tutor which provides the learners with individualized one-on-one effective tutoring, where they can interact with the tutor freely and customize their learning space as per their wish and comfort. This Tutor provides the learner with various supports helping them to complete a learning task, develop skills and acquire knowledge. As lack of motivation to learn is a major concern in rural areas and self-regulation is a must for informal learning environments, we take some of the previously mentioned inexpensive and affordable technologies into consideration for the design of scaffolds in our tutoring system.

The learning environment of the tutor is based on Problem-Based Learning (PBL) approach where the student learns by solving problems. We create a model where while problem-solving, the system supports the learner with specific scaffolds, just-in-time remedies and feedback, the status of the student's learning path, motivational elements, interactive interface, learner's control over problem representation, and instructional effect, visible/active scaffolds, audio options, and the language of the interface.

Along with cognitive scaffolds, both adaptive and adaptable scaffoldings are incorporated in our tutor but we assume that our target learners might not have the ability to control the fading function of the scaffolds, so we focus more on adaptive scaffolding. Though, we also provide options to turn the scaffolds on and off. A customizable language medium to facilitate individualized learning for them is likely to make the interface more usable and useful, as the focus of our tutor is not the language but the development of problem-solving skills of rural people for a better living.

Cognitive Load Theory (CLT) directed us to design instructional structure for our Intelligent Tutoring System, aligning with the characteristics of the context-based curriculum for the rural students as well as their own characteristics as learners. The interface for a novice will differ from that for the learner with a higher degree of expertise. The interactive elements increase for the relatively expert learner as he becomes used to the system, hence saving him from the overload of information, plus as the expertise level increases, the complexity of the task increases as well. The intrinsic cognitive load for a relatively experienced learner is more than that for a novice and the extraneous cognitive load is reduced for both so that the learners can put attention to the problem states, operators and important solution steps. Scaffolds for a novice are more in number and fading occurs as the learner develops the next level of expertise. Self-assessment is also introduced in the interface at a later stage. The system also indicates the skills and knowledge acquired by the learner at every stage in the form of badges and stars. These badges and stars can be turned into more context-specific rewards which are more appealing to them and hence add up as a motivational factor. Figures 2 and 3 show the conceptual interfaces for a novice and a learner with higher degree of expertise.

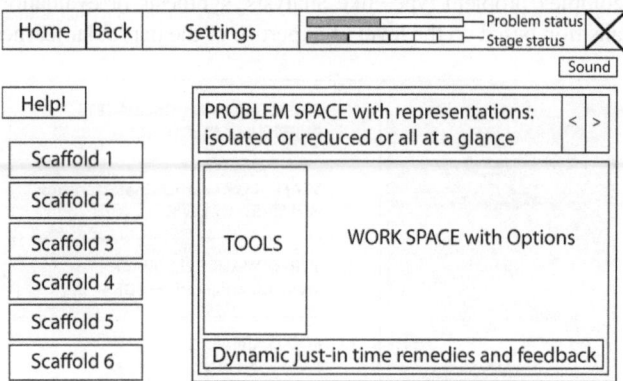

Fig. 1. Conceptual Interface for a novice learner

After the learner solves a problem, the system directs him to the next problem, based on the actions, decisions, the kind of interaction the learner had with the interface elements, the scaffolds he used and those he ignored, skills he acquired and the overall mastery level he achieved. Each learner has his own profile based on his history and the system adapts to each learner model accordingly. Figure 3 illustrates what a learner model contains.

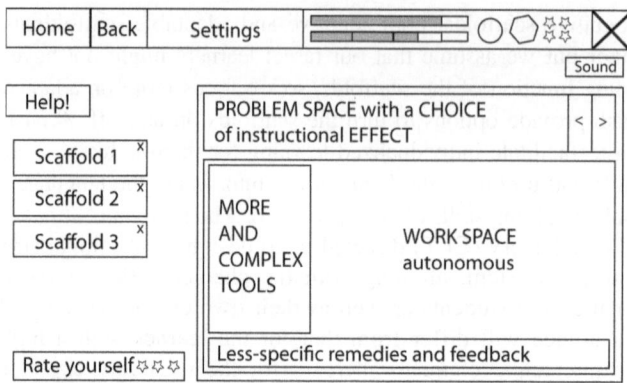

Fig. 2. Conceptual Interface for a learner with higher degree of expertise

This dynamic performance assessment along with the Transfer and Reinforcement Model (TRM) of this system is used to determine the sequence of curriculum for a particular learner profile. TRM allows learning by two approaches, (i) Transfer, and (ii) Reinforcement. The model consists of 3 sets of problems with similar conceptual knowledge, first, a set of problems with content that fall in the comfort zone of the learner (T1) (e.g. familiar, relevant situation, prior experience). Second, a problem-set with similar structural knowledge as that of the first set, but a more abstract natured problem-set which do not relate to a real-life situation and focuses more on the fundamental concept, problem states and skills (T2). Third set of problems begin with the problems which demand practical applications of the underlying concept and these might make a transition to more complex problem types like analysis, synthesis or evaluation. The system decides this transition based on the level of expertise of the particular learner (T3,T4,T5).

ACTIONS' Log	PROBLEMS and PROBLEM-SETS: CURRICULUM SEQUENCE
DECISIONS' Log	
SCAFFOLDS Used	SCAFFOLDS: Learner Characteristics and MASTERY Level
SKILLS Acquired	PERFORMANCE FEEDBACK: Dynamic and Static FEEDBACKS
MASTERY Level	
PROBLEMS' Log	FOCUS AREAS: SKILLS Targetted
STORES each learner's profile	ADJUSTS based on the previous performance

Fig. 3. Learner Mode 1

This is how we use T-Matrix method in designing the curriculum sequence of our model of the tutoring system for transfer of the structural knowledge of one question to another which further transfers the conceptual knowledge to the next question, and this is followed by more questions where this conceptual knowledge is applied practically in different contexts. Figure 4 illustrates the Transfer and Reinforcement Model (TRM).

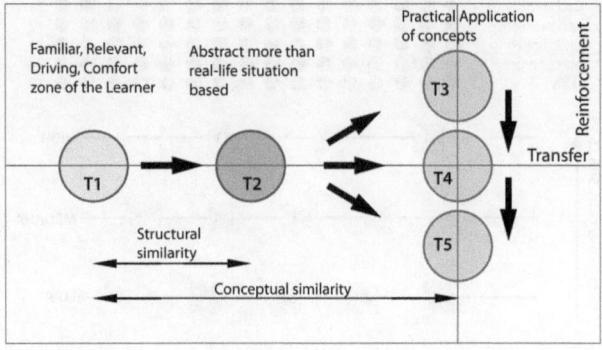

Fig. 4. Transfer and Reinforcement Model (TRM)

The first two sets T1 and T2 subject to schema construction and the last ones T3, T4, and T5 for schema automation. The number of problems in each set is decided by the system based on the learner's progress in acquiring a particular skill. A quick learner with high expertise might make a shift to the next problem set after solving only one problem. But the same shift for a slow learner might be followed by the approach of reinforcement through repeated practice of problem-solving from the same set. We name this group of three problem-sets as a cluster. The overall performance after one cluster and the level of expertise of the learner decides the next cluster-formation which starts with its first problem-set. This is demonstrated in Figure 5.

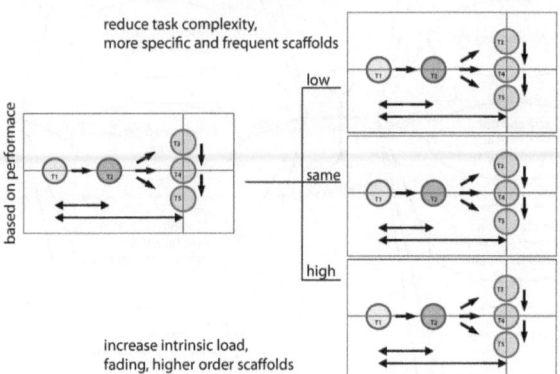

Fig. 5. Curriculum Sequencing between *cluster*

The skills which our tutor focuses on are categorized into three levels, Low, Medium and High based on their relation with surface level knowledge and deep conceptual knowledge. These skills are networked with links attached to one or more problems. A particular skill might be linked to one or more problems, problem-sets or clusters. And one problem is linked to at least one skill. This network is shown in the Figure 6 "Skill Modeling".

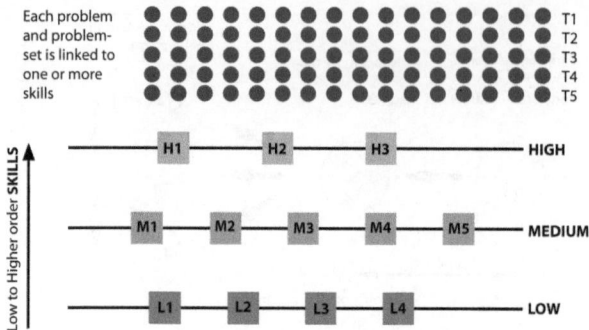

Fig. 6. Skill Modeling

The Intelligent Interactive Tutor has 3 actors, the Learner, the Interface and the System. Figure 7 shows the relations and functions of each other.

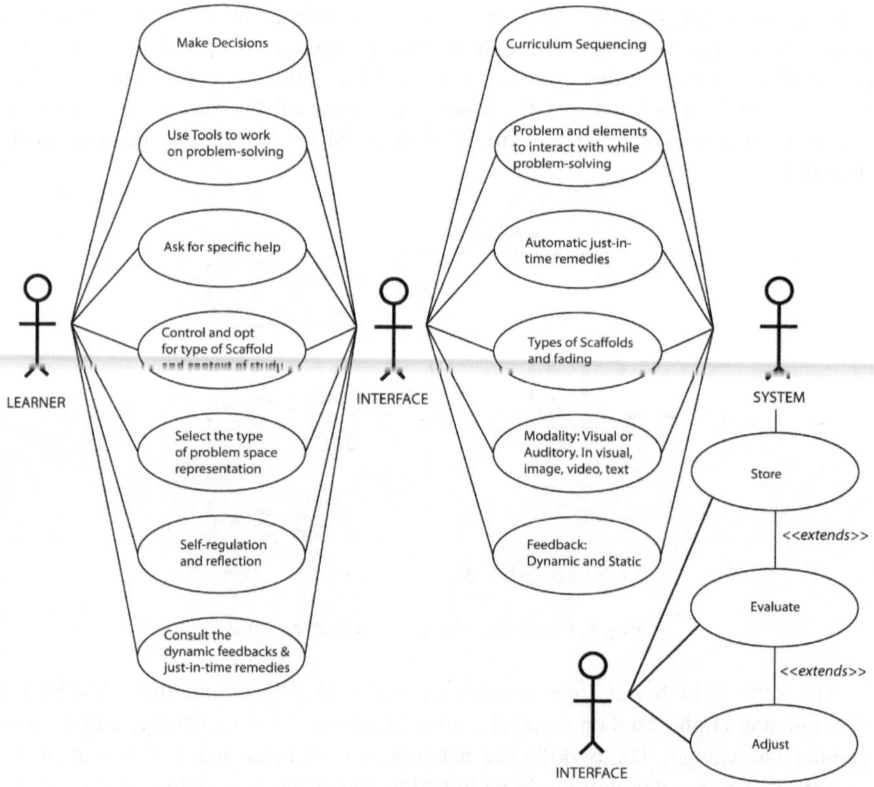

Fig. 7. Use Case Diagram of the conceptual model of Intelligent Interactive Tutor

4   Future Research

The model we propose for the Intelligent Interactive Tutoring System provides the underlying conceptual structure and explains the features and how it functions. The concept behind the content for this tutor is to make the information relevant to the learners so that they can relate to the learning tasks. As the target learners in our paper are the rural students, future researches must be aimed at ethnographic studies in various rural regions of India. These studies would help in designing a generalized curriculum for the Rural India. The curriculum would contain content based on the situations, the real-life problems they face and the skills they should develop. This could further lead to developing a database of problems for the Tutoring System based on the problem characteristics for a Problem-Based Learning environment. The specific skill models would also be made possible to develop by such research work. A management system for regularly updating the curriculum is another potential area to look into.

As this conceptual model is highly dynamic in nature in terms of learner assessment and system adaptive-ability, new methods of quick and inexpensive processing need to be developed.

This model of an Intelligent Interactive Tutor opens up many new opportunities for researchers to work on and implement this system for real in the Rural Indian Education System.

References

1. Arroyo, I., Cooper, D.G., Burleson, W., Woolf, B.P., Muldner, K., Christopherson, R.: Emotion sensors go to school. In: Dimitrova, V., Mizoguchi, R., du Boulay, B., Graesser, A.C. (eds.) Proceedings of the 14th International Conference on Artificial Intelligence in Education, AIED 2009, Brighton, UK, pp. 17–24, 6–10 (2009)
2. Baker, R.S.J.: Modeling and understanding students' off-task behavior in intelligent tutoring systems. In: Rosson, M.B., Gilmore, D.J. (eds.) Proceedings of the 2007 Conference on Human Factors in Computing Systems, CHI 2007, San Jose, CA, USA, pp. 1059–1068 (2007)
3. Baker, R., Corbett, A.: More accurate student modeling through contextual estimation of slip and guess probabilities in Bayesian Knowledge Tracing. In: Proceedings of Ninth Intelligent Tutoring System Conference (ITS 2008), Montreal, Canada, pp. 406–415 (2008), doi:10.1007/978-3-540-69132-7_44
4. Baker, R.S.J., Corbett, A.T., Aleven, V.: Improving contextual models of guessing and slipping with a truncated training set. In: Baker, R.S.J., Barnes, T., Beck, J.E. (eds.) Proceedings of EDM 2008, The 1st International Conference on Educational Data Mining, pp. 67–76 (2008a)
5. Baker, R.S.J., Corbett, A.T., Roll, I., Koedinger, K.R.: Developing a generalizable detector of when students game the system. User Model. User-Adapt. Interact. 18(3), 287–314 (2008b)
6. Beck, J.E., Chang, K.-m., Mostow, J., Corbett, A.T.: Does Help Help? Introducing the Bayesian Evaluation and Assessment Methodology. In: Woolf, B.P., Aïmeur, E., Nkambou, R., Lajoie, S. (eds.) ITS 2008. LNCS, vol. 5091, pp. 383–394. Springer, Heidelberg (2008)

7. Biswas, G., Jeong, H., Kinnebrew, J., Sulcer, B., Roscoe, R.: Measuring self-regulated learning skills through social interactions in a teachable agent environment. Res. Pract. Technology-Enhanced Learn. 5(2), 123–152 (2010)

8. Bloom, B.S.: The 2 sigma problem: the search for methods of group instruction as effective as one-to-one tutoring. Educ. Res. 13(4), 4–16 (1984)

9. Brusilovsky, P.: Adaptive and intelligent web-based educational systems. Int. J. Artif. Intell. Educ. 13, 156–169 (2003)

10. Carlson, R., Chandler, P., Sweller, J.: Learning and understanding science instructional material. J. Educ. Psychol. 95, 629–640 (2003)

11. Cen, H., Koedinger, K.R., Junker, B.: Learning Factors Analysis – A General Method for Cognitive Model Evaluation and Improvement. In: Ikeda, M., Ashley, K.D., Chan, T.-W. (eds.) ITS 2006. LNCS, vol. 4053, pp. 164–175. Springer, Heidelberg (2006)

12. Corbett, A., Anderson, J.: Knowledge tracing: Modeling the acquisition of procedural knowledge. User Modeling and User-adapted Interaction 4(4), 253–278 (1994)

13. Cetintas, S., Si, L., Xin, Y.P., Hord, C., Zhang, D.: Learning to identify students' off-task behavior in intelligent tutoring systems. In: Dimitrova, V., Mizoguchi, R., du Boulay, B., Graesser, A.C. (eds.) Proceedings of the 14th International Conference on Artificial Intelligence in Education, AIED 2009, Brighton, UK, pp. 701–703, 6–10 (2009)

14. Desmarais, M.C.: Performance comparison of item-to-item skills models with the IRT single latent trait model. In: Konstan, J.A., Conejo, R., Marzo, J.L., Oliver, N. (eds.) UMAP 2011. LNCS, vol. 6787, pp. 75–86. Springer, Heidelberg (2011)

15. Desmarais, M.C., Baker, R.S.D.: A review of recent advances in learner and skill modeling in intelligent learning environments. User Modeling and User-Adapted Interaction, 1–30 (2012)

16. Jackson, S.L., Krajcik, J., Soloway, E.: The design of guided learner-adaptable scaffolding in interactive learning environments. In: Proceedings of the SIGCHI Conference on Human Factors in Computing Systems, pp. 187–194. ACM Press/Addison-Wesley Publishing Co. (1998)

17. Jonassen, D.: Supporting problem solving in PBL. Interdisciplinary Journal of Problem-based Learning 5(2), 8 (2011)

18. Kester, L., Kirschner, P.A., van Merrienboer, J.J.G., Baumer, A.: Just-in-time information presentation and the acquisition of complex cognitive skills. Comput. Hum. Behav. 17, 373–391 (2001)

19. Koedinger, K., Cunningham, K., Skogsholm, A., Leber, B.: An open repository and analysis tools for fine-grained, longitudinal learner data. In: Baker, R., Beck, J. (eds.) Proceedings of the 1st International Conference on Educational Data Mining, pp. 157–166 (2008)

20. Lepper, M.R., Woolverton, M., Mumme, D.L., Gurtner, J.L.: Motivational techniques of expert human tutors: lessons for the design of computer-based tutors. In: Lajoie, S.P., Derry, S.J. (eds.) Computers as Cognitive Tools. Lawrence Erlbaum Associates, Hillsdale (1991)

21. Marcus, N., Cooper, M., Sweller, J.: Understanding instructions. J. Educ. Psychol. 88, 49–63 (1996)

22. Mathews, L.M., Rao, B.R.K.: A Feasible Rural Education System. International Journal 3 (2012)

23. McKeough, A., Marini, A., Lupart, J.L. (eds.): Teaching for Transfer: Fostering Generalization in Learning. Erlbaum, Hillsdale (1995)

24. Merrill, M.D.: First principles of instructional design. Educ.Technol., Res. Dev. 50, 43–59 (2002)

25. Mousavi, S., Low, R., Sweller, J.: Reducing cognitive load by mixing auditory and visual presentation modes. J. Educ. Psychol. 87, 319–334 (1995)
26. Pardos, Z.A., Heffernan, N.: Navigation the parameter space of Bayesian Knowledge Tracing models: visualizations of the convergence of the expectation maximization algorithm. In: Proceedings of the 3rd Educational Data Mining Conference, Pittsburgh, PA, June 11-13, pp. 161–170 (2010a)
27. Pardos, Z.A., Heffernan, N.T.: Modeling individualization in a Bayesian networks implementation of knowledge tracing. In: Proceedings of the 18th International Conference on User Modeling Adaptation and Personalization, Big Island of Hawai, USA, pp. 20–24 (2010b)
28. Pavlik Jr., P.I., Yudelson, M., Koedinger, K.R.: Using Contextual Factors Analysis to Explain Transfer of Least Common Multiple Skills. In: Biswas, G., Bull, S., Kay, J., Mitrovic, A. (eds.) AIED 2011. LNCS, vol. 6738, pp. 256–263. Springer, Heidelberg (2011)
29. Schmidt, R., Bjork, R.: New conceptualizations of practice: Common principles in three paradigms suggest new concepts for training. Psychological Science 3, 207–217 (1992)
30. Sockalingam, N., Schmidt, H.G.: Characteristics of problems for problem-based learning: The students' perspective. Interdisciplinary Journal of Problem-based Learning 5(1), 3 (2011)
31. Sweller, J., Chandler, P.: Why some material is difficult to learn. Cognit. Instruct. 12, 185–233 (1994)
32. Tindall-Ford, S., Chandler, P., Sweller, J.: When two sensory modes are better than one. J. Exp. Psychol.: Appl. 3, 257–287 (1997)
33. van Gerven, P.W.M., Paas, F., van Merrienboer, J.J.G., Schmidt, H.G.: Cognitive load theory and aging: Effects of worked examples on training efficiency. Learn. Instruct. 12, 87–105 (2002)
34. van Merriënboer, J.J.G., Kirschner, P.A., Kester, L.: Taking the load off a learner's mind: Instructional design for complex learning. Educ. Psychol. 38, 5–13 (2003)
35. van Merriënboer, J.J.G., Paas, F.: Powerful learning and the many faces of instructional design: Toward a framework for the design of powerful learning environments. In: de Corte, E., Verschaffel, L., Entwistle, N., van Merriëenboer, J. (eds.) Unravelling Basic Components and Dimensions of Powerful Learning Environments, pp. 1–20. Elsevier Science, Oxford (2003)
36. van Merriënboer, J.J.G., Sweller, J.: Cognitive load theory and complex learning: Recent developments and future directions. Educational Psychology Review 17(2), 147–177 (2005)
37. Yudelson, M.V., Koedinger Jr., P.I., Koedinger, K.R., Mellon, C.: Towards Better Understanding of Transfer in Cognitive Models of Practice. In: Proceedings of the Fourth International Conference on Educational Data Mining (2011)

Crop Classification Using Gene Expression Programming Technique

Omkar Subbarama Narasipura , Rithu Leena John[2], Nikita Choudhry[2],
Yeshavanta Kubusada[2], and Giridhar Bhageshpur[2]

[1] Department of Aerospace Engineering, Indian Institute of Science, Bangalore, India
`omkar@aero.iisc.ernet.in`
[2] Department of Information Technology, National Institute of Technology Karnataka,
Surathkal, Karnataka, India
`yeshavanta.kp@gmail.com`

Abstract. Precise classification of agricultural crops provides vital information on the type and extent of crops cultivated in a particular area. This information plays an important role in planning further cultivation activities. Image classification forms the core of the solution to the crop coverage identification problem. In this paper we present the experimental results obtained by using Gene Expression Programming (GEP) to classify the crop data obtained from satellite images. We have adopted supervised one-against-all learning technique to perform the classification of data. Gene Expression Programming provides an efficient method for obtaining classification rules in the form of a mathematical expression for a given data set containing input and output variables. We have also compared the classification efficiencies obtained with those of other classifiers namely Support vector machines and Artificial neural networks. Sensitivity Analysis has also been carried out to determine the significance of each input variable.

Keywords: Gene expression programming, crop classification, Sensitivity analysis.

1   Introduction

Agriculture is the process of producing food, fiber, feed and other goods by the systematic growing and harvesting of crops. Its importance in the Indian society can hardly be over-emphasized. Thus, there arises a need to make the best possible use of cultivable area. For efficient use of arable land and for the estimation of temporal changes in it, there exists a necessity for accurate information on crop cultivation. Crop classification provides the necessary information for this purpose and   it can be done on the basis of growing cycle , crop type and species, variety, season, land type, crop use (food/fodder), method of processing and cultivation techniques.

Information about crops and agricultural activities can be acquired through remote sensing [1]. Remote Sensing (RS) using space-borne sensors is the tool that can be

A. Agrawal et al. (Eds.): IITM 2013, CCIS 276, pp. 200–210, 2013.

used for obtaining observations on spectral behavior of crops as well as their growing environment, i.e., soil and atmosphere. There are satellites worldwide that provide these images. Quick-Bird [2] is an American earth observation satellite that collects high-resolution multispectral imagery at 2.4 and 2.8meter resolutions. We have utilized 4-band images acquired from this satellite as the input dataset in our experiment for classification. The classification problem can be dealt with in two ways: supervised learning and unsupervised learning. When the ground truth for the input data set is available, supervised learning is preferred over unsupervised learning to perform classification (detailed explanation in [3]). The ground truth for the Quick-Bird dataset has previously been acquired by Omkar *et al* [4] and hence we have adopted supervised learning to perform classification.

Evolutionary algorithms (EAs), such as Ant-Miner and Genetic Programming, make use of the rule induction model, which represents knowledge extracted in the form of rules which are used for classification. Evolutionary algorithms are iterative search optimization techniques that extract an optimal solution from a "population" of solutions. In Gene expression programming, the classification rules are obtained in the form of expressions that relate the attributes of samples and class labels in terms of mathematical operators. These expressions can further be analyzed to perform sensitivity analysis which helps us to gain better understanding of how the input variables influence the categorization of samples into classes. The objective of this paper is to make use of Gene Expression Programming to perform supervised classification of crop data (Quick Bird) based on crop type (sugarcane, ragi, etc.) and extract arithmetic expressions for the same. The efficiency of classification obtained with GEP has been compared with those of other classifiers. We have also carried out sensitivity analysis on the resulting expressions to determine how the output class labels are influenced by each of the input variables.

2   Gene Expression Programming

Gene Expression Programming (GEP) aims to achieve an optimum solution, in the form of a mathematical expression, which relates the input and output variables of the data set. The GEP process begins with a random set of chromosomes which represents solution to the problem in hand, that are produced to form the first generation. Subsequent populations via genetic modification are descendants of this initial population. In order to form the initial population we have to choose the symbols for the chromosomes, that is, we must choose a set of terminals (the input variables) and a set of functions that are appropriate to solve the problem at hand. For our experiment, the spectral bands of the satellite image denoted by d_0, d_1, d_2 and d_3 along with numerical constants constitute the terminal set and we have confined our operator set to the basic Arithmetic operators : addition(+), subtraction(-), division(/) and multiplication(*).Next, we must provide a fitness function against which the fitness of each individual is evaluated. Once the fitness values have been assigned to all the chromosomes of the population, the next task is to pick out the fittest chromo-somes of the population to reproduce with modification. The selection mechanism that we have chosen is roulette-wheel sampling In order to form the next population; the selected chromosomes are modified using the genetic operators. In our experi-ment we have utilized the following genetic operators:

- Mutation
- Inversion
- Transposition (Insertion Sequence, Root Insertion sequence, gene)
- Crossover (one-point and two-point)

Working of all the genetic operators has been explained in detail in [5]. The process of GEP has been schematically represented in Figure 1. In this paper we have used GEP technique to generate mathematical equations which predict possible throughput of the route. GEP is very efficient compared to other Evolutionary algorithms because it combines the advantages of both Genetic Programming (GP) and Genetic Algo-rithms (GA) [5] and it provides better results to the benchmark problems than both GP and GA [5]. Hence we have employed GEP for implementation.

3   Methodology

3.1   One against All Learning

For a two-class (binary) problem, the GEP expression performs classification by re-turning a positive or non-positive value indicating whether or not a given instance belongs to that class. To extend GEP to n-class classification problems, where n>2, we adopt the one against-all method to transform the n-class problem into n 2-class problems. These are constructed by using the examples of class i as the positive ex-amples and the examples of classes other than i as the negative examples.

In the Quick-Bird data set, there are 4 classes and hence the binary-class classifica-tion problem is extended to a *4* binary-class classification problem. In this method we obtain one expression for each class to recognize instances belonging to that class and reject instances of other classes. A threshold of 0.5 is chosen such that if a sample returns a value above 0.5 for an expression, it is classified as a positive sample for that class and is classified as a negative sample if it returns a value below 0.5.We have found the "One Against All" technique to be accurate for our experiment and thus have adopted it, though it might not be the case for every experiment.

3.2   Classifying a Given Sample

After the four expressions are obtained, in order to classify the given data sample, the sample's values of d_0, d_1, d_2, d_3 are substituted in the class expressions obtained pre-viously.

Let O_i be the output of $GEPE_i$, where $GEPE_i$ represents the gene expression for class i,

Then $O_i = GEPE_i(X)$ (1)

If $O_i >= 0.5$, $X \in Class_i$

If $O_i < 0.5$, $X \notin Class_i$

The dataset used represents a high resolution image of southern India. The study area is a region around Mysore district in Karnataka, India. It has a densely cultivated set-up and basic crop coverage classes are present. It has dimensions of 1357×5929 pixels and the geographical area it covers is 2.748×7.973 km. "One level" classification has been carried out by dividing the image into four classes representing sugarcane, ragi, paddy and mulberry. The ground truth and high resolution image were overlaid above one another using tools Erdas Imagine 8.5. There are totally 6507 entries in the dataset out of which 1601 were used for training and remaining 4906. were used for testing.

3.3   Sensitivity Analysis

Sensitivity Analysis (SA) is the study of how the changes in the output of a model (numerical or otherwise) can be apportioned to different sources of uncertainty in the model input[7]. This process is an integral part of a knowledge extraction technique, so we have performed it as well in order to provide a more distinct interpretation of the data. It was carried out for each of the arithmetic expressions obtained in the previous section. The techniques used for SA are varied. But the technique that we have used is Parametric Sensitivity Analysis which is described in detail in [8].

It provides information on factors that mostly contribute to the output variability, the region in the space of input factors for which the model output is either maximum or minimum or within pre-defined bounds, interaction between factors, optimal or instability regions within the space of factors for use in a subsequent calibration study. Sensitivity Analysis is common in physics and chemistry, in financial applications, risk analysis, signal processing, neural networks and any area where models are developed[13].Parametric Sensitivity analysis methodology involves identification of the relative contribution of each input for a particular output. For instance consider a mathematical model wherein the output Y is a function of k inputs:

$$Y = f(d_0, d_1, ... d_k)$$ (2)

The sensitivity gain for a given class with respect to each input variable- namely d_0, d_1 ,d_2, d_3 is calculated by the given formula below..

$$\left| \frac{\dfrac{dY}{Y}}{\dfrac{dd_i}{d_i}} \right|$$

Here $i=0,1,2,3$ and Y is the algebraic expression for the class being analysed. The following section is a detailed explanation of Parametric Sensitivity Analysis technique adopted. By performing differentiation with respect to $d_0(i=0)$ for the expression of class 1 we get a derivative expression for class 1. In this derivative, the values of d_0, d_1, d_2, d_3 and the constants (C_0, C_1) are substituted from the first sample of the test data set. Next the results is multiplied by d_0. This is iteratively done for all 4906 samples (since the data set is that large), yielding us 4906 different numeric values. This set of values is termed as $\mathbf{A_x}$.

$$\mathbf{A_x} = \frac{dY}{dd_i} * d_i \tag{3}$$

For each class expression, the same procedure is repeated, wherein the values of the 4 variables from the testing data set are substituted into the mathematical expression of each class. This set of values is termed as $\mathbf{B_x}$.

$$\mathbf{B_x} = Y \tag{4}$$

Every value in $\mathbf{A_x}$ is divided by its corresponding value in $\mathbf{B_x}$. After summing up these values, their average is calculated is shown below

$$M = \frac{\left(\sum_{j=1}^{4906} \left| a_j \middle/ b_j \right| \right)}{4906} \tag{5}$$

The value "M" is sensitivity gain of class C1 with respect to d_0.

4   Experiment and Results

In GEP, the expressions evolved are in the form of KARVA k- expressions[9] and these expressions can be easily converted into mathematical expressions. Table 4 has the mathematical expressions for each class. In the following expressions each gene contains random numerical constants (C_0, C_1) , these values are different for each gene. They are represented as G_1C_0, G_1C_1 for gene 1 and G_2C_0, G_2C_1 for gene 2 in a chromosome. The values of these numerical constants have been tabulated in Table 8.

The GEP parameters like head length of a chromosome, number of genes in the chromosome, number of chromosomes in each population, etc. were predefined by us . In the due course of experiment, values were changed to suit the problem and get better results. The parameter values we used are documented in Table 1.

Table 1. GEP Parameters

Parameter	Values
Exclusion Level	1.1
Mutation Rate	0.044
Inversion Rate	0.1
Number of Generations	5000
Population Size	30
Linking Function	+
Head Length	9
Number of Genes	2

Table 2. Confusion Matrix for training data using GEP

Class No	C_1	C_2	C_3	C_4
C_1	362	0	0	0
C_2	0	500	0	0
C_3	0	0	500	0
C_4	0	0	0	239

Table 3. Confusion Matrix for testing data using GEP

Class No	C_1	C_2	C_3	C_4
C_1	1182	0	0	0
C_2	0	1139	0	0
C_3	0	0	1274	0
C_4	0	0	0	1311

Table 4. Equations of the corresponding classes

Class No	Mathematical Expression
C_1	$\dfrac{\left(d_2 + (d_3 - d_0 + d_1)\right)}{G_0 C_1} - d_2 + \dfrac{(d_3 - G_2 C_1)*\left(\frac{d_3}{G_2 C_1}\right)}{G_2 C_0 - d_2} + \left((d_3 + G_2 C_1) - \left(\frac{d_1}{d_3}\right)\right)$
C_2	$\left(\left((G_1 C_0 * G_1 C_1) - (G_1 C_0 + d_3) + (d_0 + d_3)\right) - \left(\frac{d_2}{G_1 C_0} * d_3\right)\right) + \left((d_1 + d_0)*(G_2 C_0 * G_2 C_0) + \left(\frac{(d_0 + d_0)}{(d_0 * G_2 C_1)}\right)\right)$
C_3	$d_0 + \dfrac{(G_2 C_1 * G_2 C_0) - (d_0 + d_0)}{1} + (G_2 C_1 + d_1) + (d_2 - d_1)$
C_4	$\dfrac{\frac{(d_2 - d_1 + d_3 - d_1)}{d_0}}{G_1 C_0} + d_3 - d_2 - d_0 + \dfrac{\frac{(d_2 - G_2 C_1 + d_3 - d_0)}{d_0}}{G_2 C_0} + d_3 - d_2 - d_0$

Table 5. Showing the sensitivity analysis results for each of class's k-expression with respect to each input variable

Class No	d_0	d_1	d_2	d_3
C_1	0.71	0.069	3.08	12.58
C_2	3.26	3.76	7.72	7.72
C_3	6.95	--	11.48	--
C_4	0.38	--	2.04	2.98

Table 6. The constants used in the mathematical expression

Class No	$G_1 C_0$	$G_1 C_1$	$G_2 C_0$	$G_2 C_1$
C_1	-4.102569	-5.865693	-0.246673	5.819092
C_2	1.334472	8.14331	-4.936982	-6.500397
C_3	4.246368	5.066558	2.807099	-4.773468
C_4	9.373169	1.834442	-5.160522	2.094238

The Equation obtained after the sensitivity analysis is tabulated in Table 7.Sensitivity analysis is carried only on C_1 and C_2 as class C_3, C_4 expressions were dependent on two and three input variables correspondingly new expressions for these classes are not generated. The constants obtained after sensitivity analysis is tabulated in table 8.

Table 7. Equations obtained after sensitivity analysis

Class No	Mathematical Expression
C_1	$\left(\dfrac{d_2}{d_1}\right) - \left(\dfrac{G_1 C_0}{(d_0 - d_2)+1}\right) + \left(\dfrac{d_1}{((d_1 - G_2 C_0) - (d_0 * G_2 C_1))*\left(\left(\dfrac{G_2 C_1}{d_1}\right)+\dfrac{d_2}{d_1}\right)}\right)$
C_2	$(G_1 C_1 * d_0)*((d_2 * G_0 C_1)-(2 * G_1 C_0))+((G_2 C_1 * G_2 C_1)-(G_2 C_1 + G_2 C_0))*(G_2 C_1 + G_2 C_0)-\left(\left(\dfrac{d_1}{G_2 C_{11}}\right)* d_2 * d_2\right)$

Table 8. Equations obtained after sensitivity analysis

Class No	$G_1 C_0$	$G_1 C_1$	$G_2 C_0$	$G_2 C_1$
C_1	3.46347	2.785553	7.980408	2.785553
C_2	8.124633	-9.847596	-9.347534	0.673645

The following figures show the ROC curves plotted for the sake of comparison with Artificial Neural Networks and Support Vector Regression. In the figures from Figure 1 to 4 we have plotted the ROC curve to compare. In diagrams G represents Gene expression programming , S represents Support vector Regression and A represents Artificial Neural Networks. As all the three techniques give discrete values we have got points in the graphs.

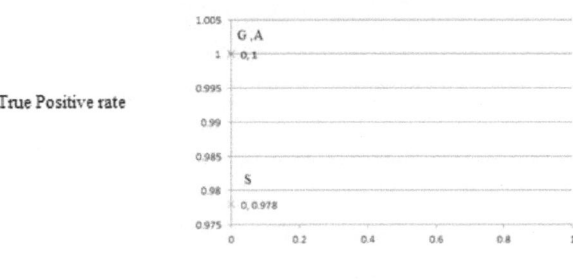

Fig. 1. ROC Curve for Class 1

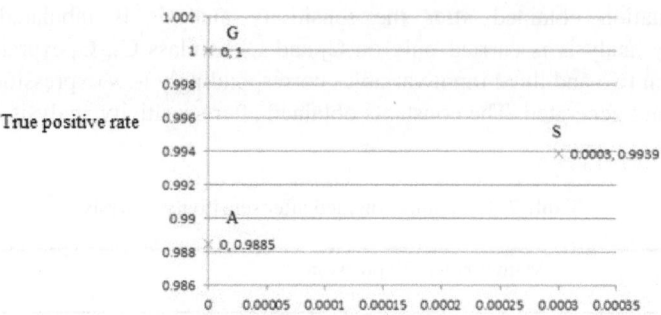

Fig. 2. ROC Curve for Class 2

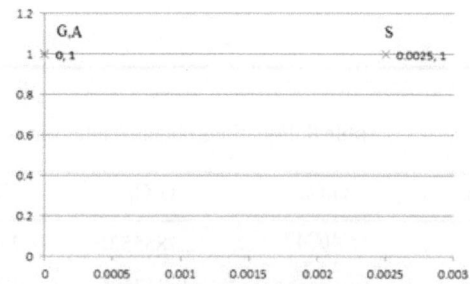

Fig. 3. ROC curve for Class 3

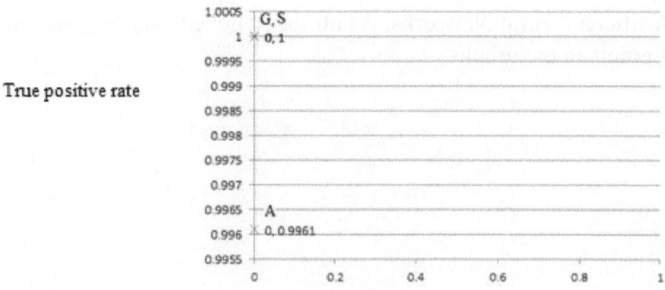

Fig. 4. ROC Curve for class 4

5   Comparison with Artificial Neural Networks and Support Vector Regression

Artificial neural networks (ANN) are simplified artificial models based on the biological learning process of the human brain .The procedure most commonly used to train an ANN is a method known as back-propagation [10]. The ANN was trained using the Fast Artificial Neural Network Library (FANN) [11].For training, a mean square error (MSE) of 10^{-5} and a maximum iteration number (epoch) of 50000 were used. The output function used is the sigmoid function. The function used in hidden layer is sigmoid function. The structure of the ANN giving best results was 4-3-1 where the 4 represent the numbers of nodes in the input layer, the hidden layer had 3 nodes and the Output layer had 1 node. The initial weights and biases of the network were selected randomly. SVMs (Support Vector Machines) are a useful technique for data classification. It is a non-probabilistic binary linear classifier which takes a set of input data and predicts, for each given input, which of two possible classes comprises the input. The idea behind SVM design is to choose support vectors that will maximize the separation between training data. For our experiment we trained a SVM using LIBSVM with the same dataset as used with GEP with one-against-all classification. The type of SVM used is C-SVC (C-Support Vector Classification). For training, 1601 samples are used and 4906 samples for testing (same as GEP).

For a better comparison of the classifiers Receiver operating characteristics (ROC) curve has been plotted for each class. ROC curve is plotted by taking true positive rate or sensitivity on y-axis and false positive rate or 1-specificity on the x-axis [12]. Any point in ROC space corresponds to the performance of a single classifier on a given distribution. Here the classifiers we compare are GEP, ANN and SVM, all of them can be considered as hard-type classifiers since they output only discrete class labels in our experiment.

6   Conclusion

In this paper we have carried out supervised crop classification using Gene Expression Programming technique to classify high resolution satellite images. Using one-against all approach we obtained arithmetic expressions specific to each class. Sensitivity analysis is carried out to determine the sensitivity of input variables, and eliminate the least sensitive input variable to obtain more compact and simpler expressions. Further principal component analysis is carried out to find the most dominant input variable, the results of principal component analysis concur with that of sensitivity analysis. A confusion matrix is obtained for the classification of each class and the classification accuracy, sensitivity and specificity are calculated. Finally crop classification with the same data is carried out using ANN and SVM. We can conclude from the ROC graphs that the predictive power of GEP is better than of ANN and SVM. GEP also has an added advantage of expressing the relationship between input variables and target class label via an algebraic expression which gives us a better understanding of the data set.

References

1. Ohkubo, N.: A New supervised learning of neural networks for satellite image classifica-tio. In: International Conference on Image Processing-ICIP 1999, vol. 1, pp. 505–509 (1999)
2. Rossi, L.: New High resolution satellite application: Quick-Bird. Presented at EFITA Conference, Hungary (2003)
3. http://gautam.lis.illinois.edu/monkmiddleware/public/analyti cs/clusterclassification.html (March 10, 2012)
4. Omkar, S.N., Senthilnath, J., Mudigere, D., Manoj Kumar, M.: Crop Classification using Biologically Inspired Techniques with High Resolution Satellite Image. Journal of the Indian Society of Remote Sensing. Springer India 36, 172–182 (2008)
5. Cheng, J., Greiner, R., Kelly, J., Bell, D., Liu, W.: Learning Bayesian networks from data: An information-theory based approach. Artificial Intelligence 137, 43–90 (2002)
6. Ferriera, C.: Gene Expression Programming, Mathematical Modelling by Artificial Intelligence, 2nd edn. Springer (May 2006)
7. Satelli, A.: Sensitivity Analysis for Importance Assessment. Risk Analysis 22, 579–590 (2002)
8. Cho, K.-H., Shin, S.-Y., Kolch, W., Wolkenhauer, O.: Experimental Design in Systems Biology Based on Parameter Sensitivity Analysis with Monte Carlo Simulation: A case study for the TNFα mediated NF-κB Transduction Pathway
9. Suresh, S., Sundararajan, N., Saratchandran, P.: A sequential multi-category classifier using radial basis function networks. Neuro-Computing 71(7-9), 1345–1358 (2008)
10. Fast Artificial Neural Network (November 19, 2011), http://leenissen.dk/ fann/wp/
11. He, H., Garcia, E.A.: Learning from imbalanced data. IEEE Transactions on Knowledge and Data Engineering 21(9), 1263–1284 (2009)
12. Wikipedia (July 15, 2011), http://en.wikipedia.org/wiki/Sensitivity_ analysis

Software Security Testing Process: Phased Approach

Suhel Ahmad Khan and Raees Ahmad Khan

Department of Information Technology
BabasahebBhimraoAmbedkar University (A Central University),
Lucknow-226025
ahmadsuhel28@gmail.com, khanraees@yahoo.com

Abstract. Early identification of defects and prevention of defects migration are key goals of the software security testing process. Early integration of security testing activities into the development lifecycle leads to secure software development. The prescribed key activities of security testing are closely interconnected with security development life cycle to deliver secure software. Software test process elaborates various testing activities and describes which activity is to be carried out when. Given the need and significance of phased approach of security testing, this paper proposes different testing activities to be carried out while integrating it within the security development life cycle.

Keywords: Software Security Testing, Security Test Life Cycle, Security Test Cases.

1   Introduction

Security testing is part of the analysis of security properties in the development systems. These security properties are verified relative to the functional specification, guidance documentation, and high level design of the system [1]. Software Security testing is a continuously growing field. Advance techniques and technologies are rapidly being developed in order to ensure continued security. The intruders or hackers targets on application level which can be easily lacerate security. The hackers exploit its vulnerabilities to obtain sensitive information to take control of the system. The possible disruption to ongoing behavior can be control through security testing.

Security testing is regarded as an important means to improve security of software. Security testing with a structured approach throughout the entire development life cycle gives a good understanding of the software quality and protects from known security risks[2]. If security testing is not considered during development, the application can contain dangerous vulnerabilities and sufficient vulnerability propagation will occur throughout the development phases making enormous risks to the organization. The security development life cycle process positioning as a separate process that has a strict interconnection with security testing activities to perform secure development actions.

A. Agrawal et al. (Eds.): IITM 2013, CCIS 276, pp. 211–217, 2013.

2   Involved Activities in Perspective Framework of Software Security Testing

The motive of software security testing is that the software behavior would be fully operative under hostile conditions. The ultimate objectives of security testing are to validate the robustness and to prevent security vulnerabilities from ever entering the software. While addressing security testing, one of the major issues to consider is to discuss how the system under design deals with possible attacks at early design stage[3, 4]. An effective security testing should test the entire phases, rather than just implementation. A test process is needed to ensure that the designed system can protect asset from attacks with the help of mitigation. An appropriate and accurate security test activity implemented during development may make the software more profitable [5]. In addition to this, an effective and prescriptive process of security testing specifying very clear prioritized activities may be advantageous in different perspectives as follows:

A.   Security Test Strategy & Security Test Plan
  • Preparation of high-level security test plan
  • Designing strategy document for various types of security testing
  • Analyzing various security testing approaches available
  • Selection of security test tools, test effort estimation and scheduling for optimal security testing
  • Planning of resources for complete security testing
B.   Design Security Test Cases
  • Include statement of purpose, what is being tested
  • Elaborate methods, how it will be tested
  • Include step environment data
  • Write the basis security test cases and security test procedures
  • Consider actual functional and security flow
C.   Execute Security Test Cases
  • Prioritize execution of security test cases, identify essential features that must be tested
  • Identify the risk or consequences of not testing some features
  • Run the security test cases, document test results and log defects for failed cases
  • Map defects to security test cases, rested the defect fixes
  • Design security test execution records containing overall results
D.   Capture Security Test Results
  • Prepare security test log
  • Document security test incidents reports
  • Identify the events requiring further analysis
  • Prepare security test summary report
E.   Captures Security Test Metrics
  • Identify base metrics for direct measures
  • Design calculated metrics for indirect measures
  • Metric calculation for software security testing

F. Qualitative Assessment
  • Prepare a set of parameters
  • Document qualitative reporting
  • Make interpretation
  • Give suggestive measures

G. Security Test Closure Report
  • Prepare a checklist
  • List out activities that must be performed after the project is closed
  • Document traceability matrix
  • Do defect trade analysis

3   Security Test Life Cycle Process Integration within the Development Process

In order to gain insight into the quality of software, an integrated approach of security testing is necessary to spot the vulnerabilities in each phase of development life cycle and to mitigate the same then and there to avoid its propagation. An integration of security testing within the development process will reduce the cost of damages and risks associated [6]. Security testing strategy for software product should be developed for each phase. Security testing aims at finding security vulnerabilities prior to making them available to end users. One of the fundamental objectives of security testing is to identify whether the security features of the software implementation are consistent with design.

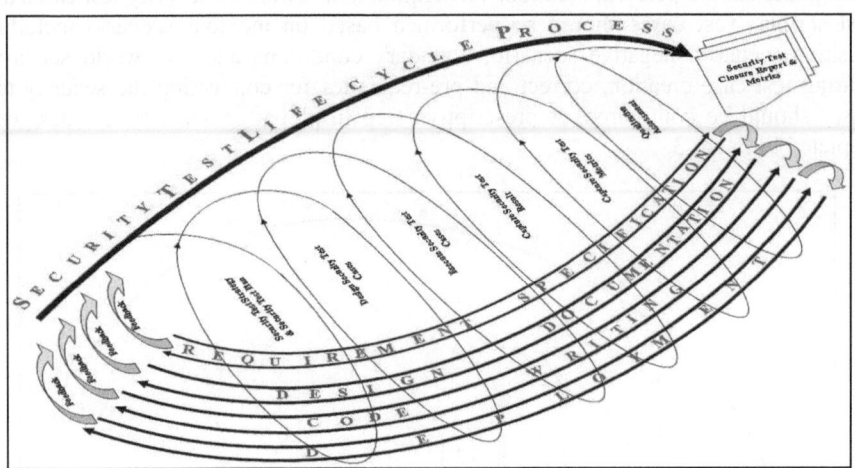

Fig. 1. (a): Security Test Life Cycle Process Integration within the Development Process

Figure 1(a) shows security test life cycle process stating as a separate process that has a very tight interconnection with development activities. Each phase is briefly described in the following section.

3.1   Security Test Strategy and Plan

An appropriate security test plan should be prepared enabling the mapping of security tests to secure requirements and defining the entry and exit criteria for each phase of testing. High level test plan should identify the items to be tested, the features to be tested, the type of testing to be performed, the personnel responsible for testing, the resources and schedule required to complete testing, and risks associated with the plan. A prescriptive step in preparing security test strategy and plan is depicted in figure 2.

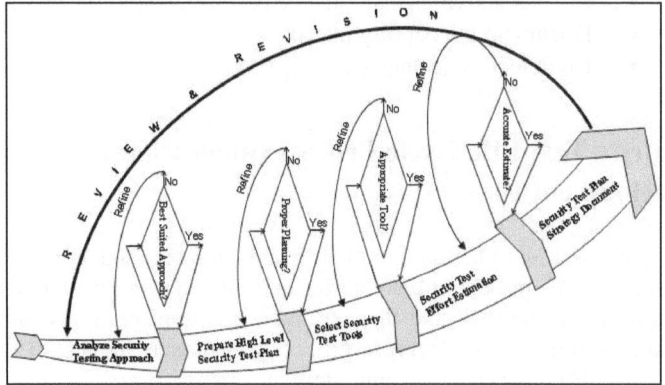

Fig. 2. Process of Security Test Strategy & Security Test Plan

3.2   Design Security Test Cases

This phase should perform creation, verification and rework of security test cases and test scripts. Test cases should be performed based on the four scenario including positive scenario, negative scenario, boundary conditions and real world scenario. During test case creation, correct and pre-requisites for conducting the security test cases should be configured. A prescriptive step in preparing security test design is depicted in figure 3.

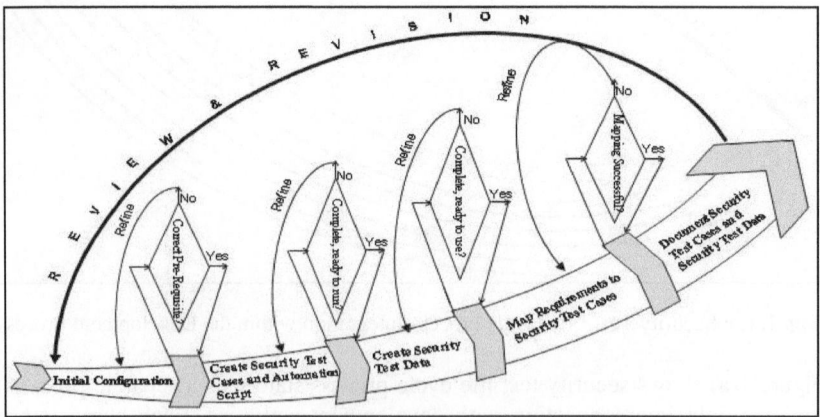

Fig. 3. Process of Designing Security Test Cases

3.3   Execute Security Test Cases

In this phase, security test scripts should be executed in a logical sequence with specific input data. The results should be monitored and output should be recorded in test sheets. Out of the larger cluster of test cases, their priorities of execution should be decided based on some rationale, non-arbitrary criteria. Test results should be documented and log should be prepared with defects for failed cases. Accordingly, security test plan and test cases should be reviewed and revised. A prescriptive step in executing security test cases is shown in figure 4.

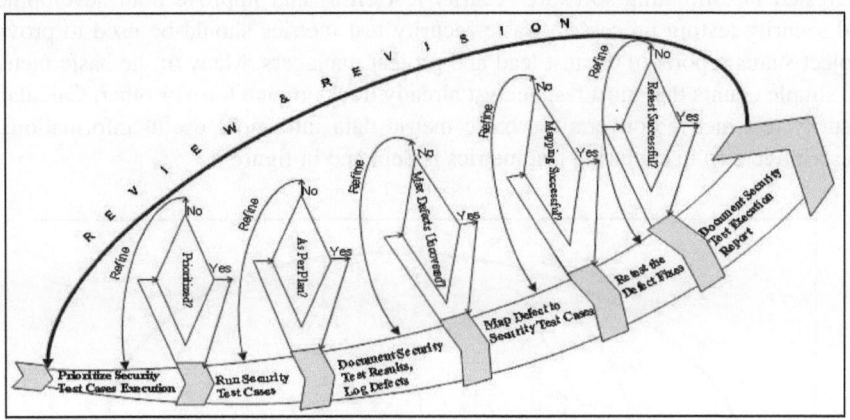

Fig. 4. Process of Executing Security Test Cases

3.4   Capture Security Test Result

After successful security test case execution, the identified bugs should be fixed and retested to declare the result as pass or fail. Test reports should be documented properly. A test log should be prepared to present chronological notes of relevant

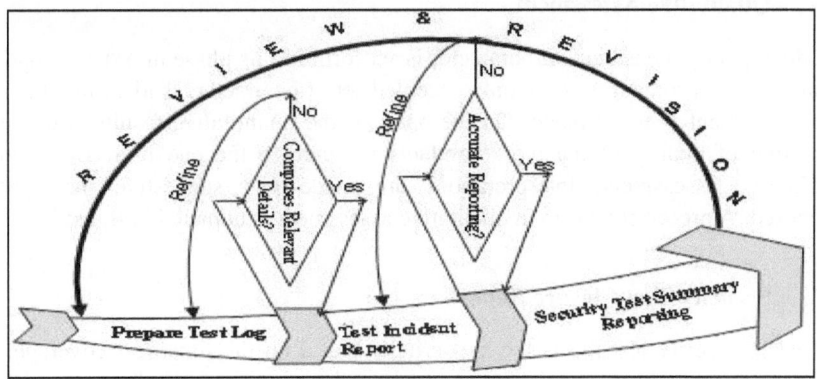

Fig. 5. Process of Capturing Security Test Result

details about the execution of tests. A test summary report should be prepared at last summarizing the results of test activities associated with one or more test design specification and provide evaluation based on such result. A prescriptive step in executing security test cases is shown in figure 5.

3.5   Capture Security Test Metrics

Security test metric should be identified which may aid in precise estimation of project effort, address the interest of metric group, software managers who are interested in estimating software security test effort and improve both development and security testing processes. Basic security test metrics should be used to provide project status reports to the test lead and project managers. Many of the basic metrics are simple counts that most test analyst already tracks in one form or other. Calculated security test metric converts the basic metric data into more useful information. A prescriptive step in capturing test metrics is depicted in figure 6.

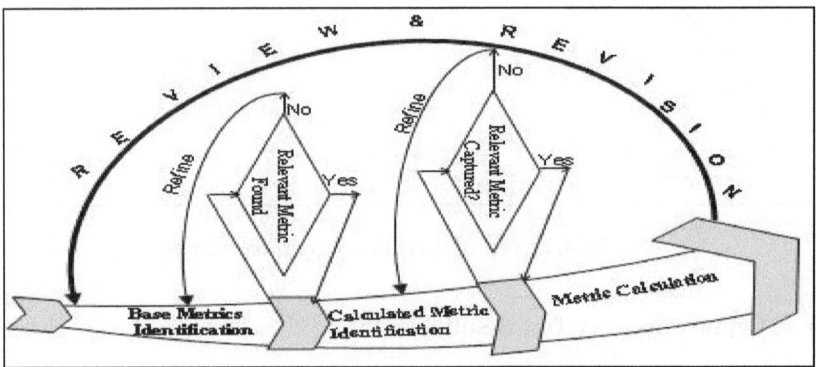

Fig. 6. Process of Capturing Security Test Metrics

3.6   Qualitative Assessment

Product quality measurement parameter is set forth in this phase in order to assess the quality of the product. A commonly accepted set of parameters is identified for which the assessment is to be made. On the basis of the quantitative results, a qualitative reporting of quality of the work products is made to the end user. Based on the qualitative assessment, interpretations are made and suggestive measures are proposed. A prescriptive step in qualitative assessment is depicted in figure 7.

3.7   Security Test Closure Report

Once the security test meets the exit criteria based on the time, test coverage, cost, software, critical business objectives, quality, the activities including capturing key outputs, lesson learned, results, logs, documents related to the project are archived

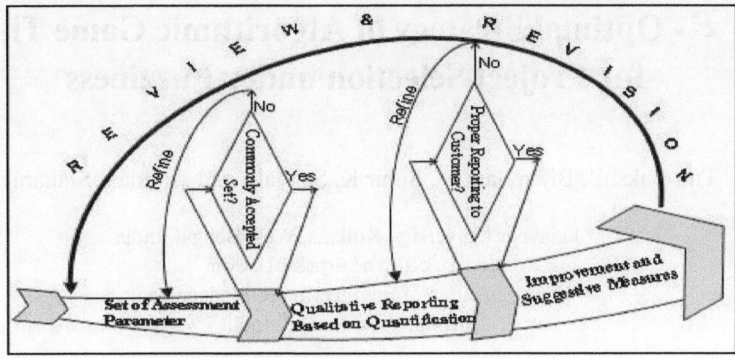

Fig. 7. Process of Qualitative Assessment

and used as a reference for future project. Test closure document should contain a checklist of all of the items that must be met in order to close a test project as well as a list of activities that must be performed after the project is closed.

4   Conclusion

It has become essential to integrate phased security testing process within the development life cycle with the intent of finding errors at each phase well in advance in order to reduce developmental cost, delivery time and rework efforts. The prescribed activities of software security testing process are interconnected with development activities. These security activities are verified through development process. The proposed work may help testers to better understand and execute test in an efficient and effective manner.

References

1. Abrams, M.D.: FAA System Security Testing and Evaluation. MITRE Technical Report (May 2003)
2. Turpe, S.: Security Testing: Turning Practice into Theory. In: IEEE International Conference on Software Testing, Verification and Validation Workshop (ICSTW 2008). IEEE Computer Society (2008)
3. He, K., Feng, Z., Li, X.: An Attack Scenario Based Approach for Software Security Testing at Design Stage. In: 2008 International Symposium on Computer Science and Computational Technology, pp. 782–787. IEEE Computer Society (2008)
4. Gu, T.-Y., Shi, Y.-S., Fang, Y.-U.: Research on Software Security Testing. World Academy of Science, Engineering and Technology, 647–651 (2010)
5. Software Security Testing, Software Assurance Pocket Guide Series: Development, Volume III, Version 1.0 (May 21, 2012)
6. Potter, B., McGraw, G.: Software Security Testing. IEEE Security & Privacy, 32–36 (2004)

An $\mathcal{E}$ - Optimal Strategy of Algorithmic Game Theory for Project Selection under Fuzziness

Tuli Bakshi[1], Bijan Sarkar[1], Subir K. Sanyal[1], and Arindam Sinharay[2]

[1] Jadavpur University, Kolkata, West Bengal, India
tuli.bakshi@gmail.com
[2] Future Institute of Engineering & Management,
Kolkata, West Bengal, India

Abstract. Software project success or failure depends on the ineffective software project management. Success or failure of any project can be attributed by incorrect handling of one or more project variables such as people, proper technology, proper project scheduling and selection. Among these attributes proper project selection is one of the most vital part of software project management. There exist many uncertainties in project management and current software engineering techniques are unable to eliminate them. So there is huge scope for developing. The current researchers have developed a unique model which is capable to take decision on the field of software project selection. This model has two embedded sub models namely fuzzy AHP (Analytic Hierarchy Process) and strategic game model. Here in the first case experts opinions are considered under fuzzy environment and in the second case, different decisions makers act as players in the game module. Different criteria are taken into consideration for choosing optimal strategy of the players. An elaborated case study is also analyzed for testing the output of the system.

Keywords: Software project management, project selection, fuzzy AHP, Strategic game, optimal strategy.

1   Introduction

With the growth in the number of organization adopting software project management system there is an advance increase in the number of multiple simultaneously ongoing and interrelated projects in organization. In this condition as organization have selected more and more projects for accomplishing their targets, objectives. It has become utmost necessary to have a logical and cost effective profit making proper software project selecting mechanism. To evaluate individual projects or group projects and there by choosing to implement some set of projects, fulfilling the objectives of the parent organization is the prime task of a strategic project selection process. This systematic mechanism can be applied to any area of organization's business in which choice must be made from the competing alternatives. Each project will have different cost, benefit and risk criteria under uncertainty. In case of such differences of characteristics, project selection is the very difficult task. It is more

A. Agrawal et al. (Eds.): IITM 2013, CCIS 276, pp. 218–230, 2013.
© Springer-Verlag Berlin Heidelberg 2013

complex to have a portfolio of choosing number of different projects. Project selection is one of the many decisions to be taken by project management system. According to Bakshi et al. [1] proper choice of project is crucial to the long run survival of every organization. This type of decision making system (DMS) comprises of multi-criteria decision making (MCDM) method. Hung Yoon [2] suggested multi criteria decision making is preferable among available classified alternatives. Therefore MCDM is one of the most widely used decision support system in project selection problem [3]. In this mechanism economic, environmental, social and technological factors are taken into consideration for selection of the project and making the choice sustainable. Decision theory for MCDM-project selection mechanism usually analyzes decision making processes from player's point of view, where game theory plays its analytical interactive role among many players. Most of the game theory is concerned with discrete, finite games which consist of finite number of players, their movements, the happening events and the outcome of the game.

The present work depicts game theory-mechanism design model for selecting projects. The mechanism has been developed considering multi criteria decision making environment as the basis. More over the studies have been carried out for project selection and evaluation under fuzziness of interleaved decision outcome.

2 Related Works

R & D project selection mechanism is a critical mediator between product development strategy of an organization and managing process of projects [4]. According to Bakshi et al [4]. To estimate, evaluate and choose the optimal project, optimization techniques are most fundamental quantitative tools. Project selection procedures can be placed in one of the following domains:

a) Unstructured peer review;
b) Project's scoring;
c) Mathematical programming such as integer programming, Goal programming;
d) Economic models, such as Net present value (NPV), Cost-benefit analysis;
e) Decision analysis, such as multi-attribute utility theory (MAUT), decision trees, Analytical hierarchy process   (AHP) and other tools;
f) Artificial intelligence (AI), including expert systems and fuzzy sets;
g) Project optimization.

According to Hwang & Yoon [2] Multi-criteria decision making (MCDM) is applied to preferable decisions among available classified alternatives by multiple attributes. So MCDM is one of the most widely used decision methodology in project selection problems [5]. The MCDM is a method that follows the analysis of several criteria, simultaneously. In this method economic, environmental, social and technological factors are considered for the selection of the project and for making the choice sustainable. Several frameworks have been proposed for solving MCDM problems, namely Analytical Hierarchy Process [AHP] [6], Analytical Network Process [ANP] [7], which deals with decisions in absence of knowledge of the independence of higher level elements from lower level elements and about the independence of the elements within a level. Other framework available are data envelopment analysis (DEA), Technique for order performance by similarity to ideal solution (TOPSIS) [8], VIKOR [9], COPRAS [10], with grey number,[11], LINMAP [12] etc.. With these techniques alternative ratings are measured, weight of the criteria are expressed in précised numbers .The projects' life cycle assessment is to be determined and the impact of all actors is to be measured. There are some mandatory axioms that the criteria describing feasible alternatives are dimensions, which are important to determine the performance.

In the research paper, project selection and evaluation studies have been carried under fuzziness [13-15]. Fuzzy methods were applied to the multi-attribute selection models [16-17]. Sevkli et al. [18] have proposed a method of project selection combining AHP and fuzzy LP. The weights of the project selection criteria are measured using AHP method.

A game is a decision making situation, with many players having objectives that partly or completely conflict with each other. The motive of the players is important in taking the optimal decision. It is better to model the design using fuzzy set theory. Nagoorgani and Revathy [19] have proposed TOPSIS for fuzzy data as the most preferable choice among the all possible choices in MCDM problem. They applied the non-cooperative games such as Prisoner's dilemma to rank the choice of alternatives. An equilibrium has been established using multi criteria decision making which gives the players choice of optimal strategy. In [20] Dytejak et al. proposed an approach for decision support system with regard to sustainable development strategy components evaluation. They presented a concept of game against nature. Each of the components considered to address devoted source of complexity. Chen and Larbani [21] studied discrimination analysis of MCDM problems from game theoretic point of view. They formulated MCDM problem as a bi-matrix zero sum game primarily. Then studied the consensus [weights] in a MCDM game by multi objective technique when many decision periods were involved. Lastly they used the weight to predict the outcome of coming decision period. Zavadsks et al. [22] have used operation research and MCDM tools for many complicated assessment problems as based on criteria values, criteria weights and opinions of stake holders in the ranking of alternatives.

3   Theory of Decision Support System

Every situation which calls for a decision is distinguishable from other. By Payne et al [23], the decision differs the following ways as in figure 1:

1. Problem context: - structural issues, uncertainties, outcomes, urgency, options etc.
2. Cognitive factors:- Decision Makers' (DM) belief and knowledge, attitude to risks, values and preferences etc.
3. Social context:- Dm's identity , numbers, stakeholders, authority over necessary resource and responsibility etc.

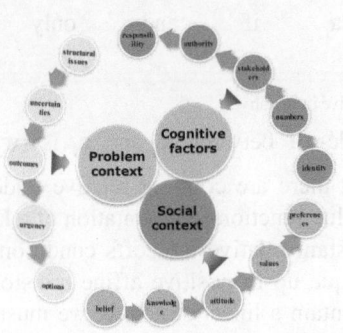

Fig. 1. Factors that affect decision making

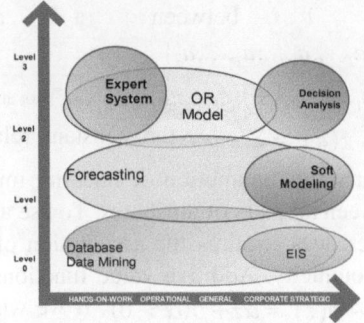

Fig. 2. Category of a variety of DSS

Different definitions are available for Decision Support Systems. We consider as in the form: A Decision Support System is a computer based system which support the decision making processes by helping the DM by to form and explore the implementations of their judgments and hence to make decisions based upon understanding.

A Decision Support System is about modeling and understanding the perspectives, views, preferences, values and uncertainties DM's. Figure 2 indicates the rough classification of the variety of Decision Support System (DSS) tools according to both domain of managerial activity and level of support. A DM's perceptions of and preferences for possible alternatives are usually a mixture of complex conflicting values. The preferential independence is a technical concept which consists of the very common (not universal) features of preferences embodied in the following manner:-

• all other things being equal, more money is preferred to less.
• all other things being equal, greater safety is preferred to less.
• all other things being equal, less environmental effects are preferred to less.

The term attribute means one of the factors which need to be taken into account in a decision. A subset of the attributes is preferentially independent of the remaining attributes if the preferences between any pair of alternatives which differ only in their levels of achievement on attributes within the subset do not depend on the levels of achievement on the remaining attributes. A multi-attribute value function is linear if

$$v\left(a_1, a_2, \ldots, a_q\right) = w_1 a_1 + w_2 a_2 + \ldots + w_q a_q.$$

The coefficients $\left(w_1, w_2, \ldots, w_q\right)$ are known as weighting factors or, simply, weights. Linear value functions are commonly assumed in many areas of economics, commerce and operational research. Comparing time streams of cash-flows according to net present value (NPV) assumes a linear value structure in which:

$$v(a_1, a_2, a_3, \ldots\ldots, a_q) = a_1 + \rho a_2 + \rho^2 a_3 + \ldots\ldots + \rho^{q-1} a_q.$$ However, there is extra structure here over that assumed by linear value theory: the weighting factors are related by $\left[\dfrac{w_i}{w_{i-1}}\right] = \left[\dfrac{\rho^{i-1}}{\rho^{i-2}}\right] = \rho$, for $i = 1,2,\ldots,q.$. Alternatives are compared according to their total financial value, $\left(w_1 a_1 + \ldots + w_q a_q\right)$ in which w_i is the financial value of one unit of the ith attribute. We shall say that there is a constant relative trade-off of

γ_{ij}:   1   between a_i and a_j if   and   only   if
$\left(a_1, a_2, ..., a_i, ..., a_j, ..., a_q\right)$

~ $(a_1, a_2, ..., a_i + \gamma_{ij}\varepsilon, ..., a_j - \varepsilon, ..., a_q)$, for any ε, a positive or negative.

If $v(a) = \Sigma_i w_i a_i$, the constant relative trade-off between $\mathbf{a_i}$ and $\mathbf{a_j}$ is $(\mathbf{w_j/w_i})$.
Clearly the assumption of linearity implies that there are constant relative tradeoffs between all pairs of attributes. To use a linear value function representation of a DM's preferences requires the assumption of the constant relative tradeoffs condition and monotonicity. Additive value functions are unique up to positive affine transformations: $\varphi(z) = \alpha z + \beta (\alpha > 0)$. If we wish to maintain a linear structure, we must further insist that $\beta = 0$. This is necessary because, if $v(.)$ is linear, $v(0, 0, ..., 0) = 0$.

4   Game Theory as Multi-criteria Decision Support System

There are numerous descriptions of the mathematical theory for the evaluation of multi criteria analysis. Game theory can be used to analyze actual strategic interaction in order to mathematically capture behavior in strategic condition in which a decision maker's (DM) depends on the choice of other, because of its focus on conflicting performance [24]. Game theory is often defined as the theory of conflict or a science of strategic decision making. It deals with the decision making in organization where the outcome depends on the decisions of two or more autonomous player, and where no single decision maker has full control over outcome.In game theory zero-sum game describes a situation in which a participant's gain or loss is exactly balance by the losses or gains of the other participants. If the total gains of the participants (here DM) are added up and the total losses are subtracted they will sum to zero. The game obeys a law of conservation of utility value, where utility value is never created or destroyed, only transferred from one player to another. A zero sum game is a game where the total utility of gained by the winning decision maker is equivalent to the total utility lost by the loosing decision maker. All zero sum games have Nash equilibrium and often solve using linear programming technique.

2-persons zero sum game model for decision maker (DM) & ε-optimal strategy

Let a strategy s_i for a decision maker player i, is defined as an element of Δ ($\mathbf{A}_i$). The term, Δ ($\mathbf{A}_i$) is considered as the set of all probability distribution over $\mathbf{A}_i$ where $\mathbf{A}_i$ is the set of real numbers for strategy s_i. Therefore, $s_i(\mathbf{x}) = \Pr [s_i = \mathbf{x}]$.Then we define the support of s_i as, $\mathbf{supp}$ (s_i) = set of all $\mathbf{a}_i \in \mathbf{A}_i$ such that $s_i(\mathbf{a}_i) > \mathbf{0}$. In words – a mixed strategy $s_i(\mathbf{x})$ is the probability that a decision player i will use as his/her pure strategy $\mathbf{x}$. the support of a mixed strategy s_i is the set of all different pure strategies that are used with non-zero probabilities. Now we can use the mixed strategies to claim a relaxation for dominant or Nash equilibrium. Next, we assume that the expected utility of a game is denoted by $\mathbf{U}_i(\mathbf{s}_i, \mathbf{s}_{-i})$.

Let v_i be the maximum over all mixed strategies for player i of the minimum over all mixed strategies of the other player.

$$\therefore v_i = \max_{s_i \in \Delta(A_i)} \left\{ \min_{s_{-i} \in \Delta(A_i)} \left\{ U_i\left(s_i, s_{-i}\right) \right\} \right\};$$

or,

$$\overline{v_i} = \min_{s_{-i} \in \Delta(A_i)} \left\{ \max_{s_i \in \Delta(A_i)} \left\{ U_i\left(s_i, s_{-i}\right) \right\} \right\}.$$

Our observation is: $\overline{v_i} = -v_{-i}$.

Proof:-By definition of zero-sum game, $U_i(s_i, s_{-i}) = -U_{-i}(s_i, s_{-i})$.

Hence, $v_i = \max_{s_i \in \Delta(A_i)} \left\{ \min_{s_{-i} \in \Delta(A_i)} \left\{ U_i\left(s_i, s_{-i}\right) \right\} \right\}$ $-\min \left\{ \min_{s_{-i}} \left\{ U_{-i}\left(s_i, s_{-i}\right) \right\} \right\} = -\overline{v_i}$, hence proved.

$$= \max_{s_i \in \Delta(A_i)} \left\{ \min_{s_{-i} \in \Delta(A_i)} \left\{ U_{-i}\left(s_i, s_{-i}\right) \right\} \right\}.$$

We consider the axiom of relations,

$\max(-f(x)) = -\min(f(x))$

& $\min(-f(x)) = -\max(f(x))$.

And by applying this, we get

Formally, then we can decide to minimizing the strategy of player i equals minus the maximizing strategy of other player.

ε - optimal strategy : - A pair of strategy (s_i, s_{-i}) is optimal if they are the best responses for other. The column DM player's best response to a non-optimal strategy s_i has value more than v, so we come to the condition: $R\left(s_{-i}\right) \leq v \leq C\left(s_i\right)$. A pair of strategies is ε - optimal strategy if $C\left(s_i\right) - R\left(s_{-i}\right) \leq \varepsilon$, i.e. no player can gain more than ε by choosing strategies.

5   Schematic Diagram of Proposed Design

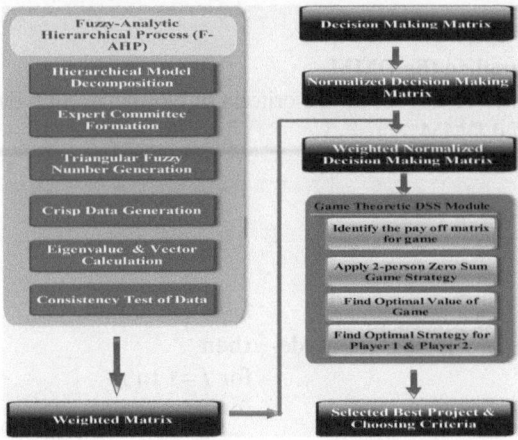

Fig. 3. Schematic Diagram of Proposed Model

6   Algorithms Developed

We have incorporated the following algorithms to construct the proposed model of ϵ - approximate game theoretic mechanism.

Algorithm of Fuzzy-AHP.

Step1:- Decomposition of the problem into the hierarchical   model.

Step 2:- Formation of expert committee.

Step 3:- Generation of triangular fuzzy numbers (TFNs).

Step 4:- Defuzzification of fuzzy data into crisp data.

Step 5:- Calculation of Eigen value and Eigen vectors.

Step 6:- Test of consistency of data derived.

Step 7:- Find the value of the alternatives.

Algorithm to Construct the Decision Making Matrix (DMM).

The DMM can be formed as m feasible alternatives (rows) and n numbers of criteria (columns) as:

$$X_{ij} = \begin{bmatrix} x_{11} & x_{12} & \cdots & x_{1j} & \cdots & x_{1n} \\ x_{21} & x_{22} & \cdots & x_{2j} & \cdots & x_{2n} \\ \cdots & \cdots & \cdots & \cdots & \cdots & \cdots \\ x_{i1} & x_{i2} & \cdots & x_{ij} & \cdots & x_{in} \\ \cdots & \cdots & \cdots & \cdots & \cdots & \cdots \\ x_{m1} & x_{m2} & \cdots & x_{mj} & \cdots & x_{mn} \end{bmatrix},$$

where x_{ij} = score/performance value for i^{th} alternative of jth criteria .

The logic behind the DMM construction is as follows:-

for column j=1 to n
{
if optimal vale of jth criteria is unknown
then
$X_{(OPT,j)} = (X_{ij})_{max}$;
else if the criteria is non-preferable
then $X_{(OPT,j)}$
$= (X_{ij})_{min}$;
}

Algorithm to Normalize the DMM.

In this step, the initial values for all the criteria of Normalized DMM is converted into weighted normalized DMM,

$$\overline{X_{ij}} = \begin{bmatrix} x_{11} & x_{12} & - & x_{1j} & - & x_{1n} \\ x_{21} & x_{22} & - & x_{2j} & - & x_{2n} \\ - & - & - & - & - & - \\ x_{i1} & x_{i2} & - & x_{ij} & - & x_{in} \\ - & - & - & - & - & - \\ x_{m1} & x_{m2} & - & x_{mj} & - & x_{mn} \end{bmatrix}$$

Here we have used the algorithm described below:-

INPUT: - DMM X_{ij} .

OUTPUT: - Normalized DMM $\overline{X_{ij}}$

while (true)
{
do {
if (column ==benefit criteria)
for j=1 to n
then
for i =1 to m
for j=1 to n

$$x_{ij} = \left(x_{ij} \middle/ \sum_j x_{ij} \right) ;$$

else if (column == cost criteria)
then
for i =1 to m

$$x_{ij} = \left(\frac{1}{x_{ij}} \right) \; ;$$

$$x_{ij} = \left(\frac{x_{ij}}{\sum_j x_{ij}} \right) \; ;$$

done

}

}

Algorithm to Calculate Weighted Normalized Matrix.

In this step, the initial values for all the criteria of DMM are normalized into the matrix.

$$\widehat{X}_{ij} = \begin{bmatrix} \widehat{x}_{11} & \widehat{x}_{12} & ... & \widehat{x}_{1j} & ... & \widehat{x}_{1n} \\ \widehat{x}_{21} & \widehat{x}_{22} & ... & \widehat{x}_{2j} & ... & \widehat{x}_{2n} \\ ... & ... & ... & ... & ... & ... \\ \widehat{x}_{i1} & \widehat{x}_{i2} & ... & \widehat{x}_{ij} & ... & \widehat{x}_{in} \\ ... & ... & ... & ... & ... & ... \\ \widehat{x}_{m1} & \widehat{x}_{m2} & ... & \widehat{x}_{mj} & ... & \widehat{x}_{mn} \end{bmatrix}$$

Here we have used the algorithm described below:-

INPUT:- 1) Normalized DMM $\overline{X}_{ij}$ **as**

N[i][j] and

2) **weight matrix W[i]**

OUTPUT: - Weighted Normalized DMM $\overline{X}_{ij}$ **as WN[i][j].**

or j = 1 to n

{

i=0

while(I < n)

{

WN[i][j] = N[i][j] * W[i];

i++;

}

}

7   Case Study

According to expert's decision, the following matrix is formed and then by using Triangular Fuzzy Number the Fuzzy evaluation matrix is formed

Table 1. Evaluation Matrix

Criteria	NPV	ROR	PB	PR
NPV	1	1	2	1
ROR	1	1	2	2
PB	0.5	1	1	1.33
PR	0.5	0.5	0.75	1

Table 2. Fuzzy Evaluation Matrix

Criteria	NPV	ROR	PB	PR
NPV	(1,1,1)	(0.75,1,1.25)	(1,2,3)	(0.75,1,1.25)
ROR	(0.8,1,1.33)	(1,1,1)	(1,2,3)	(1.33,2,4)
PB	(0.33,0.5,1)	(0.8,1,1.33)	(1,1,1)	(1,1.33,2)
PR	(0.25,0.5,0.75)	(0.33,0.5,1)	(0.5,0.75,1)	(1,1,1)

Now calculating all the values by applying Chang's [25] theory the following results are obtained:

$$\begin{cases} S_{NPV} = (3.50, 5.00, 6.50) \otimes (0.04, 0.057, 0.078) \\ = (0.14, 0.28, 0.51) \\ S_{ROR} = (4.13, 6.00, 9.33) \otimes (0.04, 0.057, 0.078) \\ = (0.17, 0.34, 0.73) \\ S_{PB} = (3.13, 3.83, 5.33) \otimes (0.04, 0.057, 0.078) \\ = (0.13, 0.22, 0.42) \\ S_{PR} = (2.08, 2.75, 3.75) \otimes (0.04, 0.057, 0.078) \\ = (0.08, 0.16, 0.29) \end{cases}$$

And

$$\begin{cases} V(S_{NPV} \geq S_{ROR}) = 0.85, \ V(S_{NPV} \geq S_{PB}) = 1, \\ V(S_{NPV} \geq S_{PR}) = 1, \\ V(S_{ROR} \geq S_{NPV}) = 1, \ V(S_{ROR} \geq S_{PB}) = 1, \\ V(S_{ROR} \geq S_{PR}) = 1, \\ V(S_{PB} \geq S_{NPV}) = 0.82 \ V(S_{PB} \geq S_{ROR}) = 0.67, \\ V(S_{PB} \geq S_{PR}) = 1, \\ V(S_{PR} \geq S_{NPV}) = 0.55, \ V(S_{PR} \geq S_{ROR}) = 0.4, \\ V(S_{PR} \geq S_{PB}) = 0.73 \end{cases}$$

Minimum of all values (0.85, 1, 0.67, and 0.4)
The weight W = (0.29, 0.35, 0.22, 0.15)

There are available different projects in an industry. Here the survey data of expansion of optical fiber for telecommunication sector in one part of Iran [26] has been reused. In this example, they were assessed five different feasible alternatives of projects. To ranking of the projects four criteria are identified.

Table 3. Initial Decision Making Matrix

	NPV	ROR	PB	PR
P1	10	3	6	7
P2	13	5	7	9
P3	9	1	8	1
P4	11	3	8	7
P5	12	5	10	5

Table 4. Normalized Decision Making Matrix

Weights	0.29	0.35	0.22	0.15
Criteria	NPV	ROR	PB	PR
P1	0.18	0.18	0.15	0.24
P2	0.24	0.29	0.18	0.31
P3	0.16	0.06	0.20	0.03
P4	0.20	0.18	0.20	0.24
P5	0.22	0.29	0.26	0.17

Table 5. Weighted Normalized Matrix

Criteria	NPV (+)	ROR(+)	PB (-)	PR (-)
P1	0.0522	0.063	0.033	0.036
P2	0.0696	0.1015	0.0396	0.0465
P3	0.0464	0.021	0.044	0.0045
P4	0.058	0.063	0.044	0.036
P5	0.0638	0.1015	0.0572	0.0255

∴ Value of the game: 0.04275
Player 1: (0, 0.82124, 0, 0, 0.17876); Player 2: (0, 0, 0.54404, 0.45596)

It is well known that a strategic game is a model of interacting decision makers [22]. In this case study, the decision makers are considered as players. A strategic game consists of a set of players; for each player, a set of actions are defined; for each player, preferences over set of action profiles are given.

In this case study, four preference criteria were selected for project selection on the basis of questionnaires of same expert.

- ❖ x_1 :-- Net Present Value (NPV) in currency.
- ❖ x_2 :-- Rate of Return (RoR) in currency.
- ❖ x_3 :-- Payback period (PB) in month or year.
- ❖ x_4 :-- Project Risk (PR).

The weight of the criteria is found by the Analytic Hierarchy Process (AHP) under fuzziness by a group of expert. The weight of the criteria and their calculation are presented in table 1 & table 2. The initial decision making matrix, normalized DMM and weighted normalized DMM are presented in table 3, table 4, table 5 respectively.

The matrix game (two person zero sum) game is applied here for the selection of the alternative. The alternatives are assigned to the first player's strategies and the criteria are assigned to the second player's strategies. For the pay off function a dimensionless evaluation numbers are used. For the decision making, there is a normalized matrix of performance (Table 4) and a weighted normalized matrix of performance (Table 5). The initial values of all criteria of the decision making matrix are normalized as:

For benefit criteria $\overline{x_{ij}} = \left(\dfrac{x_{ij}}{\sum\limits_{i=0}^{m} x_{ij}} \right)$ and the criteria whose preferable values are min-

imum are normalized by applying two stage procedures as follows:

(a) First take the reciprocal of each entry as $x_{ij} = \dfrac{1}{x_{ij}^{*}}$,

(b) Then normalized as before by $\overline{x_{ij}} = \left(\dfrac{x_{ij}}{\sum\limits_{i=0}^{m} x_{ij}} \right)$

The optimal value of the game is **0.04275**. As a calculation result there are received the following vector as:

$S_1^{*} = (0,\ 0.82124,\ 0,\ 0,\ 0.17876)$, for the first player

$S_2^{*} = (0,\ 0,\ 0.54404,\ 0.45596)$, for the second player.

8   Result Set and Computational Complexity Analysis

The calculation of the result shows that the value of the second alternative (Project 2) equals to 82% and the value of the fifth alternative (Project 5) equals to 18% (approx).The first, third and fourth alternatives are not involved into the determination of the equilibrium point because their functional influence is lower and they are dominated by the other influence.

Again, the assessments of the criteria are represented by the optimum strategy for the second player. Here the criterion 3(Payback Period) equals to 54% and the criterion4 (Project Risk) is valued by 46% (approx). The criteria 1 & 2 are not involved into the calculation of the equilibrium point, because they are dominated by criteria 3 & 4.

Theorem: In any zero-sum decomposable game, the Nash equilibrium can be found in polynomial time.

Proof: First we prove that Nash equilibrium exist at all.

We assume that every game has Nash equilibrium. Now we try to find one. We define the following variables:-
Here $L_{u,i}$ is a linear function as the game is decomposable. In particular, $L_{u,i} = \sum_{v,j} U_{u,v}(i,j).x_{v,j}$.
We considered the following linear program:

$x_{u,j} = \Pr[\text{player } u \text{ chooses action } j]$
$U_{u,v}(i,j) = \text{the payoff for a player } u \text{ if } u \text{ plays } i \text{ and } v \text{ plays } j$
$L_{u,i}(\overline{x}) = \text{the expected payoff for player } u \text{ if he / she chooses action } i \text{ given that the other players fix their strategy } x_{v,j}$

$$\begin{cases} Minimize & \sum_u w_u \\ subject\ to: & w_u \geq L_{u,i} \quad \forall u,i \\ & \sum_i x_{u,i} = 1 \quad \forall u \\ & x_{u,i} \geq 0 \quad \forall u,i \end{cases}$$

The following claim completes the proof:

Claim. The minimum is achieved at 0 which is Nash Equilibrium.

Proof: - We define: $\overline{w}_u = \sum_i x_{u,i} L_{u,i}$ --this is the average gain of player u. Obviously, $\sum_u \overline{w}_u = 0$, because this is zero sum game. From the linear programming, we can have $w_u \geq \overline{w}_u$. To minimize w_u, we can set $w_u = \overline{w}_u \quad \forall u$, yielding $\sum_u \overline{w}_u = 0$, which is minimal. Thus, for every strategy I, $L_{u,i} \leq w_u$ is no better than the average $\overline{w}_u$, which proves that it is indeed a Nash Equilibrium. Therefore, our proposed game theoretic mechanism design has a 0.04275 approximation.

9   Conclusions

In this designed mechanism, game theory offers an appropriate approach to modeling decision making process. The application of the game theoretical design in multi criteria decision making processes involves the simplification of reality in the model. These mechanism design problem can often be used in other research field as decision support tool. Equilibrium calculation derives more information which in turn be used to assess of the alternatives. With calculation of equilibrium point the same assessment is lifted for all criteria.

On the other hand, fuzzy triangular number enhances the decision maker's domain by continuing assessment. The game theoretic model over this fuzzy triangular number, used as weight of decision alternatives, makes this method more robust.

However, this model has some flaws, described below, to be overcome in the next optimistic future scope:

1   In practice players do not usually holds the complete information about the strategies and pay off functions of the other player.
2   Game theory assumptions that Decision Maker acts perfectly rational way, may never match in real life situation.

References

1. Bakshi, T., Sanyal, S.K.: A Soft-Computing approach for Software Project Selection. In: International Conference on Recent Trends in Information Systems. IEEE (2011) ISBN: 978-1-4577-0792-6/11/$26.00
2. Hwang, C.L., Yoon, K.P.: Multiple Attribute Decision Making and Introduction, p. 2. Sage Publication (1995)
3. Bakshi, T., Sarkar, B.: MCA based performance evaluation of project selection. International Journal of Software Engineering and Applications (IJSEA) 2(2) (April 2011)
4. Bakshi, T., Sarkar, B., Sanyal, S.K.: An Optimal Soft-Computing Based AHP-QFD Model Using Goal Programming for Decision Support System. International Journal of Scientific & Engineering Research 3(6) (June 2012)
5. Saaty, T.L.: The Analytic Hierarchy Process: Planning, Priority Setting. Resource Allocation, 287 p. Mcgraw-Hill (1980)
6. Satty, T.L.: The Analytic Network Process. RWS Publications Pittsburgh (1996)
7. Hwang, C.L., Yoon, K.: Multiple Attribute Decision Making: Methods and Applications. A state of the Art Survey, 1st edn, 259 p. Springer (1981)
8. Wang, T.C., Lee, H.-D.: Developing a fuzzy TOPSIS approach based on subjective weights and objective weights. Expert Systems with Applications 36(5), 8980–8985 (2009)
9. Datta, S., Beriha, G.S., Patnaik, B., Mahapatra, S.S.: Use of compromise ranking method for supervisor selection: A multi-criteria decision making (MCDM) approach. International Journal of Vocational and Technical Education 1(1), 007–013 (2009)
10. Zavadskas, E.K., Turskis, Z., Tamosaitiene, J., Marina, V.: Multicriteria selection of project managers by applying grey criteria. Technological and Economic Development of Economy 14(4), 462–477 (2008d)
11. Zavadskas, E.K., Kaklauskas, A., Turskis, Z., Tamosaitiene, J.: Multi-attribute decision-making model by applying grey numbers. Informatica 20(2), 305–320 (2009b)
12. Srinivasan, V., Shocker, A.D.: Linear programming techniques for multidimensional analysis of privileged. Psychometrika 38, 337–369 (1973)
13. Bayrak, M.Y., Elebi, N.C., Kin, H.T.: A fuzzy approach method for supplier selection. Production Planning & Control 18(1), 54–63 (2007)
14. Bevilacqua, M., Petroni, A.: Traditional purchasing to supplier management: a fuzzy logic-based approach to supplier selection. International Journal of Logistics Research and Applications 5(3), 235–255 (2002)
15. Tuzkaya, G., Ozgen, A., Ozgen, D., Tuzkaya, U.R.: Environmental performance evaluation of suppliers: a hybrid fuzzy multi-criteria decision approach. International Journal of Environmental Science and Technology 6(3), 477–490 (2009)
16. Razmi, J., Rafiei, H., Hashemi, M.: Designing a decision support system to evaluate and select suppliers using fuzzy analytic network process. Computers & Industrial Engineering 57(4), 1282–1290 (2009)
17. Sreekumar, Mahapatra, S.S.: A fuzzy multi-criteria decision making approach for supplier selection in supply chain management. African Journal of Business Management 3(4), 168–177 (2009)
18. Sevkli, M., Koh, S.C.L., Zaim, S., Demirbag, M., Tatoglu, E.: Hybrid analytical hierarchy process model for supplier selection. Industrial Management & Data Systems 108(1), 122–142 (2008)

19. Nagoorgani, A., Revathy, K.: Equilibrium Analysis in Prisoner's Dilemma using Fuzzy Numbers. International Journal of Algorithms, Computing and Mathematics 2(3), 9–13 (2009)
20. Dytczak, M., Ginda, G.: Multi-Criterion Evaluation of Development Strategy Components in the Presence of Inangibles and Uncertainty. In: 19th International Conference on Systems Engineering. IEEE (2008) ISBN: 978-0-7695-3331-5/08
21. Chen, Y.W., Larbani, M.: Multiple Attribute Decision Making in Dynamics:A Multi-Objective Game Approach. In: MCDM 2004, Whistler, B.C, Canada, August 6-22 (2004)
22. Peldschus, F., Zavadskas, E.K., Turskis, Z., Tamosaitiene, J.: Sustainable Assessment of Construction Site by Applying Game Theory. Inzinerine Ekonomika-Engineering Economics 21(3), 223–237 (2010) ISSN 1392-2785
23. Payne, J.W., Bettman, J.R., Johnson, E.J.: Behavioural Decision Research: A Constructive Processing Perspective. Annual Review of Psychology 43, 87–131 (1992)
24. Luce, R.D., Raiffa, H.: Games and Decisions: Introduction and Critical Survey. Wiley & Sons, New York (1957)
25. Chang, D.Y.: Theory and Methodology Applications of the extent analysis method on fuzzy AHP. European Journal of Operational Research 95, 649–655 (1996)
26. Dodangeh, J., Mojahed, M., Yusuff, R.M.: Best project selection by using of Group TOPSIS Method. In: International Association of Computer Science and Information Technology-Spring Conference

Factors of Influence in Co-located Multimodal Interactions

Ramadevi Vennelakanti, Anbumani Subramanian,
Sriganesh Madhvanath, and Prasenjit Dey

Hewlett-Packard Labs, Bangalore, India
{rama.v,anbumani,srig,pdey}@hp.com

Abstract. Most work on multimodal interaction in the human computer interaction (HCI) space has focused on enabling a user to use one or more modalities in combination to interact with a system. However, there is still a long way to go towards making human-to-machine communication as rich and intuitive as human-to-human communication. In human-to-human communication, modalities are used individually, simultaneously, interchangeably or in combination. The choice of modalities is dependent on a variety of factors including the context of conversation, social distance, physical proximity, duration, etc. We believe such intuitive multimodal communication is the direction in which human-to-machine interaction is headed in the future. In this paper, we present the insights we have from studying current human-machine interaction methods. We carried out an ethnographic study to observe and study users in their homes as they interacted with media and media devices, by themselves and in small groups. One of the key learning we have from this study is the understanding of the impact of the user's context on the choice of interaction modalities. The user context factors that influence the choice of interaction modalities include, but are not limited to: the distance of the user from the device/media, the user's body posture during the media interaction, the user's involvement level with the media, seating patterns (cluster) of the co-located participants, the roles that each participant plays, the notion of control among the participants, duration of the activity and so on. We believe that the insights from this study can inform the design of the next generation multimodal interfaces that are sensitive to user context, perform a robust interpretation of the interaction inputs and support more human-like multimodal interaction.

1   Introduction

Human-to-human communication is rich, evocative and truly multimodal. Humans use a number of modalities simultaneously to communicate. Each of these modalities supplements, substitutes or emphasizes the message being conveyed by another, and in unison are the symphony of human-to-human communication. These modalities are used by themselves or in combination. It is also true that humans switch seamlessly from one modality to another with ease. For example depending on the situation, they switch seamlessly between speech (whispers, indoor, outdoor voices, etc.), gestures

A. Agrawal et al. (Eds.): IITM 2013, CCIS 276, pp. 231–245, 2013.

(subtle, fine, gross, etc.), gaze (glance, steady, stare, etc.), touch (gentle, soft, hard, etc.) and so on. Humans are also complete systems in themselves, able to receive and send communication in a truly multimodal fashion.

Multimodal interaction has been an area of research interest for computer scientists and HCI researchers for nearly two decades. Interfaces that allow users to switch between modes of interaction have in general required the user to explicitly state the mode s/he wants to interact in. There has been some progress towards making these interfaces more adaptive based on the user's ability, proximity [1], the task or the environment, but this kind of research is still at a nascent stage.

Moreover, as personal computers get increasingly used for media consumption,their role is transitioning from being a single user productivity device to a potentially multi-user media consumption device. Today it is common to see a group of friends huddled around a personal computer (PC) downloading and viewing the latest episode of their favorite television (TV) show, checking out the latest posts on a social networking site, orviewing photos from a recent vacation. What, however has remained largely unchanged during this transition is the mode of interaction. The keyboard and mouse (and more recently touch) are still the most available modes of interaction. Consequently media consumption, which is quite often a group activity, becomes limited in its interaction with the device to a single user interaction experience. Given that group media consumption lends itself well to larger screens and consumption from a distance, multimodal interfaces based on gesture, speech and gaze offer considerable promise. However, much work remains to be done towards developing effective multimodal interactions, for group consumption activities, that works well in real-world situations. An understanding of these real world situations becomes necessary to inform the design of multimodal interfaces.

In this paper we describe an exploratory study, of interaction with present-day media and media devices among small groups of people in their homes, aimed at discovering factors and patterns that may influence the design of multimodal interfaces. We then present the key findings from this study, which relate to the role of user context in influencing the choice of interaction modality

2   Related Work

In this section we review briefly, the literature relevant to our work. While there are a number of areas that may be relevant, we focus on multimodal interactions, co-located experiences and floor control.

There has been significant work in the area of multimodal HCI over the past few years.This along with the availabilityofnewerand more efficient sensor technologies and more robust recognition systems has greatly shifted the focus from traditional single-user interactions with a system using a keyboard and mouse to multi-user, device-free interactions using gesture and speech among other modalities. In the survey paper [7] the authors have discussed various approaches to multimodal human computer interaction and the state of the various technology components that go into this, namely face, expression, affect and gaze recognition, gestures and large scale body movements etc. They also discuss various approaches to user and task modeling and the challenges in this space. Our work is aimed at understanding the factors that impact the multimodal interactions which in turn can be used to create models that assimilate all these factors and aid robust response and recognition.

Most work in the multimodal interaction space is focused on the robust fusion and recognition of multimodal inputs. The focus has been with the accuracy of recognition of valid input, rarely looking at reasons why the user provided invalid inputs.There has been little focus on the factors that impact multimodal input itself. In [6], the authors survey the various issues associated with multimodal interfaces. In [10] and [12] the emphasis is on the need for multi-disciplinary research approach towards advancing the state of the art multimodal systems.In[11],the authors set out to define guidelines for multimodal user interface design including systems that should be designed for the broadest range of user's and contexts, taking into account the user preference of modality and so on. They go on to state that multimodal systems should easily adapt to user contexts, applications and profiles. In our work we provide a deeper understanding of the user context and the factors that impact multimodal inputs.

Co-located, co-present or co-experience as it is varyingly called to describe physically co-present sharing, is another area of relevance to our work. In [4],the focus shifts from a single user experience to the experiences that are created when users share and experience together with others. In [6] the authors, in their work explore display factors that influence co-located collaboration and are focused on the display (size, angle and numbers) and user arrangement (side-by-side or face-to-face). Our work focuses on the multi-user, co-located interactions and factors that influence it.

Co-present interactions naturally open the space of ownership of command and control. In their recommendations from an ethnographic study [3] on activities and interactions in the living room state that, future technologies should support social interactions and personal activities while addressing communication and personalization needs. The concepts of entry point and access points in a social interaction experience are introduced in [5]. In [9] the focus is on moderator assisted floor control in highly collaborative co-located tasks. In our work we are more interested in unsupervised control sharing in the context of input device free interactions and explore the various possibilities in our work.

Both active input modes such as speech, gesture etc. that the user intends as a command to the system and passive input modes that comprise user presence, gaze, body position etc. are discussed in [10]. In our work we explore both active input modes and the factors that impact active inputs and passive input modes, information about which can be used to more intelligently process the active inputs.

While there is a body of work in each of the related areas, we believe there is a scope for a more holistic approach to the design of intuitive multimodal interactions. In our work we set out to study this in a more exploratory manner towards gaining insights that will help us design and build more adaptive, robust and responsive systems, interfaces and interactions. In our work we focus is not on what the user needs to learn to interact, but on understanding the user and his/her context so that we build more responsive and intuitive multimodal interactions and systems.

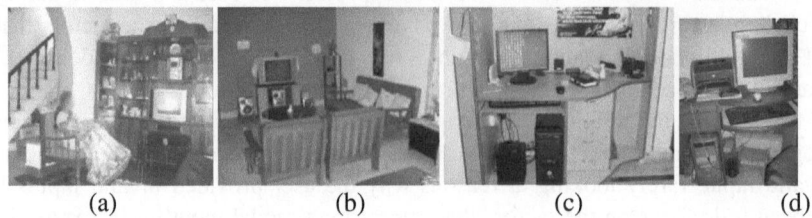

(a)   (b)   (c)   (d)

Fig. 1. (a, b) The TV is placed in the living room and the furniture (seating) arranged around it. (c, d) The PC is placed in a corner of the bedroom with just enough space for a chair in front of it.

3   The Study

3.1   Design and Methodology

In order to identify and understand the various factors that impact multimodal interaction design in a co-located media consumption scenario, we designed an ethnographic study to analyze user's interactions with their digital media and media devices in small group settings in their home environments.The focus of the study was to find factors and patterns that may influence the design of multimodal interactions. We observed activities as they occurred normally. For example, in one case, we studied a group of friends as they shared photos from a recent picnic one evening. In another case, we observed a family share a movie time on a Sunday afternoon.

Studying users in their homes requires that we make the most of the time we are allowed and at the same time be as nonintrusive as possible. We also wanted to observe activites as they would happen normally (without having to stage them), so we needed to understand the media activities in a household to be able to plan around them. On day one time was spent time with the primary respondent gathering profiling information, getting a general picture of the layout of the house and understanding the use of space (what were considered shared, private and personal spaces). The various media devices, their configuration and their placement in the homes were noted. In addition, we noted information like, who owned(even notionally) the media, what devices were used, what were the types of media consumed on what devices, with whom and at what times were the media sharedso as to identify the activities we wanted to observe.   If a family usually watched a movie on Sunday afternoon, we designed and planned our observations around that occassion. Some respondents had just returned from a picnic or from attending a celebration and were anyway planning to get together with friends to view the photos from that event, we observed these sessions. When an activity of interest to our study was not scheduled for the next few days, we asked them to have one organised (Why don't you invite your friends over to show them your holiday pictures ? We sponsored pizzas for such group activity).   Observation and interaction sessions with each respondent (and their family and friends) were spread over three to four days.

3.2   Participants and Procedure

Since we   wanted to understand interaction patterns that would give us an insight into the design of multimodal interactions, we decided to study heavy media users.This would not only give us many activities to observe, but also provide us with richness of information that comes from familiarity of use, Participants recrutied for the studyowned and used at least three of the following media devices : an MP3 player, digital camera, personal computer, high-end mobile phone, music system, gaming console. Participants were also active on social networking sites and shared photos online.We had 12 respondents: five female and seven male, in the   16 to 23 years age group and were recruited across two metro cities in India. The participants mostly belonged to nuclear families with their family consisting of parents and one or two siblings. While the primary participant was the focus of the interactions, other family members were encouraged to join the interactions. These impromptu interactions (especially when initiatied by a curious sibling) provided very natural interaction scenarios to observe. All sessions were video recorded with consent. In case of female participants, a family member (usually an elder female family member) was encouraged to look through the camera monitor to give them a sense of comfort that the recordings were impersonal and this gave them the confidence to allow the rest of the interactions to happen unsupervised. The two member research team consisted of the moderator, who also made notes, and the observer who also kept an eye on the camera. The camera was mounted on a tripod and mostly left stationary thus helping the participant to get used to its unintrusive presence.

Pre-designed questionnaires, data sheets and observation sheets(not attached due to space constraints) were used to record information and observations all through the sessions. Group activities were observed passively while single user activities were often interactive with observations followed by specific questionning to eleicit information and understanding. The ethnographic technique of observation was used extensively to supplement video recording. Post analyis of the video along with the notes and photographs were used to identify interaction patterns, influencing factors and draw insights.

4   Observations

In this section we detail our observations around media interactions. While the study covered a number of other media devices we noted that the target group used the PC for most of their media activities, sharing photographs, downloading, watching and sharing movies and TV shows, listening to and sharing downloaded music, social networking etc., so most of our observations and insights in the context of the PC. However, we believe though that observations, insights are relevant across media devices and media types. The study was carried out in India, so some observations regarding the layout of the home and the ownership, placement and use of devices may be more culturally specific. However we believe that the interaction patterns and insights we draw from these observations are relevant across cultures

4.1   Media Devices - Their Ownership and Use

Most Indian homes do not conceive a separate family room. The living room doubles up as a space used for many purposes: to receive and entertain guests, to watch TV, to catch up with the family and have dinner. In the homes of the participants we studied, the TV was usually placed in the living room (Figure 1 a, b). The TV is the center of focus in the living room and seating is arranged around the TV, as in a horseshoe arrangement facing the TV (Figure 1b). The location of the TV lends itself to easy access and viewing for all. Different family members (mostly the adults) had preferred TV viewing slots that were not easily traded. While the female participants followed some of the local TV shows the male participants said they rarely watch TV unless there was a game being broadcast. This does not mean that these youngsters do not watch TV. Both male and female participants closely followed some American TV shows and regularly downloaded the latest episode to watch with friends. Only two of the homes we visited had a second TV, and it was placed in the parent's bedroom. It was not uncommon for the family to gather around the TV close to dinner time. While the program was not of interest to all present, it was considered family time. The adults were absorbed in the show while the youngsters barely glanced at the TV as they were engrossed texting on their phones. The game console was tethered to the TV. The family music system was also placed in the living room.

The PC is used mainly by the youngsters (our participants) in the house. While most houses had a single PC that was shared by the siblings, four homes had a second PC- a laptop that belonged to the elder, college going sibling. This laptop was considered more personal and rarely shared. The shared PC, since it was rarely used by others in the house, was placed in a corner of their bedroom (Figure 1c, d). The PC usually has its own table fixed into a corner in the bedroom and typically has a single straight back chair in front of it. The only other furniture in the bedroom that can be used for sitting on is the bed. When friends come over to share media, they gather around the PC sitting on the only chair and the bed.   The personal computer was used for a variety of activities – surfing the web, downloading and watching movies and video, storing and viewing photographs, playing music, email, chat, social networking, etc.Participants regularly downloaded and saved the latest movies, songs and episodes of TV shows they followed; for viewing with friends.

The digital camera is shared among the family but iskept in the youngster's wardrobe. The mobile phone is one device that is not shared and is considered strictly personal.

4.2   Media Activities

Media activities themselves are classified by the participants as those to share with family andthosewithfriends. Broadcast TV was watched with family, movies were watched with family and friends (though the genres differed), and music was mostly an ambient activity. The music system in the living room was shared by the family but music (different genre) downloaded from the internet was played on the PC and shared with friends. Photos on the PC were mainly shared with friends. However occasionally, the family gets together to view photos from a recent family vacation or a wedding. Most participants had a large photo collection stored on the PC, mostly from trips and events with friends, and these were viewed with friends. The participants also kept track of TV shows and downloaded these from the internet (to stay one up on the episodes that were being broadcast) and were saved for viewing with friends. Games were played with siblings and friends. While the participants had a large friends circle, they regularly shared media with a smaller group of four to five people. This is also the size of the most co-located group activities during the course of our study.

4.3   Media Interactions

We observe that interactions with the media are itself impacted by a number of factors: the type of media being consumed, which in turn impacts the interaction frequency or intensity, the interaction distance, the notion of control over the media and the interactions, the shape of the cluster that the people in the group form in front of the PC, roles in the cluster (group), interaction postures, etc.

In a co-located media consumption scenario, like viewing photos or a video on the PC, the members of the group interact both, with each other and with the media. While interaction between the group members is unregulated and free, the interactions with the PC are directed through a keyboard and mouse controlled by one person. A shared media experience is thus reduced to a single person interaction experience.

However this is also not entirely true though, as members of the group who do not have physical control of the input device, still interact with the media (i) directly: pointing at photographs; and (ii) indirectly: by telling the person who is in possession of the input device what input to give the system – say, to pause or increase/ decrease the volume. So while some interactions are direct, others are through a proxy (the group member in possession of the input device). Proxy interactions are necessary because the system has just one input device.

These scenarios, where shared experience are reduced to single person interaction experience are however opportunity areas when considering device independent multimodal gestural interactions.

4.4   Interaction Frequency

Different media types have different interaction frequencies or the frequency at which command and control inputs are directed at the media device. Audio-visual media have interaction peaking towards the beginning and end of the media activity. Visual media like photos have uniform interaction intensity through the session. Video games are another example of an interaction intensive media. Music, an ambient activity has low interaction intensity.

4.5   Cluster Shape

During the study we observed that the cluster shape of seating patterns also varies by device and media type (Figure 2). The cluster shape for TV is determined primarily by the seating arrangement and the show being viewed. The form factor and the screen size also ensures that the users have a good view from wherever they sit and a remote allows them to interact seamlessly irrespective of their seating position and distance. The cluster shape in front of a PC varies depending on the media type. The media type also determines the interaction frequency. A media activity like photo viewing has a high interaction frequency and typically lasts for half an hour. So the cluster becomes a straight line in front of the display (Fig 2 a) so as to provide a clear view of the display to each of the viewers. In the case of an audio-visual medium like a video (movie, TV show) the interaction frequency is low and the activity typically lasts for over an hour and half. The cluster then tends to move away from the display and find comfortable postures. However, the typical seating available in front of the PC mostly allows only a linear cluster shape.

4.6   Roles in a Group

Members in a group take up various roles during the co-located media activities we observed. The four roles primarily observed were those of the:

1. Doer - one who executes the command and control and has physical possession of the input device (keyboard, mouse or remote) and so has direct control over the media device
2. Controller - one who issues the actual command which is executed by the Doer; the Controller hasa proxy control over the media device through the Doer
3. Doer & Controller - One who not only has physical possession of the input device, but also issues the commands
4. Passive Spectator - one who consumes media passively

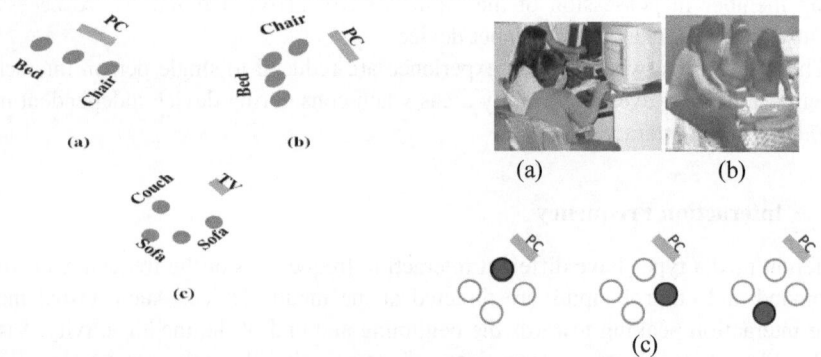

Fig. 2. Cluster shapes of seating patterns observed based on media device and type. Viewing (a) photos on aPC, (b) movie/video on a PC, and (c) movie/video on aTV.

Fig. 3. (a,b) The struggle for control. (c) Shifting position of the *controller* (indicated by ●) during a media activity.

These roles played, by the group members, were not determined by either the ownership of the media or media device, and are also not static over a media consumption activity. The Controller asserts control over the media by specifying what inputs the Doer should give the system.

4.7   Control and Shifting Control

Control over the media,was observed to be often assumed by the one initiating the session. However control itself does not remain static with one group member and shifts from one person to another depending on the roles they play in the group (Figure 3) and the duration of the interaction. Control is assumed or sometimes given with consent and sometimes without (Figure 3 a). In case of the PC the person in possession of the keyboard and mouse is in control of the device. The affordance of the device itself – the tethered keyboard and mouse makes it difficult for physical control to shift easily, unlike in the case of the TV remote that can be passed on from one hand to another. The cluster then tends to move away from the display ensuring that one person, the doer, is within arm's reach distance of the input devices for any interaction. The cluster formed is hockey stick shaped. Gaming is another high interaction intensity activity and the cluster stays close to the display.

4.8   Interaction Distance

The interaction distance varies both by the device and media type. It was observed that the interaction distance for a TV remains relatively constant as the seating in the living room (where the TV is usually placed) is constant. Viewers take up various positions in this seating arrangement. The seating position does not impact interactions with the TV as the input device, the remote control can be operated from anywhere in the room by anybody. The seating and the cluster shape is constant for the media type that is most often watched on TV – video. The interaction distance in most homes varied from seven to 12 feet.

The PC has more dynamic interaction distance depending upon the type of media being consumed When the media interaction frequency is high, as with photos and games, the interaction distance is around two feet and when the interaction frequency is light, as with movies and video, the users tend to sit farther away at a distance of five to 10 feet.

4.9   Interaction Postures

We observed that the duration of the interaction session, the interaction intensity and other factors like seating available, etc. influence the positions and postures each of the group members gets into during the session. These are also factors that determine if the user will make the effort to interact with the system by taking / asking for the input device or use a proxy interaction mechanism.

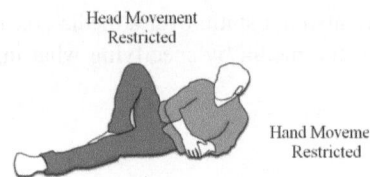

Completely relaxed posture, with minimal body movement
possible leading to higher dependence on speech

Fig. 4. Lounge posture and possible interaction
modalities

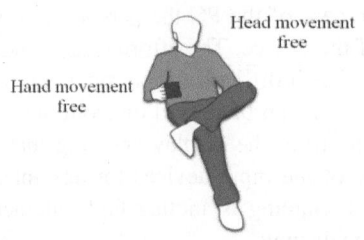

Lean back posture, easy movement possible so all faculti
available for interaction

Fig. 5. Comfort posture and possible interaction
modalities

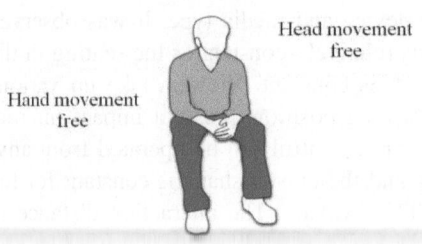

Lean forward posture, easy movement possible so a
faculties available for interaction

Fig. 6. Attentive posture and possible interaction
modalities

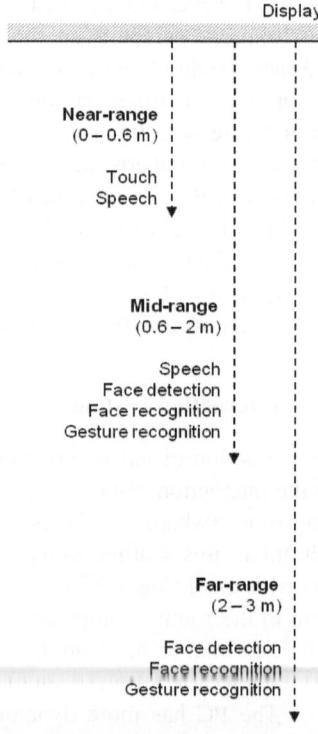

Fig. 7. Technologies available for
interaction based on the distance of
interaction

The seating postures of users can broadly be classified into three groups: Lounge,
Comfort and Attentive. Each of these postures has a bearing on the faculties (and so
modalities) available for use and interaction.

Lounge Posture. The hands may be used to prop the upper body off the ground so
as to be able to get a view of the media. This posture locks the movement of hands.
The head movement is also restricted with the torso being propped up. Therefore the
use of hands to gesture and head movement is restricted. There is greater dependence
on speech as an input and interaction modality.

Table 1. Gesture-speechco-occurrence and possible metadata

Speech	Gesture	Speech	Possible Tags
Who is that?	Pointing	That is Ron	Ron
Where is this?	Pointing	This is in Agra / TajMahal	TajMahal / Agra
What is that?	Pointing	This is the TajMahal	TajMahal

Comfort Posture. This is a relaxed but upright posture adopted by users while seated in a sofa or a chair with armrests and a slightly inclined back rest (see Fig. 5). The torso is upright and inclined slightly back, however there is no restriction of body movement or user of hands. All modalities – hand gestures, speech, head and face – are available for interaction. However, the availability of the hands for interaction is dependent upon the seating. The viewer may rest their elbows on the armrest thus restricting hand movement to a reduced area.

Attentive Posture. The attentive posture is similar to the comfort posture but is a lean forward posture with the user in an attentive mode having all faculties available for interaction (see Fig. 6). However, the user may rest elbow on the knee and thus restrict the availability of the hand for interaction, thus increasing the dependence on speech.

4.10 Gesture-Speech Patterns

We observed an evident gesture-speech pattern when the users interacted with images (photos) – the co-occurrence of gestures and speech. When sharing photos, people point-to and talk-about things of interest in a picture. A pointing gesture is used to indicate regions of particular interest in a picture while the speech that co-occurs contains information about the picture and also contains keywords such as 'who', 'what', 'this', 'that', 'where' etc. The subsequent speech patterns are typically about specific information about the photograph in context – names of people and places, occasions, etc. (Table 1). Therefore, such multimodal interactions captured in an interaction, and extracted intelligently can aid in the creation of implicit metadata creation for pictures in context. Such implicitly captured data is referred to as 'interaction metadata' [13].

5   Discussion and Conclusion

In this section we discuss the impact of the interaction factors on the design of multi-modal interactions with focus on the impact of postures, control passing and interaction metadata.

The role of seating posture, which in turn is influenced by the type of media being consumed, was observed to be significant. Other key factors that influence the interaction include placement of media devices in the home, groups with whom media is shared, media type that is shared with specific groups, interaction distance and intensity, cluster patterns that these groups form, the roles played by people in these groups , and the passing of control over the media and media device.

Interaction Distance and Its Impact on Interaction Modalities. Based on our observation of participants and a follow-up interview, we observe a pattern in choice of interaction modalities based on the distance of the user to the display, as shown in Figure 7. In a near-range (up to 0.6m) from the display, users rely on touch and speech modalities for interaction. In mid-range (0.6 – 2 m), users prefer to depend on speech and gesture modalities for interaction. Face-detection and face-recognition is also suitable for this distance interaction. At far-range (beyond 2m), speech may not be reliable as an input and also recognizing fine gestures may not be possible. Therefore, only coarse gestures, face-detection and face-recognition may be suitable for interaction at this distance.

Postures and Their Impact on Interactions. In addition to gestural interactions, we observed several posture variations in users while interacting with their systems. We identify at least three kinds of postures in an interaction. An 'attentive posture' (Fig. 6) is exhibited by users during an active interaction (like when typing a document) and this posture allows a user to freely move his/her hands and head free thereby making related modalities possible. Also, in this posture, the user is less likely to depend on speech as a modality, given the quantum of input required for interaction. A 'comfort posture' (Fig.5) is generally adopted by users when an interaction does not require active intervention and this posture also enables the use of all faculties for interaction. In a 'lounge posture' (Fig.4), as is typically seen when users do not plan to interact often with a PC (as in watching a movie on a PC), the hand and head movements are restricted and so the user would generally rely on speech as a modality for interaction. It is evident that the modalities available for interaction are dependent upon the posture the user is in. If the system is able to detect the posture of the user based on the images from, say a depth camera, the system can use this information to evaluate and refine the confidence of   the input modality for each user. This early information on expected interaction modality can be used for more intelligent multimodal fusion and result in better recognition.

Control Passing. In the context of accessory-free multimodal gestural interactions, there is a need to ensure that the interactions with the media are channeled in some way. Currently the channeling of inputs to the system is done by the sequential nature of inputs from a keyboard or mouse. But in the absence of such a channeling device there is a chance for the system to receive simultaneous inputs from more than one of the co-located viewers. There needs to be a method of dealing with these simultaneous inputs and preventing a chaos situation. There is a need to maintain discipline, while making sure that no participating users feels completely left out of the interaction experience. Interaction control can be divided into multiple levels and can be user configurable. One example of levels of control: controls can be divided into two levels disruptive and non-disruptive. Disruptive controls are controls that will change the media / media object that is being interacted with and disrupt the current interaction. These controls may not be handled by multiple users since it may cause a lot of disruption of the ongoing activity. Non-disruptive controls are those that can be used to manipulate the media or object of current interaction. These controls may be with multiple users since they lead to a very small effect on the activity in focus. For example in the context of a photo sharing application, the two levels of controls are: (i) disruptive: go to another photo / album / collection, close album / application; and

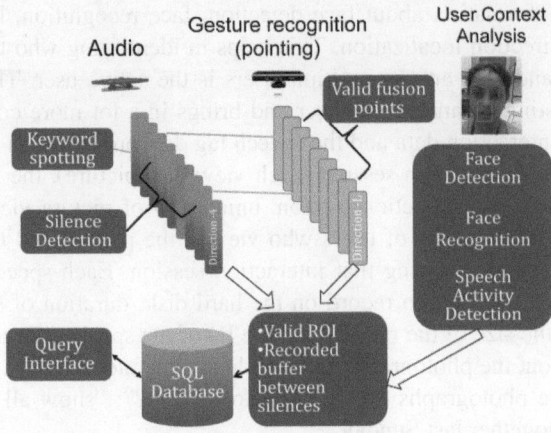

Fig. 8. Architecture of the prototype that captures interaction metadata

(ii) non-disruptive: pause, zoom in, and zoomout.In the context of a video application they are:(i) disruptive: go to another video, play, close application; and (ii) non-disruptive: pause, volume control

Controls can be can be layered based on any of, but not limited to, the following factors:(i) the first users to start the interaction and the others; (ii) the first user to be registered by the system and the others; (iii) the registered owner of the media/ device and the rest; (iv) demographics of the user group – only one of the adults in the group can take control.

Interaction Metadata..Interactions with photos in the context of co-located photo sharing contain rich information: people who saw it, who said what, the region of interest pointed at when they said it, who did they see it with, for how long and how often and so on. All this information if captured and analyzed can create interesting memories about the photograph. Interaction information so captured can be used to create a new type of data called interaction metadata [13], a new type of metadata which gives information about who interacted with the photo and with whom and what were the regions of interest in the photo and the speech associated with these regions of interest (stored as voice snippets). Interaction metadata also helps with organizing photos better by providing mechanisms for filtering based on who viewed, most viewed etc. Interaction metadata is an under explored implicit metadata type created from interactions with media.We have integrated these insights into the design of systems and experiences to provide more intuitive and robust interaction experiences in our work [13] [14]. Figure 8 shows a prototype of a system that we built to capture the above mentioned interaction metadata [7], [14]. It uses a gesture recognition engine to identify the regions of a photograph the user is pointing to. The audio module detects speech activity and captures a recording of the audio where a predefined keyword is spotted. The captured audio is truncated from beginning to the end of an audio activity in the region where the keyword is spotted. This helps in limiting the amount of audio that is stored and captured as metadata. The user context analysis block provides information about face detection, face recognition, lip motion detection and audio direction localization. This helps in identifying who the user is during the interactions and who among multiple users is the active user. This helps in attributing an interesting comment to a user and brings in a lot more context to the captured data. The interaction data and the speech tag data are stored in a SQL Database. At the end of each interaction session (each view of a picture), the following data is stored: a unique ID of interaction session, unique ID of picture viewed, duration of viewing for that picture, IDs of users who viewed the picture and the list of speech tags that were generated during that interaction session. Each speech tag contains a unique ID, a link to the audio record on the hard disk, duration of speech, ROI (the coordinates and the size of the region) and the ID of the speaker. These stored interaction metadata about the photographs can also help generate interesting queries such as "show me all the photographs I have not shown Bob?"; "show all the photographs Alice and I saw together last Sunday".

6   Summary

This paper attempts to identify and explain as many interaction patterns that occur in a co-located shared media consumption scenario, as possible. The understanding of these patterns and the factors that lead to them are essential towards the design of intuitive multimodal gestural interactions for a co-located media consumption experience. Current media interactions channel command and control input to the media device through the single remote, keyboard and mouse attached to the device. However, envisaging a scenario devoid of these accessory devices would mean being cognizant of the interaction patterns.

In our work we set out to provide a holistic perspective of user context understanding required for the design of intuitive multimodal interaction. The factors that impact multimodal interactions are identified. The systems we have prototyped not only enables creation of interaction metadata, but also provides a multiuser experience with levels of control sharing as discussed in this paper.

It is important that real world interaction patterns are kept in mind when designing multimodal systems and interactions. This paper provides a real world view of how media interactions are played out, and emphasizes the need for a multidisciplinary approach towards the design of multimodal interactions. It is necessary to evaluate the performance of various sensors that support multimodal technologies against behavior patterns described in the paper. Current state of user interfaces and sensor technologies are far from being able to address these complexities, but that is the direction that they need to work towards.

Acknowledgements. Thanks are due to the study participants and their families for letting us into their homes and lives and sharing their experiences with us. Thanks are also due to the teams that helped with the data collection and hours of video data analysis.

References

1. Ballendat, T., Marquardt, N., Greenberg, S.: Proxemic interaction: designing for a proximity and orientation-aware environment. In: ACM International Conference on Interactive Tabletops and Surfaces (ITS 2010). ACM, New York (2010)
2. Batterbee, K., Koskinen, I.: Co-experience: user experience as interaction, vol. 1(1). Taylor & Francis CoDesign (2005)
3. Bernhaupt, R., Obrist, M., Weiss, A., Beck, E., Tscheligi, M.: Trends in the living room and beyond: results from ethnographic studies using creative and playful probing. Computers in Entertainment - Social Television and user Interaction 6(1) (January 2008)
4. Dumas, B., Lalanne, D., Oviatt, S.: Multimodal Interfaces: A Survey of Principles, Models and Frameworks. In: Lalanne, D., Kohlas, J. (eds.) Human Machine Interaction. LNCS, vol. 5440, pp. 3–26. Springer, Heidelberg (2009)
5. Hornecker, E., Marshall, P., Rogers, Y.: From entry to access: how shareability comes about. In: Proc. of the Conference on Designing Pleasurable Products and Interfaces (2007)
6. Inkpen, K.M., Hawkey, K., Kellar, M., Mandryk, R.L., Parker, J.K., Reilly, D., Scott, S.D., Whalen, T.: Exploring Display Factors that Influence Co-Located Collaboration: Angle, Size, Number, and User Arrangement. In: Proceedings of HCI International 2005, Las Vegas, USA (July 2005)
7. Jaimes, A., Sebe, N.: Multimodal Human Computer Interaction: A Survey. In: IEEE International Workshop on Human Computer Interaction in Conjunction with ICCV (2005)
8. Madhvanath, S., Vennelakanti, R., Subramanian, A., Shekhawat, A., Dey, P., Rajan, A.: Designing multiuser multimodal gestural interactions for the living room. In: Proceedings of the 14th ACM International Conference on Multimodal Interaction (ICMI 2012), pp. 61–62. ACM, New York (2012)
9. Myers, B., Chuang, Y., Tjandra, M., Chen, M., Lee, C.: Floor control in a Highly Collaborative Co-Located Task (2004), http://www-2.cs.cmu.edu/~pebbles/papers/pebblesfloorcontrol.pdf (accessed: June 01, 2009)
10. Oviatt, S., Cohen, P.R.: Multimodal Interfaces That Process What Comes Naturally. Communications of the ACM (2000)
11. Reeves, L.M., Lai, J., Larson, J.A., Oviatt, S., Balaji, T.S., Buisine, S.P., Collings, P., Cohen, P.R., Kraal, B., Martin, J.-C., McTear, M., Raman, T., Stanney, K.M., Su, H., Wang, Q.Y.: Guidelines for multimodal user interface design. Communications of the ACM 47(1), 57–59 (2004)
12. Turk, M., Bailenson, J., Beall, A., Blascovich, J., Guadagno, R.: Multimodal Transformed Social Interaction. In: ICMI (2004)
13. Vennelakanti, R., Dey, P., Shekhawat, A., Phanindra, P.: The Picture says it all! Multimodal Interactions and Interaction Metadata. In: 13th International Conference on Multimodal Interaction, Alicante, Spain, November 14-18 (2011)
14. Vennelakanti, R., Madhvanath, S., Subramanian, A., Sowndararajan, A., David, A., Dey, P.: Pixene: Creating memories while sharing photos. In: Proceedings of the 14th ACM International Conference on Multimodal Interaction (2012)

Hierarchal Structure of Community and Link Analysis

Seema Mishra and G.C. Nandi

Indian Institute of Information Technology, Allahabad, India
{seema.mishra.phd,gcnandi}@gmail.com

Abstract. Discovering the hierarchy of organizational structure in a dynamic social network can unveil significant patterns which can help in network analysis. In this paper, we formulated a methodology to establish the most influential person in a temporal communication network from the perspective of frequency of interactions which works on hierarchal structure. With the help of frequency of interactions, we have calculated the individual score of each person from Page Rank algorithm. Subsequently, a graph is generated that showed the influence of each individual in the network. Rigorous experiments we performed using Enron data set to establish a fact that our proposed methodology correctly identifies the influential persons over the temporal network. We have used Enron Company's email data set that describes how employees of company interacted with each other. We could analyze from our methodology and verify from the facts in the Company's dataset since after bankruptcy, the result of interactions and behaviors of the individual of the network are absolutely known. Our result shows that the proposed methodology is generic and can be applied to other data sets of communication to identify influential at particular instances.

Keywords: Dynamic social network analysis, social network analysis, hierarchal structure.

1 Introduction

A network structure is the perfect epitome provides a formal way of representing data that emphasizes the association between entities. This representation has a substantial importance gives the insight of knowledge into the data. Since for the work to be done many entities these days are interconnected and behaviors of individual entity reflect the function of whole system at large extent. The entity could be people, organization [15], computer nodes [16]. Networks are primarily studied in mathematical framework i.e. graph [1].

In modern era, social network analysis is proliferated area of research, has been in existence for quite some time and experiencing a surge in popularity to understand the behavior of the users at individual and group level [Wasserman & Faust, 1994, Wellman, 1996]. Understanding the behavior of individual social networking methods assuage the analysts to revealing hidden patterns from social communication. In order to model the social network mathematically, most popular data structure typically known as graphs are used where the nodes depict the individual or group of person, or event or organization etc and each link/edge represents connection/relationship

A. Agrawal et al. (Eds.): IITM 2013, CCIS 276, pp. 246–254, 2013.

between two individual. Social network analysis attempts to understand the network and its components like nodes (social entities commonly known as actor or event) and connections (inter-connection, ties, and links). It has main focus of analyzing individuals and their interdependent relationships among them rather than individuals and their attributes as we deal in conventional data structure.

The target of this paper is to proposing a hierarchical structure of social network changing with time.

Types of social network

Sociometric: It involves the entire population and focus on global structure pattern of social network.

Egocentric: It focus individual interaction pattern for analyzing social network. Limitation of this kind of analysis is that it is very difficult to collect case by case data.

2 Dynamic Social Network Analysis

Versatile power of social network is being applied to mining pattern of social interaction in wide ranging applications including disease modeling [4] information transmission and behavior analysis [2, 3, 16] and business management and behavior analysis. Network analysis came in to picture as its practical applications in intelligence and surveillance [5] and has become popularized paradigm to uncover anti-social network such like criminal, terrorist and fraud network majorly after the tragically event of September 11th, 2001 which has shattered the whole world. Traditional social network analysis are incorporated with several computational techniques like artificial intelligence, machine learning, data mining to develop empirical research on human behavior, groups and organizational behavior within links among them with varying level of uncertainties.

There are two level of analysis in DNA. Firstly, it focuses on relational data, i.e.; data about a link between group of people, events and locations, organizations. Identifying associations between these entities is a crucial part of unveiling different types of activities in order to discover knowledge about network. The second is the focus on dynamism of the relations; i.e., how these relations likely to change in the future and what are the interesting consequences of these changes in the system.

Social interaction could be in any form that depends on the type of data available [6]. It might be verbal or written communication (cell phones, emails, and blogs chatting), scientific collaboration (co-authorship network, citation network), browed websites, and group of animals. This mathematical network model is very successful in analysis of social network but major drawback is that it may miss the temporal aspect of interaction because social interaction is inherently dynamic in nature. The static model of interaction can give the information that could be inaccurate and decision made based merely on this contributed information might lead analyst to faulty direction.

Several shortcomings can be highlighted when dealing with static model of social network that could forbid acknowledging the casual relationship of pattern of social interaction [6]:

• What is the rate of spreading diseases while modeling diseases and who is the central person whom should be vaccinated to control spread of it among group of person.

• What are the causes and consequences of social structure evolution?

Dynamic social network analysis is emerging research area play a crucial role to fill gap between traditional social network analysis and time domain. Dynamic study of network includes classical network analysis, link analysis, and multi-agent systems.

Dynamic network analysis facilitates the analysis of multiple types of nodes (multi-node) and multiple types of links (multi-plex) simultaneously. On the contrary, static network analysis can only focus at most two mode data and analysis one type of link at a time. There are several characteristics of dynamic network:

• Nature of nodes are dynamic, there properties changes with respect to time.

• Deals with meta-network.

• Network evolution is consequent of agent-based modeling.

Furthermore the network analysis exists in four levels [15]: Attribute oriented analysis, Position oriented analysis, and Structure oriented analysis, Dynamic network analysis. Fig1 shows the categorization. The attribute analysis captures the properties of vertices and edges and finds the causal relation with the structure of network.

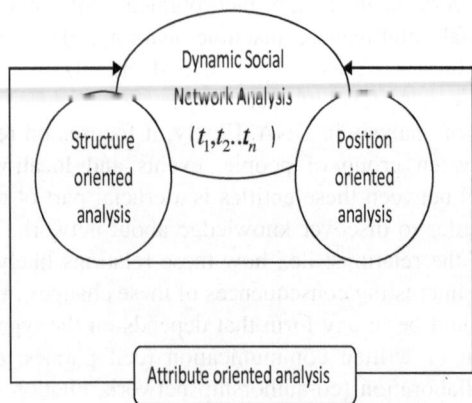

Fig. 1. Level of network analysis

Position oriented analysis aims to investigate the mico level stage of network. It looks into every single entity i.e. node or organization and their characteristic in the network. Structure analysis is macro level analysis of network and investigates the average metrics of social network. Dynamic analysis can utilizes the all measures of aforementioned analysis in order to identify progressive behavior of network and individual.

ROLE OF DATA MINING IN SOCIAL NETWORK

Social computing can make use of data mining techniques in following analysis

- Community Detection
- Classification
- Link Prediction
- Network Modeling

COMMUNITY IN SOCIAL NETWORK

A community is sub part of whole network between which inter-community interaction is relatively frequent and strong than intra-community interaction. It can be in any form for example group, subgroup, and cluster. It may: a) citation network represents related papers on single topics, b) web pages on related topics.

Community detection is a classical problem in social network analysis. Commonly, it can be the problem of identifying sub-graphs of original graph and called vertex sparsifier [12]. These small networks uphold the relevant information of original group. Four levels of analyses are being conducted in community identification as shown in fig 1:

ANALYSIS OF PREVIOUS RESEARCH

Hierarchical methods for community detection falls into two categories: agglomerative and divisive. In former case each node is assumed to be a community and repetitively group together. Similarly, in later case initially whole network is considered a community and divided subsequently into smaller one. Most methods are graph clustering and partition. Distance based structural equivalence [7] uses distance metrics to identify similar entities. In graph partition methods several algorithms has been proposed [8, 9]. Newman- Girvan method and spectral clustering methods [10, 11] uses a notion of modularity and utilizes edge between-ness metric to divide into groups.

In analyzing dynamic pattern, many methods use the temporal snapshots of interaction over the times [13, 14].

3   Discovering Hierarchy of Group

Before analyzing community hierarchy we define several basic terminologies. Hierarchy of community provides the power of each individual in a group. If somehow we know this chain we can find the leader of group. Regarding this we used well known algorithm PageRank which calculate the individual score I_score of each person to represent importancy of person. Higher the score of person more powerful the person is.

Definition: If $P = \{p_1, p_2 ... p_n\}$ be the collection of persons involved in communication. For any members p_i and p_j if I_score (p_i) $\geq$ I_score(p_j) then p_i can be the leader of p_j.

3.1   Proposed Model

Figure 2 shows architecture of our system proposed

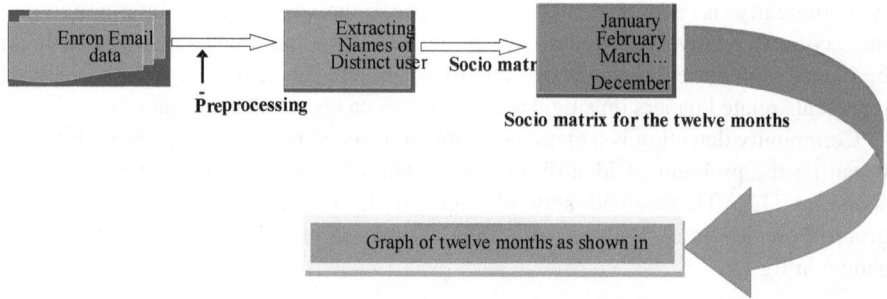

Fig. 2. Model for extracting graph over months

First the Individual score of each member calculated with the help of Page Rank algorithm described following.

Input: Social Network G.

Output: Individual score of each person

Steps:

1.   d = 0.85
2.   epi = 0.01
3.   del = 0,delta[150]
4.   del_prev=0
5.   float sum1 = 0
6.   float sum2 = 0
7.   float e = 0
8.   do loop:
9.   del_prev=del
10.   iter++
11.   fort i = 1 to 150

```
12.              R[1][i] = ((1 - d) / N) +    d*fun(i)
13.              for j = 0 to 150
14.                      sum2 += R[1][j]
15.                      sum1 += R[0][j]
16.
17.              e = sum1 - sum2
18.              for j = 1 to 150
19.                      R[1][j] = R[1][j] +   e*L[j]/sum_all
20.              For j = 1 to 150
21.                 sum2 += R[1][j] - R[0][j]
22.                 del = sum2
23.                 for j = 1to 150
24.                 R[0][j] = R[1][j]
25               while(epi > del && del_prev!=del)
26.    for i=0 to150
27.    R[0][i]=10000.0*R[0][i]
```

In I_score (), d is damping factor generally assumed to be around 0.85. R is vector stores the individual score of each person. N denotes the total number f persons in the network. Sum_all defines the sum of the weight of all edges. Fun() defines

$$\sum_{p_j \in M(p_i)} W(p_{ij}) \cdot \frac{P_k(j)}{L(p_j)}$$ where $L(p_j)$ sum of weights of all edges linked with p_j

and $W(p_{ij})$ weights of edges linking p_i and p_j.

4   Practical Implementation and Analysis

In this section, we evaluate the capability of the proposed approach on discovering organizational structure and to exploring evolution of organizational structure in a dynamic social network and link between individuals. We performed the experiments on Enron email data set. Email communication data has become a practical source for research in network analysis like social network. Mostly the experiments are carried out on the artificial data due to the non-availability of real life communication data. The Enron email data set [17] has become a benchmark for this sort of research domain in network analysis. This data set was made public and posted on web by the Federal Energy Regulatory Commission during its investigation for fraud happened in company, in order to make it test bed for validating and testing the efficacy of methodologies developed for counter-terrorism, fraud detection and link analysis. Data is about 150 users communication mostly senior managers organized into folder. But this set has still lots of issues like integrity issue and duplicate messages issue. For preprocessing, first the names of distinct users were extracted and duplicated ids were neglected.

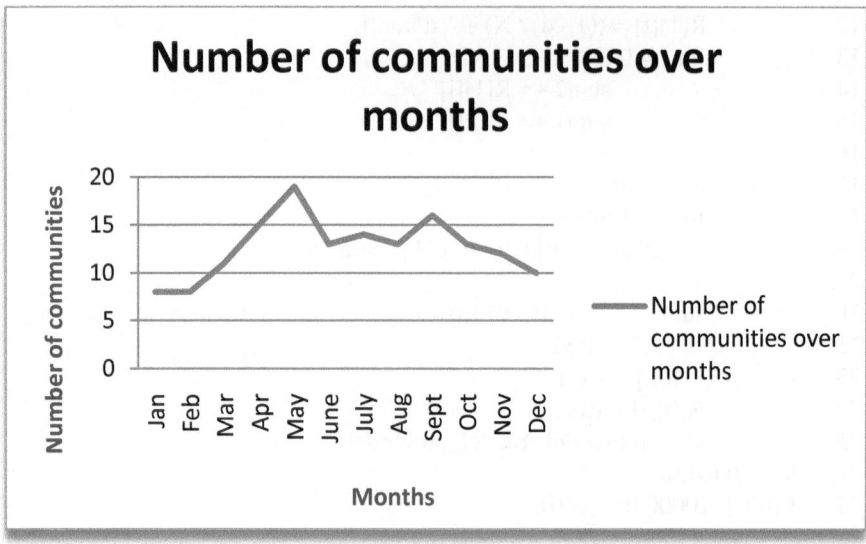

Fig. 3. Number of communities over months

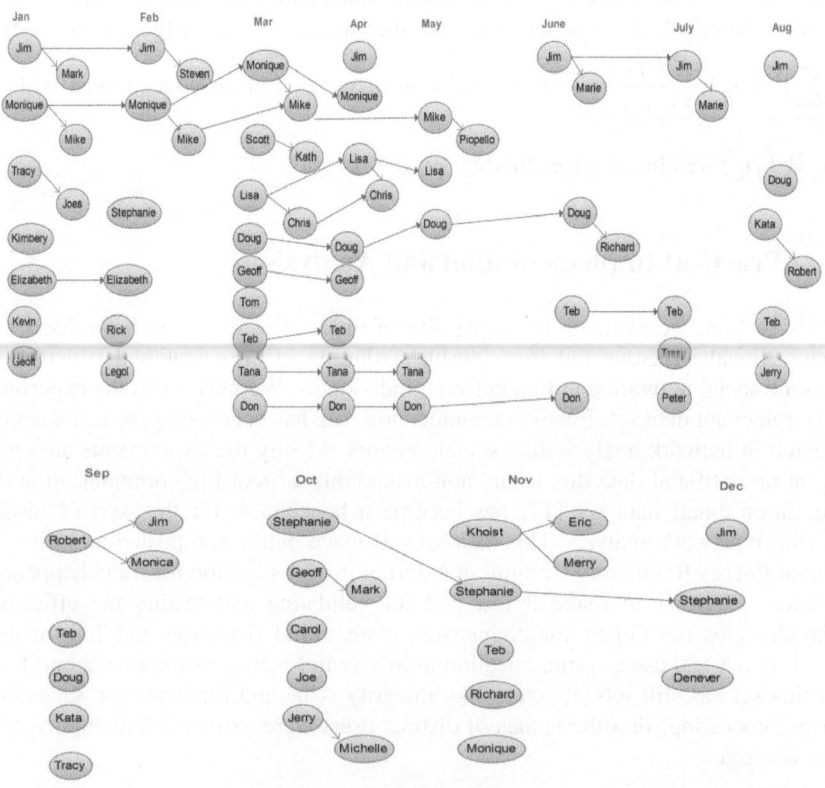

Fig. 4. Evolution of community from months Jan to Dec

The proposed approach is implemented in DEV C++. The experiments were conducted on a 2.1GHz PC with Core(TM)2 Dual- Core Pentium 4 processor with 2 GB RAM.

On examining the results in figure 3, we analyzed the number of grouping in the month of May was maximum. Figure 4 shows that Jim was the person who headed the group from Jan to Feb. Monique was leader throughout the months form Jan to April.

5   Conclusion and Future Scope

In this paper we introduced a concept of hierarchy of positions in group by taking temporal interaction data of twelve months in organization that shows how the position and link of group members changes when people joining and leaving the group. This hierarchal group interaction is significant to facilitate link analysis of individuals with the time period In the future we are planning to improve the integrity issues of preprocessed Enron data results of experiments.

References

[1]   Hanneman, R.A., Riddle, M.: Introduction to social network methods University of California, Riverside (2005), published in digital form
      http://faculty.ucr.edu/~hanneman/

[2]   Baumes, J., Goldberg, M., Magdon-Ismail, M., Wallace, W.: Discovering hidden Inform. (2004)

[3]   Tyler, J., Wilkinson, D., Huberman, B.: Email as spectroscopy: Automated discovery of community structure within organizations. In: Proc. 1st Intl. Conf. on Comm. and Tech. (2003)

[4]   Kretzschmar, M., Morris, M.: Measures of concurrency in networks and the spread of infectious disease. Math. Biosci. 133, 165–195 (1996)

[5]   Baumes, J., Goldberg, M., Magdon-Ismail, M., Wallace, W.: Discovering hidden groups in communication networks. In: Proc. 2nd NSF/NIJ Symp. on Intel. and Security Inform. (2004)

[6]   Berger-Wolf, T.Y., Saia, J.: A framework for analysis of dynamic social networks. In: Proc. KDD 2006, pp. 523–528 (2006)

[7]   Fortunato, S., Castellano, C.: Springer's Encyclopedia of Complexity and System Science. Community Structure in Graphs (2008)

[8]   Chekuri, C., Goldberg, A., Karger, D., Levin, M., Stein, C.: Experimental study of minimum cut algorithms. In: Proc. 8th SAIM Syposium on Discreet Algorithm, pp. 324–333 (1997)

[9]   Wu, A.Y., et al.: Mining scale-free networks using geodesic clustering. In: Proc. KDD 2004, pp. 719–724 (2004)

[10] Newman, M.E.J., Girvan, M.: Finding and evaluating community structure in networks. Phys. Rev. E 69, 026113 (2004)

[11] Newman, M.E.J.: Modularity and community structure in networks. PNAS 103(23), } 8577–8582 (2006)

[12] Moitra, A.: Approximation algorithms for multi commodity type problems with guarantees independent of the graph size. FOCS, 3–12 (2009)

[13] Zhou, D., Councill, I., Zha, H., Lee Giles, C.: Discovering Temporal Communities from Social Network Documents. In: Proc. of ICDM 2007, pp. 745–750 (2007)

[14] Tantipathananandh, C., Berger-Wolf, T., Kempe, D.: A Framework For Community Identification in Dynamic Social Networks. In: Proc. of KDD 2007, pp. 717–726 (2007)

[15] Wasserman, S., Faust, K.: Social network analysis: Methods and applications. Cambridge University Press, New York (1994)

[16] Wellman, B.: Computer networks as social networks. Science Magazine 293, 2031–2034 (2001)

[17] The original dataset can be downloaded from William Cohen's web page, http://www-2.cs.cmu.edu/~enron/

A Model to Calculate Knowledge from Knowledge Base

Anurag Singh, Kumar Anurupam, Rajnish Sagar, and Shashi Kant Rai

Indian Institute of Information Technology
Allahabad, India
beinganuragsingh@gmail.com,
kanurupamjha@gmail.com,
rajnish.sagar@yahoo.com,
shashikant@iiita.ac.in

Abstract. Knowledge base can be defined as the database of knowledge. It comprises of several factors including information, intelligence, skill set and experience. Experience is the most important factor amongst these. This paper talks about the model to calculate the knowledge of an entity in terms of mathematics. Knowledge will be calculated by taking the above mentioned four elements. This will be beneficial for any organizations in the sense that they will be able to calculate their current knowledge and the knowledge required at a particular instance. This will in turn save the wastage of resources that the organization holds knowledge can be created through various factors and utilization of resources of the organization. The second benefit will be reduction in the amount of time taken to create knowledge. These two benefits shall be discussed in detail in the later sections.

Keywords: Experience, information, knowledge, knowledge base.

1   Introduction

In the present scenario, various organizations need quality knowledge that can be implemented immediately and effectively in times of need. This in turn creates a need to produce more and more knowledge and to store it for future use. Management of the produced and stored knowledge is also very much required because this management will help in sharing the knowledge and its proper use.

This paper deals with the basic things related to knowledge. It includes which type of knowledge is available for a particular purpose and how to enhance our knowledge for a competitive edge. Therefore it is very much necessary to calculate how much potential knowledge we have. This paper will help in calculating a close value of knowledge mathematically from knowledge base which will again help in proper utilization and effective management of time as well.

In the later sections, we will define the various components for calculating knowledge and how to calculate knowledge from them. In the last part, we will be discussing the future scope of this perspective.

A. Agrawal et al. (Eds.): IITM 2013, CCIS 276, pp. 255–261, 2013.
© Springer-Verlag Berlin Heidelberg 2013

2   Related Work

In the field of knowledge base several works have been done specially in the areas like populating knowledge base for news, metadata from unstructured text and web data by Rosa Stern and Benoit Sagot. They used Web data resources to create an entity database, which is linked to the entities mentioned in French news wires [1]. There is also some work done for evaluating the quality of a knowledge base from text by James Mayfield and Tim Finin. They described a method for direct evaluation of a knowledge base and an instantiation [2]. Kunihiko Higa,and Olivia R. Liu Sheng proposed object oriented methodology for database/knowledge base coupling. They focused on lack of semantic support and they tried to provide use of Structured Entity Model [3]. There is some mathematical representation done on knowledge base transformation by Gosta Grahne, Alberto O. Mendelzon and Peter Z. Revesz. For expressing queries and updates on knowledge bases they proposed a language of finite sets of relational structures [4]. Regarding the future of knowledge base management Annie Saunders proposed some online solution. Here she developed a help desk knowledge based system for Princeton University [5]. But there is less work reported in order to get knowledge as a value. Here in this paper we are proposing a model which can help us to get close to the exact value of knowledge. This model is a direct function of knowledge with respect to information and experience.

3   Knowledge and Its Components

3.1   Knowledge

Knowledge can be defined as an acquaintance with something or someone. It includes information, facts, skills or descriptions. Intelligence is also a prime factor of knowledge in any organization. These factors are obtained through experience or often with proper education for example, obtaining knowledge is also a time dependent process.

Information. In layman's language, information is anything which has the ability to be interpreted as a message. In the field of computers, information means a useful data. Data is nothing but a collection of raw facts and when it provides certain value then it is termed as information. It can be accurate as well as specific and is meant only for a particular context. It decreases the situation of uncertainty and increases the understanding related to a particular instance. Information can be processed, stored, shared and transmitted over a channel [11].

Fact. Fact can be defined as anything that is true and can be verified. It is always related to a real occurrence and there is always some proof that certain fact either exists or happened corresponding to certain experience. This quality makes a fact to be believed as true and establishes that the particular thing or situation has been existed in real. Through actual experience and constant observations, facts can be acquired [12].

Skills. Skill comes with learning and learning is a continuous and lifelong process. Beside this, effective use of knowledge to achieve some goal or task is also a skill. Basically with the use of skill the expected results can be obtained by minimal usage of factors like time and energy. Skills can broadly be classified into three types: work specific, self-managed and transferable. Work specific skills are acquired through proper training and guidance in any specific field and in most of the cases it is time specific. Transferable skills cover the concepts of communication skills and management skills and are important for the organizations. Self-managed skills on the other hand are a part of an individual's personality [6].

Description. When any information is presented in an elaborative manner for better understanding of the subject then it is called description. Description gives a complete and thorough knowledge about any information and helps to form a critical mental faculty of the information which helps in its usage as per the requirement [13].

Intelligence. Intelligence is a reflection of high usage of mental abilities. By the use of information, knowledge of any subject and skills can easily be acquired and applied. It is not restricted to any particular domain and helps in decision making and problem solving. If there is a new situation created in front of an entity, its intelligence will help to adapt the same and react accordingly. It also covers how a person or an organization applies his knowledge that has been acquired over a period of time.

Experience. Experience can be defined as a procedural way to observe something over a period of time specified or unspecified to enhance knowledge and skill set. When a person observes something by his involvement in the subject or passes by a particular situation, he is supposed to gain experience for that particular subject and situation. For gaining experience in any area any individual or organization must have to undergo or encounter the happenings leading to boost up the volume of information and knowledge.

4   Knowledge Base

A knowledge base is a repository to store knowledge. It is similar to database replacing data with knowledge and is a major part of the field artificial intelligence. It helps to store, organize, create or modify knowledge. Over the web, knowledge base is used to share and more specifically search the information. In present scenario Frequently Asked Questions (FAQs) are one of the stellar examples of knowledge base. Also tutorials and references are the commonly used knowledge base. Some even count procedures and other types of graphics as a part of knowledge base. These are human readable knowledge bases. Another type of knowledge base is Machine readable knowledge base; these knowledge bases consist of knowledge stored in logically consistent manner and include logical operators.

5   Knowledge Base Management

The term Knowledge base management system was first introduced by Nonaka in 1991[7]. He has given SECI model for knowledge base management. SECI represents Socialization, Externalization, Combination and Internalization respectively.

In similar fashion of a database we adopt certain strategy to manage knowledge and create a knowledge base. By this the knowledge can be easily stored and modified. It also helps in resource optimization. In case of knowledge base time is one of the major resources. It is because the factors determining knowledge like experience, skill, intelligence etc. increases primarily along with time.

6   Mathematical Realization

We are considering knowledge as a function of information, intelligence, skill set, and experience. Although other elements can also be a part of knowledge but here we are focusing on the above mentioned elements only. These elements can be used to calculate the knowledge value collectively, but some of these elements may depend upon each other. Like intelligence and skill may depend upon experience and may not play a major role in the calculation of knowledge. We are not taking fact as part of function as the verifiability of fact depends on experience. If the fact is proven then it is a fact and is relevant to experience and if not then it cannot be considered as a fact. So fact can be neglected as a part of experience. This can be mathematically written as

$$K = f (E, I, S, i) \qquad (1)$$

Where, E is experience, I is Information, S is Skill Set, i is Intelligence, K is knowledge.

Now we know that intelligence can be defined in term of decision making ability, and we can say that with experience the decision-making ability increases resulting into increase in the intelligence as well. So we can basically say that intelligence is a function of experience, or intelligence is directly related to experience. So we can replace intelligence with experience and can deduce our equation to:

$$K = g (E, I, S) \qquad (2)$$

Also, as per definition, experience comprises of skills. Skill is defined to be the ability to perform any pre-determined tasks, and with experience skills are gained and honed. Thus, skill can also be said to be dependent on experience, further reducing our equation to

$$K = h (E, I) \qquad (3)$$

Since there is no direct correlation between information and experience we have two different parameters which are required to calculate this equation. E is Experience and I is Information.

Now we can have two cases related to experience and information. The first case is when Experience and Information are from different field.

If experience is from a different field then this experience has little, or no significance on the knowledge synthesis from the available equation. But if the information is related to the field then it will be the value of the knowledge. So,

E=0 and therefore K= I

If information is from a different, unrelated field, i.e., the piece of information is simply noise; therefore it can be safely assumed that whatever be the experience, no knowledge can be extracted from it. So,

K= 0

The second case will come into picture when Experience and Information will be from the same field.

In that case we have

$$K = h (E, I) \qquad (4)$$

Now from Shannon's theorem [9] of Entropy, Information can be calculated as:

$$H(X) = E\ [I(X)] \tag{5}$$

This can be explicitly written as:

$$H(X) = \sum P\ (xi)\ I\ (xi)\ over\ 1<=i<=n \tag{6}$$

Where, H(X) = Entropy of X, P(X) = Probability mass function,
I is Information of X, X is possible values {x1......xn}. [9]
And from Henderson law [8] we can calculate Experience as a function of time as:

$$Cn = C1n\text{-}a \tag{7}$$

Where,
C1 is Cost of first production of 1st unit of knowledge from the available information,
Cn is Cost of production of nth unit of knowledge from the available information,
n is Total volume of information,
a is Elasticity of experience regarding to output that is knowledge.

Following figures were plotted by Henderson [8] himself for a research work conducted for Boston Consulting Group, in the late 1970s. The figures show the experience curve as a function of Cost per unit and Cumulative units of Knowledge production. By these two figures we can analyze that the cost of knowledge production decreases with the increase in experience. It means by acquiring experience over time, the time taken or other factors contributing the knowledge production are used less comparatively to initial period.

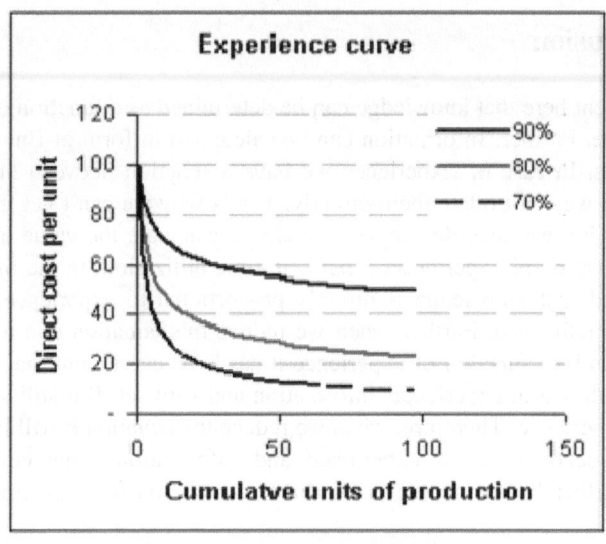

Fig. 1. Relation between Cost per unit and Cumulative Knowledge production per unit [10]

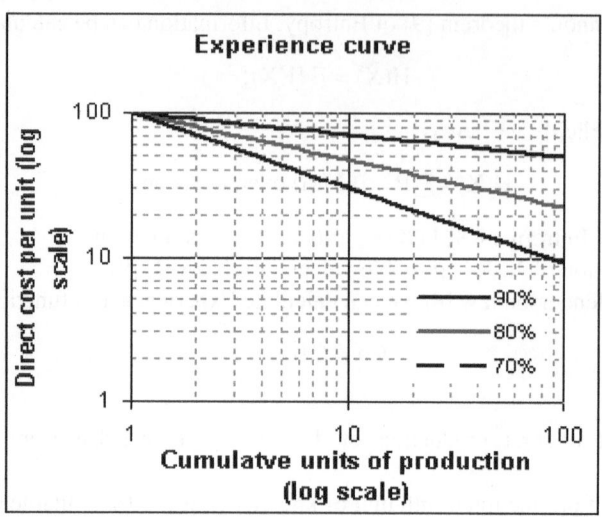

Fig. 2. Relation between Cost per unit and Cumulative Knowledge production per unit in terms of log [10]

In the above cases we have calculated knowledge taking into consideration the different scenarios. In first two cases where information and experience belong to different fields then the value of knowledge will be K=I (when experience is from different field) and K=0 (when information is from different field) respectively. While in third case we have given a function which can be used in the future to calculate knowledge. So we can say that as the experience increases, the cost of creating knowledge from any piece of information decreases as a result of improved learning.

7   Conclusion

Thus it is evident here that knowledge can be determined as a function of Information and Experience. Further, Information can be calculated in form of Entropy by Shannon's Theorem. In case of Experience we have a function between knowledge and experience but we can't relate them directly. That's why we can't get the exact value of Knowledge but we have developed a model to calculate the value of Knowledge. Also in the equation of experience, it helps in time utilization. In the first equation it has been stated that knowledge is directly proportional to experience, information, skill set and intelligence. Further when we reduce this equation due to the fact that intelligence can be a function of experience it has been carved out that knowledge in directly proportional to experience, information and skill set. But still skill sometime depends on experience. Therefore, when we reduce the equation it will be evident that knowledge depends only on experience and information. This equation cannot be reduced further because there is no direct correlation between information and experience.

When experience and information belong to two different fields then experience will have no significance and when these two elements belong to the same field then knowledge is a function of experience and information.

8   Future Work

This paper is a model to calculate the value of knowledge. It's a stepping stone to generate the formula for deriving an approximate value of knowledge. For exact value of knowledge we have to deploy this model further to create a specific equation. Future work can be done in formulating a direct equation between experience and knowledge. Some work can also be done in quantitative calculation of experience to get the exact value of Knowledge. Knowledge calculation cannot be confined to the above mentioned four constraints. So there can be possibilities to add or remove factors to calculate the knowledge, more accurately.

References

1. Stern, R., Sagot, B.: Population of a knowledge base for news metadata from unstructured text and web data (2012), https://akbcwekex2012.files.wordpress.com/2012/05/13_paper.pdf
2. Mayfield, J., Finin, T.: Evaluating the quality of knowledge Base Populated from text (2012), http://ebiquity.umbc.edu/_file_directory_/papers/633.pdf
3. Higa, K., Sheng, O.R.L.: An object-oriented methodology for knowledge base/database coupling (1992), http://dl.acm.org/citation.cfm?id=129888.129895
4. Grahne, G., Mendelzon, A.O., Revesz, P.Z.: Knowledge base transformation, http://dl.acm.org/citation.cfm?id=137097.137882andcoll=DLand dl=ACMandCFID=150042091andCFTOKEN=76377614
5. Saunders, A.: Online solutions: Looking to the future of knowledge base management (2004), doi:10.1145/1027802.1027848
6. Steele, M.: Leverage your transferable skills. Futures in motion, Inc., http://www.slideshare.net/joongie69/m-steele-leverage-your-transferable-skills-1
7. Ikujiro, N., Krogh, V., Georg: Tacit knowledge and knowledge conversion: Con-troversy and advancement in organizational knowledge creation theory. Organization Science 20(3), 635–652 (2009), doi:10.1287/orsc.1080.0412
8. Henderson, B.: Experience curve effects (1970), http://dinarstandard.com/leadership/strategy-concepts-the-experience-curve
9. Shannon, C.E.: The Bell System Technical Journal (1948), http://www.alcatel-lucent.com/bstj/vol27-1948/articles/bstj27-3-379.pdf
10. http://www.sqaji.com/ExperienceCurve/screenshot.gif
11. http://www.businessdictionary.com/definition/information.html
12. http://www.merriam-webster.com/dictionary/fact
13. http://grammar.about.com/od/d/g/description2ter.ht

Information Extraction from High Resolution Satellite Imagery Using Integration Technique

Pankaj Pratap Singh and R.D. Garg

Geomatics Engineering, Department of Civil Engineering, IIT Roorkee, India
pankajps.iitr@gmail.com, garg_fce@iitr.ernet.in

Abstract. This paper presents an integration technique for extraction of Information from high resolution satellite image and also demonstrates the accuracy achieved by the final extracted information. The integration technique comprises of an improved mathematical morphology based watershed transform and a non-linear derivative method. It overcomes all the disadvantages of existing region based and edge based methods by incorporating aforesaid integration methods. It preserves the advantages of multi-resolution and multi-scale gradient approaches. Using these approaches, it avoids excessive fragmentation into regions. The watershed segmentation is proved to be a powerful and fast technique for both contour detection and region-based segmentation. In principle, watershed segmentation depends on ridges to perform a proper segmentation, a property that is often fulfilled for contour detection where the boundaries of the objects have been expressed as ridges. On the other hand, the non-linear derivative method is used for resolving the discrete edge detection problem. Since it automatically selects the best edge localization, which is very much useful for estimation of gradient selection. The main benefit of univocal edge localization is to provide a better direction estimation of the gradient, which helps in producing a confident edge reference map for synthetic images. This nonlinearity will effectively improve global filtration process and regarded to be an effective technique for regularization in order to provide information extraction in a valid manner. The practical merit of this proposed method is to derive an impervious surface from emerging urban areas. Hence this proposed method gives a major contribution in the field of satellite image for information extraction.

1 Introduction

In the advent of remote sensing technology, a high resolution satellite image exhibits lot of information in particular region. Therefore, it is indeed a better extraction process, which has been proposed by researchers. The segmentation process is already a big issue in available extraction methods, due to the impact of variability in spatial values and correlation of spectral values for different objects. There is also a big problem which evolves in segmentation process, due to over-segmentation and under-segmentation. Over-segmentation problem can be reduced with the incorporation of multi-resolution method in watershed segmentation algorithm [1]. Edge detection

A. Agrawal et al. (Eds.): IITM 2013, CCIS 276, pp. 262–271, 2013.

with the univocal localization plays a crucial role in segmentation of images for suppressing the noise. This approach can be achieved with the help of non-linear scheme by incorporating linear regularization. This regularization generally induces delocalization for neighboring edges [2]. This new Non Linear Filtering Scheme (NLFS) combines good localization, Signal to Noise Ratio (SNR) improvement, robustness against mutual-edge influence and a very low computational cost. The gain of NLFS is inversely proportional to regularization due to localization factor.

2   Related Work

To achieve a high level of correctness in segmentation of image, an integration method is required. This integration method comprises of a gray scale morphological approach, which is used to find out structures of image corresponding to shapes and marker-controlled watershed segmentation. This marker controlled watershed technique is based on region based segmentation, which helps in contour detection and to find out boundaries of the objects [3]. Multi-resolution approach is quite effective to improve the segmentation results, which is based on the measurement of different dissimilarity measurement in different level of resolution. It also incorporates the global clustering information of image [4]. Image segmentation methods is now become an important field of satellite image processing, because of availability of high resolution satellite data with varying spatial properties. Therefore, segmentation techniques are used to obtain better segmented results by keeping into consideration of high quality results in comparison to the existing one. Reference data can be used to get supplementary information in order to improve the evaluation criteria by visual inspection [5]. In another work, a pixel based approach is used to segment the images of road and building areas; thereafter an object based classification approach is incorporated to classify non-road and non building like impervious surface [6]. Rizvi et al. proposed a framework to achieve multiresolution segmentation of high resolution satellite imagery by incorporating first marker controlled watershed approach. Initially markers are selected from satellite data to identify objects in low and high resolution images. These markers are also helpful to divide image into homogenous segments, thereafter, watershed approach is applied to partition the image. This method treats image as a set of pixels for classification, which can improve segmentation results [7] [8].

3   Information Extraction Using Marker-Controlled Watershed Segmentation Technique and a Non-linear Derivative Method

In the proposed methodology, the whole process is executed by two methods. A high resolution satellite image consists of high volume of data, which cannot be easily classified. Due to standard pixel based approach and spatial variability in objects, classification process becomes more complicated. Therefore, a satellite image is to be divided in homogeneous regions prior to classification. It will classify satellite images in segments not only on the basis of spectral values, but also using neighborhood information such as size, texture and so on. First of all, a high resolution multi spectral satellite image is taken as input to drive gradient magnitude thereby using low gradient for borders of objects and high gradient for objects inside the image. This outcome image is segmented with the help of watershed transform. It can be over-segmented or under-segmented due to some factors like objects' variability, shadows and noise. So, it has to be passed through preprocessing steps, before calculating markers which controlled watershed drawbacks. A variety of procedures can be applied to find the foreground markers, which must be connected blocks of pixels inside each of the foreground objects. Applying the operation of opening followed by closing can remove the dark spots and stem marks. The results of reconstruction-based opening and closing process are more effective than standard opening and closing operation for removing small blemishes without affecting the overall shape of the objects. The calculated value of regional maxima will help to obtain good foreground markers.

Edge detection function is based on nonlinear derivatives. This function differentiates the image to estimate the gradient. This calculated gradient magnitude is used for image segmentation, but the problem of over-segmentation used to occur in this way, because of watershed transform method without preprocessing step. Separating touching objects in an image is one of the most difficult image processing operations. The watershed transform method is often applied to this problem. It can be achieved by computing the watershed transform and distance transform of threshold image output, thereafter looking for the watershed ridge lines of the result. It computes the Euclidean distance transform of the binary image. To remove small blemishes without affecting the overall shape of the objects, the regional maxima of resulted image is calculated from 'opening-closing by reconstruction' operation for foreground marker image. While superimposing the foreground marker image on original image, most of the occluded and shadowed objects are not found to be marked properly. The 'opening-closing by reconstruction' operation cleans the image with the help of some operator and also removes stray isolated pixels from image. Let us evaluate some of the basics of edge detection technique using a derivative approach. The classical continuous model of edge detection involves the Heaviside function: $C(x) = H(x)$. Edge detection corresponds to gradient computing which is achieved by two directional filtering operations, regularized by presence of a low-pass filter h or not ($h = \delta$):

$$\overline{g(x,y)} = \begin{pmatrix} \frac{\partial}{\partial x} h * I(x,y) \\ \frac{\partial}{\partial y} h * I(x,y) \end{pmatrix} = \begin{pmatrix} f_x * I(x,y) \\ f_y * I(x,y) \end{pmatrix} = \begin{pmatrix} g_x(x,y) \\ g_y(x,y) \end{pmatrix} \tag{1}$$

Where $I(x,y)$ is the original image and $f_x(x,y)$ and $f_y(x,y)$ are the directional regularized detectors. When $h(x,y)$ is separable, $f_x(x,y) = f(x) h(y)$ and $f_y(x,y) = h(x) f(y)$. From the gradient images, the gradient modulus and edge orientation images are calculated, followed by the local maxima of the image. Finally, a segmentation stage (for example, a simple Thresholding process) leads to the representation of the edges in the image.

$$PG_+ = \begin{pmatrix} PG_{x+} \\ PG_{y+} \end{pmatrix} = \begin{pmatrix} T\left(F_+(z)\, I(z,\ .)\right) \\ T\left(F_+(z)\, I(.,\ z)\right) \end{pmatrix},$$ (2)

$$PG_- = \begin{pmatrix} PG_{x-} \\ PG_{y-} \end{pmatrix} = \begin{pmatrix} -T\left(-F_-(z)\, I(z,\ .)\right) \\ -T\left(-F_-(z)\, I(.,\ z)\right) \end{pmatrix}.$$ (3)

$$|g_{ed}| = \sqrt{(g_{x+} + g_{x-})^2 (g_{y+} + g_{y-})^2}$$ (4)

Polarized gradient (PG_+) is required parameter to take consideration of pixel values. It will approach with the use of edge detection modulus (g_{ed}). It will also help to provide regularization way to estimate gradient of images along with the lines (columns). Since, this NLFS scheme considers the orientation of edges, which is coming through as an outcome in shifted pixel localization from anti-symmetric linear filter. This orientation of edges shows the variation of sign and it provides univocal localization.

$$y_k^r = -y_{-k}$$ (5)

This localization depends on the variation of edges. This all shows improvement in results of edge detection with this NLFS scheme without use of regularization comparatively better from traditional method without regularization [9].

4   Proposed Methodology for Integration Technique Based Classifier

In the proposed methodology, an integration approach is used to classify satellite imagery for extracting existing classes from the image. This completes process evolves each step to complete this task and its complete processing flowchart is shown below in figure 1 & 2. To calculate Gradient magnitude as a segmentation function, the minimum and maximum values of gradient helps to find border of objects and inside the objects respectively. Now, watershed transform uses aforesaid derivative values for segmentation of image, but eventually a problem of over-segmentation occurs, due to the lacking of preprocessing step such as marker computation. To overcome this problem, a foreground and background marker evaluates segmentation with the help of resulted image in successive steps of 'opening-closing by reconstruction' operation. It eventually, results that don't come up to the mark by using calculated markers, therefore calculated markers replace by a non-linear derivative method. Gradient modulus (gm), components of nonlinear derivatives and polarized derivatives compute for localized edges inside the object shape. Finally the outcome of these aforesaid methods extracts the information from satellite imagery.

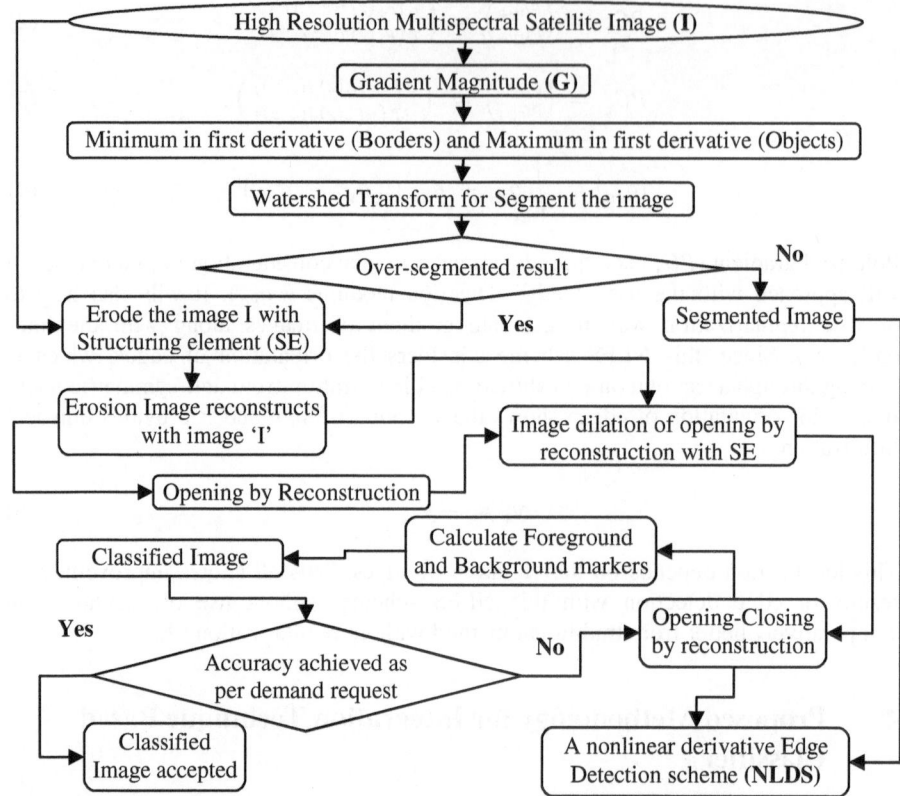

Fig. 1. Detailed representation of an integration approach for information extraction contd

5   Results of the Proposed Integration Classifier

The proposed integration method has been tested on urban areas of emerging region. First of all, proposed Integration classifier tested on emerging urban area, which is shown below in Figure 3 (a-f) shows the successive results of aforesaid method. Initially an input image converted into grayscale for retrieving Gradient magnitude image, which helps to evaluate watershed transform image as shown in figure 3(c). Due to the occurrence of over-segmented result after evaluating watershed transform of gradient magnitude image, another image reconstruction method is used. Thereafter, image reconstruction followed by multiple erosions calculates a resulted image as shown in figure 3(d). It also says as resulted image after applying opening by reconstruction operation. Now, these results are not sufficient to achieve the higher degree of accuracy.

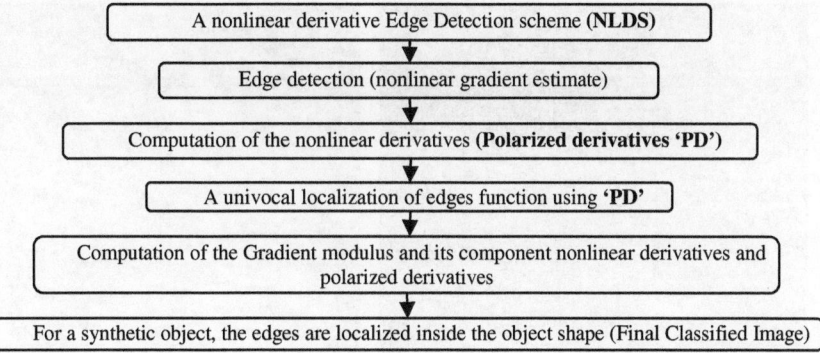

Fig. 2. Detailed representation of an integration approach for information extraction

Therefore, A NLDS method applies on figure 3(d) to suppress the effect of over-segmentation. The resulted Final Edge detection output of satellite imagery is shown in figure 3(e) and finally, Figure 3(f) shows extracted classes in different colors from satellite imagery with the help of an integration classifier approach. These different classes are carrying distinct information in form of colors such as dark blue, sky-blue, light blue, green-yellow, light orange and dark orange-maroon colors indicate, shadow, roads, trees, building's roof, building's outer walls and concrete surface respectively. Figure 3(f) shows quite different colors for building classes, due to the different spectral values of emerging urban area. It shows buildings roofs shows diversity, due to different material like steel or red cement are shown as yellow, orange and light green color respectively. Apart from it, constructed side wall shows as mild orange color, which will reflect elevation factor in image.

(a)   (b)

Fig. 3. Results of extracted classes from satellite image (emerging urban) in successive steps. (a) Input image, (b) Converted grayscale image, (c) Calculated watershed transform image by using gradient magnitude image, (d) Resulted image after applying opening-by-reconstruction operation,(e) Final Edge detection on satellite imagery, (f) Extracted classes from satellite image.

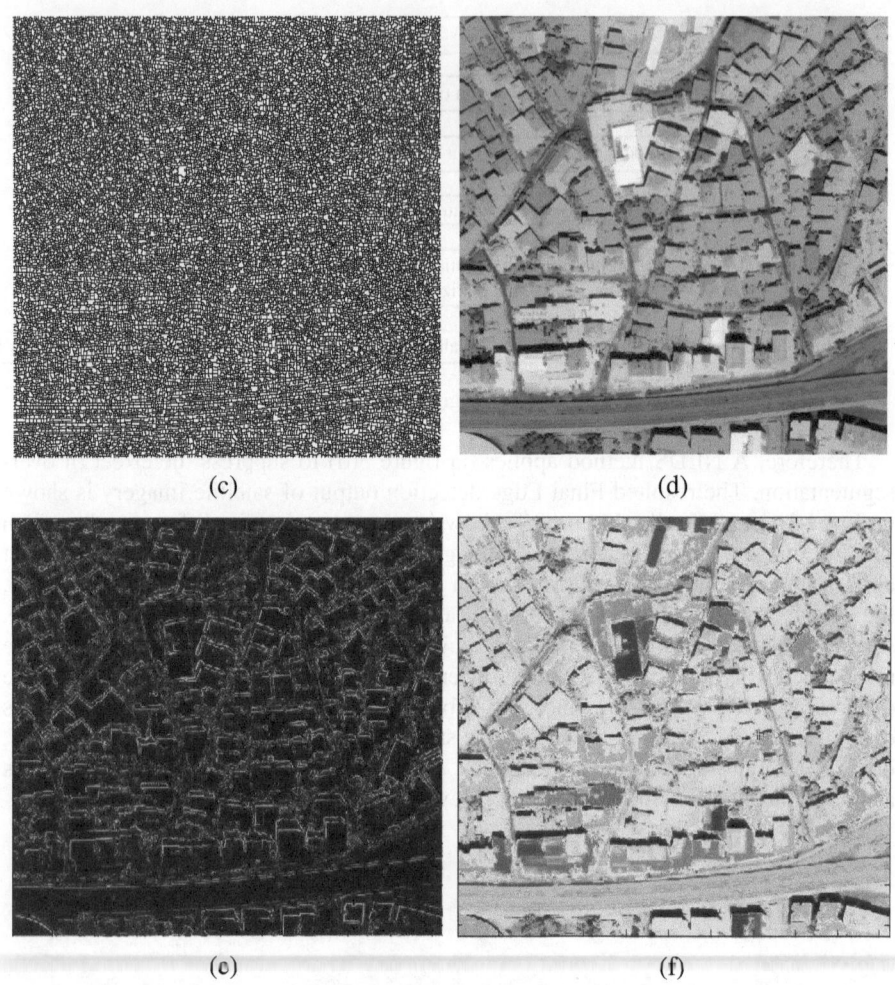

Fig. 3. (*Continued*)

6 Accuracy Assessment of the Proposed Algorithm

An accuracy assessment is the comprehensive discussion about classification. Accuracy assessment is a general expression for comparing the classification to satellite data that are assumed to be true, in order to determine the accuracy of the classification process. Ground truth data is generally used for deriving reference true data. It is usually not practical to ground truth or otherwise test every pixel of a classified image. Therefore, a set of reference data is usually used. Reference data are continuum portion of features on the classified image for which actual features are (or will be) known. The complete satellite image is selected as reference data. Accuracy assessment is an important step in the classification process. The goal is to quantitatively determine how effectively continuum variation of features was grouped into the correct feature classes in the area under investigation.

6.1   Fuzzy Error Matrix

Fuzzy error matrix compare, on category-by category basis, the relationship between known reference data (ground truth) and the corresponding results of an automated classification. The accuracy assessment for the soft classified and reference data is estimating by calculation the fuzzy error matrix which is given in Table 1 for emerging urban area. The value of Kappa Coefficient (K) = 68.20% means the classification has achieved an overall accuracy (OA) that is 79.01% better than would be expected from random assignment of pixels to features.

Table 1. Fuzzy error matrix of classification for emerging urban area

		Soft Classified Data			
		Shadow	**Building**	**Roads**	**(Column) Total agreement**
Reference Data	**Shadow**	0.1989	0.2045	0.2046	0.2188
	Building	0.2660	0.2981	0.3072	0.4102
	Roads	0.2614	0.2911	0.2930	0.3710
	(Row) Total agreement	0.2943	0.3475	0.3582	

6.2   Producer's Accuracy

Producer's accuracies (as shown in Table 2) result from dividing the number of correctly soft classified class proportion in each category (on the major diagonal) by the training set as class proportion from reference data used for that category (the column total agreement).

Table 2. Producer's accuracy of classification for emerging urban area

Feature	Accuracy calculation	Producer's accuracy (%)
Shadow	0.1989 / 0.2188	90.90
Building	0.2981 / 0.4102	72.69
Roads	0.2930 / 0.3710	78.98

This indicates a drastic improvement in the accuracy of the results obtained by the integration approach which is able to classify, in particular the shadow and the roads features, with almost 91% and 79% efficiency in Table 2. The calculated Overall producer's accuracy (OPA) is 80.86%.

6.3   User Accuracy

User's accuracies (as shown in Table 3) result by dividing the number of correctly soft classified class proportion in each category by the total reference data that are classified in that category (the row total agreement). The calculated Overall user's accuracy (OUA) is 78.40%.

Table 3. User's accuracy of classification for emerging urban area

Feature	Accuracy calculation	User's accuracy (%)
Shadow	0.1989 / 0.2943	67.59
Building	0.2981 / 0.3475	85.78
Roads	0.2930 / 0.3582	81.81

7   Conclusion

Integration method is effective to extract information from satellite imagery, which incorporates two techniques such as an improved mathematical morphology based watershed transform and a non-linear derivative method. With the help of non-linear derivative method, it will automatically select the best edge localization, based on the correct estimation of gradient selection. Its main contribution is to derive univocal edge localization with the help of noise reduction in presence of finding best edges. The main benefits are univocal edge localization for synthetic and real images, noise reduction with no regularization and better direction estimation of the gradient. It can produce a confident edge reference map for synthetic images, extremely efficient on salt and pepper noise. However, an impervious surface is still a challenging task to extract from urban areas. The satellite image with 1-m/pixel resolution has been acquired from Wikimapia. In our case, the place and date are not critical factor. The major objective is evaluation of the content of the image. Experimental results indicate possible use of proposed integrated approach in information extraction from high resolution satellite image in a reliable manner. The accuracy assessment parameters overall accuracy and kappa coefficient values are calculated as 79.01% and 68.20% respectively, which show good degree of extraction of information from emerging urban area. A producer's accuracy value of 80.86% also shows better extraction, due to the occurrence of better accuracy of shadow and roads information from emerging urban area. A User's accuracy value of 78.40% also shows better extraction, due to the occurrence of better accuracy for all class information from emerging urban area. The resulted classified image shows good level of accuracy for derived classes (Road, building and shadow – can also be termed as information) from imagery. It shows good degree of information extracted from HRSI. The practical merit of this proposed method is to derive an impervious surface from urban and suburban areas. Hence this proposed method gives major contribution in the field of satellite image for information extraction.

References

1. Kim, J.B., Kim, H.J.: Multiresolution-based watersheds for efficient image segmentation. Pattern Recognition Letters 24(1-3), 473–488 (2003)
2. Laligant, O., Truchetet, F., Meriaudeau, F.: Regularization Preserving Localization of Close Edges. IEEE Signal Processing Letters 14(3), 185–188 (2007)
3. Parvati, K., Rao, B.S.P., Das, M.M.: Image Segmentation Using Gray Scale Morphology and Marker Controlled Watershed Transformation. Discrete Dynamics in Nature and Society, Article ID 384346, 8 pages(2008), doi:10.1155/2008/384346
4. Liu, J., Yang, Y.H.: Multiresolution Color Image Segmentation. IEEE Transactions on Pattern Analysis and Machine Intelligence Archive 16(7), 689–700 (1994)
5. Meinel, G., Neubert, M.: A comparison of segmentation programs for high resolution remote sensing data. In: Proceedings of the 20th International Archives of Photogrammetry and Remote Sensing (ISPRS) Congress, XXXV(Part B), Istanbul, Turkey, pp. 1097–1102 (2004)
6. Shackelford, A.K., Davis, C.H.: A combined fuzzy pixel-based and object-based approach for classification of high-resolution multispectral data over urban areas. IEEE T. Geoscience and Remote Sensing 41(10), 2354–2363 (2003)
7. Rizvi, I.A., Mohan, B.K., Bhatia, P.R.: Multi-resolution segmentation of high-resolution remotely sensed imagery using marker-controlled watershed transform. In: ACM Proceedings of the International Conference Workshop on Emerging Trends in Technology (ICWET 2011), vol. 14(9), pp. 674–678. TCET, Mumbai (2011)
8. Rizvi, I.A., Mohan, B.K.: Object-Based Image Analysis of High-Resolution Satellite Images Using Modified Cloud Basis Function Neural Network and Probabilistic Relaxation Labeling Process. IEEE T. Geoscience and Remote Sensing 49(12), 4815–4820 (2011)
9. Laligant, O., Truchetet, F.: A Nonlinear Derivative Scheme Applied to Edge Detection. IEEE Transactions on Pattern Analysis and Machine Intelligence 32(2), 242–257 (2010)

Multilevel Semi-fragile Watermarking Technique for Improving Biometric Fingerprint System Security

M.V. Joshi, Vaibhav B. Joshi, and Mehul S. Raval

DA-IICT, Gandhinagar, Gujarat, India
{mv_joshi,vaibhav_joshi,mehul_raval}@daiict.ac.in

Abstract. Classical biometric system are prone to compromise at several points. Two of the vulnerable points are : 1. biometric database 2. biometric feature matcher subsystem. We propose a two level watermarking scheme to secure these vulnerable points. Watermark W_1 is used for database authentication and made resistive to lossy compression. It is derived using block based singular values (SV's) of a fingerprint image. W_1 establish linkages between watermark and fingerprint image. Watermark W_2 is used to secure feature matcher subsystem. It is computed using second and third order moments of the fingerprint image. W_2 is made resistive to mild affine transformation and lossy compression to incorporate practical aspects of biometric fingerprint system. The proposed watermarking method not only provides protection to database and matcher subsystem, it also gives security against copy attack.

Keywords: Fingerprint, moments, semi-fragile, singular value decomposition (SVD), watermarking.

1   Introduction

The systematic and scientific approach for human identification started in 19th century using an identification number or random symbols. In early 20th century as technology progressed these approaches for human identification became obsolete and biometric features gained popularity for human identification. The rapid development of computer networks and increased use of multimedia data via the Internet has resulted in fast and convenient mechanism for information exchange. With the ease of editing and availability of manipulating softwares the authenticity of digital images becomes an important concern. Over the last decade, digital watermarking has presented excellent techniques for image authentication. Fragile or semi-fragile watermarks [1],[2],[3],[4] are mainly applied for content authentication and integrity attestation because they are sensitive to modifications. These modifications may results in unauthorized embedding of watermark which is a major threat from the authentication perspective. Unauthorized embedding can be attempted via two ways. 1) Adversary embeds new and customized watermark in the existing legal watermarked content. This threat classified as an ambiguity attack is a major menace for copyright application of the watermarking system. 2) Adversary gains access to the

A. Agrawal et al. (Eds.): IITM 2013, CCIS 276, pp. 272–283, 2013.
© Springer-Verlag Berlin Heidelberg 2013

original watermark used in authentication system and add it to another illegal content. The watermark detector will be spoofed and it will authenticate illegal content by detecting presence of original watermark in it. This type of attack is classified as a copy attack [5],[6]   and it can have very severe consequences for biometric authentication system.

Many watermarking techniques use variety of transforms for embedding watermark. Singular value decomposition (SVD) has emerged as one of the popular transform for watermarking applications as it uses optimal bases for representation derived from data [7],[8]. Authors in [9],[10],[11] proposed combining SVD and discrete wavelet transform (DWT) based watermarking techniques. E.Ganic et.al decomposed the cover image into four bands using DWT (LL, LH, HL and HH) and added identical gray scale watermark to all the four sub-bands. In order to create watermarked image, scaled singular values (SV's) of the watermark was added to SV's of all the sub-bands. While recovering, SV's were extracted from the sub-bands of possibly noisy image and combined with orthogonal matrices to reconstruct the watermark from each sub-band. These approaches suffer from severe security flaws due to requirement of original watermark or the eigen vectors of the watermark during recovery at the receiver. This enhances the threat of copy attack on biometric system.

In the biometric authentication system watermark is generally used to check the authenticity of the biometric images stored in the database. In one such approach [12] authentication scheme was based on SVD and least significant bit (LSB) embedding. Even though LSB embedding resulted in excellent perceptual quality, the method is susceptible to unauthorized removal of watermark. In this scheme, due to malicious manipulation, a false positive may occur in the matcher subsystem. This will authenticate the illegal test sample. Authors in [13] presented multimodal biometric authentication that provides additional security along with fingerprint matching. They used facial features as watermark which is inserted into the respective fingerprint images. Authors in [14] also used facial features to watermark fingerprints using DWT and an embedding key. Even though these approaches improve security, requirement of two separate biometric modalities make them operationally costly. Many of the SVD based watermarking methods focus on the issue of improving robustness with fixed perceptual fidelity. Very little attention has been paid to the security aspect of SVD based watermarking schemes. In most of the SVD based algorithms, a pair of right and left orthogonal matrices are used to regenerate the watermark at the decoder. Changing these bases may regenerate illegal watermark [15]. The proposed method does not require "original" orthogonal matrices for watermark reconstruction which is one of its main advantage over other SVD based watermarking schemes.

In a classical biometric system, the test image suffer from mild form of affine transformation while sensing. This happens since no user places finger in the same position every time while using system. Due to this fact distortion in terms of rotation, scaling and translation (RST) is introduced in the test image. In an automatic fingerprint identification system, the matcher subsystem handles these distortions [16]. From watermarking perspective, this affine transformation of the test image will cause a loss of synchronization at the watermarking detector and may cause a complete failure in the detection system. Hence for a successful detection in the proposed approach one of the watermark is made RST invariant. To the best of our knowledge no biometric watermarking system has been proposed with RST invariance in the test sample. It can be argued that noise cleaning process of biometric system will take care of affine transformation but it adds computational burden. In [17] authors suggested many RST invariant watermarking algorithms. Out of them, we chose moment based approach due to its simplicity. Second and third order moments are found to be RST invariant for any image and thus used for generating RST invariant watermark. Keeping these factors in mind we introduce multiple semi-fragile watermarks for authentication at database and matcher subsystem of a biometric fingerprint system. Here the database image is divided into several blocks and SVD is calculated for each of them. Our algorithm then utilizes the relationship between SV's in a block to calculate W_1. It also calculates the moments of the test fingerprint image to generate W_2. Watermark W_2 is inserted in such a manner that it is resistive to image compression. As both watermarks are computed from image features they are linked to fingerprint image and provide protection against copy attack.

2   Proposed Method

We first review few basics of SVD and RST invariant moments as watermark embedding and extracting process depends on them.

2.1   Singular Value Decomposition

Any m × n real valued matrix A, with m ≥ n can be written as the product of three matrices.

$$A = U \times S \times V^T \qquad (1)$$

The columns of the m × m, U have mutually orthogonal unit vectors, as are the columns of the n × n, V matrix. S is a pseudo-diagonal matrix, having diagonal elements as singular values. There are n singular values $\sigma_1, \sigma_2, \sigma_3, ..., \sigma_n$ with the condition that:

$$\sigma_1 \geq \sigma_2 \geq \sigma_3 \geq \cdots \geq \sigma_n \qquad (2)$$

While both U and V are not unique, the singular values σ_i are fully determined by A.

2.2   Moments

For a 2D continuous function $f(x, y)$, the moment of order (p + q) is defined as:

$$m_{pq} = \int_{-\infty}^{+\infty} \int_{-\infty}^{+\infty} x^p y^q f(x,y) dx dy, \qquad p, q = 0,1,2, \dots \dots \dots \qquad (3)$$

The central moments are defined as

$$\mu_{pq} = \int_{-\infty}^{+\infty} \int_{-\infty}^{+\infty} (x - \bar{x})^p (y - \bar{y})^q f(x,y) dx dy, \qquad \bar{x} = \frac{m_{10}}{m_{00}}, \bar{y} = \frac{m_{10}}{m_{00}} \qquad (4)$$

If $f(x, y)$ is a digital image, then equation (4) becomes

$$\mu_{pq} = \sum_{-\infty}^{+\infty}\sum_{-\infty}^{+\infty} (x - \bar{x})^p \; (y - \bar{y})^q \; f(x,y) \tag{5}$$

A set of seven invariant moments can be derived from the second and third moments as in [18] to generate watermark W_2. Next we describe embedding and extraction process for watermarking algorithm. Some of the assumptions in proposed method are:

1. Fingerprint images in biometric database are stored in lossy format (JPEG2000) to conserve the storage space.
2. It is assumed that test image at sensor will undergo mild affine transformation due to inconsistency in finger placement by the user.
3. Following are shared between embedding and extraction process.
   - Distance between two quantizer (δ).
   - Rules for computing watermark.
4. It is assume that watermarking authentication phase will follow the biometric recognition phase. Final authentication decision is rolled out only after both phases are cleared

2.3   Embedding Process

The embedding process has following steps:

1. Take an input fingerprint image I of size $M \times N$ and calculate it's higher order moments.
2. Use decimal to ASCII conversion and generate moment based watermark (W_2).
3. Decompose I using DWT to generate LL_1, LH_1, HL_1, HH_1 bands.
4. Divide LL_1 band into blocks of size $P \times Q$.
5. Apply SVD on each blocks and compute watermark W_1 based on the following relation:

   $W_1(k) \;=\; 0 \;$ if $\; \delta \;<\; ((S_i(2,2)\text{-} \; S_i(3,3))/2)$,
   $W_1(k) \;=\; 1 \;$ if $\; \delta \;\geq\; ((S_i(2,2)\text{-} \; S_i(3,3))/2)$,

   where, i indicates i^{th} block in an image, $W_1(k)$ denotes k^{th} bit of W_1 and δ is minimum distance between the two quantizers of SQ.
6. Use scalar quantization (SQ) to embed W_1 in σ_{max} of each block. Quantize SV to an even or an odd value following the embedding rule as: if $W_1(k) = 0$ quantize to an even value else quantize it to an odd value.
7. Apply inverse SVD over each block to get watermarked version of LL_1 band (LL_{1w}).
8. Apply second level of DWT decomposition on LL_{1w} to generate LL_2, LH_2, HL_2, HH_2 bands.
9. Use SQ to embed W_2 in the coefficients of LH_2 band. Quantize coefficients to even or odd value with embedding rule same as for W_1 i.e. if $W_2(k) = 0$ quantize

the selected   coefficient to an even value else quantize it to an odd value. Here k indicates k^{th} bit of W_2. LH_2 coefficients for embedding are selected based on the key. Since DWT coefficients having maximum value are not affected by lossy compression embedding watermark in them provides high resistivity to lossy compression [19],[20].

10. Apply inverse DWT to generate final watermarked image I_w.

2.4   Extraction Process

Extraction is divided into two parts: 1) watermark extraction and, 2) authentication.

Watermark Extraction

The watermark extraction process has following steps:

1. Apply one level DWT decomposition on noisy watermarked image I_{wn} to generate LL_{1n}, LH_{1n}, HL_{1n}, HH_{1n} bands.
2. Apply SVD on blocks of the LL_{1n} band.
3. Find the σ_{max} in each block of LL_{1n}. Apply following rules to extract watermark W_1^{re}.

$$W_1^{re}(k) = 0 \text{ if } \sigma_{max} \text{ of block}(i) \text{ is even,}$$
$$W_1^{re}(k) = 1 \text{ if } \sigma_{max} \text{ of block}(i) \text{ is odd,}$$

where, i indicates i^{th} block and $W_1^{re}(k)$ denotes k^{th} bit of W_1^{re}.

4. Compute SVD based watermark W_1^{rc} based on the relation between SV's from LL_{1n} band as done in embedding process.
5. Get the test image I_i from the sensor of biometric fingerprint system and obtain the moment based watermark W_2^{rc} by computing the higher order moments on it.
6. Apply second level wavelet decomposition on LL_{1n} to generate LL_{2n}, LH_{2n}, HL_{2n}, HH_{2n} bands.
7. Extract watermark W_2^{re} from LH_{2n} band using the following rules.

$$W_2^{re}(k) = 0 \text{ if selected DWT coefficient of } LH_{2n} \text{ band is even,}$$
$$W_2^{re}(k) = 1 \text{ if selected DWT coefficient of } LH_{2n} \text{ band is odd,}$$

where, $W_2^{re}(k)$ denotes k^{th} bit of W_2^{re}.

Authentication.

In the proposed method we use two watermarks for two level authenticity checks. One at the database to check any manipulation on stored fingerprint images and another to secure matcher subsystem of a biometric fingerprint system. Thus, these watermarks add another security layer over biometric fingerprint system.

Authenticity check at database:

It should be noted that this check can run on stored database at any instance without requiring test fingerprint image from sensor of the biometric fingerprint system. The steps of authentication process are:

1. Compare W_1^{re} and W_1^{rc} and find matching scores between them (Euclidean distance in our case).
2. Compare matching score with predefined threshold value.
3. Declare stored image to be authentic if   matching score $\geq$ threshold value.

Authenticity check at matcher subsystem of biometric fingerprint system:
This check is carried on test fingerprint image available from the sensor of the biometric fingerprint system. The steps for authentication are:

1. Compare W_2^{re} and W_2^{rc} and find matching value.
2. Compare matching value with predefined threshold.
3. Declare test image to be authentic if matching value $\geq$ threshold value.

In normal circumstances above mentioned authentication mechanisms may run independently. In case of security threat the process requires two level sequential authentication mechanism. The steps followed after test fingerprint is available at the sensor are:

1. Run authenticity check for a test fingerprint image at database.
2. After clearing this first level authentication, proceed to second level authentication at matcher subsystem.
3. Authenticate only if the steps 1 and 2 are cleared.

3   Experimental Result

Performance of the algorithm is evaluated using a database containing fingerprint samples from FVC2004 [21]. For experiments 8 bit gray scale fingerprint images *I* with 500 dpi [22] are selected. The size of M $\times$ N   = 320 $\times$ 320 is selected to improve fingerprint detection [23]. For LL_1 band, block of size P = Q = 4 is used and the entire

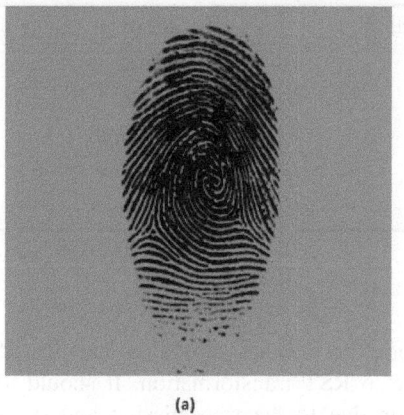 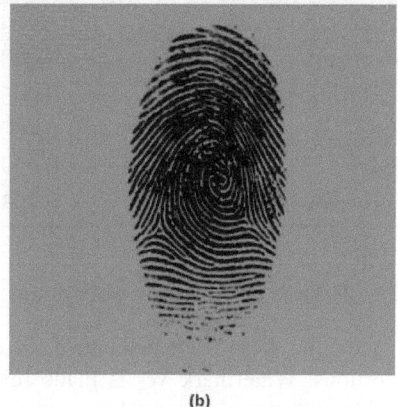

(a)   (b)

Fig. 1. (a) Original fingerprint image (b) Watermarked fingerprint image

image is divided into 1600 non overlapping blocks. Watermarking capacity of proposed method is 1bit per block. For SQ, minimum distance between two quantizers is chosen as 0.1 at both the levels of watermarking.

Invisible watermarking methods should have excellent perceptual fidelity and it is reflected in PSNR of 93.29 dB for watermarked images in the proposed method. Figure 1 (a) and (b) show original and watermarked biometric images, respectively. As two watermarks are used for multiple authenticity checks, we show experimental results on a database as well as on matcher subsystem.

3.1   Results on Database

Under the scenario of image transmission and storage in database, watermark W_1 must survive natural image processing operations like image compression. Therefore, to check robustness of watermark W_1 against lossy compression we apply JPEG2000 compression with compression ratio (CR) of 5. In order to study behavior of the method against compression, we apply this attack over 800 images and compute bit error rate (BER). We also apply histogram equalization (Hseq), Gaussian noise (GN) with zero mean and 0.1 variance and copy attack over 50 images and compute their BER. Table 1 shows average BER for different attacks on W_1. The threshold value for authentication decision is selected empirically based on mean values of BER.

In the proposed work, JPEG2000 compression is considered as non-malicious attack on database with all other attacks considered as malicious ones. In order to showcase security of the method, copy attack was mounted against watermarked image. Copy attack is simulated in the following manner. Watermark used in the database fingerprint is assumed to be available with the attacker in perfect form and this watermark is inserted in to the illegal fingerprint template using the algorithm proposed in section 2 with known watermarking key.

Table 1. Average BER for different attacks on W_1

Attacks	Average BER	Decision
No attack	0.000000	Authentic
JPEG2000 (CR = 5)	0.00653	Authentic
Hseq	0.46099	Unauthentic
GN	0.49994	Unauthentic
Copy attack	0.19305	Unauthentic

3.2   Results on Matcher Subsystem

In automatic fingerprint authentication system, the matcher subsystem handles RST distortions. Watermark W_2 is made resistive to RST transformation. It should also provide robustness against lossy compression due to the transmission and storage requirements. Once again in order to study method's behavior for matcher subsystem different manipulations (attacks) are applied on each of the test fingerprint image and average values of results are as shown in table 2. The threshold value for authentication decision is selected empirically. It is based on the mean value of BER obtained against each attack. Following attacks are considered.

1. JPEG2000 compression with CR = 5.
2. Rotation of +5° on test fingerprint image.
3. Rotation of -5° on test fingerprint image.
4. Up scaling by 2 on test fingerprint image.
5. Down scaling by 2 on test fingerprint image.
6. Gaussian noise (GN) addition with $\mu = 0$ ane $\sigma = 0.1$ on test fingerprint image.
7. Copy attack.

Table 2. Average BER for different attacks on W_2

Attacks	Average BER	Decision
No attack	0.000000	Authentic
JPEG2000 (CR = 5)	0.00040	Authentic
Rotation of -5°	0.04645	Authentic
Rotation of -5°	0.03634	Authentic
Up scaling by 2	0.00137	Authentic
Down scaling by 2	0.00229	Authentic
GN	0.46308	Unauthentic
Copy attack	0.62645	Unauthentic

Attacks No. 1 to 5 are considered as non-malicious and 6,7 as malicious for matcher subsystem. Resistivity against JPEG2000 for both watermark W_1 and W_2 are showcased in figure 2 (a) and 2 (b). We selected 800 fingerprint images from FVC2004 database to showcase the results.

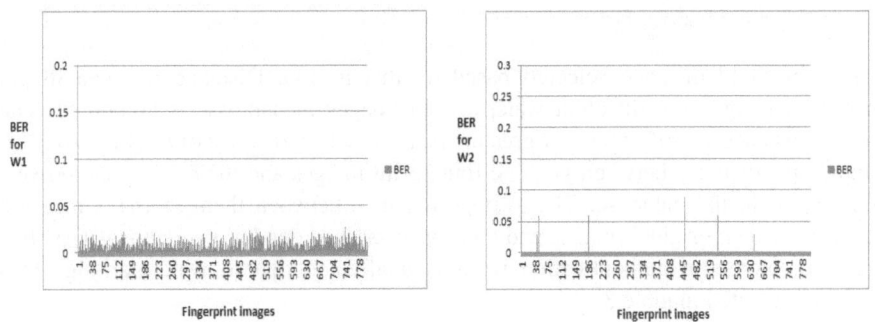

Fig. 2. (a)BER for W_1 against JPEG2000(CR = 5)   (b) BER for W_2 against JPEG2000(CR = 5)

3.3   Watermarking Effect over Biometric Authentication System

In the proposed approach watermarking is used to create an additional security layer on the top of existing biometric fingerprint system. Watermark is a "foreign" content to fingerprint image, therefore it is essential that insertion of watermark should not cause significant change in the biometric authentication decision. In order to showcase the effect of watermark on fingerprint authentication, we use fingerprint matching algorithm developed in [24],[25]. We selected it because it is fast and scalable. Output of this algorithm gives Euclidean distance between test fingerprint image and it's closest match in the database. We stored 100 watermarked versions of genuine fingerprint images in a database and used 100 genuine and 100 illegal images as query images to the database. From the result, obtained using matching algorithm based on thresholds, false positive and false negative probabilities are calculated to plot receiver operating characteristics (ROC) curve for proposed watermarking technique as shown in figure 3.

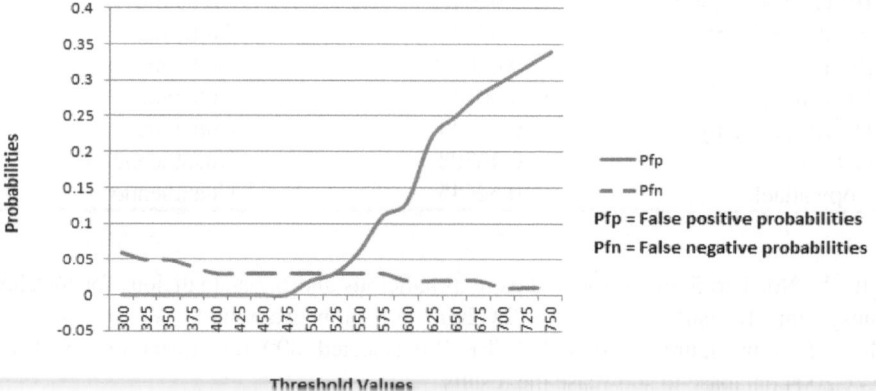

Fig. 3. ROC curve for proposed watermarking technique

The threshold distance selected based on this is 400. Distance between illegal fingerprint image with different watermarked images in database is computed. The average distance is 995 which is greater than the selected threshold value. We also compute the distance between genuine fingerprint images and their watermarked versions stored in the database. The average distance between them is 141. Since the distance between original images and their watermarked database versions is less than threshold, biometric authentication remains unaffected due to watermarking. This result are depicted in table 3.

Table 3. Average distance between watermarked, original and fake fingerprint images (for 100 images)

Average distance between watermarked and original fingerprint image	Average distance between watermarked and fake fingerprint image	Threshold
140.5677	994.6301	400

4 Conclusion

A moments and SVD based multipurpose watermarking technique for fingerprint authentication, has been presented. The proposed algorithm is robust against JPEG2000 compression and it is extremely sensitive to other malicious manipulations. The method is secure against copy attack as reflected in table 1 and 2. The method not only provides authenticity checks at multiple levels to increase security but also biometric detection accuracy remains unchanged due to watermark insertion. The qualitative comparison of proposed method with [12] and [13] is as shown in table 4 to indicates it's efficacy. Results indicate that proposed method is better than [12] and [13].

Table 4. Feature based comparison of proposed method, [12] and [13]

Feature	Lamiaa et.al [13]	Wang et.al [12]	proposed method
Method Nature	Fragile	Fragile	Semi-fragile
Number of watermark	One	One	Two
Survive against JPEG2000	No	No	Yes
Survive against copy attack	No	Yes	Yes
RST invariance for matcher subsystem	No	No	Yes

Acknowledgment. The authors would like to thank Board of Research in Nuclear Science (BRNS), Department of Atomic Energy, Government of India for providing research grant to carry out this work.

References

1. Barreto, P.S.L.M., Kim, H.Y., Rijmen, V.: Toward secure public-key blockwise fragile authentication watermarking. Proc. IEE. 149(2), 57–62 (2002)
2. Celik, M.U., Sharma, G., Saber, E., Tekalp, A.M.: Hierarchical watermarking for secure image authentication with localization. IEEE Trans. Image Process. 11(6), 585–595 (2002)

3. Jaejin, L., Chee, S.W.: A watermarking sequence using parities of error control coding for image authentication and correction. IEEE Trans. Consum. Electron. 46(2), 313–317 (2000)
4. Kundur, D., Hatzinakos, D.: Digital watermarking for telltale tamper proofing and authentication. Proc. IEEE 87(7), 1167–1180 (1999)
5. Kutter, M., Voloshynovskiy, S., Herrigel, A.: The Watermark Copy Attack. In: Proc. of the SPIE, Security and Watermarking of Multimedia Contents II, vol. 3971, pp. 371–379 (January 2000)
6. Barr, J., Bradley, B., Hanniga, B.: Using Digital Watermarks with Image Signatures to Mitigate the Threat of the Copy Attack. In: Proc. ICASSP, vol. 3, pp. 69–72 (April 2003)
7. Liu, R., Tan, T.: An SVD-based watermarking scheme for protecting rightful ownership. IEEE Trans. on Multimedia 4(1), 121–128 (2002)
8. Zhou, B., Chen, J.: A geometric distortion resilient image watermarking algorithm based on SVD. Chinese Journal on Image and Graphics 9, 506–512 (2004)
9. Ganic, E., Eskicioglu, A.M.: Robust DWT-SVD domain watermarking: Embedding data in all frequencies. In: Proc. Workshop Multimedia Security, Magdeburg, Germany, pp. 166–174 (September 2004)
10. Bhatnagar, G., Raman, B.: A new robust reference watermarking scheme based on DWT - SVD. Comput. Standards and Interfaces 31(5), 1002–1013 (2009)
11. Lai, C.-C., Tsai, C.-C.: Digital image watermarking using discrete wavelet transform and singular value decomposition. IEEE Trans. Instru. and Measur. 59(11), 3060–3063 (2010)
12. Wang, D.-S., Li, J.-P., Wen, X.-Y.: Biometric Image Integrity Authentication Based on SVD and Fragile Watermarking. In: IEEE Congress on Image and Signal Processing, CISP 2008, vol. 5, pp. 679–682 (May 2008)
13. El Bakrawy, L.M., Ghali, N.I., Hassanien, A.E., Peters, J.F.: Strict Authentication of Multimodal Biometric Images Using Near Sets. In: Gaspar-Cunha, A., Takahashi, R., Schaefer, G., Costa, L. (eds.) Soft Computing in Industrial Applications. AISC, vol. 96, pp. 249–258. Springer, Heidelberg (2011)
14. Vatsa, M., Singh, R., Noore, A., Houck, M.M., Morries, K.: Robust biometric image watermarking for fingerprint and face images. IEICE Electronics Express 5(2), 23–28 (2006)
15. Wu, Y.: On the security of SVD-Based ownership watermarking. IEEE Trans. on Multimedia 7(4) (August 2005)
16. Ratha, N.K.: Effect of controlled image acquisition on fingerprint matching. In: IEEE Fourteenth International Conference on Pattern Recognition, vol. 2, pp. 1659–1661 (1998)
17. Zheng, D., Liu, Y., Zhao, J., El Saddik, A.: A survey of RST invariant image watermarking algorithms. ACM Computing Surveys 39(2), Article 5 (June 2007)
18. Gonzalez, Woods: Digital Image processing using MATLAB, pp. 610–613. Tata McGraw Hill (2010)
19. Lin, C.Y., Chang, S.-F.: A Robust Image Authentication Algorithm Surviving JPEG Compression. In: SPIE, Storage and Retrieval of Image/Video Database, pp. 296–307 (1998)
20. Raval, M.S., Rege, P.P.: Discrete wavelet transform based multiple watermarking scheme. In: Proceeding IEEE TENCON 2003, pp. 935–938 (October 2003)
21. http://bias.csr.unibo.it/fvc2004/databases.asp
22. http://egovstandards.gov.in/standardsandFramework/biometrics tandards/fingerprin_image_data_standard_ver1.0.pdf

23. Watson, C.I., Wilson, C.L.: Effect of Image Size and Compression on One-to-One Finger-print Matching, National institute of standard and technology, U.S, NISTIR 7201 (February 2005)
24. Jain, A.K., Prabhakar, S., Pankanti, S.: A Filterbank-based Representation for Classification and Matching of Fingerprints. In: International Joint Conference on Neural Networks (IJCNN), Washington DC, pp. 3284–3285 (July 1999)
25. Prabhakar, S.: Fingerprint Classification and Matching Using a Filterbank, Ph.D. thesis, Michigan State University (2001)

Implementation of Fractal Dimension for Finding 3D Objects: A Texture Segmentation and Evaluation Approach

T. Pant

IIIT Allahabad
Deoghat, Jhalwa
Allahabad (UP), India 211012
tpant@iiita.ac.in

Abstract. In present paper, a non-Euclidean approach for finding high dimensional objects has been proposed. The approach is based on the fact that fractal dimension represents the roughness of 2D objects in digital images which can be measured and used to infer about the structure of objects. Since fractal dimension varies in the range 2.0 to 3.0, where the objects having higher value of fractal dimension represent more dense objects in terms of their space filling property, the measurement of fractal dimension leads to discriminate various objects. The image texture obtained from fractal map has been used for this discrimination. The texture map is segmented on the basis of fractal dimension values and segmentation evaluation has been done. The results obtained for the test images are promising and show that the image texture can be segmented using fractal dimension values. The possible future scope of the work has also been highlighted with the applications in real life, e.g., computer vision.

Keywords: Fractal dimension, Image segmentation, Segmentation evaluation, Texture.

1   Introduction

Vision is one of the special features of human senses which machines can only mimic due to the complexities in vision mechanism [1], [2]. The 2D projection of 3D objects is a complex issue which utilizes human heuristics. However, machine vision is superior in the sense that human vision is only limited to the visible spectrum whereas machine vision can utilize the whole electromagnetic (EM) spectrum [3]. One point is to be highlighted here is that all the imaging systems must provide the images in such a form that human can interpret them visually. In this respect, most of the images are recorded and then converted to visible formats. However, for machine vision, it is not a necessary constraint as machine vision is able to interpret the images in their raw format as far as visual interpretation is concerned. Thus, human vision is limited to the visible band, whereas machine vision is having no such obstacle. Once the images are available their interpretation is necessary. For this purpose, various image

A. Agrawal et al. (Eds.): IITM 2013, CCIS 276, pp. 284–296, 2013.

processing and analysis techniques are available and these applications are in a rapid growth of improvements till date.

There are certain parameters to study and analyse the images, e.g., tone, size, shape, texture and others, which again depend on individual pixel or combination of pixels. As an interest of present research, textural analysis is a major field in image interpretation which deals with the pixel neighbourhood. Since, few image features and image objects are depending on their neighbourhood pixels for correct identification, instead of individual pixel, it is necessary to study such objects on the basis of their contextual information. The contextual analysis dealing with texture can be done with numerous parameters like Gabor filter, autocorrelation length, fractal parameters, gray level co-occurrence matrix and others [4]. One of the interesting facts in such analysis is the lack of geometry to explain such measures, leading to search for other tools and fractal geometry is one of these tools.

Image segmentation is an important task in image processing and image analysis. Since image analysis can be done on a pixel by pixel basis or on the basis of pixel neighbourhood, segmentation may also be performed on pixel by pixel basis or pixel neighbourhood. Since texture is a property of neighbourhood, texture segmentation refers to segmentation of pixel neighbourhood, i.e., segmentation is to be performed for a group of pixels instead of single pixel. Although there are various methods available for image segmentation which are equally applicable for texture segmentation, their evaluation is also important. Segmentation evaluation is a complex process and requires extensive research work, since no uniform method is available for a perfect segmentation evaluation.

A fractal based segmentation has been performed, in present paper where image texture is identified using fractal dimension values. The segmented image has been evaluated by using the approach of Liu and Yang as described by Borsotti *et al.* [5] and Zhang *et al.* [6]. Segmentation evaluation is one of the tedious jobs to be performed for assessment of image segmentation. Although segmentation is ultimately assessed by human aid, a suitable method is always required which minimizes human assistance in evaluation process.

2   Fractal Dimension for Image Interpretation

The traditional Euclidean geometry fails in certain cases to explain the objects accurately which led to explore beyond Euclidean geometry and consequently fractal geometry came to the existence. B.B. Mandelbrot [7] proposed the basics of fractal geometry and used to explore the world where conventional geometry ceases to explain various natural phenomena. Further, the evolution of fractal based image interpretation is based on the work of A.P. Pentland [8] where modeling of natural scene with fractals was proposed using a fractional Brownian motion (fBm) process. The fBm is a random function, $f(x)$, characterized by

$$\Pr\left(\frac{f(x+\Delta x)-f(x)}{\|\Delta x\|^{H}} < y\right) = F(y)\,\forall x \text{ and } \Delta x \tag{1}$$

where $0<H<1$ is the Hurst parameter and $F(y)$ is the cumulative density function, which in general assumed to be a cumulative distribution of a Gaussian probability density function with zero mean and variance σ^2 The concept can be extended for 2-variable function $f(x,y)$ and is the very suitable model for images. In case of 2D image, the function $f(x)$ becomes two variable function $I(x,y)$ and thus 2D fBm process is defined as the pdf

$$\Pr\left(\frac{I(x+\Delta x, y)-I(x,y)}{\|\Delta x\|^{H}} < z\right) = F(z) \tag{2}$$

where $F(z)$ is the cdf.

It is now a ubiquitous fact that images can not only be modeled but also interpreted with the help of fractal geometry. Further, fractals are useful to interpret the image elements, majority of the features among them are texture, namely fractal dimension, self-similarity, lacunarity, Hurst index and others.

Although a number of fractal parameters to interpret the image elements are available, fractal dimension is of special interest because it gives a measure of roughness, when image is viewed as a 2D surface. The value of fractal dimension (D) lies between 2.0 and 3.0 which otherwise represents the distribution of image elements, i.e., pixels in image matrix and is defined by [7], [8], [9]

$$D = \frac{\log(N_r)}{\log\left(\frac{1}{r}\right)} \tag{3}$$

where N_r represents the number of similar parts of an object scaled down by the ratio r representing any real number.

Estimation of fractal dimension is performed in a number of ways [9], [10] and in the direction of calculating fractal dimension for images, triangular prism surface area method (TPSAM) by K. C. Clarke [11] is a milestone. The method is very popular and from the day of availability it is widely used [9], [12]. A brief discussion of the method is now presented. In this method, the image pixels are considered as columns with heights equal to their pixel values leading a hypothetical image pixel forest. These columns are used to generate an imaginary prism in 3D with four pixels at four corners and their average value in the center. This central pixel is purely assumed pixel since it represents the mean of pixel values and actually does not exist. Thus, these points generate four triangular prisms in 3D space and the total surface area of the four triangles at upper surface is estimated. The base surface area is estimated for this particular configuration. This process is repeated for various base resolutions, starting from 2×2 pixels in multiple of 2. Corresponding upper surface area and base area is used to estimate the slope (s) of best fit line in a log-log plot and the fractal dimension D is calculated by the formula

$$D = 2.0 - s \tag{4}$$

Since total upper surface area decreases with an increase in base resolution, the slope in equation (4) estimates to be negative and comes to be greater than −1, in general, so that the fractal dimension of surface lies between 2.0 and 3.0. The simplicity and ease of use led for the choice of TPSAM for application in present study, however other methods are also in vogue. There are certain issues in estimation of fractal dimension for images, a description of these issues is available in [9] and [13]. However, summarizing them, one of the issues is related to the uniqueness of the fractal dimension value. The fractal dimension of two or more fractals may be same despite of their different construction and orientation; an example could be referred from Pant et al. [13]. TPSAM covers all the image pixels equally if considered from different image configurations, i.e., if the images is rotated by a multiple of 90°, TPSAM estimates same value. The other issue is related to fractal dimension estimation methods. Since numerous methods are available for estimation of fractal dimension, there is no unique or unified method which could estimate the fractal dimension of digital images accurately. All the methods have respective pros and cons and they can be used on a requirement basis, like complexity and faster estimation. TPSAM is again suitable in these both factors and hence popular. Third important issue to be highlighted here is the outbounds of fractal dimension. Since the digital images are discretized images, they do not estimate the slope in log-log plot accurately in few cases leading an outbound value of D, which may be less than 2.0 or greater than 3.0. The only reason for the error in estimation of the slope is discrete values of image pixels. However, this fact does not affect the study too much [9], [13].

One of the important properties of fractal dimension with digital data is statistical self-similarity instead of self-similarity. In fact, digital images are statistically self-similar rather than exact self-similar, which affects the study while local and global fractal features are to be identified individually. Theoretically, for any fractal object local and global fractal dimension is same as it is independent of scale, but in case of images, this independency diminishes. Consequently, the terms local and global fractal dimensions get evolved and studied for various purposes. It is axiomatic that these two measures, i.e., local and global fractal dimension values are context dependent and they are specific when utilized for the desired applications.

Study of local fractal dimension, which is estimated in a local neighbourhood, called local window, has also an impact on fractal based analysis. A window size of 5 by 5 pixels is minimum suitable window as explained by Pant et al. [13]. On the basis of window dependency, the local fractal dimension (D_w) can be formulated by modifying equation (3) as

$$D_w = \frac{\log(N_{rw})}{\log\left(\frac{1}{r}\right)} \tag{5}$$

where w represents the size of local window.

3   Fractal Dimension for 3D Object Identification

One of the basic facts for fractal dimension is that it represents any object in such a way that the minimum dimension of that object is its topological dimension. Here, minimum dimension means that the object may have higher dimension than its topological dimension but at least it will possess its topological dimension, however not exactly equal to topological dimension. The topological dimension (D_T) is the usual dimension of the objects whereas a new dimension, called Hausdorff-Besicovitch dimension (D_{HB}) is defined on the basis of Hausdorff measure. Formally, for a set F, following constraints are needed to be satisfied [14]–

$$\left.\begin{aligned}
&\exists s_0 \in [0,\infty] \text{ s.t.} \\
&H^s(F) = \infty \,\forall\, s < s_0 \\
&H^s(F) = 0 \,\forall\, s > s_0
\end{aligned}\right\} \tag{6}$$

where H^s is the s dimensional Hausdorff measure and s_0 is a unique value, called Hausdorff's dimension or more suitably Hausdorff-Besicovitch dimension. For a rigorous mathematical description of dimension and measures [14] is referred. Thus, we have

$$D_{HB} = s_0 \tag{7}$$

Basically, any object is fractal if its Hausdorff-Besicovitch dimension is strictly larger than its topological dimension [7], i.e.,

$$D_{HB} > D_T \tag{8}$$

This fact is trivial but useful for the point of machine vision. The analogy can be explained with basic objects of geometry, i.e., Euclidean geometry. A point is zero dimensional object, however, a set of points always leads a curve of one dimension since there many points try to constitute a curve when collected. Thus, collection of zero dimensional objects tries to become a one dimensional object. Here, the Non-Euclidean geometry was introduced to explain such a phenomenon and consequently, a number of geometrical objects could be explained on its ground. Cantor's dust is the most suitable example of it, which is a collection of points and tends to comprise a curve. In fact Cantor's dust, specifically, a triadic Cantor's dust is a subset of the line R, i.e., set of real numbers [14]. The dimension, i.e., fractal dimension, of Cantor's dust is 0.63 [7], [14]. In other words, Cantor's dust fills 63% space in one dimensional space. This concept can be generalized and consequently it can be concluded that, in general, any n dimensional object when collected, tends to fill $n+1$ dimensional space and possesses a dimension between n and $n+1$. Thus, the term minimum dimension cannot have a value equal to n or more than $n+1$.

It can now be explained how fractal dimension is useful to assist machine vision. On the basis of above explained theory, the 2D objects tend to generate 3D objects when they are collected together. In terms of pixel values, the object will be treated as 3D when the pixel values are distributed in random sequence showing big crests in

3D if image is seen in this space and thus the object possesses a fractal dimension closer to 3.0. However, the sparsity of 2D objects will generate 2D heaps which are not 3D objects or closer to 3D objects. Such objects will have a dimension between 2.0 and 3.0. A flat surface, on the other hand, having no crests in third dimensions, so that it could be treated as a smooth surface exhibits the fractal dimension near to 2.0. This is the hypothesis of present study and sought to be verified experimentally.

4   Methodology

The methodology of the present study is shown in figure 1. As the data flow diagram shows, the input digital image is used for local D estimation at first. The local D estimation is done on a 5×5 window as discussed in section 2. Summarizing the discussion regarding window size, it can be said that 5×5 window is the minimum suitable window for which texture features are estimated. The local D values provide corresponding D map which is obtained by plotting D values as image pixels. Since this image has single pixels representing neighbourhood and its properties, D map is not equivalent to actual image. As a matter of fact, each value of D map is a representative of small neighbourhood, i.e., the window of original image with corresponding textural property. In next step, the D map is used for segmentation purpose, where D based texture is being segmented instead of original image. An adaptive segmentation approach has been followed in which the threshold values are fractal dimension values since the process is done on fractal images.

The segmented image is used for 3D object identification on one hand and for segmentation evaluation on the other hand. The image objects are used for various fractal dimension values so that their tendency towards 3D could be checked from the segmented image. However, in segmentation evaluation, using the method of Liu and Yang, the accuracy is tested. The robustness of present study lies in segmentation evaluation in which the F index has been estimated for each segmented image. Theoretically, the smaller value of F represents a better segmentation for various segmented images. The index is estimated by [5], [6]

$$F = \frac{1}{1000(r \times c)} \sqrt{R} \sum_{i=1}^{R} \frac{e_i^2}{\sqrt{A_i}} \qquad (9)$$

where r and c represent number of rows and columns in the image, R represents number of segmented regions, A_i represents area of the ith segmented region and e_i represents average error in pixel values in ith region.

In the study, a digital camera image form Nikon Coolpix P100 in jpeg format has been used. The image is having 3648×2736 pixels with 24-bit pixel depth which is analysed in all the three colour components. Since each component of the jpeg image represents three visible bands namely red, blue and green, the image is divided into three sub-images of red green and blue colour components respectively and each of the sub-images is used for fractal analysis. In order to perform the fractal analysis, a local fractal dimension has been estimated using a moving window and corresponding image is generated. These images are named as fractal images whose detailed description is available in [13].

Since image segmentation is an important task in the field of vision, its evaluation is more important. There may be supervised or unsupervised evaluation which depends on the availability or unavailability of reference data respectively. This task therefore becomes tedious in case of unsupervised evaluation. It is a well known fact that a good segmentation is always problem dependent and to be judged by the users [5].

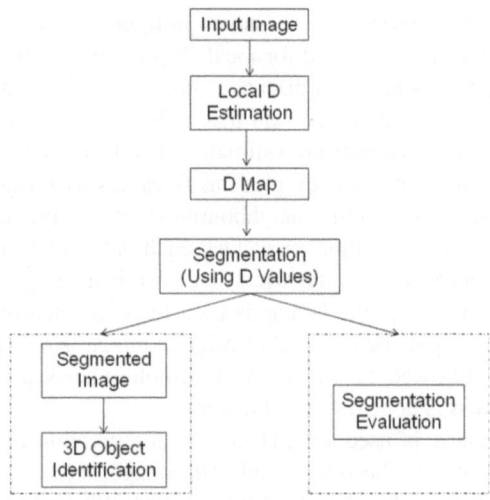

Fig. 1. Methodology of the proposed approach

5   Results

As a practical point of view, all the objects having fractal dimension near to 3.0, say more than 2.9, can be considered to be a dense structure whereas others may be treated as rare ones. Although this threshold, i.e., 2.9 is a matter of measurement, it can also be affected by various other parameters, e.g., noise, estimation methods and others. Since, it is not always possible practically to have all the objects with nearly 3.0 dimension value, it is natural to find the objects with highest value of dimension first. On the basis of this highest value, various objects could be identified. A bit of caution is necessary at this juncture, since few of the values may go beyond 3.0 and this overflow can occur due to various reasons, noise being one of them [13]. These out flowing values are neglected for the sake of brevity. Rest of the image is used for finding out the desired objects.

The three component images are shown in figure 2 (a), (b) and (c) and their corresponding fractal images are shown in figure 3 (a), (b), (c). The image components are named as ImR, ImG and ImB for red, green and blue components respectively.

Similarly, the fractal images are named as DImR, DImG and DImB in analogy to the image components. The fractal dimension values for each component showing top three maximum, minimum and average values are shown in table 1. The segmented images of DImR, DImG and DImB are shown in figure 4 (a)–(c), 5 (a)–(c) and 6 (a)–(c) respectively.

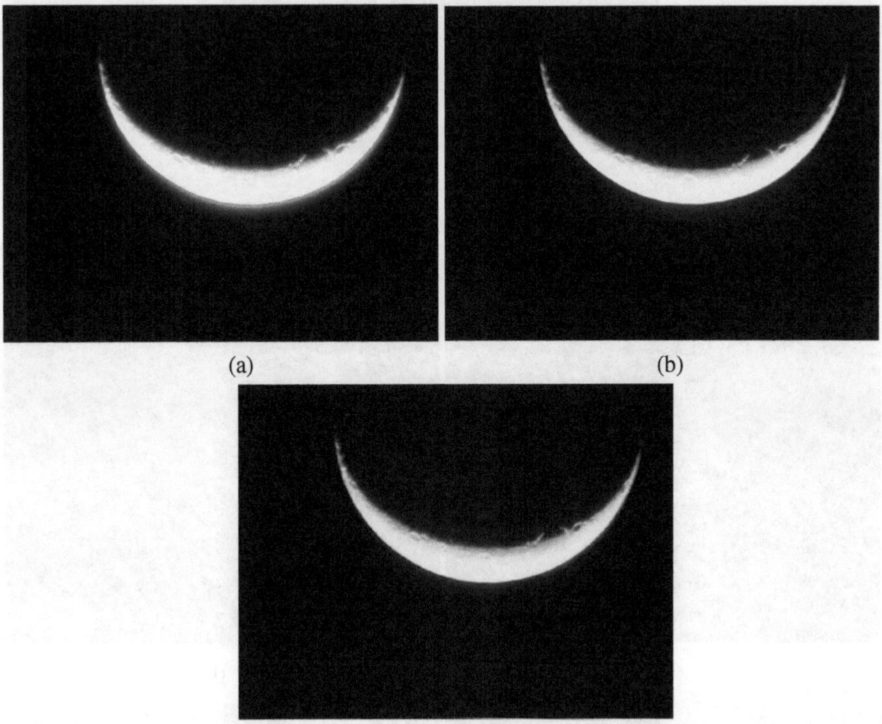

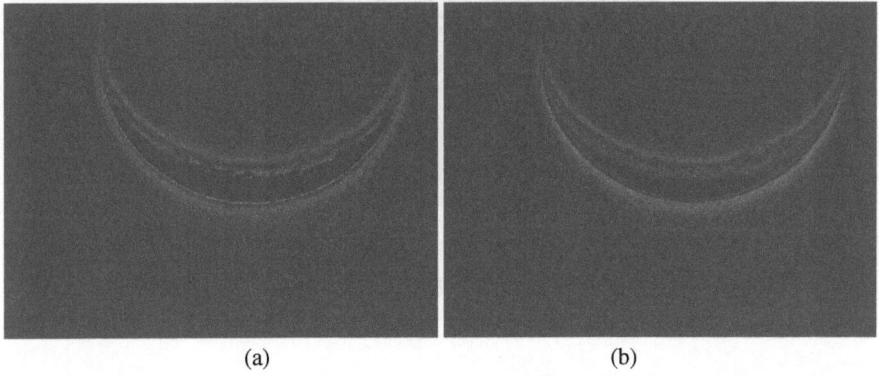

(a)   (b)

(c)

Fig. 2. (a) Red component, (b) Green component, (c) Blue component of image

(a)   (b)

Fig. 3. (a) Fractal image of red component of image, (b) Fractal image of green component of image, (c) Fractal image of blue component of image

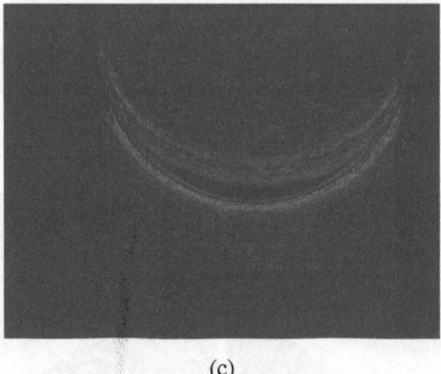

(c)

Fig. 3. (*Continued*)

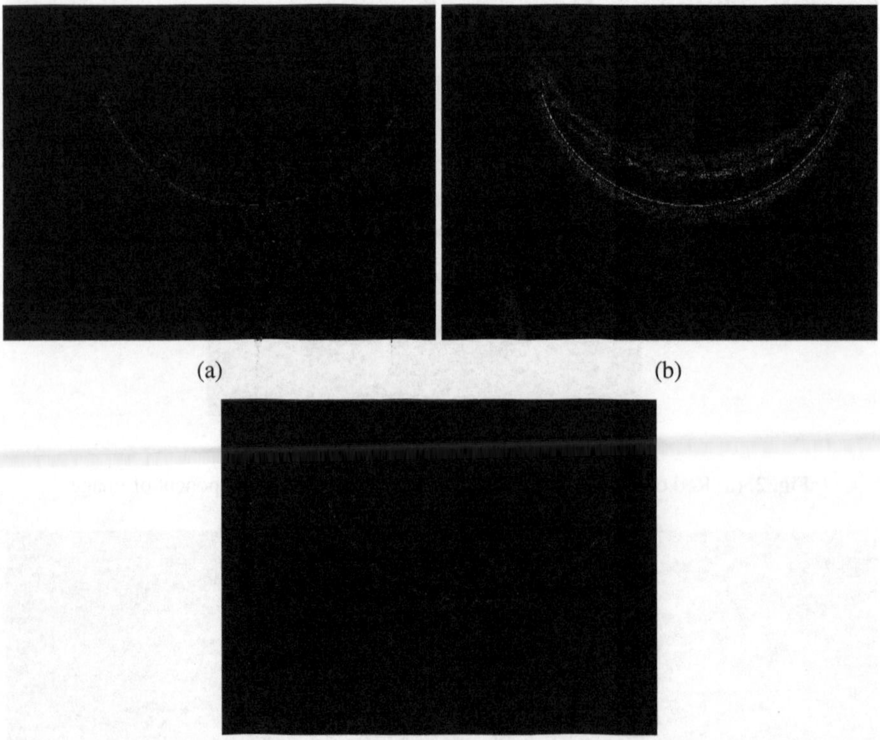

(a)   (b)

(c)

Fig. 4. (a)-(c) Segmented image of figure 2 (a) with three threshold values

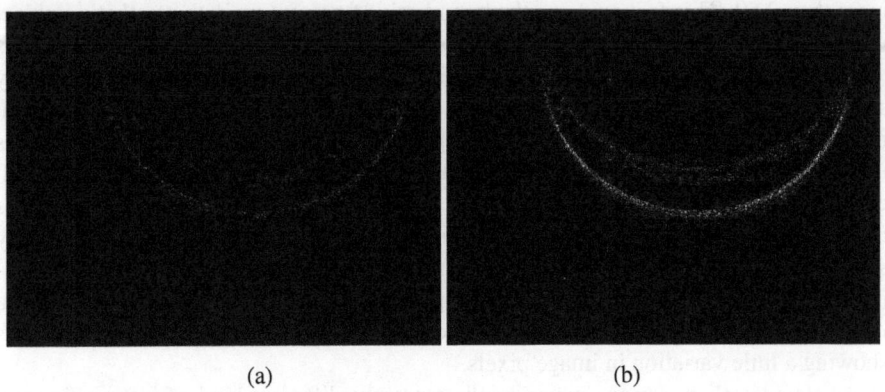

(a)   (b)

(c)

Fig. 5. (a)-(c) Segmented image of figure 2 (b) with three threshold values

(a)   (b)

Fig. 6. (a)-(c) Segmented image of figure 2 (c) with three threshold values

(c)

Fig. 6. (*Continued*)

Table 1. Values of local fractal dimension for various image components

Image Component	D_{max1}	D_{max2}	D_{max3}	D_{min}	D_{avg}
DImR	2.559	2.548	2.544	1.808	2.010
DImG	2.571	2.549	2.547	1.798	2.011
DImB	2.589	2.526	2.520	1.782	2.013

Table 1 contains the fractal dimension values at local level for each image component. The top three values of fractal dimension, named as D_{max1}, D_{max2}, D_{max3}, minimum value, named as D_{min} and average value, named D_{avg} of fractal dimension in each image component have been extracted. A closer look at table 1 reveals that the value of fractal dimension for various objects in the image under observation is not more than 2.59. This fact explains the hypothesis of present work to say that no object in the image is so much dense that it tends to be a 3D object, however, the value says that there are sufficiently rough objects present in the image. This fact is confirmed by second and third maximum values of fractal dimension. A variation in maximum, minimum and average value for each component image clearly indicates that various image types possess different kind of information, for example, the roughness which can be identified by fractal dimension. The minimum value, as shown in table 1, goes beyond the theoretical limits of fractal dimension, the reason for which is already stated above. A final conclusion can be drawn from the average value of fractal dimension which is close to 2.0 in each component image. This value indicates that the image under present study is almost smooth, i.e., most of the part of this image is showing a little variation in image pixels.

As stated earlier, various image bands represent different kind of information depending on the specific band, this fact can visually be observed in figure 2 (a)–(c) where each component is different and represents some specific detail. Figure 2 (c) shows an image with sharp edges compared to the other two bands. However, it has hidden information that is highlighted in corresponding fractal image, i.e., figure 3 (c). There is a region surrounding the object possessing more contour lines which is not observable in other component images. Although the blue component of image is sharper than other two, the fractal image indicates a sharper image showing better boundaries in red component image. It indicates that fractal features are band specific and hence represent the things differently in various EM bands.

The segmented binary images based on fractal dimension values are generated and displayed in figure 4, 5 and 6. Figure 4 (a)–(c) show three segmented images for fractal images of red component, i.e., figure 3 (a) with different threshold values. An adaptive thresholding has been applied and corresponding segmented images are generated. The threshold values 2.10, 2.20 and 2.30 are obtained for figure 4 (a), (b) and (c) respectively. It can be observed that smaller value of fractal dimension gives better segmented image for red component image. A similar statement can be drawn for figure 5 (a)–(c) and 6 (a)–(c) which represent the segmented images for green and blue component fractal images. The threshold values for figure 5 are 2.10, 2.15, 2.20 and those for figure 6 are 2.15, 2.20 and 2.25 respectively.

One interesting but concealed point is to be noted from the segmented images, which reveals a different perspective of fractal analysis. It says that fractal dimension is able to highlight the variation in pixel neighbourhoods and consequently identifies the edges of various objects. It can be shown from the segmented red component image where uniform background is suppressed as displayed in figure 4 (a). The sharp investigation of fractal images in figure 3 (a)–(c) shows that although fractal dimension is able to highlight the edges, it is rarely good as the conventional edge detectors. Nevertheless, this feature can be used for finding the edges where the edge width is higher which is again obviously explained by figure 4 (a), 5 (a) and 6 (a). Summarily, the fractal features are able to separate the boundaries of different object to a limited extent.

The segmentation results have been evaluated for each image. For this purpose, the method of Liu and Yang has been used. Since segmentation evaluation methods have been proposed by various researchers time to time and they have worked successfully in various images, it is still required to find a universal method or measure to evaluate image segmentation. In present study, this fact has been faced and supported. It is also observed that segmentation evaluation always requires human assistance at some extent for obtaining good segmentation results, since the term good is only defined by human [5], [6].

6   Conclusions

The study concluded in following results. Fractal analysis of individual bands of optical images gives a possibility to use it to any kind of image generated form EM spectrum. For each band, the effect of fractal dimension is observed which can be reflected on various kinds of images. Since the behavior of fractal features is different with different image components as fractal dimension is different for each component, it implies that different bands possess different kind of information. Digital images can be segmented on their fractal features, which is an aid in machine vision when texture analysis is concerned. Different objects can be separated at the boundaries by fractal dimension as fractal dimension is able to detect the variation in pixel values in small neighbourhood.

A Non-Euclidean dimension measure, i.e., fractal dimension has been used to identify 3D objects in the images. For identification of such objects, the concept based on fractal dimension has been proposed and verified on optical images. The dense objects possessing higher fractal dimension values can be separated from other objects with application of proper threshold values. The segmentation performed with the help of fractal dimension is successful and evaluated using the method of Liu and Yang. The results are acceptable and conclude that texture can be classified with the fractal dimension. It is concluded that the present study can be applied on various types of images generated from wide electromagnetic spectrum like X-ray, UV, thermal, gamma ray images.

References

1. Dee, H.M., Velastin, S.A.: How Close are We to Solving the Problem of Automated Visual Surveillance? A Review of Real-world Surveillance, Scientific Progress and Evaluative Mechanisms. Machine Vision and Applications 19, 329–343 (2008)
2. Thacker, N.A., Clark, A.F., Barron, J.L., Beveridge, J.R., Courtney, P., Crum, W.R., Ramesh, V., Clark, C.: Performance Characterization in Computer Vision: A Guide to Best Practices. Computer Vision and Image Understanding 109, 305–334 (2008)
3. Cubero, S., Aleixos, N., Moltó, E., Gómez-Sanchis, J., Blasco, J.: Advances in Machine Vision Applications for Automatic Inspection and Quality Evaluation of Fruits and Vegetables. Food and Bioprocess Technology 4, 487–504 (2011)
4. Petrou, M., Sevilla, P.G.: Image Processing Dealing with Texture. John Wiley and Sons, Ltd., England (2006)
5. Borsotti, M., Campadelli, P., Schettini, R.: Quantitative Evaluation of Color Image Segmentation Results. Pattern Recognition Letters 19, 741–747 (1998)
6. Zhang, H., Fritts, J.E., Goldman, S.A.: Image Segmentation Evaluation: A Survey of Unsupervised Methods. Computer Vision and Image Understanding 110, 260–280 (2008)
7. Mandelbrot, B.B.: The Fractal Geometry of Nature. W.H. Freeman and Co., New York (1982)
8. Pentland, A.P.: Fractal-based Description of Natural Scenes. IEEE Transactions on Pattern Analysis and Machine Intelligence PAMI-6, 661–674 (1984)
9. Sun, W., Xu, G., Gong, P., Liang, S.: Fractal Analysis of Remotely Sensed Images: A Review of Methods and Applications. International Journal of Remote Sensing 27, 4963–4990 (2006)
10. Huang, Q., Lorch, J.R., Dubes, R.C.: Can the Fractal Dimension of Images be Measured? Pattern Recognition 27(3), 339–349 (1994)
11. Clarke, K.C.: Computation of the Fractal Dimension of Topographic Surfaces using the Triangular Prism Surface Area Method. Computers and Geosciences 12(5), 713–722 (1986)
12. Ju, W., Lam, N.S.-N.: An Improved Algorithm for Computing Local Fractal Dimension using the Triangular Prism Method. Computers and Geosciences 35, 1224–1233 (2009)
13. Pant, T., Singh, D., Srivastava, T.: Advanced Fractal Approach for Unsupervised Classification of SAR Images. Advances in Space Research 45, 1338–1349 (2010) Edgar, G.: Measure, Topology, and Fractal Geometry. Springer, New York (2008)

Fuzzy Clustering of Image Trademark Database and Pre-processing Using Adaptive Filter and Karhunen-Loève Transform

Akriti Nigam, Ajay Indoria, and R.C. Tripathi

Indian Institute of Information Technology, Allahabad
akriti.nigam@yahoo.co.in,
iiita.ajayindoria@gmail.com,
rctripathi@iiita.ac.in

Abstract. In this paper an efficient preprocessing module has been described which focuses on building a trademark database that can be used for developing a trademark retrieval system. The preprocessing module focuses on noise removal from the trademark images using an adaptive filtering technique using Wiener filters, followed by Karhunen-Loève Transform that makes the trademark search process rotation invariant by rotating the object along positive y direction. Since the registered trademarks are huge in number and will increase invariantly in the future it will be strenuous for the search system to search for similarity in such huge database. Intention is to reduce the search space hence Fuzzy Clustering has been applied.

Keywords: Noise removal, Weiner filter, Hotelling transform, Karhunen-Loève transform, Fuzzy Clustering.

1   Introduction

The Intellectual Property office worldwide, in compliance with the recommendations of World Trade Organization, assures protection to the trademark owners on their goods and services. Since the trend of branding of goods and services has been increasing rapidly in the recent times, the amount of registered trademark images that the Govt. needs to maintain is huge. The Indian Trademark office uses automated system for checking similarity of word mark images but the search for similarity of figurative or device marks is still manual.

Not only in India but even in countries like US and UK, the search method is still based on keywords. There is no automatic system that matches the image trademark applied for, with the country's database of registered trademarks and prior pending applications, to prevent a likelihood of infringement.

The table below shows a comparative study of the trademark registration scenario in several countries-

A. Agrawal et al. (Eds.): IITM 2013, CCIS 276, pp. 297–305, 2013.

Table 1. Comparative study of the trademark registration scenario in several countries

Country	Trademark registration time	Official Search tool availability	Registration fee in INR	Pre grant publication availability worldwide
China	14-18months	Word mark only	9200Rs. Approx.	Not available
South Africa	34-36 months	Not available	8000Rs. Approx.	Not available
Mexico	6-9 months	Word mark only	12800Rs. Approx.	Available
Brazil	2-3 years	Not available	12800Rs. Approx.	Only word marks available
Czech Republic	6-12 months	Word mark only	15400Rs. Approx	Not available
Slovak	6-9 months	Not available	13700Rs. Approx.	Not available
Turkey	12-15 months	Word mark only	19000Rs. Approx.	Not available
Yugoslavia	6-9 months	Word mark only	8400 Rs. Approx.	Not available

Manual search in trademark registration system has it's repercussions in the form of backlog latency time for e.g. registration time of a new trademark in India ranges from 14 to 36 months in an average.

This paper describes the development and maintenance of a trademarks database. The prime considerations in the paper are on noise removal from trademark images, handling rotation invariance and clustering of database.

Most of the noise removal techniques are based on application of noise removal algorithms on a global basis, without considering the noise present in the image for e.g. in [1] median filtering has been considered for trademark image cleaning only if noise is a necessary concern.For impulse noise models there are variations in techniques that have been used for noise removal. In [2] a discrete noise model has been developed that considers noise having 0 or 255 value only. Results obtained are good for discrete noises but fails for noise that is distributed uniformly.

In [3] Garnett et al., the Lena image is corrupted with various levels of impulse noise and then removed using technique called ROAD (Ranked ordered absolute difference) and trilateral filters.A simpler approach has been discussed in [4] where similar neighbor criterion has been used to remove noise, wherein any pixel is considered as original image pixel if it has sufficient similar neighbor pixels else it is considered as noise. Clustering has been considered as a preprocessing step for database building in by Peng-Yeng Yin et al.[5] but they did not show the outperformance of soft clustering over hard clustering and hence not justified the use of soft clustering technique. The original retrieval efficiency obtained by them is 76%.

2   Overview of the Proposed Methods

2.1   Trademark Image Noise Removal

The Department of Intellectual Property of most of the countries worldwide, publishes the scanned copy of the registered trademark images along with their details for e.g. the Indian Govt. publishes it in the form of pdf's every fortnight on its official website ipindia.nic.in [15]. These images have been used to compile the database. Most of the image noise removal approaches either apply on all the image pixels or are based on manual judgment of noise type. Both these approaches have their explicit disadvantages, hence to avoid this we have used the adaptive filtering method [6] using Weiner filters (linear filter) as it adjusts itself according to the local variations in the image.

2.2 Working

Consider a noisy image 'I' having a size of P x Q pixels. We consider a window of M X N size and apply the following steps:

1) At each pixel in the centre of the M X N window the local mean and variance is computed using

$$\mu = \frac{1}{MN} \sum_{n_1,n_2 \in \eta} a(n_1, n_2) \tag{1}$$

$$\sigma^2 = \frac{1}{MN} \sum_{n_1,n_2 \in \eta} a^2(n_1, n_2) - \mu^2 \tag{2}$$

where μ represents the N X M neighborhood pixels in the image I and σ^2 denotes the variance .

Using the above estimates the Weiner filter modifies the pixel values at (n_1, n_2) by

$$b(n_1, n_2) = \mu + \frac{\sigma^2 - v^2}{\sigma^2} (a(n_1, n_2) - \mu) \tag{3}$$

where v^2 is the noise variance which is taken as the average value of all the local variance estimates.

Fig. 1. Results of noise removal. Left image is noisy, right one is obtained after noise removal

Many medical image retrieval systems also need preprocessing of their medical images for e.g. retina images, X-Rays, ultrasound reports etc. The above mentioned noise removal technique when applied to a retina image used for retinopathy treatment gives the following result-

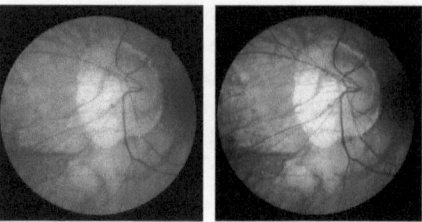

Fig. 2. On the left side is image of retina and on the right side is its preprocessed version having more clear details

2.3   Hotelling Transform

An effective trademark retrieval system should be resistant to any form of transformations done to it like rotation, translation and scaling. The cases of translation and scaling can be very well handled by the use of chain codes for representing object boundaries. The chain codes of an image and its scaled version can be normalized to same value [16]. Similarly translated objects will also have the same chain code values. The practice of rotating and pasting of objects can create confusion in the eyes of the consumer and the forged trademarks can be mistaken to be the original trademark. Lot of work has been done to make images rotation invariant like the use of moment invariants introduced by Hu et al. in [18], Zernike moments[19] and by using Fourier descriptors in [20].To handle this kind of infringement and make the trademark retrieval system rotation invariant, Hotelling transform is used to make sure that 0-direction remains invariant always, it is also known as Karhunen-Loève Transform [8, 9] androtates the object by using the angle to positive y-axis as the measurement direction.

The idea is to convert a set of interdependent vector elements say$x_1, x_2, ... x_n$ into another set of vector say $y_1, y_2, ... y_n$ in such a way that if we compute the covariance matrix of the transformed vector, it will be a diagonal matrix. In other words the elements of the vectors n the transformed matrix will be uncorrelated.

2.3.1 Working
We have M data points, which are a collection of points representing a particular area of an image.

Following are the steps of the proposed approach-

1. Convert the RGB image of trademark to binary image.
2. Find all the black pixels in the binary image (assuming the background to be white and object on it as black).
3. Scan the gray scale image top to bottom going from left to right to find the first and the last black pixel. The first black pixel (say a) is the top most pixel of the object while last black pixel (say b) is the bottom most pixel of the object.

4. Similarly scan the gray scale image from left to right going from top to bottom to find the first and the last black pixel. The first black pixel (say c) is the left most pixel of the object while the last pixel (say d) is the right most pixel of the object.
5. Using a, b, c and d as four vertices of a rectangle, crop the image to fit inside this rectangle.
6. Resize the image to 128 x 128 pixels in size.
7. Suppose we have M black pixel points $x_1, x_2, x_3 \ldots \ldots x_n$, we first compute the mean of the these data points using-

Mean- $\underline{m_x} = E\{x\} \approx \frac{1}{M}\sum_{k=1}^{M} x_k$ (4)

8. Next we compute the covariance matrix of the population of the data points. The covariance matrix is computed using:

$$\text{Covariance- } \underline{\underline{C_x}} = E\left\{ \left(\underline{x} - \underline{m_x}\right)\left(\underline{x} - \underline{m_x}\right)^T \right\}$$

$$\approx \frac{1}{M}\sum_{k=1}^{M} \underline{x_k}\,\underline{x_k}^T - m_k m_k^{\,T} \qquad (5)$$

The diagonal elements of C represent the variance of elements in x_i.

9. Now we can create a transformed vector 'y' which can be taken as a linear combination of 'x'. To do so the Eigen values of the covariance matrix obtained above is computed (say).
10. The final transformation of 'x' is done according to-

$$y = ^T(x - m_x) \qquad (6)$$

a)   b)

Fig. 3. Results of applying Hotelling transform

In the above figure 3, the images on the right show the result of applying the proposed method on the images shown on the left. If a registered trademark image like one's in the left above are infringed by rotating the object and pasted, any edge detection technique that computes the edge directions and magnitude will be not be able to detect this case of infringement, however if the above preprocessing step is applied before detecting edge directions, both original and rotated objects will be alligned in a common direction hence can be detected easily.

2.4   Database Clustering

Several thousands of trademarks are registered in the world every month. Considering the size of the database that would be reached within few years and the time it would require to search and compare among such huge number of images, it is essential to reduce the search space by clubbing together similiar trademark images, similar in terms of features used to represent the trademarks. Clustering has it's applications in various fields for e.g. in [18] a medical image retrieval system survey has been mentioned that also uses clustering for its databsae management. Many medical databases required clustering for discovering useful patterns and information for e.g. in [21] density based clustering has been described for spatial cancer database. Here in this work basic color, texture and shape features have been used to assign a position to each trademark in the 3 features space. Broadly there are two main types of clustering- hard clustering and soft (fuzzy) clustering[5, 12].

2.4.1 Hard Clustering

This is one of the traditional clustering methods where each image is assigned a class label based on it's characteristic features. There are several shortcomings of this clustering method, first of all it is heavily infulenced by the starting cluster points, secondly in situations where a point on the feature space is equally distant to two or more cluster centroids, the decision of cluster assignment is dicey as shown in the figure 8 below, thirdly for situations shown in figure , usually the assignment based on distance to centroid can give wrong results.

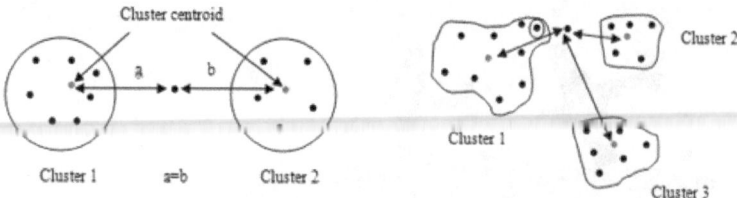

Fig. 4. Problems with hard clustering

Figure 4 shows a case where the feature point is equally qualified to be a member of more than one cluster. As shown in figure 4, the feature point is at equal distance to the centroids of cluster 1 and cluster 2. In such a case the decision as to which cluster the point should be assigned becomes arbitrary and can affect the cluster structure.

In case b shown in figure 4 above we can see that the feature point is closest to centroid of cluster 2 but is more closer to a point in cluster 1, however the centroid of cluster 1 is far from that of cluster 2. In such a case the feature point will be assigned to cluster 2 based on the hard clustering algorithm but as is evident the feature point will have properties similar to the encircled point in cluster1.

2.4.2 Soft Clustering

Also called Fuzzy c means clustering algorithm (FCMA) is a clustering method that takes care of the above dicey situations that can occur in hard clustering.

The fuzzy clustering algorithm allows each element to belong in various clusters simultaneously with various membership scales.

Algorithm:

Let $X = \{x_1, x_2, x_3 ..., x_n\}$ denote the feature vectors of length 'n' and $V = \{v_1, v_2, v_3 ..., v_c\}$ denote the set of cluster centroid.

1) First we choose any 'c' arbitrary cluster centroids.

2) Next for each feature vector we compute the membership values in each clusters using:

$$\mu_{ij} = \frac{1}{\sum_{k=1}^{c}(d_{ij}/d_{ik})^{(\frac{2}{m}-1)}} \quad (7)$$

Here 'n' represents the number of cluster points taken. 'vj' is the jth cluster centroid. 'm' is the factor of fuzziness and it belongs in the range $[1, \infty]$. Total number of cluster centroids is represented by 'c'. 'μ_{ij}' represents the by how much is i^{th} pointa member of jth cluster. The distance between any point 'i' and the jth cluster centroid is represented by 'dij'. The distance considered here is Euclidean distance.

3) After getting a new population list for each cluster we compute/recomputed the cluster centroids using:

$$v_j = (\sum_{i=1}^{n}(\mu_{ij}{}^m) \, x_i / \sum_{i=1}^{n}(\mu_{ij})^m) \text{ for every } j=1, 2... \text{ 'c'} \quad (8)$$

Steps 2 and 3 are repeated till we get no variations in the cluster centroids.

3   Experimental Results

The proposed work has been implemented using MATLAB R2010a. The database contains 1000 trademark images extracted from the journals published at ipindia.nic.in. All the database images have been pre processed using noise removal techniques mentioned in section 2, followed by Hotelling transform to make them invariant to rotation. To test how efficiency can be seen to be improved, the clustering technique has been used on a CBIR system that uses color as a feature for similarity matching of trademark images and retrieval of similar images. The color feature has been extracted using color histogram for dominant Red, Green and Blue color channels (RGB). The database images are partitioned using Fuzzy C Means clustering into 3 clusters.The initial testing is done using 500 database images. In the first half of the experimental test hard clustering has been used to show the reduction in the search space size achieved. To get over the problem of deciding the number of clusters, ISO

DATA algorithm has been used that considers the splitting and merging of the clusters based on the cluster size and inter/intra cluster distance.

Table 2 shows the search space size when applying CBIR for trademark database using color histograms. The result shows a significant reduction in the number of images that the retrieval system has to search from when no clustering is done and when hard/soft clustering is applied.

Table 2. Experimental Results

Query Image	Database Size	Search Space Without Clustering	Search Space using Hard Clustering	Search Space using Fuzzy-c Means Clustering
1	200	200	90	95
2	200	200	74	80
3	200	200	68	76

We can justify the increase in the amount of search space in case of fuzzy C means clustering by considering the fact that a single data point/image can be a member of more than one cluster in this case for e.g. in case of an image having contributions of red and blue colors in it, the hard clustering will assign it to either the cluster having red colored images or to the one having blue colored images, however fuzzy c means will assign it to both the above clusters with varying level of membership.

4   Conclusion

In this paper, an efficient pre processing approach has been presented for building a trademark retrieval system. The noise found in trademark images has been categorized and the noise removal algorithm has been discussed that uses Wiener filters. Implementation of Karhunen-Loève Transform (Hotelling transform) has been discussed to make the retrieval process rotation invariant. The results of applying Karhunen-Loève Transform have been shown that rotates inclined objects in image to a normalized angle. To reduce the trademark retrieval search space, clustering of the database has been done. Fuzzy c means clustering has been shown to outperform the hard clustering technique.

References

1. Wei, C.-H., Li, Y., Chau, W.-Y., Li, C.-T.: Trademark image retrieval using synthetic features for describing global shape and interior structure. Pattern Recognition 42, 386–394 (2009)

2. Pok, G., Liu, J.-C., Nair, A.: Selective Removal of Impulse Noise Based on Homogeneity Level Information. IEEE Transactions on Image Processing 12(1), 85–92 (2003)
3. Garnett, R., Huegerich, T., Chui, C.: A Universal Noise Removal Algorithm with an Impulse Detector. IEEE Transactions on Image Processing 14, 1747–1754 (2005)
4. SaidAwad, A., Man, H.: Similar neighbor criterion for impulse noise removal in images 64, 904–915 (October 2010)
5. Yin, P.-Y., Yeh, C.-C.: Content-based retrieval from trademark databases 23, 113–126 (January 2002)
6. Patel, P., Tripathi, A., Majhi, B., Tripathy, C.R.: A New Adaptive Median Filtering Technique for Removal of Impulse Noise from Images. In: Proceedings of the 2011 International Conference on Communication, Computing & Security, ICCCS 2011, pp. 462–467 (2011)
7. Sanchez-Marin, F.J.: Image Registration Of Gray-Scale Images Using The Hotelling Transform. In: Conference on Video I Image Processing and Multimedia Communications, pp. 119–123 (July 2003)
8. Ben Hamza, A., Luque, P., Martinez, J., Roman, R.: Removing noise and preserving details with relaxed median filters. J. Math. Image Vision 11(2), 161–177 (1999)
9. Marcos, E., Acuna, C.J., Vela, B., Cavero, J.M., Hernandez, J.A.: A database for medical image management. Computer Methods and Programs in Biomedicine 86, 255–269 (2007)
10. Shyu, M.-L., Chen, S.-C., Chen, M., Zhang, C.: A Unified Framework for Image Database Clustering and Content-based Retrieval. In: MMDB 2004, pp. 19–27. ACM (November 2004)
11. Luo, W., Dang, D.: An efficient method for the removal of impulse noise. In: IEEE International Conference on Image Processing, Atlanta, pp. 2601–2604 (October 2006)
12. Nigam, A., Garg, A.K., Tripathi, R.C.: Content Based Image Retrieval by integrating shape with color and texture information
13. Gonzalez, R.C., Woods, R.E.: Digital Image Processing. Prentice Hall (2002)
14. Intellectual Property India website, http://www.ipindia.nic.in
15. Ur Rehman, M.A.: A New Scale Invariant Optimized Chain Code for Nastaliq Character Representation. In: IEEE Conference on Computer Modeling and Simulation, pp. 400–403 (2010)
16. Hu, M.K.: Visual pattern recognition by moment invariants. IRE Trans. Inf. Theory 8, 179–187 (1962)
17. Bhagat, A.P., Atique, M.: Medical Image Retrieval, Indexing and Enhancement Techniques: A Survey. In: ICCCS 2011, pp. 387–390. ACM (2011)
18. Kim, W.Y., Kim, Y.S.: A region based shape descriptor using Zernike moments. Signal Processing: Image Communications 16(1-2), 95–102 (2000)
19. Zhang, D.S., Lu, G.: A comparative study on shape retrieval using Fourier descriptors with different shape signatures. In: Proc. International Conference on Intelligent Multimedia and Distance Education, ICIMADE 2001 (2001)
20. Chauhan, R., Kaur, H., AfsharAlam, M.: Data Clustering Method for Discovering Clusters in Spatial Cancer Databases. International Journal of Computer Applications (0975 – 8887) 10(6) (November 2010)

Lesion Detection in Eye Due to Diabetic Retinopathy

Pankaj Badoni[1] and R.C. Tripathi[2]

[1] Headstrong Services India Pvt Ltd, Noida
badoni18pankaj@gmail.com
[2] Department of IT, IIITA, Allahabad, India
rctripathi@iiita.ac.in

Abstract. Diabetic Retinopathy (DR) is one of the chronic diseases which has caused stir in the medical world, since initial symptoms are hard to detect or predict and if it goes unnoticed then it may lead to permanent blindness. So the need arises for fast and efficient systems which can detect whether the patient is suffering from DR or not. In automatic detection of lesion in eye due to diabetic retinopathy the lesions are detected based upon the lesion's characteristic for e.g. exudates are bright spots and hemorrhages are dark lesions. The detection of lesions facilitates in initial screening step of the disease, with this we can perform automatic screening of images whether they are DR infected or not. In present system with the help of morphological image processing techniques, we are trying to detect lesions in two categories i.e. dark and bright lesions. The present system is able to detect 90 % exudates in image and 85% dark lesions.

Keywords: Morphology, Exudates, HAMs, Diabetic retinopathy, Haemorrhages.

1 Introduction

Diabetic Retinopathy (DR) is very acute problem and if goes unnoticed then may lead to undesirable results, if properly monitored and diagnosed; it can be reduced by a major factor. As per the leading news articles, medical organizations and ophthalmology journals ,India is having most number of cases of Diabetes mellitus, which favors the occurrence of DR ,moreover its considered fourth common diseases causing blindness. As per a survey on retinopathy from Madurai revealed that among 1,863 new patients of DR, 37% had observable DR [10]. It becomes a need for automatic screening of the images, so that the patients suffering from Diabetes could be tested for regular interval of time. India being second largest populated country where medical resources are not that frequently available. If we can come up with some system which can assist medical practitioners, it will be of immense help to the medical world.

2 Previous Works

Last few decades have seen the rapid development in the field of medical image processing and computer vision. Detection of lesions due to Diabetic Retinopathy is

A. Agrawal et al. (Eds.): IITM 2013, CCIS 276, pp. 306–315, 2013.
© Springer-Verlag Berlin Heidelberg 2013

not a new term in the context of Image processing. Researchers like Chutatape and Zhang [1] have detected the lesions based on top down and bottom up strategy, they have divided the problem in two broad categories like bright lesions and dark lesions, for detection of dark lesion they have used top down approach and then for classification SVM has been used, whereas for the bright lesions bottom up strategy with fuzzy c-means is used to extract out bright lesions, Ravishankar et al. [2] have used morphological image processing for extracting blood vessels and exudates , they used convergence of major blood vessels for optic disc localization. For HAMs color model of lesions is created and based on that the classification is done. They have accuracy of 97.1% in detecting optic disk and 95.1% detection of exudates, 90.5% for HAMs.

Sinthaniyothin et al. [3] used region growing segmentation techniques for detection of exudates and maximum variance technique for detection of optic disk. Sensitivity and specificity of the system is 80.21% and 70.66% respectively. Langroudi and Sadjedi [4] have used pre-processing steps to enhance images, for instance simple power-law transform is used for enhancing quality of image. Yuji Hatanaka et al.[5] have given an improvement over existing system for detection of hemorrhages, they have used image normalization techniques for enhancing the quality of images, as the HAMs and normal blood vessels are ill illuminated, they used image normalization techniques like intensity variation in HSI domain and hemorrhages are detected using density analysis, their systems efficiency was roundabout to 80%. Atif Manssor et al [7] have proposed a novel approach to enhance exudates with the help of fuzzy morphological operators and detected soft exudates which were ignored in general cases, their detection rate of lesion is nearly 93%. Meindert Niemeijer et al. [8] have combined the previous works of Spencer et al. and Frame et al, extra features for detection of the lesions like area, compactness, aspect ratio, circularity, total intensity of the object were calculated in original image, their system achieves sensitivity of 100% and specificity 87 %. Our approach is morphological based where main emphasis is on lesion detection irrespective of any cost. Köse C et al. [13] have given an inverse segmentation approach for detection of lesions their accuracy is 95% in detection of Optic disc and 90% in segmentation of DR.

3   Methodology

In present approach, we are detecting lesions based on their intensity values; the main focus is on two categories, bright lesions and dark lesions. Bright lesions correspond to Exudates and dark lesions correspond to Hemorrhages and Micro aneurysms. While approaching the problem we have clubbed MAs and Hemorrhage into one category i.e. dark lesion (HAMS), it's based on the color properties of both lesions.

The work is divided in four steps

- Image Acquisition.
- Blood vessel extraction.
- Exudates detection.
- HAMs detection.

3.1   Image Acquisition

Images are acquired from DIARETDB0 Dataset, there are all total 130 images supplied with their binary masks. A mask removes that part which are ill illuminated or having dark contrast. The resolution of images is 1500*1152, its size is approximately 1.5 MB.

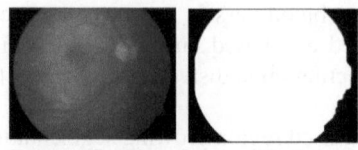

Dataset Image.   Image Mask

Fig. 1. Sample image with Mask

3.2   Blood Vessel Extraction

Images are resized to [576,720] resolution with bilinear interpolation techniques; this resizing technique keeps all the information with very small loss in it. Resized images are complemented, histogram equalized and then morphologically opened. Enhanced image is morphologically opened with 'ball' structuring element (S), radius and height values are calculated manually for number of images and 6 comes out to be perfect value (let morphologically opened image be image B).

The mathematical representations of morphological operators are

Dilation:

$$A \oplus B_1 = \{x | \hat{B}_{1x} \cap A \neq \emptyset\} \tag{1}$$

Erosion:

$$A \ominus B_2 = \{x | B_{2x} \subset A\} \tag{2}$$

Opening:

$$(B = (A \circ S)) = (A \oplus S) \ominus S \tag{3}$$

Closing:

$$A \cdot B = (A \ominus S) \oplus S \tag{4}$$

Where A is input image, B_1 and B_2 is the structuring element used for dilation and erosion respectively. $\circ$ is an opening operator, $\cdot$ is closing operator, $\oplus$ is dilation operator and $\ominus$ is erosion operator. In next step subtraction of B is done from A (A-B) , it gives us subtracted image which consist of dominant blood vessel map and rest other part goes in background. Since after subtraction we have major intensity difference in the pixel values of image, we can apply Otsu's method for calculating global threshold value. On subtracted image threshold is applied to give binary image which consist of blood vessel map and small artifacts. Small artifacts are removed with the help of connected component approach; components which are below certain range are subtracted giving us only blood vessels.

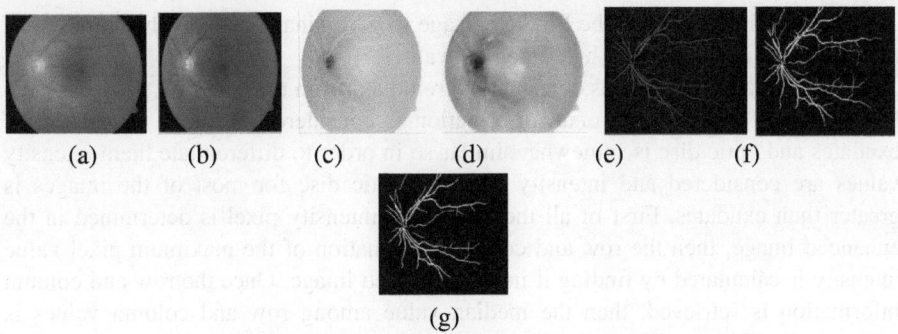

(a)   (b)   (c)   (d)   (e)   (f)

(g)

Fig. 2. Illustration of BV algorithm on fundus image

(a) Original image, (b) green channel of image, (c) complemented image of green channel, (d) morphologically opened image (e) subtracted image from enhanced image, (f) image after applying thresholding, (g) final image of extracted BV after removing small connected components.

3.3   Exudates Detection

Major hurdle in detection of exudates is optic disc, optic disc have same color and little higher intensity in comparison to the exudates, so in detection of exudates our prime duty is to remove optic disc(OD) first and then remove it from the fundus image.

It's a two-step process

> Step 1: Detection of bright intensity pixel in fundus image.
> Step 2: Detection of optic disc and subtracting it from output of step 1.

Initially grayscale image of original image is histogram equalized, since intensity of the exudates is high in comparison to the blood vessels and normal background, so it makes a useful channel for detection of lipids, in order to make the difference more clear and visible, the grayscale image is histogram equalized to enhanced image. Once image is enhanced, that image comprises all sort of lesions which occur in eye like hemorrhages, cotton wool spots, MAs and other lesions, since our main objective is to detect only exudates, so our task is to remove small objects from our image. In order to remove unwanted objects from image, the enhanced image is morphologically closed, in order to remove small objects and blood vessels; morphologically opened image comprises only of major intensity objects like optic disc and exudates. Morphologically opened image is then passed to a filter which calculates the variance of image on local basis i.e. it calculates a variance of 7*7 window and then slides the window to calculate variance of other pixel values, it slides window on whole image to calculate local variance of pixel values.

Thresholding is applied on the Filtered image to give binary image, which consist of those parts which are having high intensity values.

In second step optic disc is detected and removed from the output of previous step. For detection of optic disc pixel information is considered, as color orientation of exudates and optic disc is somewhat similar so in order to differentiate them intensity values are considered and intensity value of optic disc for most of the images is greater than exudates. First of all the maximum intensity pixel is determined in the enhanced image, then the row and column information of the maximum pixel value intensity is calculated by finding it in the enhanced image. Once the row and column information is retrieved, then the median value among row and column values is selected, then this median value for row and column gives us one coordinate values which are considered as the value of high intensity or somewhere near the center of the optic disc. The optic disc is having radius of 60-70 pixels, considering the coordinates from above finding as center and a mask of 60-70 pixels radius is drawn which acts as mask in the optic disc detection(let masked image be OD.) Now the masked image is subtracted from the output of previous step to give optic disc removed image. The enhanced image from the first step is enhanced again and thresholding is applied with higher threshold value i.e. '.85' it removes all other unnecessary information keeps only higher value pixel.

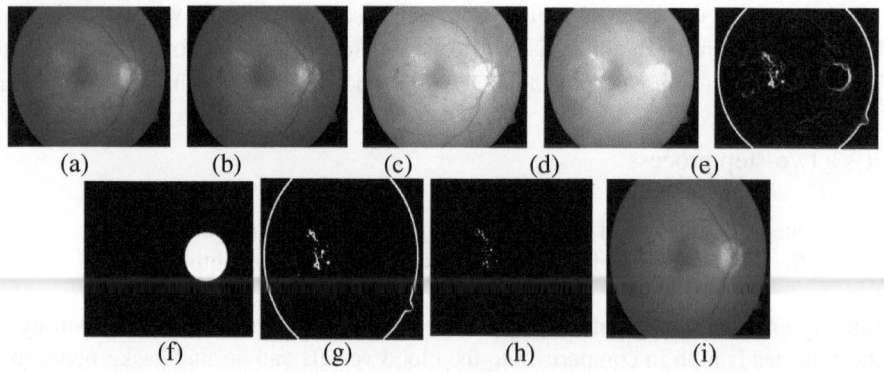

Fig. 3. Illustration of Exudates algorithm

(a) original image (O),(b)-(e) various step involved in finding high pixel value areas,(f) optic disk mask,(g) optic disc removed image,(h) morphologically closed image, (i) final output image with lesions depicted in green color.

3.4   HAMs Detection

HAMs i.e. Hemorrhage and Micro aneurysms, have been grouped in one category based on color and intensity properties. Detection of HAMs is a two-step process.

Step 1: Preprocessing stage.
Step 2: Lesion (HAMs) detection.

Preprocessing Step

For preprocessing the image it is converted to the HSI domain and their intensity of image is increased, since some of the time the intensity of lesions is very dark and it very hard to deduce whether they are artifacts occurred due to hardware restriction or bad illumination, images are converted from RGB to HSI and changes are made to intensity part of the image (I) in HIS domain. Once our task is fulfilled in HSI domain, image is restored to RGB domain for further detection of HAMs.

$$\text{Image\_HSI} = \sqrt{(1 - (\text{image\_HSI}(i, j, k) - 1)^{\wedge}2))} \qquad (5)$$

For increasing the value of intensity above formula is used, for k=3 value of intensity is changed by a considerable factor. The figures represent the intensity variation after applying the illumination technique on the original image.

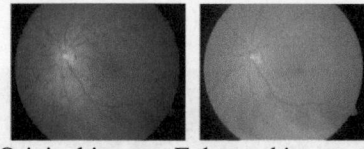

Original image   Enhanced image.

Fig. 4. Illumination enhancement

Lesion (HAMs) Detection

Green channel of illuminated image is selected for further processing as it contains more information in comparison to red and blue channel.

In the initial step grayscale image of original image is morphologically filled to fill the holes, holes are those regions which are having dark intensity and are followed by lighter intensity pixels, since this solves our purpose because our concern is about the dark pixels which come under the haemorrhage category.

Mathematical representation for morphological filling.

$$F_i = (F_{i-1} \oplus S) \cap M^c \qquad (6)$$

The iteration stops at $F_i = F_i - 1$. Here, M^c is the mask provided for reconstruction, S is a structuring element and for i=1, F_0 acts as the seed point. Region will be filled to that extent or boundary which is defined by mask.

Green channel of the processed image is subtracted from morphologically filled image to give us a grayscale image, in which we can clearly distinguish the haemorrhages from background and they can be further processed to give HAMs.

Threshold (T) when applied to the grey scale images converts the image present approach subtracted image undergoes thresholding to give only the to binary image, in which only shape information is retained, in shapes of defected areas. Here manually 'T=.30' is selected, numerical value which is supplied to the system was manually calculated for 60 images and after careful scrutinizing and examination this value is selected.

Since blood vessels and HAMs have same color intensity, so it's quite probable that they can also appear in form of lesions. Generally they were removed in the filling and subtraction process but to remove artifacts caused due to BVs, original image is passed to the blood vessel extraction algorithm and blood vessel extracted image is subtracted from the thresholded image. Final image contains HAMs detected regions.

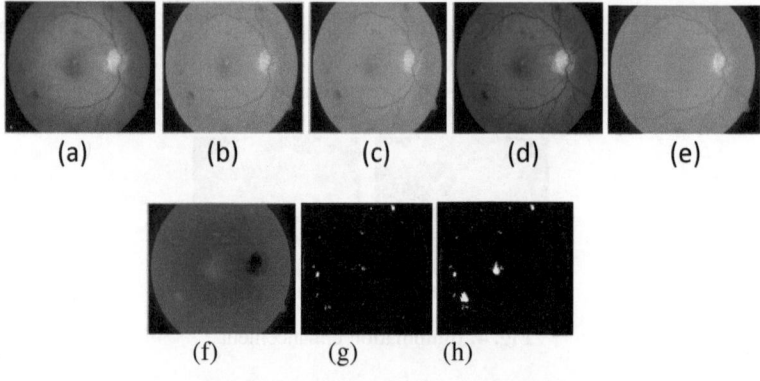

Fig. 5. Illustration of HAMs algorithm

a) Original image, (b) Intensity modified image (I), (c) conversion of I to gray scale(G), (d) green channel of I, (e) morphologically filling performed on G,(f) subtracted image, filled image from green channel,(g) thresholded image,(h) image consisting of HAMs(final output image.)

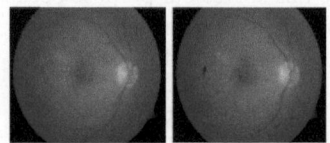

Fig. 6. HAMs superimposed over original image

4   Results and Discussion

This section shows the comparative study between other techniques and our proposed technique.

Our approach has shown considerable improvements over other morphological techniques and their combinations.

Table 1. Results of optic disc detection for all type of images either normal or abnormal from different dataset

Source of image /dataset.	Comparison in Optic Detection		
	Number of Images	Correct Results	% Success
Stare dataset	81	68	83.9
Diaretdb0	130	105	80.76
Drive	40	34	85
Messidor	1200	1000	83.33

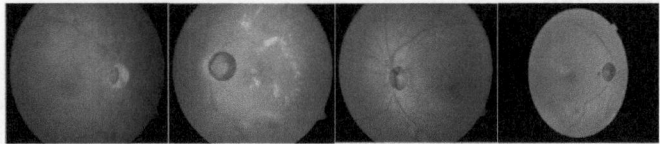

Fig. 7. Results of OD localization from different datasets

Table 2. Results of HAMs detection and comparison with other authors

Author name	Comparison of HAMs detection.			
	NI	NIHAMs	SNVY	SPCY
Sinthanayothin	30	14	77.5	88.7
Ravishankar et al.	516	348	95.1	90.5
Our approach	130	95	89.6	85

NI- Number of images used, NIHAMs-Number of Images with HAMs, SNVY-Sensitivity, SPCY-Specificity.

Table 3. Comparison of Exudate detection with other authors

Author name	Comparison of Exudate detection			
	NI	NIEx	SNVY	SPCY
Sinthanayothin	30	21	88.5	99.7
Ravishankar et al.	516	345	95.7	94.2
Chutatape	35	28	100	71
Our approach	130	81	93.1	80.7

NIEx- Number of images with exudates.

Table 1, Table 2 and Table 3 shows our results for OD localization, HAMs detection and Exudates detection. For testing we used 130 images provided by Diaretdb0 and for cross testing we used 1200 images from MESSIDOR dataset.

The present approach is only restricted to HAMs and exudates detection, it is not robust enough to detect delicate vessels Of Neo vascularisation (NVs). Manual supply of threshold value to the system is also a major drawback as it directly impacts sensitivity and specificity of the system. For implementation MATLAB 7.10.0(R2010a) is used which gives output in 10-15 seconds, many inbuilt Image processing functions were used for coding and implementation [9].

5   Conclusion

In present system we have detected lesions in two main categories and a perfect tool for early detection of lesions due to diabetic retinopathy is developed, we have achieved 90 % efficiency in exudates detection and 85% in HAMs detection. With the little help of classification techniques we can make it more efficient and perfect system.

References

1. Zhang, X., Chutatape, O.: Top-down and bottom-up strategies in lesion detection of background diabetic retinopathy. In: IEEE Conference on Computer Vision and Pattern Recognition, vol. 2, pp. 422–428 (2005)
2. Ravishankar, S., Jain, A., Mittal, A.: Automated feature extraction for early detection of diabetic retinopathy in fundus images. In: IEEE Conference on Computer Vision and Pattern Recognition, pp. 210–217 (2009)
3. Sinthanayothin, C., Kongbunkiat, V., Phoojaruenchanachai, S., Singalavanija, A.: Automated screening system for diabetic retinopathy. In: Image and Signal Processing and Analysis, ISPA, vol. 2, pp. 91–920 (2003)
4. Langroudi, M.N., Sadjedi, H.: A new method for automatic detection and diagnosis of retinopathy diseases in colour fundus images based on Morphology. In: ICBBT, pp. 134–138 (2010)
5. Yuji, H., Toshiaki, N., Yoshinori, H., Takeshi, H., Hiroshi, F.: Improvement of automated detection method of haemorrhages in fundus images. In: EMBS 2008. 30th Annual International Conference of the IEEE, pp. 5429–5432 (2008)
6. Grisan, E., Ruggeri, A.: Segmentation of candidate dark lesions in fundus images based on local thresholding and pixel density. In: EMBS 2007, International Conference of the IEEE, pp. 6735–6738 (2007)
7. Bin Mansoor, A., Khan, Z., Khan, A., Khan, S.A.: Enhancement of exudates for the diagnosis of diabetic retinopathy using Fuzzy Morphology. In: Multi topic Conference IEEE, pp. 128–131 (2008)
8. Niemeijer, M., van Ginneken, B., Staal, J., Suttorp-Schulten, M.S.A., Abramoff, M.D.: Automatic detection of red lesions in digital colour fundus photographs. IEEE Transactions on Medical Imaging 24, 584–592 (2005)
9. Gonzalez, R., Woods, R.: Digital Image Processing using MATLAB, 2nd edn. Addison-Wesley Press (2009)

10. Kumar, A.: Diabetic blindness in India: The emerging scenario. Indian J. Ophthalmology 46, 65–66 (1998)
11. http://www2.it.lut.fi/project/imageret/diaretdb0/index.html
12. http://messidor.crihan.fr/
13. Köse, C., Şevik, U., İkibaş, C., Erdöl, H.: Simple methods for segmentation and measurement of diabetic retinopathy lesions in retinal fundus images. Computer Methods and Programs in Biomedicine 107(2), 274–293 (2012), doi:10.1016/j.cmpb.2011.06.007, ISSN 0169-2607

Classification and Live Migration
of Data-Intensive Cloud Computing Environment

Sandip Kumar Pasayat[1], Sarada Prasanna Pati[2], and Prasant Kumar Pattnaik[1]

[1] School of Computer Engineering,
KIIT University, Bhubaneswar, India
pasayatsandip@gmail.com, patnaikprasantfcs@kiit.ac.in
[2] Department of Computer Science and Engineering,
ITER, S'O'A University, Bhubaneswar, India
saradapati78@gmail.com

Abstract. Cloud computing is an emerging technology providing software and hardware resources to the users' as pay-per-use basis, on the other hand in surge demand of current needs of anywhere and anytime the concept of mobile computing came into view. Both aims to provide service to the users as per their requirements and cloud computing provide better flexibility in terms of PaaS, SaaS and IaaS. Database handling is the important consideration of above type of computing environments. Many researchers are proposed issues of database using SQL and NoSQL space suitably for cloud computing scenario. Again available classification for the cloud database sited as a structured and unstructured schema-based along with small and big databases concepts. In this paper we have conducted a study of cloud databases as well as its classification in terms of ACID and NoACID. Again our work focuses on the architectural issues on Database as a Service (DaaS) based on the live migration from ACID based Database to NoACID based Database and vice-versa.

Keywords: Cloud Computing, Mobile Computing, DaaS, CDS, DBMS, ACID, NoACID, Live Migration, UDB, DPSN.

1   Introduction

Cloud computing [1] or Internet computing is becoming popular term in industry as well as in the research field. Cloud services provided by third party render services to the client all the times without interruption and with non uniform workloads may be in terms of pay-per-use basis. Cloud framework includes the services as PaaS (Platform as a Service), IaaS (Infrastructure as a Service) and SaaS (Software as a Service). Software as a Service enable applications offered as a service on demand and small software sit on the cloud serves many clients. DaaS (Database as a Service) may be an instant solution provider for users during storing/retrieval of information [3, 4]. The rapid advancements in the wireless communication and computer miniaturizing technologies have enabled users to utilize computing resources anywhere in the computer network. For example, one can even connect to Intranet

A. Agrawal et al. (Eds.): IITM 2013, CCIS 276, pp. 316–324, 2013.

from an aero plane. Mobile database technology allows the development and deployment of database applications for handheld devices, thereby making relational database based applications available in the hands of mobile workers. Employees using handheld can link to their corporate networks, download data, work offline, and then connect to the network again to synchronize with the corporate database. For example, with a mobile database embedded in a handheld device, a package delivery worker can collect signatures after each delivery and send the information to a corporate database at the end of the day. The traditional database systems do not provide special facilities for specific update operations in a mobile computing environment. One of the constraints for such databases is related to the size of the program that can be run on the limited memory handheld devices. The commercially available mobile database systems allow operation across a wide variety of platforms and data sources. They also allow users with handheld to synchronize with Open Database Connectivity (ODBC) database content and personal information management data and email from Lotus Development's Notes or Microsoft's Exchange. These database technologies support either query-by-example (QBE) or SQL statements. Some of the commercially available Mobile Relational Database systems includes IBM's DB2 Everywhere 1.0, Oracle Lite' and Sybase's SQL [2]. Traditional database design is static and simplifies many issues while mobility change the way we design databases. In mobile database [2] many aspects are dynamic, from sporadic accesses by individual users to particular data to continuous access of a particular data by a large group of users. Mobile hosts have to deal with planned or unexpected disconnections when they are mobile; they are also likely to have scarce resources such as low battery life, slow processor speed, and limited memory, their applications are required to react to frequent changes in the environment such as new location, high variability of network bandwidth; their data interests are changing from time to time and from location to location; even data semantics in mobile hosts may vary according to data access patterns, connection duration and disconnection frequencies, etc. Again data partition, location and replication seem to be dynamic and require a dynamic database design and reconfigure scheme. DaaS is the core service in cloud computing environment that may include centralized database management system (DBMS) as wells as distributed DBMS [3]. Generally, centralized DBMS are adopted by the small datasets of companies, since the entire database infrastructures are made available as a service and it will reduce the cost of building the database infrastructure, recruiting the professionals to tuning and manage the Database operations. On the other hand DaaS may play a vital role in case of large scale distributed storage system say Internet or Big data. Accessing the Big Data or metadata and some transaction over this sort of data on-demand with lower latency, greater availability, and scalability are the key concerns in distributed system in cloud environment. Some of the popular DaaS are Amazons Relational Database Services (RDS), SimpleDB, Microsoft Azure, Apache Cassandra, MongoDB, Redis, Xeround cloud database services.

This paper is organized as follows: In section-2, we have discussed the framework of Cloud Database System (CDS). Our main focus is on classification for Cloud Database and Live Migration scenarios, which are illustrated in section-3 & 4 respectively. Finally, in Section-5 we conclude our work.

2   Framework of Cloud Database System

Multiple database systems integrated into the Cloud Database System (CDS) framework with respect to three dimensions are shown in Figure 1. CDS supports multiple Database systems namely Peer-to-Peer Database Systems, Client-Server Database Systems and Multi-Database Systems [5]. Client-Server Database System is the first attempt at distributing functionality. The communication duties are shared between the client machine and the server. These systems concentrate data management responsibilities at servers while the client focuses on providing the application environment including the user interface. Whereas in Peer-to-Peer Database System each machine has the full DBMS functionality and can communicate with each other to execute queries and transactions. Multi-Database System is the integration of several independent heterogeneous database systems in the cloud computing environment. It can be further classified into two categories federated database system and nonfederated database system [6]. Federated databases may administrate and synchronize the manipulation of Component Databases [7]. Multidatabase DBMS provide layer of software that runs on top of the individual DBMSs and provides user with the facilities of accessing various databases. It can also be possible that multiple users can access the same federated database or multiple federated databases. In case of design sovereignty, individual DBMSs are free to use data models and transaction management that they prefer. Communication sovereignty is about individual DBMSs being free to make decision as to what type of information it want to provide to the other DBMSs or to the software that controls their global execution. Execution sovereignty refers to the concept that each DBMS can execute the transactions that are submitted to it in any way that it want to. Diversity refers to the physical distribution of data over multiple sites, but user sees data as one logical pool. Non-Homogeneity depicts the distinct features (NonHomogeneous hardware and differences in networking protocols to variations in data managers) of each of the independent user database system in the cloud computing paradigm. However the basic issues deal with data models, query language and transaction management protocols. For example: DB2 uses SQL while INGRES uses QUEL but both are using same data model.

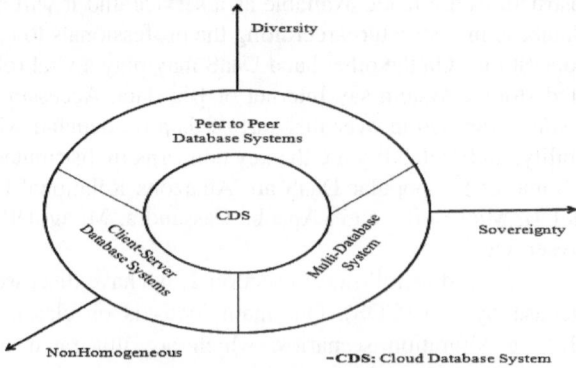

Fig. 1. Framework of Cloud Database System

3   Classification of Cloud Databases

Cloud Database classification may vary and many researchers have classified Cloud Database as Structured-Unstructured Databases [1]; Relational-NonRelational Databases [1]; SQLbased-NoSQLbased Databases [9]. Our vision of classification for the Cloud Database System is based on transaction processing. Any database transaction must satisfy some criteria and all these criteria are grouped together to form a standardized form called ACID Characteristics. So here we classify the Cloud Database in two ways ACID-based Cloud Database & NoACID-based Cloud Database as indicated in Fig. 2.

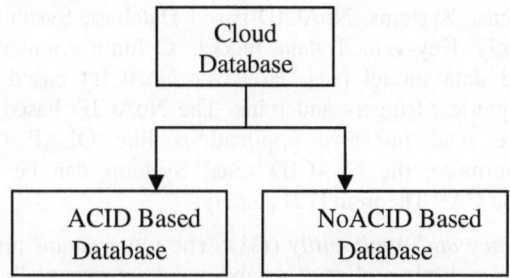

Fig. 2. Cloud Database Classification

3.1   ACID Based Database Systems

Transaction Processing is the heart of any traditional Database systems. Whereas ACID (Atomicity, Consistency, Isolation & Durability) properties are the necessary and sufficient criteria of any database transactional operations. Atomicity refers to "all or nothing" rule, which means part of transaction failure due to hardware failure, power failure or any sort of the resource failure will lead to abort the transaction otherwise after a successful transaction it may commit the transaction. Consistency states that database remain in a consistent state before and after transaction by the use of constraints, cascades and triggers and any of the combinations. If it faces any failure during transaction then the whole transaction will be aborted and database maintains the same valid state as it was before transaction. Isolation requires that concurrently executed transactions have no impact on each other's execution. It can be possible only when multiple transactions executed sequentially to maintain a valid system state. Durability refers to the persistency of committed transactions, which means in any sort of failures the committed transaction will not be corrupted or lost. It can be easily recovered with a valid system state. All the DBMSs under ACID based system adopts only relational data model. Some of the commercially available ACID based DBMSs are MySQL, Oracle, Microsoft SQL Server, PostgreSQL etc. ACID-based DaaS are well suited for OLTP (Online Transaction Processing) operations. Most popularly used ACID based Database as a Services in Cloud are Microsoft SQL Azure which can support Microsoft SQL Server T-SQL, Amazon EC2 supporting many ACID based systems through Amazon Machine Images like Oracle, DB2, Postgress, Sybase, MySQL, Microsoft SQL server. However the ACID based

Database System suffers from several challenges such as no support for Database replication (deals with the better availability in a cloud computing environment) and bottleneck problem caused by heavy application load. In addition to that it is very time consuming and cost expensive to accomplish serializability during concurrent execution.

3.2   NoACID-Based Database System

NoACID based Database Systems are getting popular as the strictness of ACID transactions is reduced. Some authors articulate the relaxed ACID transaction as BASE (Basically Available Soft-state Eventually consistent) transaction [10]. Unlike ACID-based Database Systems, NoACID-based Database Systems support multiple data models namely Key-valued data model, Column-oriented data model and Document-oriented data model [11]. However NoACID based Databases do not support complex queries, triggers and joins. The NoACID based DBMSs are well-matched for large read intensive applications like OLAP (Online Analytical Processing). Furthermore, the NoACID-based Systems can be classified in three categories as per the CAP Theorem [12] namely:

Based on Consistency and Availability (CA): The CA systems are more focused on availability through multiple replica of database and are eventually consistent [12]. In the contrary part of the system are not concerned about tolerance to network partitioning. Some of the commercial Cloud DBMSs under this category are Vertica (Column-oriented), Aster Data (Relational), and Greenplum (Relational) and so on.

Based on Availability and Partition tolerance (AP): AP systems are most widely used in Cloud DBMS, where they sustain replication and partition tolerance accomplishing the consistency [12]. Examples of those systems are: Voldemort (Key-value), Tokyo Cabinet (Key-value), KAI (Key-value), CouchDB (Document-oriented), SimpleDB (Document-oriented), Riak (Document-oriented).

Based on Consistency and Partition tolerance (CP): Moreover, the systems belonging to CP category are not well enough for replication but are eventually consistent and support tolerance to network partitioning [12]. Some of the available Cloud DBMS under this categories are BigTable (Column-oriented), Hypertable (Column-oriented), HBase (Column-oriented), MongoDB (Document-oriented), Redis (Key-value), Terrastore (Document-oriented), Scalaris (Key-value) , MemcacheDB (Key-value), Berkeley DB (Key-value).

4   Live Migration in Cloud Database

Live Migration [14] in cloud database allows a server administrator to move the running virtual machine or database transactions between different CDS nodes without disconnecting the client. Many a time migration of database transaction suffers from some of the cost affecting factors such as system downtime, service interruption due to aborted transactions of user database (UDB) and migration overhead. But live migration of database transactions may provide low overhead migration and minimized overall system downtime [15]. Some of the added benefits of live migration over traditional migration are energy conservation, load balancing and online maintenance [14].

4.1   Traditional Migration Techniques

We now discuss about the various techniques developed in the past for UDB migration in the cloud computing environment [15] are follows.

Stop and Copy: Stop and Copy is the simplest way of migrating UDB [15]. Initially the source CDS node stop serving the UDB and copy the data to destination CDS node and restarts the UDB transactions at destination CDS node. This approach has also some limitations such as the overall system downtime (due to the stopping of source CDS node) increases with the increase of UDB size. Apart from that the entire database cache lost due to restarting the transaction at destination node and hence post migration overhead time is highly increased to warm up the cache. Because of these weaknesses this is not well suited for live migration.

On demand migration: The downtime period of source CDS node may be reduced by the use of on demand migration approach [15], where a minimal data of the UDB is migrated to the destination node to avoid the disruption of services. Once the UDB comes online at destination node the corresponding transaction start executing. But the only problem is if the transaction requires the data, which has not been migrated to the destination then an expensive cache miss occurred. The post migration overhead increases with the increase in warm up time for caching the data at destination, because of this reason on demand migration approach also does not fit for live migration.

4.2   Proposed Hybrid Model for Cloud Computing Environment

Figure-3 shows our proposed model for cloud computing environment. The top most layers is composed of a large number of user/client applications. The users are accessing the Cloud Database transaction features by logging in to the desired DaaS provider. After getting the login credential from the authorized users the DaaS provider hands over the control to the DaaS server for the next transaction operation. A DaaS server acts as a gateway between the user application and the CDS node of the cluster, which may have the client library and metadata table to map the source user to the target CDS node. Furthermore, the DaaS server hides the internal complexity of cloud transaction management to the users and provides efficient services for their transaction operation. Whenever the query request from the clients reaches to the CDS node via DaaS server, it executes the query in the corresponding UDB and sends the result back to the source client through DaaS server. Every CDS node in the cluster may have the capability to control multiple UDBs along with that it preserves caching (for enhancing the read-write performance) ;maintaining UDB and transaction state information; log tables to support the fault tolerance during failure. The master CDS node in the cluster administrate the transaction operation of other cluster CDS nodes, in addition to that it also initiate the process of transaction migration. The actual physical data is stored in the bottom layer of the architecture called Distributed Physical Storage Network (DPSN). The DPSN hides the actual physical location of the storage system. UDBs along with that it preserves caching (for enhancing the read-write performance) ;maintaining UDB and transaction state information; log tables to support the fault tolerance during failure. The master CDS node in the cluster administrate the transaction operation of other cluster CDS nodes, in addition to that it also initiate the process of transaction migration. The actual physical data is stored in the bottom layer of the architecture called Distributed Physical Storage Network (DPSN). The DPSN hides the actual physical location of the storage system.

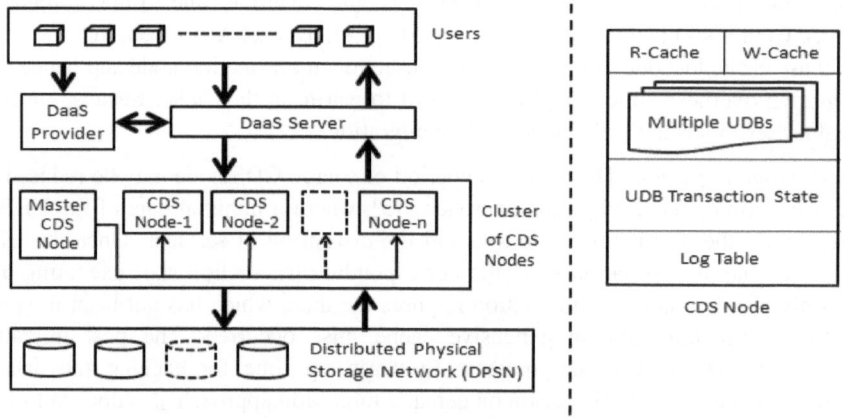

Fig. 3. A scenario of Multidatabase System model in Cloud for Live Migration

4.3   Transaction Processing in Live Migration

Live Migration of UDB in the Cloud computing environment may be viewed from the following scenarios [15, 16].

Scenario-1: All the CDS nodes within the cluster may have the ownership of one or more UDBs. When a user commits a transaction, simultaneously the UDB get updated in the corresponding CDS node (which is also called local transaction committed in UDB). Migration of Database transactions may be done between the CDS nodes. On the other hand while the source node is become unavailable to the user transaction processing, the whole uncommitted transactions are aborted to maintain the atomicity and consistency of ACID transaction. This scenario triggers before migration.

Scenario-2: At first the source CDS node sends the transaction migration request to the target node under the control of the master CDS node. The target node will reply with an approval to the source node when it finds all the required resources available to execute the transaction. After getting the approval from the target node the source node take the snapshot of the client UDB and send it to the target node, in the mean time the source node will executing some of the transactions. Since some of the transactions are executing in the source CDS node, there may be a chance of getting ambiguous data in the UDB at the destination node. To overcome this issue source node has to send the result after committing each of the transactions iteratively to the destination for synchronization of UDB state. The source node will keep a track of changes to the UDB snapshots with the aim of ensuring no changes are lost during migration. Whenever the UDB states equally matches with both source and destination node, at that very moment onwards source node stop serving UDB due to which uncommitted active transactions are aborted at source node and the complete UDB will be migrated to the destination node. In the next step the ownership of UDB decommissioned from the source node and the control is handed over to the destination. As the UDB migrated to new CDS node so the new node has to report to the Cloud Server about the new location information of the UDB. This scenario activates during the migration.

Scenario-3: This is analogous to before migration phase, but the only difference is the user transactions can be administrated and managed by the destination CDS node. It also accomplishes the atomicity and consistency of ACID transaction. The destination CDS node stores the committed transaction in DPSN and maintains a log table for failure recovery which satisfies the durability of ACID transaction. This scenario will undergo after migration.

5   Conclusion

Database as a Service in the cloud computing environment is gradually increasing its popularity due to which new scenarios will emerge with their own challenges. In order to that we describe different dimensions of cloud databases and their impact on cloud computing environment. Transaction management is the heart of every database industry and ACID property is the most necessary characteristics for the transaction processing since there may be small mobile devices. In this context in order to get access to cloud from anytime from anywhere with any type of devices compels the cloud computing environment to relax the ACID properties during some database transaction operations. Hence we classify the whole cloud database into two categories such as ACID based and NoACID based Database along with that we also discussed the significance of each of these databases. The ACID based database is well suited for the OLTP web application whereas the NoACID based database fits for OLAP application. Furthermore, safety and liveness are the two key points during transaction failure where safety refers to the correctness of system's state or data consistency and liveness ensures the progression. Therefore we have also illustrated the live migration scenarios for cloud database transactions with reference to our proposed model. In the future we can plan to extend our work by live migration of database from ACID based Database System to NoACID based Database System and vice-versa in the cloud computing environment.

References

1. Mocanu, E., Andreica, M.I., Țăpus, N.: Current Cloud Technologies Overview. In: International Conference on P2P, Parallel, Grid, Cloud and Internet Computing, pp. 291–293 (2011)
2. Pattnaik, P.K., Mall, R.: Foundamental of Mobile Computing. PHI Publication (2012)
3. Mateljan, V., Cisic, D., Ogrizovic, D.: Cloud Database-as-a-Service (DaaS) – ROI. In: MIPRO, 33rd International Convention, pp. 1185–1188 (2010)
4. Database as a Service: Reference Architecture – An Overview. An Oracle White Paper on Enterprise Architecture (September 2011)
5. Ali, M.G.: A Multidatabase System as 4-Tiered Client-Server Distributed Heterogeneous Database System. International Journal of Computer Science and Information Security 6(2), 10–14 (2009)
6. Sheth, A.P., Larson, J.A.: Faderated Database Systems for managing Distributed, Heterogeneous and Autonomous Databases. ACM Computing Surveys 22(3), 183–236 (1990)
7. Brown, P.: Distributed component database management systems, pp. 29–70. Morgan Kaufmann Publishers Inc., San Francisco (2001)
8. Ozsu, M.T., Valduriez, P.: Principles of Distributed Database Systems, 2nd edn., pp. 82–100. Pearson Education Asia (2001)
9. Sharma, V., Dave, M.: SQL and NoSQL Databases. International Journal of Advanced Research in Computer Science and Software Engineering 2(8), 20–27 (2012)
10. Kraska, T.: Building Database Applications in the Cloud. Technical report MSIS, Westf alische Wilhelms-University at Munster, MIT,University of Sydney, p. 20 (2010)
11. Burtica, R., Mocanu, E.M., Andreica, M.I., Țăpuş, N.: Practical application and evaluation of no-SQL databases in Cloud Computing. In: IEEE International Systems Conference (2012)
12. Han, J., Haihong, E., Le, G., Du, J.: Survey on NoSQL Database. In: 6th International Conference on Pervasive Computing and Applications (ICPCA), pp. 363–366 (2011)
13. Chodorow, K., Dirolf, M.: MongoDB: The Definitive Guide. O'Reilly Media Publication (September 2010)
14. Ye, K., Jiang, X., Huang, D., Chen, J., Wang, B.: Live Migration of Multiple Virtual Machines with Resource Reservation in Cloud Computing Environments. In: 4th International Conference on Cloud Computing IEEE International, pp. 267–274 (2011)
15. Das, S., Nishimura, S., Agrawal, D., El Abbadi, A.: Live Database Migration for Elasticity in a Multitenant Database for Cloud Platforms. UCSB Computer Science Technical Report, pp. 1-14 (2010-09)
16. Clark, C., Fraser, K., Hand, S., Hansen, J.G., Jul, E., Limpach, C., Pratt, I., Warfield, A.: Live migration of virtual machines. In: NSDI, pp. 273–286 (2005)

Speed Invariant, Human Gait Based Recognition System for Video Surveillance Security

Priydarshi, Anup Nandy, Pavan Chakraborty, and G.C. Nandi

Robotics & AI Dept., Indian Institute of Information Technology,
Jhalwa, Allahabad, India, 211012
{priydarshi999,nandy.anup}@gmail.com,
{pavan,gcnandi}@iiita.ac.in

Abstract. Human gait provides an important and useful behavioral biometric signature which characterizes the nature of an individual's walking pattern. This inherent knowledge of gait feature confirms the correct identification of a person in a video surveillance footage scenario. In this paper, we attempt to use computer vision based technique to derive the gait signature of a person which is a major criterion for the gait based recognition system. The gait signature has been obtained from the sequence of silhouette images at various gait speeds varying from 2km/hr. to 7km/hr. The OU- ISIR Treadmill walking speed databases have been used in our research work. The joint angles of knee and ankle are computed from the stick figure of corresponding human silhouettes which lead to construct our feature template together with the other gait attributes such as width, height, area and diagonal angle of human silhouette. The combined gait features will make the system robust in different gait speeds. The major concept behind making the gait recognition speed invariant is that the human can walk in finite speed so instead of training the classifier for a single speed the classifier is to be trained for multiple speeds. A minimum distance classifier is used to separate out different cluster of subject with combined feature vectors at different gait speeds.

Keywords: Human Gait, Minimum Distance, Gait Cycle, Speed Invariant.

1   Introduction

The human way of walking is called as Gait. Gait biometric is new and quite emergent technology in the field of unique identification system. Human gait basically deals with recognizing a person by his or her way of walking. The major advantages of gait biometric over other biometrics are, that can be captured from a distance and without the knowledge of the subject and it does not require costly hardware. It recognizes people automatically. The use of gait in the field of biometric is new technology and thus it attracts many researchers for its use in surveillance security and medical fields.

A gait-based recognition/verification system involves input video captured from a camera of good resolution because the recognition rate depends on the silhouette

A. Agrawal et al. (Eds.): IITM 2013, CCIS 276, pp. 325–335, 2013.

image quality followed by the segmentation of the human blob then extracting the gait feature, and gait recognition/ verification. Gait features are extracted using the video feed from camera after the foreground segmentation. The segmentation of background is an important task as the quality of silhouette depends on segmentation. This process is not perfect as it is hampered by the sudden light changes and shadow which makes the system implementation difficult in the outdoor environment. The human gait recognition can be classified into two sections, Model-free analysis and Model-based analysis. In model-free analysis, it is considered a sequence of silhouette's moving shape and shape with motion where as in model-based analysis; structural parameters and different models like articulated modelling [1], dual oscillator model [2] can be taken into consideration. The advantage of model based approach over the model free approach is producing potentiality against the effects of changing different cloths and different viewpoint. This approach is computationally very complex to evaluate the parameters while constructing the human model. Kale et al. and Sundaresan et al.'s have used Hidden Markov Model (HMM) [3, 4] technique on two different gait features: the silhouette's width of the outer contour and whole binarized silhouette frame of a person. Sarkar et al.'s has applied baseline algorithm [5] on determining the temporal correlation of binarized silhouette images. In this work, a bounding box was constructed to match the moving silhouette shape. Lee et al. applied model based approach to fit ellipsoidal [6] on human silhouettes. The gait feature vectors were derived from different segmented region of human silhouette. The parameters of different moment features were evaluated for recognition. The silhouette was divided into seven sections after determination of body centroid. Bhanu et al. [7] used 3D kinematic model applied on 2D human silhouettes in order to estimate the 3D gait parameters known as stationary and kinematic gait features. The silhouette shape and structure was derived separately and then combined them for recognition. Moreover, the stationary features are length of different body parts and flexion which has been estimated by key silhouette frames. This paper has been depicted in the following manner. Section 2 begins with the description of different aspects of human gait analysis. In this section a segmentation approach, feature extraction method and classification technique has been described in an elegant manner. In section 3, different results obtained from different gait features are mentioned respectively. Finally, the paper is concluded with some remarks.

2   Human Gait Analysis

Existing approaches for gait feature extraction, attempt to analyze gait sequences and capture information known as gait signature that is subsequently used for recognition/verification purposes. Of particular interest are techniques which try to tackle the gait recognition problem using only sequences of silhouette images.There are two approaches for gait recognition named as follows:

- Mark free
- Marker based

In marker based approach , marks can be used on hips , knee , ankle ,which are the main point of feature extraction using marker the most challenging task "Feature Extraction" can be accomplished easily,but it cannot be useful in real time surveillance. In Mark free approach, no marks are used. Features are extracted using different image processing technique.

In this paper we have used Mark free approach for gait identification. The training and identification process require few step those are:

- Segmentation
- Feature Extraction
- Classification.

The most important task is Feature Extraction. Features should be selected carefully taking the periodic nature of the gait into consideration.

Features or Gait Signatures can be extracted in two ways

- Model Based.
- Model Free.

In model based approach we try to create a model of the human blob and try to find the feature from that model, whereas in model free approach, we directly find the feature from the silhouette Images. In this paper we have worked on both the ways of features extraction. To make whole recognition system speed invariant we will capture the features for multiple speeds. We are working on sagittal plane of the gait, so the camera should be in such a direction that it could take sagittal plane video.

2.1   Segmentation

Segmentation basically deals with the separation of human blob from the whole captured video frames. This task is mainly hampered by sudden illumination changes and shadow which is detected as foreground during this process. False detection is an issue. Mixture of Gaussian method for foreground segmentation is used followed by converting the segmented image in binary image. Once it is determined the foreground, then the segmented RGB image is converted to greyscale and then in binary image by the following way:

$$Fore(x,y) = \begin{cases} 255 & if(Image(x,y) > 0) \\ 0 & otherwise \end{cases} \quad (1)$$

Since after applying the MoG the background is black so the pixel value greater than 0 is set to 255.The different Morphological operation is applied to get good quality binary images. This is a way of segmentation of foreground object from the dynamic scene.

2.2   Feature Extraction

As stated the feature selection and extraction is important task. In this paper we have talked about two approach of features extraction.

- Model Free.
- Model Based.

All we have now is the segmented gait of the subject in sagittal plane. A Gait database of OU-ISIR, Japan [9] has been used for deriving gait signaturesof different people at different gait speeds varying from 2 km/hr. to 7km/hr.

Model Free Approach

After lot of observation and literature survey [10] we found the periodic nature of width, height, area, diagonal angle of the rectangle that bounds the silhouette image. The attributes of the rectangle bounding the human blob are extracted .These gathered information are useful as gait signature and also used for calculating the gait cycle thus finding the frame under a cycle which is used in Model based approach and while the recognition also. The values of these attributes for all the frames under one or more gait cycle are extracted. Gait cycle is determined using these attributes trends as in one gait cycle width reaches to minima twice. Diagonal angle reaches to maximum twice and so on. Fig. 1 depicts the bounding rectangle box covers the silhouette.

Fig. 1. Bounding Rectangle

Bounding Rectangle Height

Rectangle height attribute is determined by subtracting the top and the lowest value of the Y coordinate of human blob. It is taken from the starting of the head to the lowest part of the foot.

$$H_i = y_{HeadStart} - y_{Foot} \tag{2}$$

The measurement values not only specify the person height but also the change on tip-toe position in the gait cycle. The height will be used in the model based approach.

Fig. 2. Bounding Rectangle Height

Bounding Rectangle Width

Bounding rectangle width represents the width value for a person. It is obtained by subtracting the right most and left most point on x axis for each frames

$$W_i = x_{rightmost} - x_{leftmost} \tag{3}$$

The width gives a measure of hands and legs rhythm with their variation. It is also significant as it capture the minute change in the gait cycle. The silhouette width covered by rectangle bounding box has been depicted in Fig 3.

Fig. 3. Bounding Rectangle width

Bounding Rectangle Area

Bounding rectangle area is obtained by multiplying rectangle height and width for each frame. The entire silhouette area has been calculated using the following formula and it is also signified in the following Fig 4.

$$Area_i = H_i * W_i \tag{4}$$

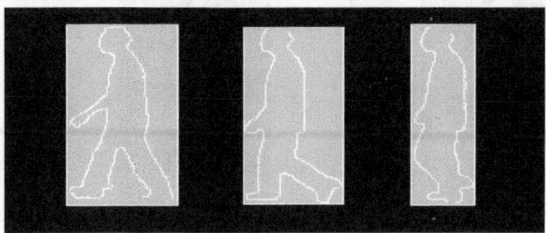

Fig. 4. Bounding Rectangle Area

Bounding Rectangle's Diagonal Angle

Bounding Rectangle's diagonal angle is obtained by calculating the tan inverse of the height by width of rectangle for each frame.

$$\theta_i = \tan^{-1} {H_i}/{W_i} \tag{5}$$

Where H denotes height and W denotes width of bounding rectangle of the blob. Fig. 5 describes the diagonal angle.

Fig. 5. Bounding Rectangle's Diagonal angle

Model Based

In this approach, we are trying to model the silhouette image into a stick figure with the help of skeleton images and then finding joints angles which will act as features. To model it into stick figure basically requires the joints position and the alignment of the body parts. For this we have used body part ratio with respect to the height. The major difficulty is in the knee and ankle joints as they are moving parts and key joints for gait feature extraction, so the modelling part is divided into two parts.

- Upper body (Head to Hip)
- Lower body(After hip to Ankle)

In upper body modelling we basically used the segment ratio and the skeleton image of the blob. Thus we have determined the skeleton of silhouette image for feature extraction. The skeleton can be determined by Distance transform. We have used Zhang-Suen/Stentiford/Holt Combined Algorithm [11] for this.

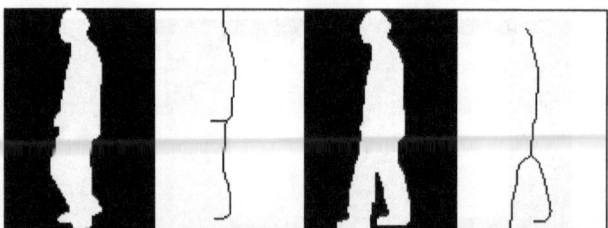

Fig. 6. Binary image with corresponding skeleton

Then the Skeleton is used along with the segment ratio to get the joints location i.e. head, neck, shoulder and hip. For this we first need the height. For the height we use the bounding rectangle's height though it is only the approximation of the height not the exact one. We vary the Y coordinate of the scan line by the segment ratio and search the point in the skeleton in that scan line. For example for the head we find the point at $0*H$ on the skeleton if we don't find the point valuing zero in the skeleton at $0*H$, we increment he till we find the head then after the head we change the scan line be segment ratio i.e. for the neck we search at $0.13*h+\alpha$, where α is the y co-ordinate of the head.Proceeding in this manner, till we reach to hip joint. Fig. 6, the extraction of skeleton figure from the binarized image has been illustrated. Then we apply body segment ratio to get the approximate length of thigh then using that length we collect all the pixels in the contour from the front of the contour starting from the hip to the hip + thigh length. After collecting the point from hip to knee we remove the outlier from those set of points using the variance analysis i.e.

$$\text{Pixel}_{\text{Final}}(x, y) = \begin{cases} \text{Pixel}(x, y) \, if \, \overline{x} - \alpha * \mu < x < \overline{x} + \alpha * \mu \\ \emptyset \; \text{Otherwise} \end{cases} \tag{6}$$

Where $\text{Pixel}_{\text{Final}}(x, y)$ is set of pixels after outlier removal, $\text{Pixel}(x, y)$ is the set of pixel before outlier removal ,$\overline{x}$ is the mean of all x values of the pixels, μ is the variance of x value and β is a constant.

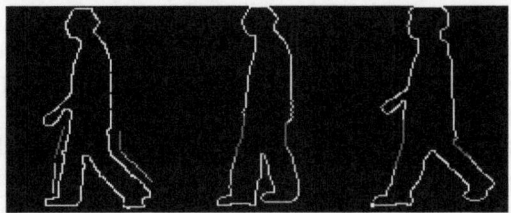

Fig. 7. Points to be taken for regression Red for thigh angle and yellow for calf

Then we apply the linear regression on the Point to get the angle of alignment of the thigh.

$$\theta = \tan^{-1} \left\{ \frac{\sum_{i=1}^{n}(x_i - \overline{x})^2}{\sum_{i=1}^{n}(x_i - \overline{x})(y_i - \overline{y})} \right\} \tag{7}$$

Where $\overline{x}, \overline{y}$ are the respective mean of the x and y value of the pixels. We take a pixel below the hip at length equal to the thigh length. Then we apply the rotation transform to the pixel to get exact location of the knee. Let $\text{Joint}_{\text{temp}}(x, y)$ be that arbitrary pixel then the joint position is given by the formula

$$\text{Joint}(x, y) = \begin{bmatrix} \cos \theta & -\sin \theta \\ \sin \theta & \cos \theta \end{bmatrix} * \text{Joint}_{\text{appox}}(x, y) \tag{8}$$

Then we proceed to the ankle in the similar manner instead of taking hip as previous joint we take knee as the previous joint and find the angle of alignment of the calf. Then we draw the point at a distance equal to the calf below the knee and then doing the rotation transform by that angle and get the ankle position.Similarly doing for the back of the contour below the hip, this will give the position of the joint of the two legs.

The problem arises during the overlapping of the two legs, because we cannot proceed with regression. Then we can take the joint angle be 0 degree in these cases. We can track the overlapping by counting the color change in a row between the knee and ankle. If the count is equal to 4 then the leg are not overlapping and the calculation is done for the angles else if the count is 2 then it is considered as overlapping. Taking joints angles zero during overlapping will not affect much because frames under overlapping are less. In Fig 8 the overlapping condition has been shown for understanding the occlusion of two legs together. Pre-processing of data i.e. feature should be done to remove noise before going to the classification of the features.

Fig. 8. Color change criterion for overlapping

2.3   Classifier

For classification and identification we have used minimum distance algorithm [13]. In this algorithm we take the features of one subject for different speed as one cluster during features acquisition. All the feature such as height, width, area, diagonal angle, knee angle, ankle angel is taken as a cluster and the distance is calculated from each point of respective attribute is taken or the distance between the centroid of the value in the attribute is taken during the recognition phase. The subject having the minimum distance less than some threshold is taken as the subject Id. If the minimum distance is greater than the threshold then the subject is considered as not registered Id. The distance is calculated for all the speeds of a person thus making the system speed invariant.

3   Result and Analysis

For background subtraction to be perfect we need a controlled environment with no shadow and constant light. Currently we are working on treadmill data set consist of the 420 silhouette image of a person for one speed and so for six different speed [9]. Following Graphs are the plot of the feature of a random subject.

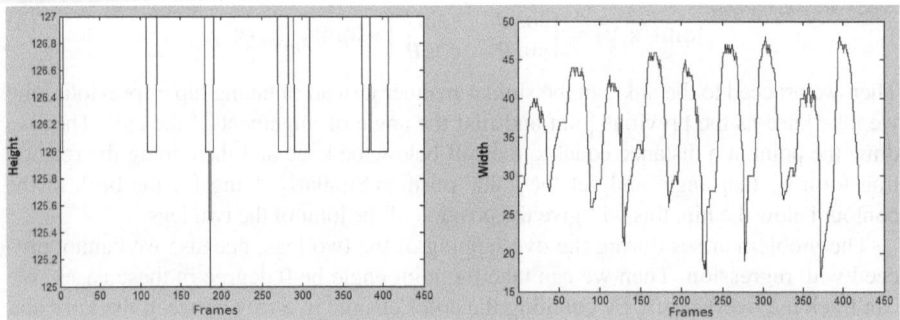

Fig. 9. Plot between Bundle Box Attributes (Height & width in pixel)& Frames

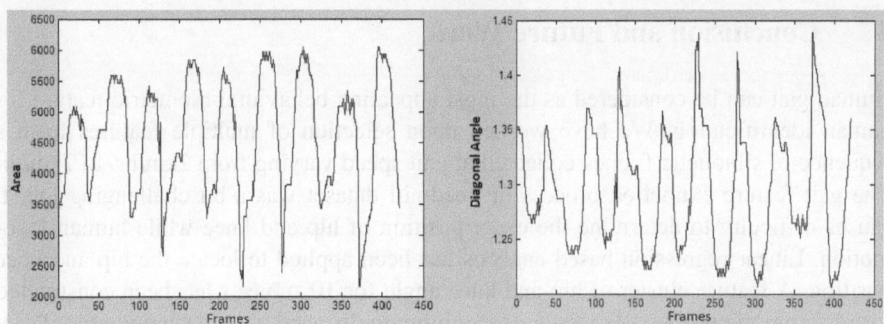

Fig. 10. Plot between Bundle Box Attributes (Area in Sq. Pixel& Diagonal Angle in radian)& frames

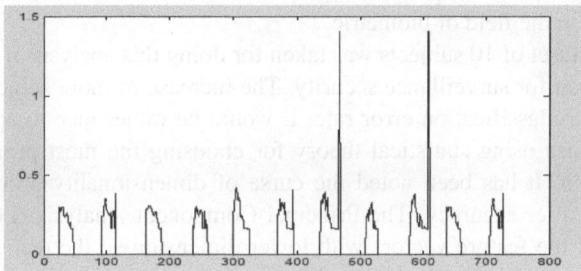

Fig. 11. Plot between Knee angle and frames [X axis represents frame. Y axis represents Knee Angle in radian].

The model free features are quit periodic which is a property of gait. These features are shown in the form of graph as shown in Fig 9 to Fig 11.The Model Based features are also periodic. The picture below in the Fig 12 is a results of the regression and joints are marked in the images.

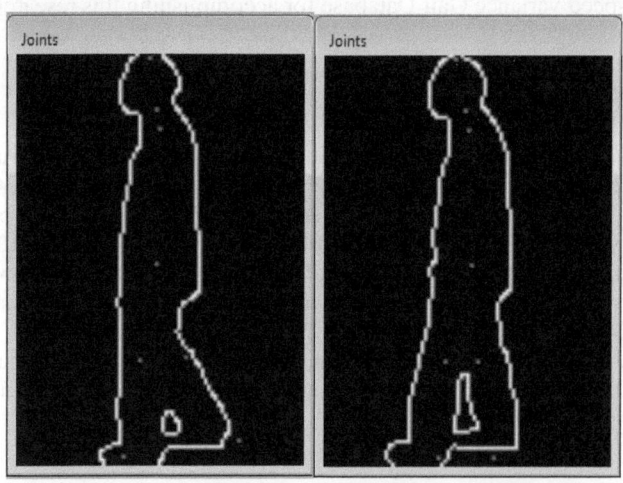

Fig. 12. Jointsmarking after regression Analysis

4   Conclusion and Future Work

Human gait can be considered as the most appealing behavioral biometric feature for human identification. We have worked upon selection of multiple features from a sequence of silhouette frames collected at gait speed varying from 2km/hr. to 7km/hr. The gait feature extraction process in treadmill dataset was a bit challenging job. It causes difficulty to determine the exact position of hip and knee while human loco-motion. Linear regression based analysis has been applied to locate the hip and knee position. A feature cluster of hip and knee angle for 10 subjects has been constructed for recognition purposes. We have used minimum distance based technique for classi-fying the unknown gait pattern among all the trained walking patterns. We have achieved satisfactory gait recognition accuracy by this method. Security Applications are very important and will play an important role in future. Gait is definitely to be a good approach in the field of biometric.

A limited dataset of 10 subjects was taken for doing this analysis of speed invariant gait classification for surveillance security. The increase of more subject leads to pro-ducing more misclassification error rate. It would be rather nice to apply feature se-lection techniques using statistical theory for choosing the most prominent features for classification. It has been noted the curse of dimensionality problem which de-grades the classifier accuracy. The Principal Component Analysis (PCA) can be ap-plied to extract the feature vectors with lower dimension so the recognition rate and computational complexity will be sensible. A concrete mathematical model is to be developed for modeling the human gait so that automatic feature extraction could be done for fast gait recognition. We plan to create a repository of human gait oscilla-tions which we will extensively analyze for person identification. We will also like to extend this work towards biomedical problems seen through gait disorder.

Acknowledgement. We would like to take the opportunity to thanks Prof Yasushi Yagi and his entire Research team of ISIR lab, Osaka University, Japan for providing us different speed variance Gait Database for accomplishing this research work.

References

1. Wang, D.K., Nixon, M.S.: On Automated Model-Based Extraction and Analysis of Gait. In: Proceeding of the IEEE Int. Conf. Face and Gesture Recognition, vol. 04 (2004)
2. Yam, C.-Y., Nixon, M.S., Carter, J.N.: Automated Person Recognition by Walking and Running via Model-Based Approaches. Pattern Recognition 37(5), 1057–1072 (2004)
3. Sundaresan, A., Roy Chowdhury, A., Chellappa, R.: A Hidden Markov Model Based Framework for Recognition of Humans from Gait Sequences. In: Proceedings IEEE Int. Conf. on Image Processing, pp. 143–150 (2003)
4. Kale, A., Rajagopalan, A.N., Sundaresan, A., Cuntoor, N., Roy Chowdhury, A., Kruger, V., Chellappa, R.: Identification of Humans using Gait. IEEE Transactions on Image Processing, 1163–1173 (September 2004)

5. Sarkar, S., Phillips, P.J., Liu, Z., Vega, I.R., Grother, P., Bowyer, K.: The HumanID Gait Challenge Problem: Data Sets, Performance and Analysis. IEEE Trans on PAMI 27(2), 162–177 (2005)
6. Lee, L., Grimson, W.E.L.: Gait Analysis for Recognition and Classification. In: Proceedings of the IEEE Int. Conf. Face and Gesture Recognition, pp. 155–162 (2002)
7. Bhanu, B., Han, J.: Human Recognition on Combining Kinematic and Stationary Features. In: Kittler, J., Nixon, M.S. (eds.) AVBPA 2003. LNCS, vol. 2688, pp. 600–608. Springer, Heidelberg (2003)
8. Yoo, J.-H., Nixon, M.S., Harris, C.J.: Extracting Human Gait Signatures by Body Segment Properties
9. OU-ISIR Gait Database,
   http://www.am.sanken.osaka-u.ac.jp/GaitDB/index.html
10. Guillen, E., Padilla, D., Hernandez, A., Barner, K.: Gait Recognition System: Bundle Rectangle Approach
11. Thinning Algorithm Page [4-6],
    http://www.massey.ac.nz/~mjjohnso/.../Thinning%20Algorithm.doc
12. Canny and Hough Transform,
    http://www.indiana.edu/~dll/B657/B657_lec_hough.pdf
13. Chen, C., Liang, J., Zhu, X.: Gait recognition based on improved dynamic Bayesian networks. Elsevier Ltd. (2010)
14. Bouwmans, T., El Baf, F., Vachon, B.: Background Modeling using Mixture of Gaussians for Foreground Detection - A Survey. Recent Patents on Computer Science 1, 3 219-237 (2008)
15. Au, O.K.-C., Tai, C.-L., Chu, H.-K., Cohen-Or, D., Lee, T.-Y.: Skeleton Extraction by Mesh Contraction. ACM (2008)
16. Sasivarnan, C., Jagan, A., Kaur, J., Jyoti, D., Rao, D.S.: Gait Recognition Using Extracted Feature Vectors. IJCST 2(3) (2011)
17. Kewatkar, S., Kathle, S.: Human Gait Recognition byOpenCV. International Journal of Computational Biology 3(1), 35–37 (2012) ISSN: 2229-6700 & E-ISSN: 2229-6719
18. Yoo, J.-H., Hwang, D., Moon, K.-Y., Nixon, M.S.: Automated Human Recognition by Gait using Neural Network. IEEE (2008)
19. Minimum Distance Algorithm,
    http://www.cs.princeton.edu/courses/archive/fall08/cos436/Duda/PR_simp/min_dist.htm

Multiresolution Framework Based Global Optimization Technique for Multimodal Image Registration

Arpita Das[1] and Mahua Bhattacharya[2]

[1] Department of Radio Physics and Electronics, University of Calcutta
[2] Indian Institute of Information Technology and Management, Gwalior
dasarpita_rpe@yahoo.co.in, mb@iiitm.ac.in

Abstract. This study has examined the problem of accurate optimization for fully automatic registration of brain images. Though the proposed global optimization techniques produce encouraging results, their speed of convergence is slow in compare to other local optimization techniques. To speed up the optimization techniques, we introduce multiresolution framework and gain a hierarchical knowledge of transformation parameters. This approach has tried to avoid the stuck in problem of local optimization technique and enhances the speed of convergence of high-dimensional searching algorithms.

Keywords: Registration, Multiresolution, Global Optimization, Convergence rate.

1   Introduction

It is common to study multiple sensor radiological images for the purpose of medical diagnosis, treatment planning and surgical operation of the patients. The physicians also recommend multi modal medical images to capture complete information of the region of interest (ROI) under investigation. But due to the change of patient's / sensor's orientation, it is difficult for a physician to integrate all imaging information in a common coordinate frame. An essential step in this integration process is bringing the images from different modalities involved into spatial alignment, which is referred to as *Registration* [1]-[3]. Registration procedure requires geometric transformations like translation, rotation, scaling and sometimes skewing such that the generated image aligns with some standard / reference image.

Major steps of registration process include *preprocessing, transformation, similarity measure* and *implementation*. Preprocessing entails any image processing to prepare or improve the images for registration. The most common preprocessing step is low-pass filtering and thresholding to remove noise [4]. In the registration process, one of the images is selected to be the *reference* image. The other image, known as the *floating* image, is attempted to align with the *reference*. These floating images which are acquired at different times and/or using different techniques, need some transformation before they can be registered with the reference image. Affine transformations are typically used in MR images to map geometric distortions [1].

A. Agrawal et al. (Eds.): IITM 2013, CCIS 276, pp. 336–347, 2013.

An affine transformation extends the degrees of freedom of the rigid transformation with a scaling factor and, additionally, a skewing in each dimension [5]-[7]. Next major step of registration method is the measurement of similarity of the images to be registered. Gray value cross-correlation can be applied to the full image to determine the best match [1]. The resulting matching is fully automatic and assumed to be maximal if both images are geometrically aligned.

Optimization of similarity measure is a function of transformation and defined as n-dimensional search for n degrees of freedom of the transformation. The optimum of similarity measure is assumed to correspond to the transformation that correctly registers the images. Unfortunately, the similarity measure is generally not a smooth function of transformation parameters and contains many local optima. Because of the existence of local optima, the choice of optimization routine has a large influence on the results of correct registration and particularly on the robustness of the method [8]. In the literature there are many global optimization techniques to find out the correct solution. However, main drawback of these exhaustive global optimization techniques is their slow convergence. Evolutionary optimization techniques such as simple model of Genetic Algorithm (GA) and Particle Swarm Optimization (PSO) have been used in medical image registration [9]-[12] with fair degree of success but leads to long execution times.

We have proposed to use a multiresolution framework in the GA and PSO based global optimization techniques to speed up the process and at the same time avoid any local optima. It has been shown that the proposed approach produces superior results compared to other common optimization techniques such as simulated annealing and hill climbing.

2   Proposed Registration Methods

The registration problem studied here is to find the best geometrical alignment of two multimodal brain images of a patient in 2D/2D dimensionality. We consider two images; the *reference* and *floating* images. Registration procedure aims to find that transformation which, when applied to the floating image, optimizes the similarity between this transformed floating image and the reference image. The details of registration steps are described below:

2.1   Transformation of Floating Image

Affine transformation is one which includes scaling and skewing in addition to translation and rotation. This type of transformation maps straight lines to straight lines and preserves the parallelism between lines. In this study we have considered only affine transformation with six degrees of freedom which will produce a 6-dimensional searching space for optimization. Various forms of affine transformations we have used here are described below:

Translation: Translation of the object can be expressed in functional form as $x' = x + t_x$ and $y' = y + t_y$, where t_x and t_y are translations in x- and y-directions respectively. Corresponding matrix form is —

$$\begin{bmatrix} x' \\ y' \\ 1 \end{bmatrix} = \begin{bmatrix} 1 & 0 & t_x \\ 0 & 1 & t_y \\ 0 & 0 & 1 \end{bmatrix} \begin{bmatrix} x \\ y \\ 1 \end{bmatrix} \tag{1}$$

Rotation: The matrix form of rotation by an angle θ in counter-clockwise/clockwise direction about the origin can be given as

$$\begin{bmatrix} x' \\ y' \\ 1 \end{bmatrix} = \begin{bmatrix} \cos\theta & \mp \sin\theta & 0 \\ \pm \sin\theta & \cos\theta & 0 \\ 0 & 0 & 1 \end{bmatrix} \begin{bmatrix} x \\ y \\ 1 \end{bmatrix} \tag{2}$$

Scaling: For scaling of an object, the functional form is $x' = s_x.x$ and $y' = s_y.y$, where s_x and s_y are scaling factors along x- and y-directions respectively.

$$\begin{bmatrix} x' \\ y' \\ 1 \end{bmatrix} = \begin{bmatrix} s_x & 0 & 0 \\ 0 & s_y & 0 \\ 0 & 0 & 1 \end{bmatrix} \begin{bmatrix} x \\ y \\ 1 \end{bmatrix} \tag{3}$$

Skewing: For a skew parallel to the x axis, we have $x' = x + ky$ and $y' = y$, where k is positive real number.

$$\begin{bmatrix} x' \\ y' \\ 1 \end{bmatrix} = \begin{bmatrix} 1 & k & 0 \\ 0 & 1 & 0 \\ 0 & 0 & 1 \end{bmatrix} \begin{bmatrix} x \\ y \\ 1 \end{bmatrix} \tag{4}$$

Similarly, for a skew parallel to the y axis, we have $x' = x$ and $y' = y + kx$, which have matrix form:

$$\begin{bmatrix} x' \\ y' \\ 1 \end{bmatrix} = \begin{bmatrix} 1 & 0 & 0 \\ k & 1 & 0 \\ 0 & 0 & 1 \end{bmatrix} \begin{bmatrix} x \\ y \\ 1 \end{bmatrix} \tag{5}$$

Above mathematical expressions show that to determine the transformation matrices we have to compute two parameters (t_x, t_y) for translation, two parameters (s_x, s_y) for scaling, one parameter (θ) for rotation and one parameter (k) for skewing. These parameters are independent of each other. Hence to determine affine transformation completely in our case, we have to compute these 6 independent parameters, called 6-degrees of freedom. So our optimization procedure involves 6-dimensional search space.

Although determination of the optimum parameter for affine transformation is a complex and involved process, we have derived an efficient optimization technique for finding the global optimum by the use of multiresolution approach.

2.2   Computation of Similarity Measure

Gray value cross-correlation can be applied to the full images or extracted feature of images to determine the degree of match [13]. Since in MR images intensity inhomogeneities appear due to unpredictable illumination [14], we have considered normalized cross-correlation (NC) as a similarity measure for the present study and maximize it to obtain correct registration. In this measure, the images are first normalized. This is typically done at every step by subtracting the mean and dividing by the standard deviation.

However, NC is also sensitive to the local intensity changes, caused by noises or different sensor techniques. As the transformation parameter (rotation) is varied smoothly, the local behavior of NC shows small discontinuities [*Ref Fig. 1*]. This creates local optima traps for the optimization methods.

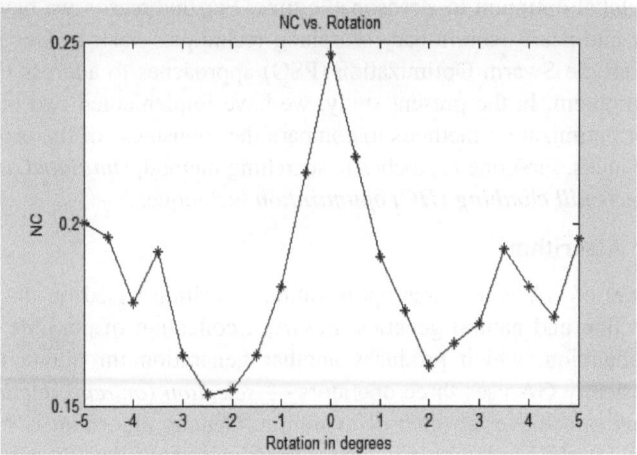

Fig. 1. Local optima of NC for MR T1 and MR T2 images

2.3   Optimization Techniques

Once a similarity measure has been chosen it is necessary to search for the transformation which will yield the optimum measure value. To do this, an optimization method is used which searches through the parameter space of allowable transformations. We have mentioned that affine transformation (in our case) is specified by 6 parameters for 2D images. Therefore, the optimization takes place in a search space; R^n, where n = 6.

As we see that similarity measures used in this study (NC) contain many local optima, exhaustive global optimization technique is appropriate to search the entire range of all possible parameters.

In most of the literatures we have found that local optimization methods are attempted to solve this problem in a multiresolution framework, which typically involves starting with low-resolution images to avoid the local minima traps. However, present study shows later, these local approaches in multiresolution framework are not always sufficient for avoiding local minima. On the other hand sophisticated global optimization methods can solve this problem substantially. Of the many different approaches to global optimization, we have investigated two evolutionary multistart searching strategies - Genetic Algorithm (GA) and Particle Swarm Optimization (PSO) to estimate the correct transformation. GA and PSO are developed in analogy of complex biological evolutionary processes and offer the capacity of population based systematic random searches. Therefore, GA and PSO will have little chance of leading to incorrect registration. These are described in the following section.

2.4   Proposed Global Searches

We know that affine transformation based searching space is high dimensional and it is difficult to identify any knowledge of initial searching point that can be capable of producing global optimum in a reasonable time. For this reason we have paid greater attention to multistart evolutionary searching techniques such as Genetic Algorithm (GA) and Particle Swarm Optimization (PSO) approaches to address the present optimization problem. In the present study, we have implemented two other derivative free popular optimization methods to compare the robustness of the proposed optimization techniques. First one is stochastic searching method, *simulated annealing (SA)* and next one is *hill climbing (HC) optimization* technique.

A   Genetic Algorithm

Simple model of GA is a search/optimization algorithm based on the mechanics of natural selection and natural genetics. In GA, a collection of possible chromosomes forms a population, which produces another generation through a natural search process. Basically GA uses three operators — *selection (or reproduction)*, *crossover* and *mutation* to achieve the goal of evolution. Genetic algorithm is not just simple random walk; it efficiently exploits the information to speculate on new search points with expected improved performance. This method allows making escapes from local optima and reaches to the global optima for the given dataset.

B   Particle Swarm Optimization

Particle swarm optimization is proposed in analogy to the social behaviour of a shoal of fish or a flock of birds, called the *swarm*. It is a heuristic approach for finding the global optimum. The individual swarm members are called *particles*. In the simplest form of PSO, each particle remembers its own best position called the *individual best or 'pbest'*, as well as the best position found by the whole swarm, and called the *global best or 'gbest'*. Global best is known to all and immediately updated when a new best position is found by any particle. PSO is iterative in nature; it updates the position and velocity of particles by utilizing the *inertia* coefficient, responsible for imparting randomness to the flight of the swarm and the *acceleration* coefficients, which allow the particle to tune the cognition and the social terms respectively.

C Simulated Annealing

Simulated annealing explores the search spaces in a stochastic manner for finding the global optimum of the function. By analogy with physical annealing process in metallurgy, each step of the SA attempts to replace the current solution by a random solution. New solution may then be accepted with a probability that depends both on the difference between the corresponding function values and also on a global parameter T (called the *temperature*), that is gradually decreased during the process [15]. Though SA is demanded as a popular global optimization technique, it is not suitable for capturing the global optimum in a high dimensional search space, because it sometimes takes a step in the wrong direction (towards a local optimum when the goal is to achieve the global optimum).

D Hill Climbing

HC is a local optimization technique, starts with a random solution and iteratively makes small changes to the solution, each time improving it a little. When the algorithm cannot see any improvement, it terminates and indicates the last solution as optimal solution. HC provides the fastest speed of convergence, but it often gets stuck in the local optima and hence yields poor accuracy [16].

E Multiresolution Framework

We have found that it is convenient to adapt a sequence of images at progressively low resolutions. These low resolution images are down sampled versions of the original image and contain fewer pixels which mean that evaluating similarity measure requires less computation. Since gross features remain at these low resolutions, it is expected that there will be fewer local optima for the optimization methods to get stuck in. These are the fundamental motivations of multiresolution processing.

Intuitively it seems that if all transformation parameters are estimated at low resolution, speed of the global optimization techniques will be enhanced. However, at the low-resolution we may not obtain the same optimum transformation parameters as obtained at full resolution and hence registration accuracy may be compromised. On the contrary, if we estimate all transformation parameters at full resolution, best accuracy will be achieved but speed of the global optimization procedure will be poor. The best trade-off between speed and accuracy are estimated experimentally in this study. Since hill climbing is a fast optimization technique, multiresolution framework is not applied on this approach. Two evolutionary searching methods, GA and PSO and simulated annealing are developed using the proposed multiresolution framework.

3   Experimental Results

This section presents several experimental results that demonstrate the robustness of the proposed registration procedure. We begin by presenting the choices of multiresolution framework that gives best experimental results. The down-sampled images are determined using Haar wavelet transform.

In this study, we have applied the proposed approaches on whole brain images to predict the early signs of Alzheimer's disease. Details of these benchmarked images can be obtained from ICALAB Image Processing Unit [17].

In this study, translation parameters (t_x, t_y) are ranged within ± 10 pixels shift. Rotation parameter θ is within 5° in clockwise direction to 5° in anticlockwise direction. Global scaling factors (s_x, s_y) are ranged from 0.8 to 1.12 and skewing factor k is ranged from -0.05 to +0.05. Optimum transformation parameter values for rotation (θ), translation (t_x, t_y), global scaling factor (s_x, s_y) and skewing factor (k) at different resolutions for T1 and T2 weighted brain MR images of original resolution 256×256 pixels are summarized in Table-1 to Table-3.

We find from the data presented in Table-1 that down to 64×64 image resolution, computed angle of rotation for best registration is close to that obtained with the original image resolution of 256×256 pixels. Further reduction of resolution starts producing markedly different results. Thus we may conclude that for rotational transformation, image resolution as low as 64 × 64 pixels, can be used to reduce the computational time without significant loss of accuracy.

Table 1. Estimation of rotation (θ) required for registration at different resolutions

Image Resolution	Rotation (θ) in degree	GA based Similarity Measure
256 × 256	2.5	0.3701
128 × 128	2.5	0.3689
64 × 64	2.4	0.3722
32 × 32	1.8	0.3669

Table 2. Estimation of (t_x, t_y) and (s_x, s_y) at different resolutions

Image Resolution	Horizontal translation t_x (pixel)	Vertical translation t_y (pixel)	Horizontal scaling factor	Vertical scaling factor	GA based Similarity Measure
256 × 256	8	6	0.92	1.05	0.3706
128 × 128	4	3	0.91	1.06	0.3692
64 × 64	0	1	0.98	1.00	0.3596

It is expected that as the image resolution is down-sampled by a factor of n, horizontal and vertical translation in terms of number of pixels also reduces by a factor of n. We find from the quantitative analysis of the data presented in Table-2 that this rule is followed while image resolution is down-sampled by a factor of 2. However, if the image resolution is down-sampled by factor of 4, horizontal and vertical translation parameters are not reduced by the same factor. Therefore we may conclude that for horizontal/vertical translation, image resolution can be down-sampled by a factor of 2 only to reduce computational time without significant loss of accuracy.

Table-2 also shows that for horizontal and vertical scaling factors, image resolution can be down-sampled by a factor of 2. This is because, optimum result is obtained with almost the same horizontal and vertical scaling factors as the full resolution.

Analysis of Table -3 shows that the skewing factor (k) must be estimated at original image resolution of 256×256 pixels. Any reduction of resolution starts producing markedly different results. The results obtained for the other images are also the same.

Table 3. Estimation of skewing factor (k) at different resolutions

Image Resolution	Skewing factor (k)	GA based Similarity Measure
256×256	0.032	0.3702
128×128	0.021	0.3504
64×64	0.013	0.3127

B Registration Results

Some of the registration results using the proposed multiresolution framework are described below. Effects of optimization techniques on the accuracy of registration method are also studied here.

Registration of Brain MRI of an 86 year old man presenting with dementia is given below. This is an example of MR T1 and MR T2 benchmark images with resolution 256×256 pixels. Registration is obtained by using the proposed global optimization technique.

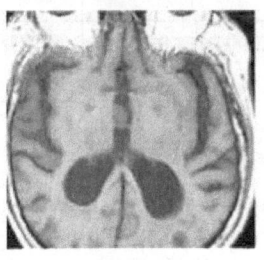 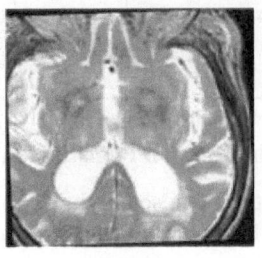 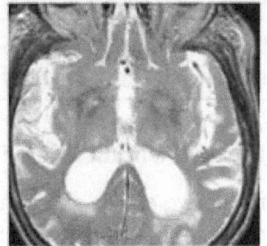

MR T1   MR T2   Registered MR T2

Fig. 2. Registration example of Brain MRI of an 86 y/o man presenting with dementia

Table 4. Optimization of NC based similarity measure (Bold-face types indicate the correct results)

Patients Details	Modalities of the images	Global Optima reached by different Optimization Techniques			
		GA	PSO	SA	HC
Patient with mild Alzheimer's disease	4 pairs of MR-T1 and MR-PD with resolution 256 × 256	**0.2466**	**0.2467**	**0.2466**	0.2412
		0.1765	**0.1764**	0.1758	0.1703
		0.1928	**0.1930**	**0.1930**	**0.1929**
		0.2108	**0.2106**	**0.2108**	0.2027
Patient with mild Alzheimer's disease	4 pairs of MR-T1 and MR-T2 with resolution 256 × 256	**0.3423**	**0.3423**	**0.3424**	**0.3422**
		0.3701	**0.3702**	**0.3702**	0.3583
		0.3745	**0.3746**	0.3681	0.3695
		0.3198	**0.3240**	0.3106	**0.3240**
Patient presenting with Alzheimer's disease	4 pairs of MR-T2 and MR-PD with resolution 280 × 280	**0.2766**	**0.2765**	**0.2766**	0.2698
		0.2839	0.2786	0.2730	0.2743
		0.2952	**0.2951**	**0.2952**	0.2736
		0.2873	**0.2873**	0.2714	**0.2874**
Patient presenting with Alzheimer's disease	4 pairs of MR-T2 and MR-PD with resolution 256 × 256	0.1941	**0.1983**	0.1903	0.1958
		0.1726	**0.1727**	**0.1726**	0.1638
		0.1828	**0.1826**	0.1803	**0.1826**
		0.1709	**0.1709**	**0.1708**	0.1622
86 y/o man with dementia	MR-T1 & MR-T2 with resolution 356 × 356	**0.3189**	**0.3190**	**0.3188**	**0.3190**
75 y/o man with dementia	MR-T1 & MR-T2 with resolution 380 × 380	**0.2003**	**0.2004**	**0.2004**	0.1838

C Effect of Optimization Techniques on Registration Procedure

Quantitative results show that the proposed optimization methods (GA and PSO) are consistent on a set of difficult benchmarked images. Robustness of the proposed optimization methods is examined by comparing several other available techniques. This robustness is due to the proposed optimization methods, not just the choice of similarity measure and multiresolution framework.

However, this study also reveals that in very few cases desired global optima are not captured by the proposed optimization techniques. This is because, though GA and PSO are developed in analogy of complex biological evolutionary processes and offer the capacity of population based systematic random searches, occasionally these optimization starts outside the capture range of desired optimum. For those cases, GA and PSO have a little chance of leading to a mis- registration of the images. Although, by using more number of initial search points of GA and PSO, the likelihood of finding the global optimum can be increased but it slows down the convergence rate.

The stochastic optimization routines like SA, is not suitable for capturing the global optimum in a high dimensional searching, because it sometimes takes a step in the wrong directions (towards a local optimum when the goal is to achieve the global optimum). In GA and PSO, this move is often controllable by exploiting a set of evolutionary parameters, however SA is trapped in the local optima.

HC optimization technique starts with a random solution, and iteratively makes small changes to the solution, each time improving it a little. However this progress may stick in a local optimal solution. Therefore HC is unable to reach the global optimum for present study.

D. Convergence of Different Optimization Techniques

Two evolutionary global optimization techniques, GA and PSO produce encouraging results for the present study. However, both PSO and GA are slow to converge to the desired optimal solution even in multiresolution framework. Though HC is stuck in the local optima very often and yields poor accuracy, it is the best optimization technique in terms of speed of convergence among other methods studied here. If the starting point is favorable then HC reach the global optima faster than other methods however, if any local optima appear during the journey, HC is trapped in that local optimum solution.

Table 5. Convergence time of four optimization techniques with different image sizes

Image size in pixels	Average Convergence time (minute)				Rate of increase of convergence time for PSO w.r.t. HC	Rate of increase of convergence time for GA w.r.t. HC
	PSO	GA	SA	HC		
152×152	10	10	8	5	5	5
232×172	15	14	11	7	8	7
230×215	18	16	13	8	10	8
256×256	25	22	18	11	14	11
280×280	31	28	22	14	18	14
356×356	60	54	46	28	32	26
380×380	76	68	57	36	40	32

In this work we have studied the convergence time of four optimization techniques with variation of different image sizes. To study the increased rate of convergences for PSO and GA techniques using the proposed multiresolution framework in compare to the standard HC technique, we have used the well known mathematical curve fitting technique on the data as shown in Table-5.

Fig. 3 reveals that the rate of increase of convergence time of PSO in comparison with HC is not exponential, rather it is bounded by a 4th degree polynomial function of time. This 4th order polynomial increase of convergence time seems reasonable for obtaining consistently accurate result.

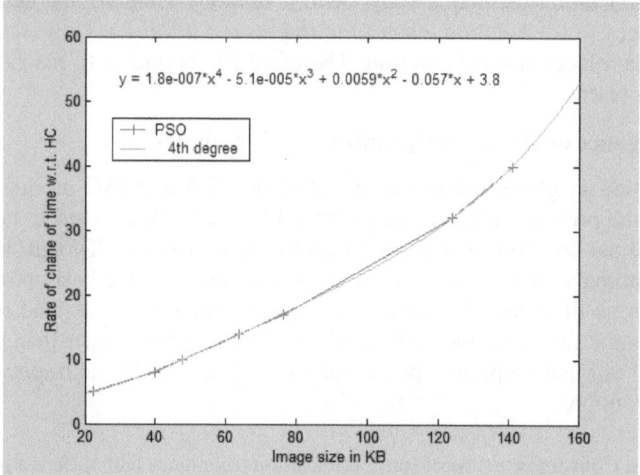

Fig. 3. Curve fitting for rate of increase of convergence time of PSO w.r.t. HC

4   Conclusion

This study has examined the problem of optimization for fully automatic registration of brain images. It is mentioned that to speed up GA, PSO and SA, a hierarchical knowledge of transformation parameters is gained from the proposed multiresolution framework. We find that though HC is stuck in the local optima very often, it is the best optimization technique in terms of speed of convergence compared to other methods. Therefore the speed of convergence of GA, PSO and SA using the multiresolution framework is compared to HC approach without considering multiresolution framework.

We also find that as the input image size increases, convergence time of GA and PSO also increases but is bounded by the order of 4th degree polynomial function of time in compare to HC. As the accuracy of GA and PSO based optimization technique is encouraging, this 4th order polynomial increase of convergence time seems reasonable.

However, the proposed evolutionary optimization methods may not give guarantee to find the global optimum in all registration problems. It has been found empirically that both of these strategies are relatively capable of avoiding to get trapped in local minima than other two optimization methods.

References

1. Maintz, J.B.A., Viergever, M.: A Survey of Medical Image Registration. Medical Image Analysis 2(1), 1–36 (1998)
2. Radau, P.E., Slomka, P.J., Julin, P., Svensson, L., Wahlund, L.-O.: Evaluation of linear registration algorithms for brain SPECT and the errors due to hypoperfusion lesions. Medical Physics 28(8), 1660–1668 (2001)
3. Shekhar, R., Zagrodsky, V.: Mutual information-based rigid and nonrigid registration of ultrasound volumes. IEEE Trans. Medical Imaging 21(1), 9–22 (2002)
4. Ding, L., Goshtasby, A., Satter, M.: Volume image registration by template matching. Image and Vision Computing 19(12), 821–832 (2001)
5. Erdi, Y.E., Rosenzweig, K., Erdi, A.K., Macapinlac, H.A., Hu, Y.-C., Braban, L.E., Humm, J.L., Squire, O.D., Chui, C.-S., Larson, S.M., Yorke, E.D.: Radiotherapy treatment planning for patients with non-small cell lung cancer using positron emission tomography (PET). Radiotherapy and Oncology 62(1), 51–60 (2002)
6. Kagadis, G.C., Delibasis, K.K., Matsopoulos, G.K., Mouravliansky, N.A., Asvestas, P.A.: A comparative study of surface and volume-based techniques for the automatic registration between CT and SPECT brain images. Medical Physics 29(2), 201–213 (2002)
7. Zagrodsky, V., Shekhar, R., Cornhill, J.F.: Multifunction extension of simplex optimization method for mutual information-based registration of ultrasound volumes. In: Sonka, M., Hanson, K.M. (eds.) Medical Imaging: Image Processing. Proc. SPIE, vol. 4322, pp. 508–515. SPIE Press, Bellingham (2001)
8. Jenkinson, M., Bannister, P., Brady, M., Smith, S.: Improved Optimization for the Robust and Accurate Linear Registration and Motion Correction of Brain Images. NeuroImage 17, 825–841 (2002)
9. Wachowiak, M.P., Smolíková, R., Zheng, Y., Zurada, J.M., Elmaghraby, A.S.: An Approach to Multimodal Biomedical Image Registration Utilizing Particle Swarm Optimization. IEEE Trans. Evolutionary Computation 8(3), 289–301 (2004)
10. Lomonosov, E., Chetverikov, D.: Pre-registration of arbitrarily oriented 3D surfaces using a genetic algorithm. Pattern Recognition Letters 27(11), 1201–1208 (2006)
11. Chen, Y.W., Lin, C.-L., Mimori, A.: Multimodal Medical Image Registration Using Particle Swarm Optimization. In: 8th Int. Conf. on Intelligent Systems Design and Applications (2008)
12. Das, A., Bhattacharya, M.: Affine Based Registration of CT and MR Modality Images of Human Brain using Multiresolution Approaches: Comparative Study on Genetic Algorithm and Particle Swarm Optimization. Int. Journal of Neural Computing & Applications 2(2), 223–237 (2011)
13. Lehmann, T., Goerke, C., Schmitt, W., Kaupp, A., Repges, R.: A rotation-extended cepstrum technique optimized by systematic analysis of various sets of X-ray images. In: Loew, M.H., Hanson, K.M. (eds.) Medical Imaging: Image Processing, vol. 2710, pp. 390–401. SPIE, Bellingham (1996)
14. Avants, B.B., Epstein, C.L., Grossman, M., Gee, J.C.: Symmetric Diffeomorphic Image Registration with Cross-Correlation: Evaluating Automated Labeling of Elderly and Neurodegenerative Brain. Medical Image Analysis 12(1), 26–41 (2008)
15. Granville, V., Krivanek, M., Rasson, J.-P.: Simulated annealing: A proof of convergence. IEEE Trans. Pattern Analysis and Machine Intelligence 16(6), 652–656 (1994)
16. Russell, S., Norvig, P.: Artificial Intelligence: a modern approach, 2nd edn. Prentice Hall, Upper Saddle River (2003)
17. Whole Brain Atlas,
    http://www.bsp.brain.riken.jp/ICALAB/ICALABImageProc/benchmarks

References

1. Moore, T.L.: A Survey of Medical Image Registration. Medical Image Analysis 2(1), 1–36 (1998)
2. Maintz, J.B., Viergever, M.A.: A Survey of Medical Image Registration (...)

Author Index